Nightschool

Svetlana Chmakova's

The Weirn Books

VOLUME ONE

Yen Press

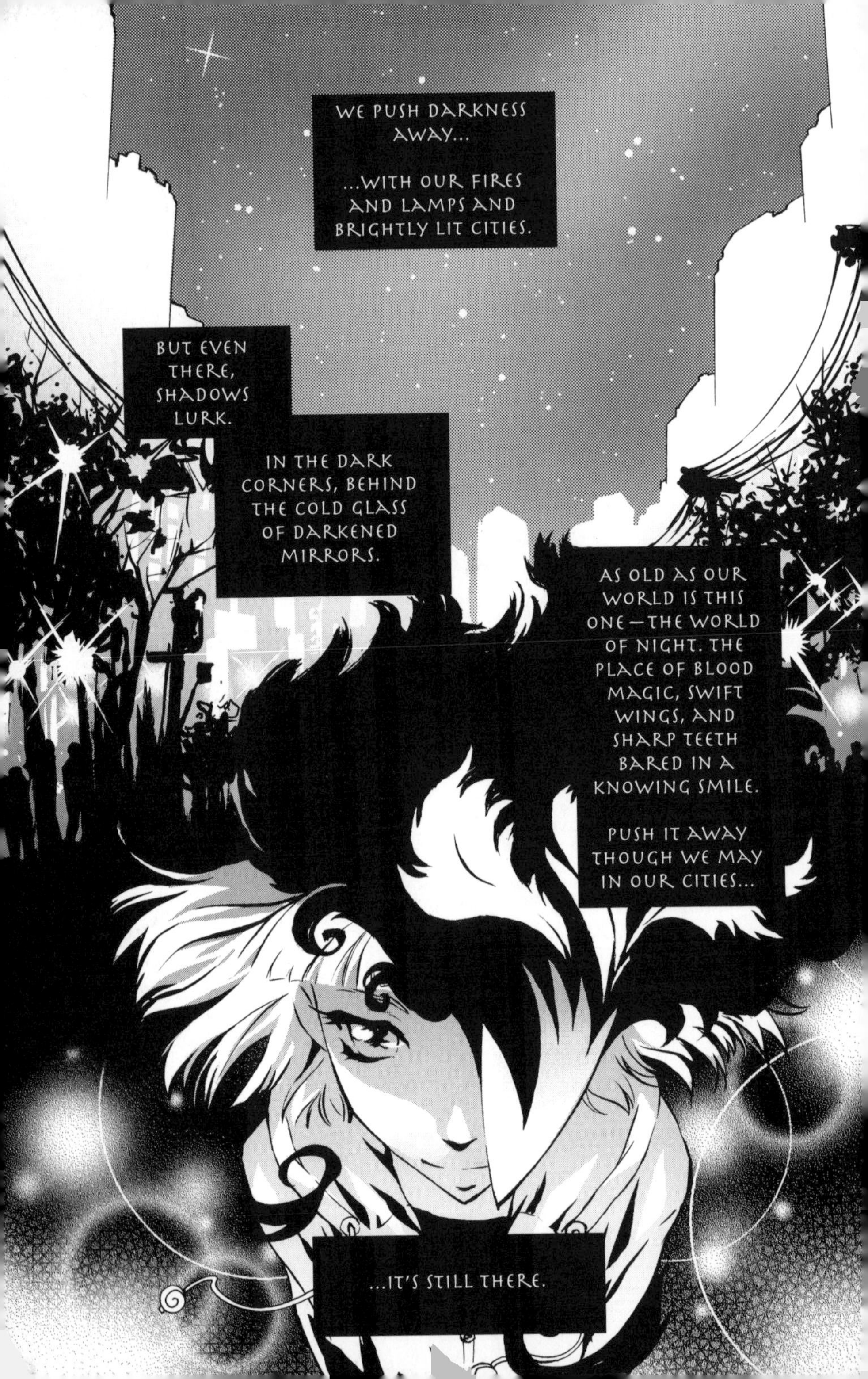
WE PUSH DARKNESS AWAY...
...WITH OUR FIRES AND LAMPS AND BRIGHTLY LIT CITIES.
BUT EVEN THERE, SHADOWS LURK.
IN THE DARK CORNERS, BEHIND THE COLD GLASS OF DARKENED MIRRORS.
AS OLD AS OUR WORLD IS THIS ONE—THE WORLD OF NIGHT. THE PLACE OF BLOOD MAGIC, SWIFT WINGS, AND SHARP TEETH BARED IN A KNOWING SMILE.
PUSH IT AWAY THOUGH WE MAY IN OUR CITIES...
...IT'S STILL THERE.

Dedicated to my parents
and
Barry McCarthy

Thank you ♡

CONTENTS

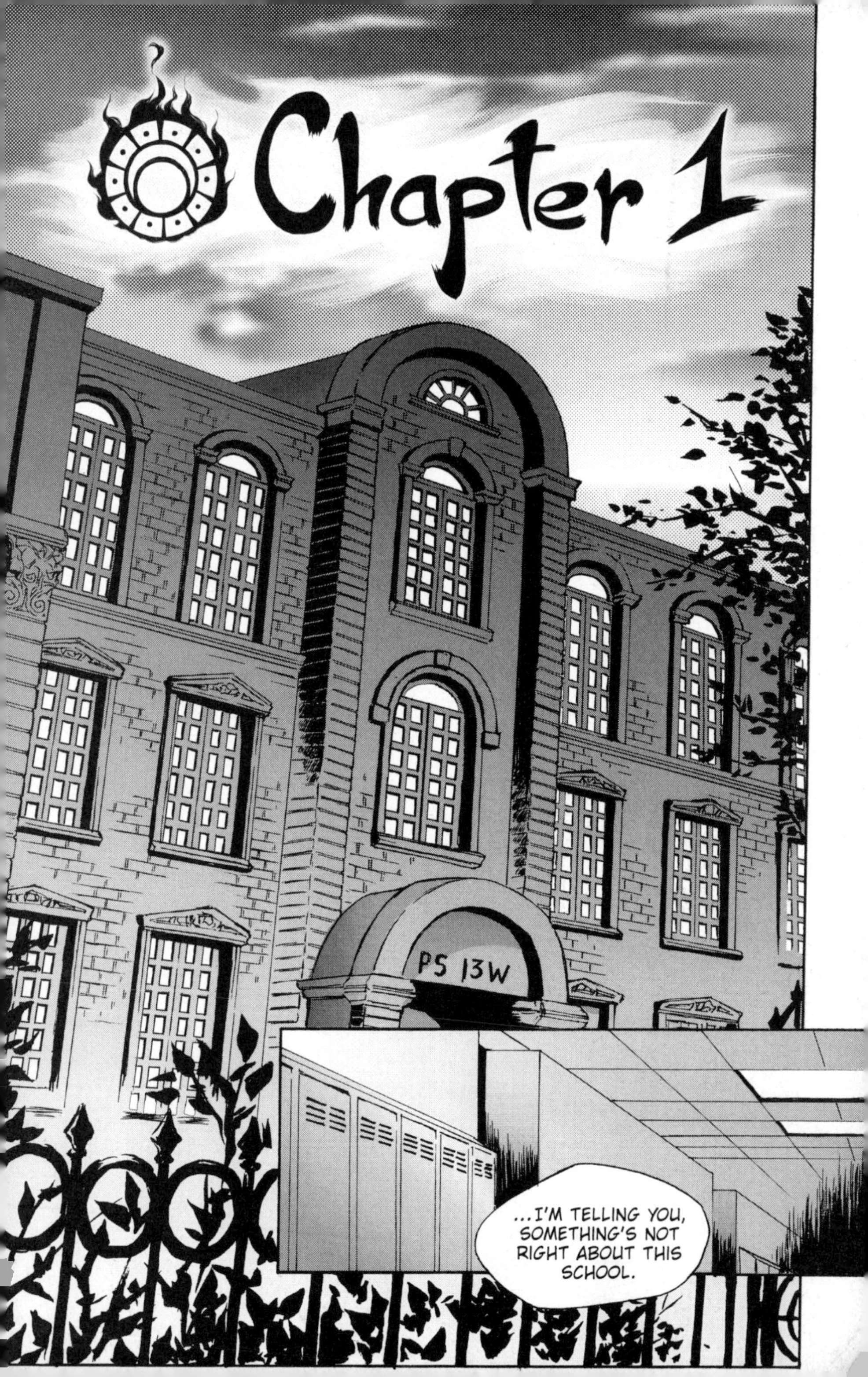
Chapter 1
PS 13W
...I'M TELLING YOU, SOMETHING'S NOT RIGHT ABOUT THIS SCHOOL.

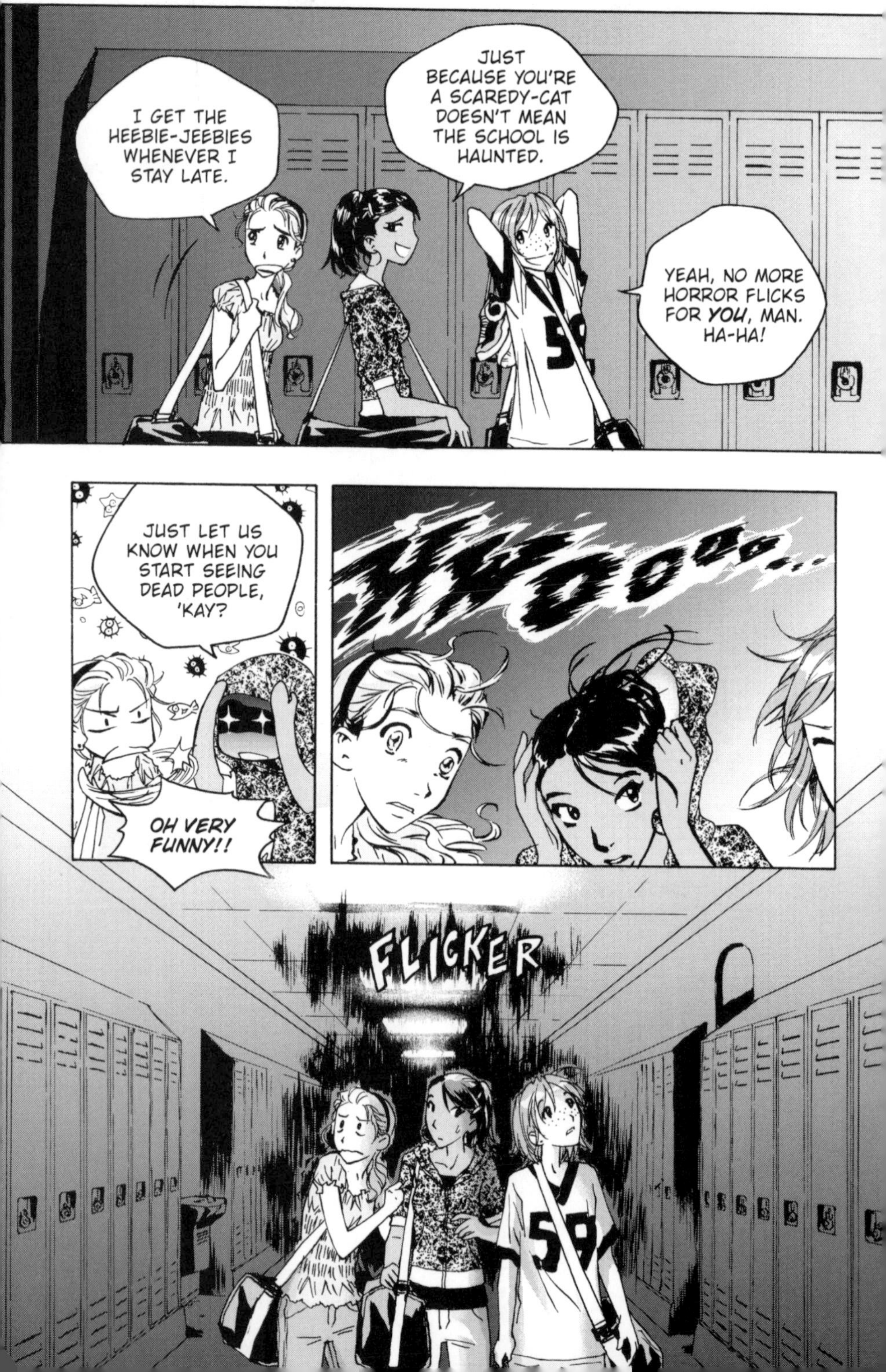
I GET THE HEEBIE-JEEBIES WHENEVER I STAY LATE.
JUST BECAUSE YOU'RE A SCAREDY-CAT DOESN'T MEAN THE SCHOOL IS HAUNTED.
YEAH, NO MORE HORROR FLICKS FOR *YOU*, MAN. HA-HA!
JUST LET US KNOW WHEN YOU START SEEING DEAD PEOPLE, 'KAY?
OH VERY FUNNY!!
ZZZOOOoo...
FLICKER

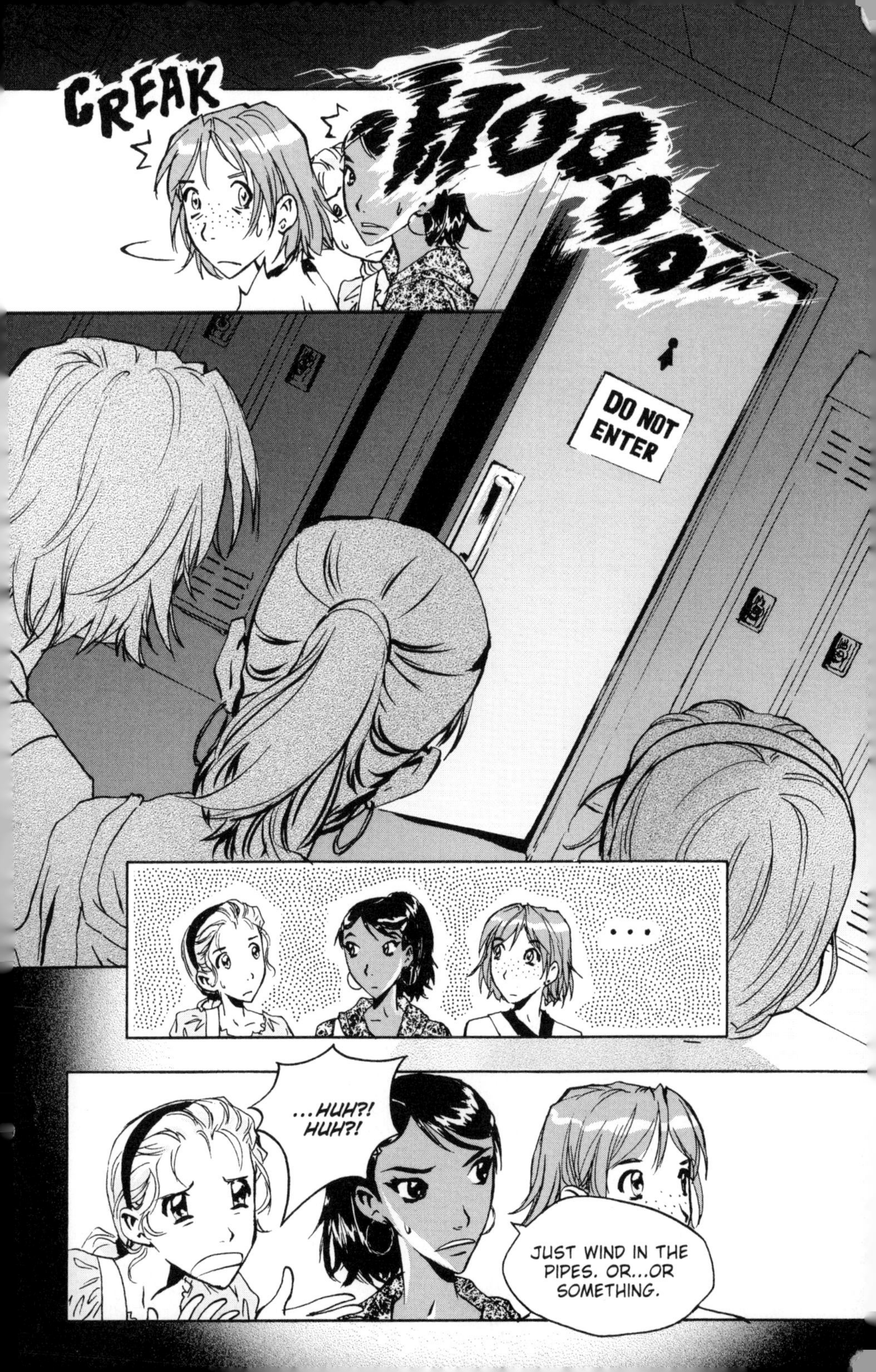
CREAK
HOOOOO
DO NOT ENTER
. . .
...HUH?! HUH?!
JUST WIND IN THE PIPES. OR...OR SOMETHING.

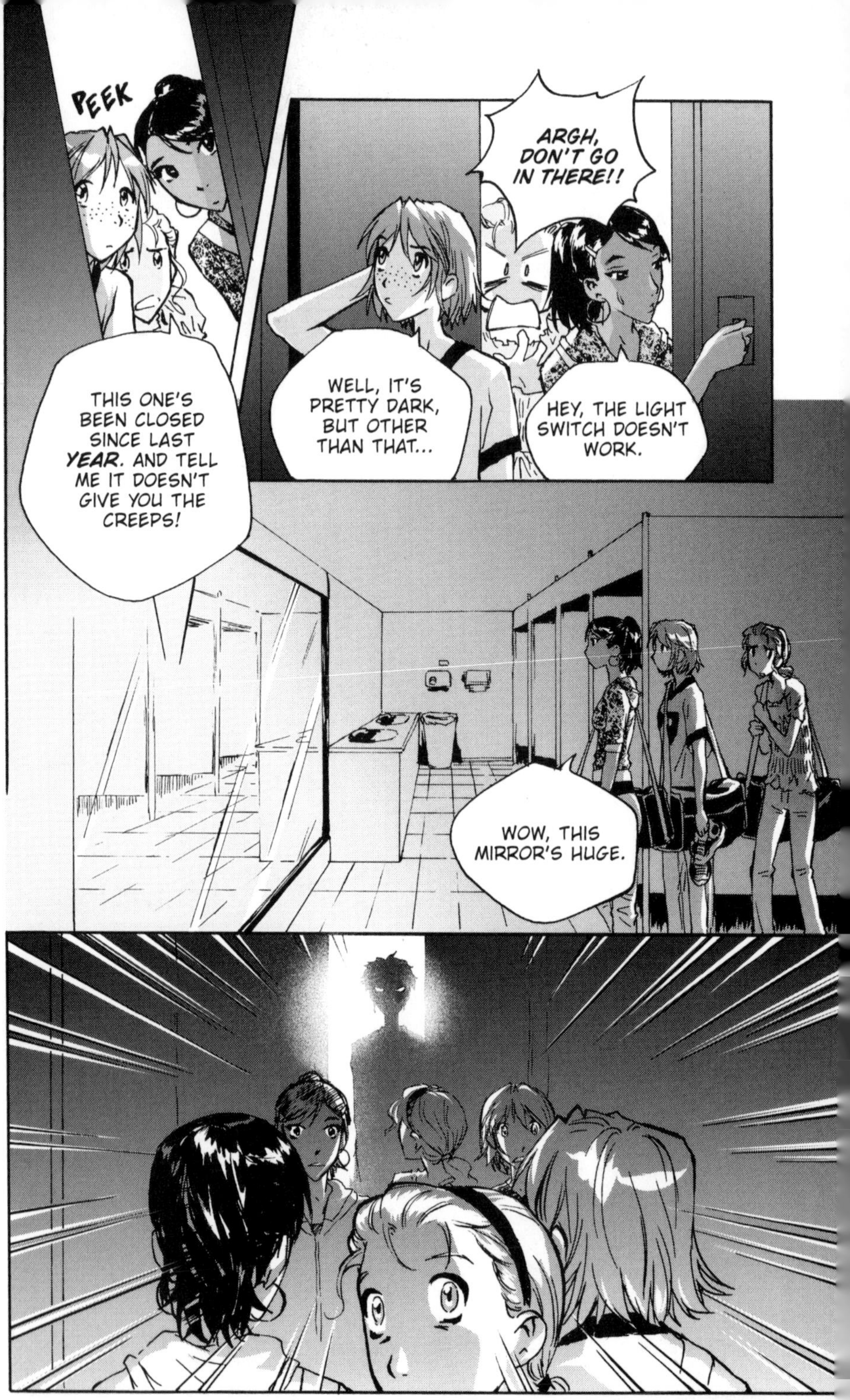
PEEK
ARGH, DON'T GO IN THERE!!
THIS ONE'S BEEN CLOSED SINCE LAST YEAR. AND TELL ME IT DOESN'T GIVE YOU THE CREEPS!
WELL, IT'S PRETTY DARK, BUT OTHER THAN THAT...
HEY, THE LIGHT SWITCH DOESN'T WORK.
WOW, THIS MIRROR'S HUGE.

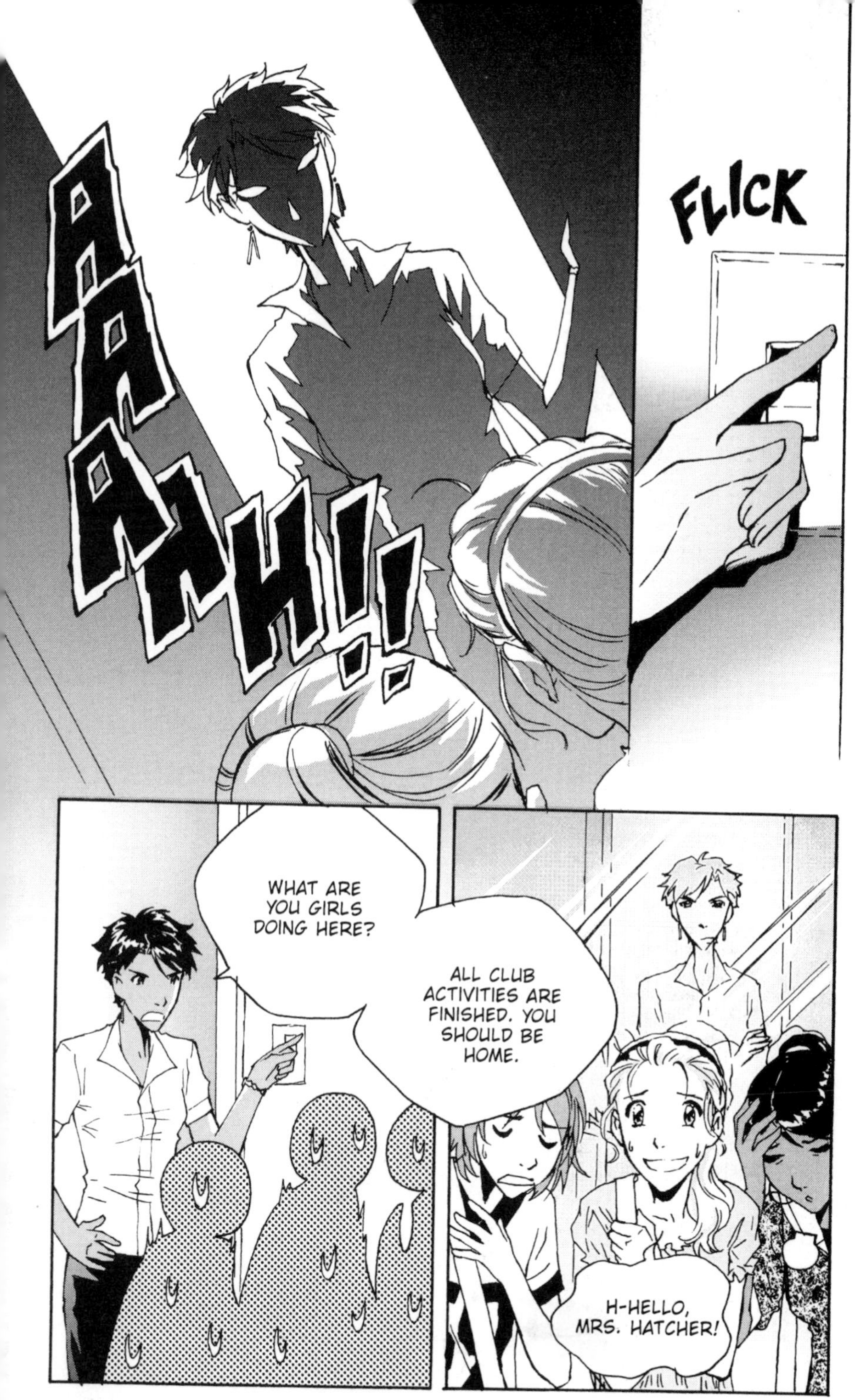
FLICK
AAAAAHH!!!
WHAT ARE YOU GIRLS DOING HERE?
ALL CLUB ACTIVITIES ARE FINISHED. YOU SHOULD BE HOME.
H-HELLO, MRS. HATCHER!

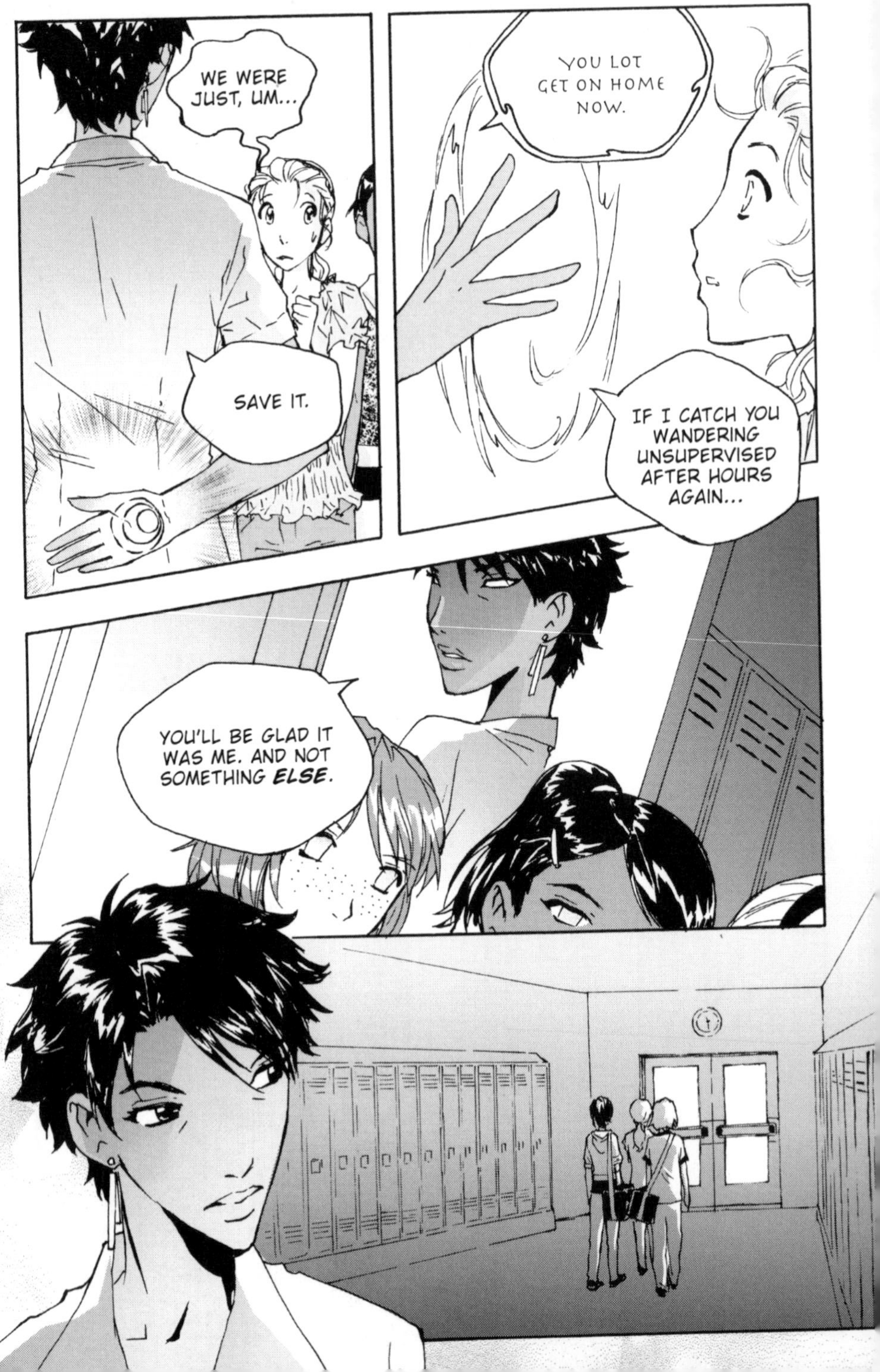
WE WERE JUST, UM...
SAVE IT.
YOU LOT GET ON HOME NOW.
IF I CATCH YOU WANDERING UNSUPERVISED AFTER HOURS AGAIN...
YOU'LL BE GLAD IT WAS ME. AND NOT SOMETHING ELSE.

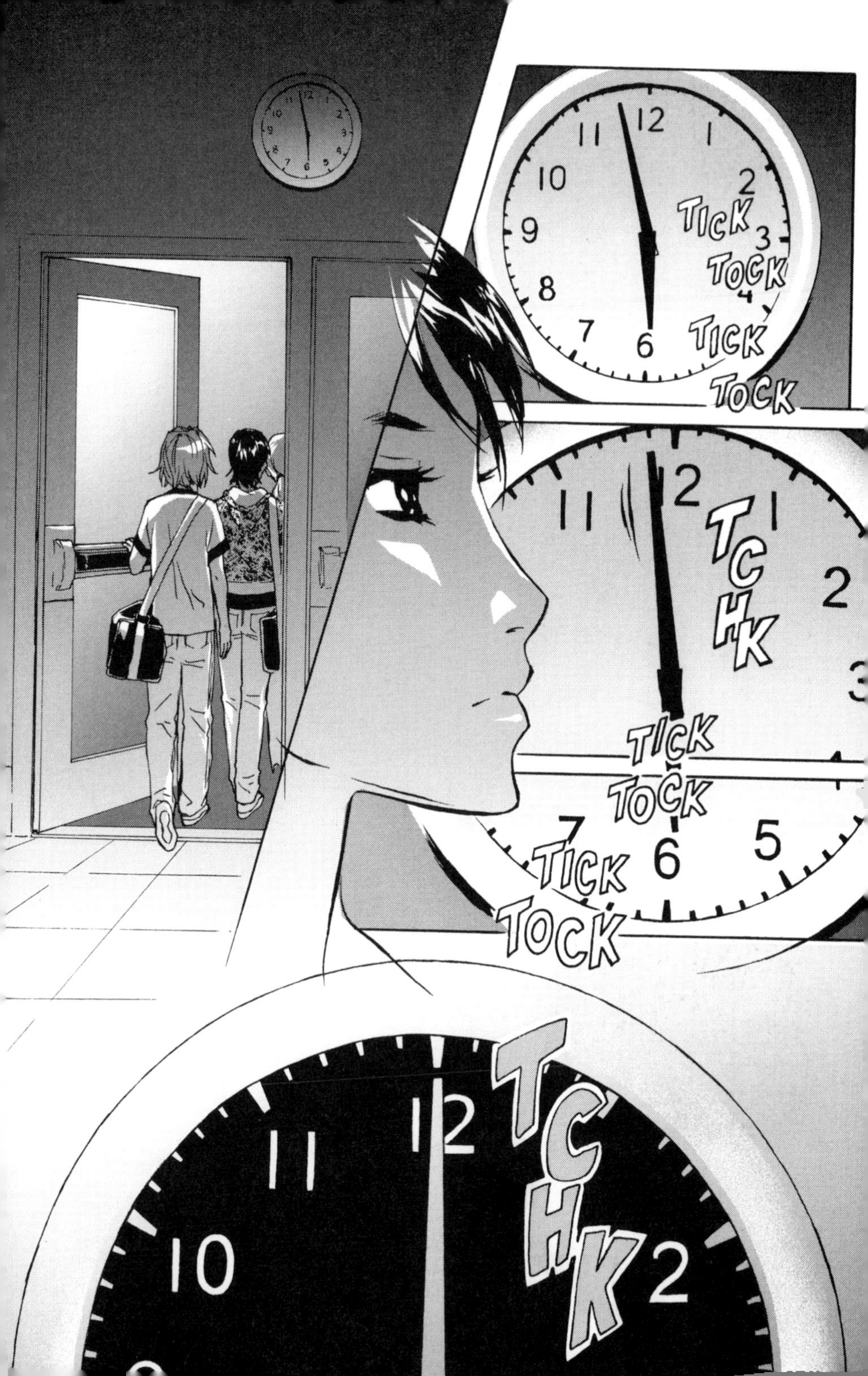
TICK
TOCK
TICK
TOCK
TCHK
TICK
TOCK
TICK
TOCK
TCHK

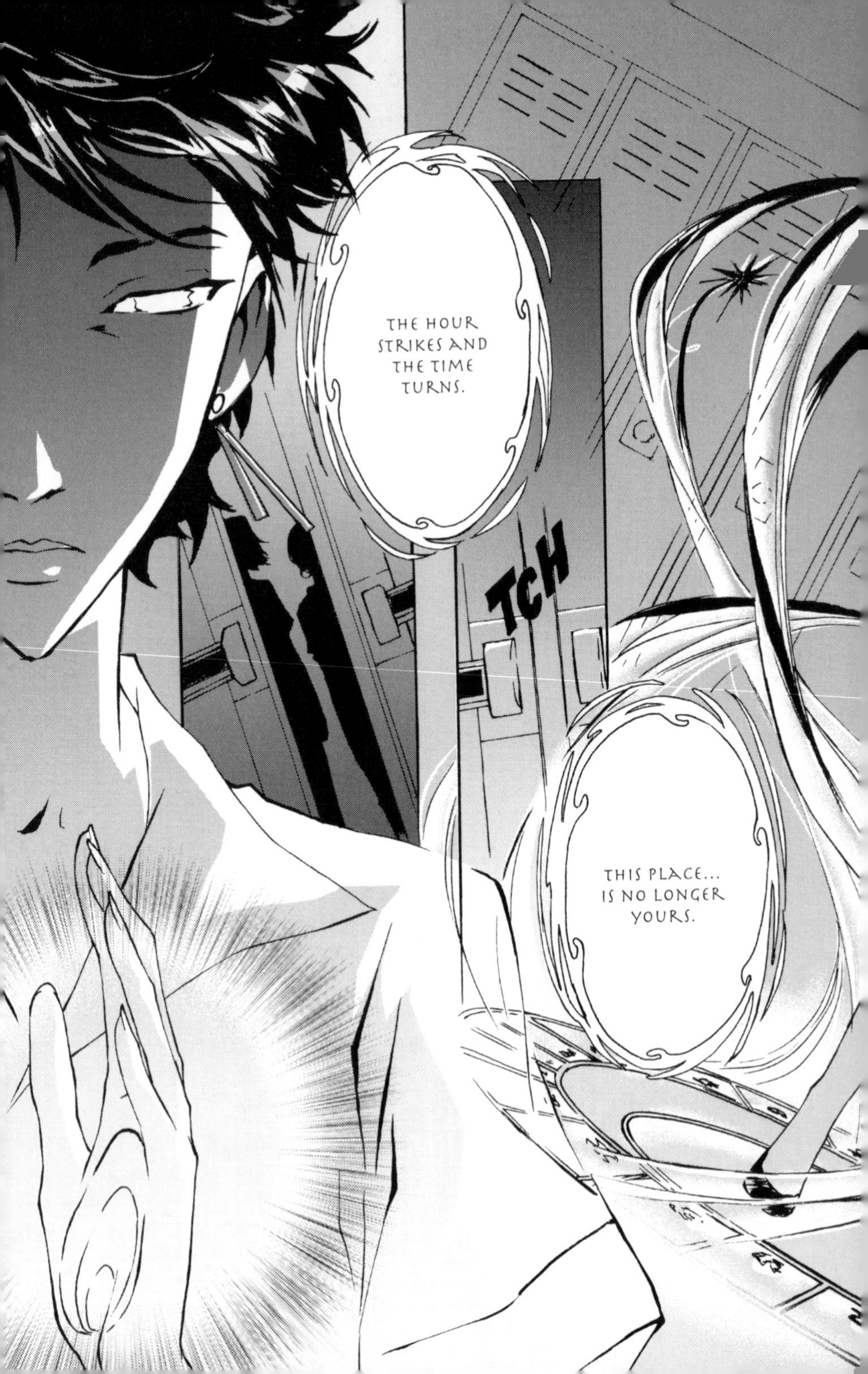
THE HOUR STRIKES AND THE TIME TURNS.
TCH
THIS PLACE... IS NO LONGER YOURS.

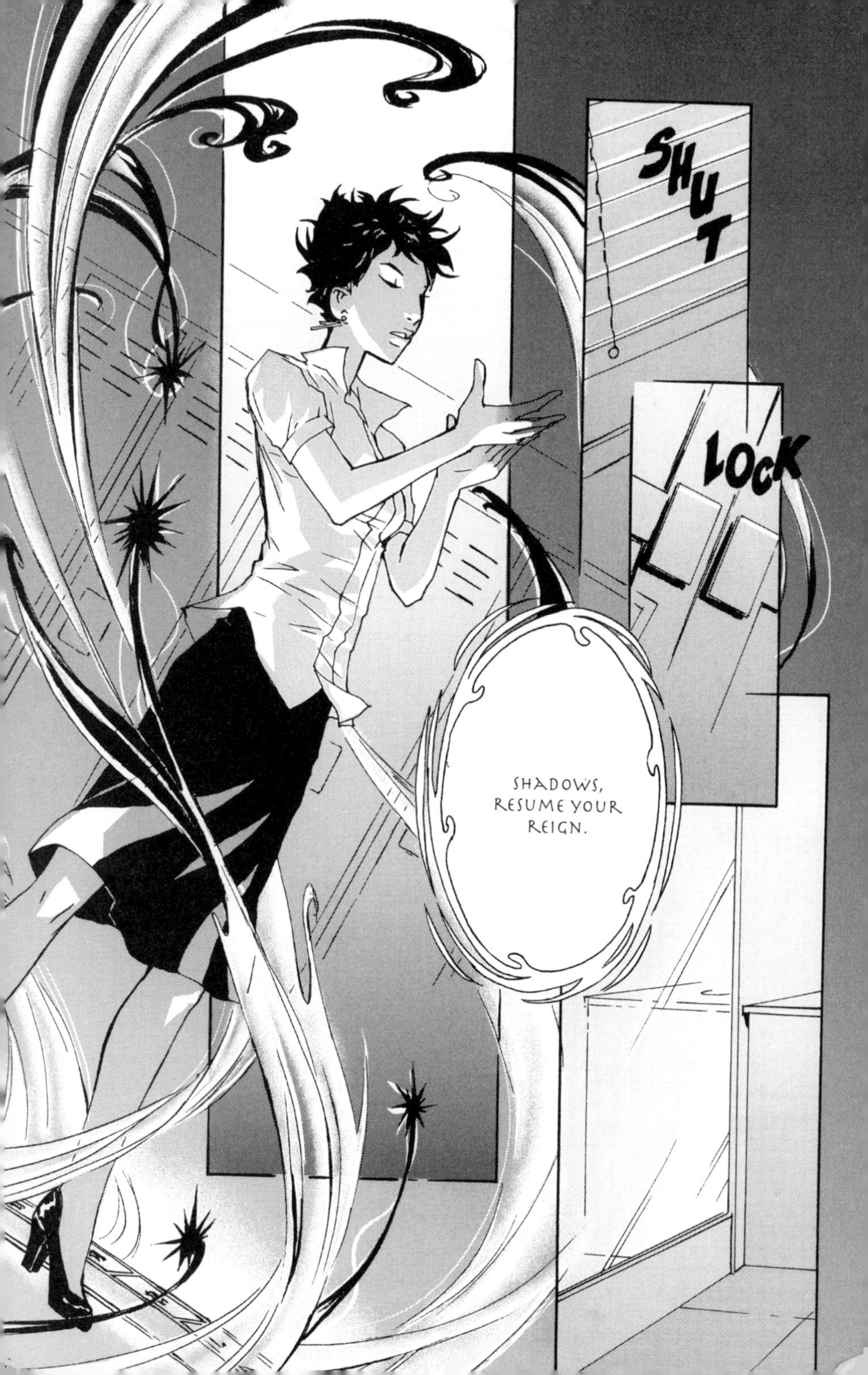
SHUT
LOCK
SHADOWS, RESUME YOUR REIGN.

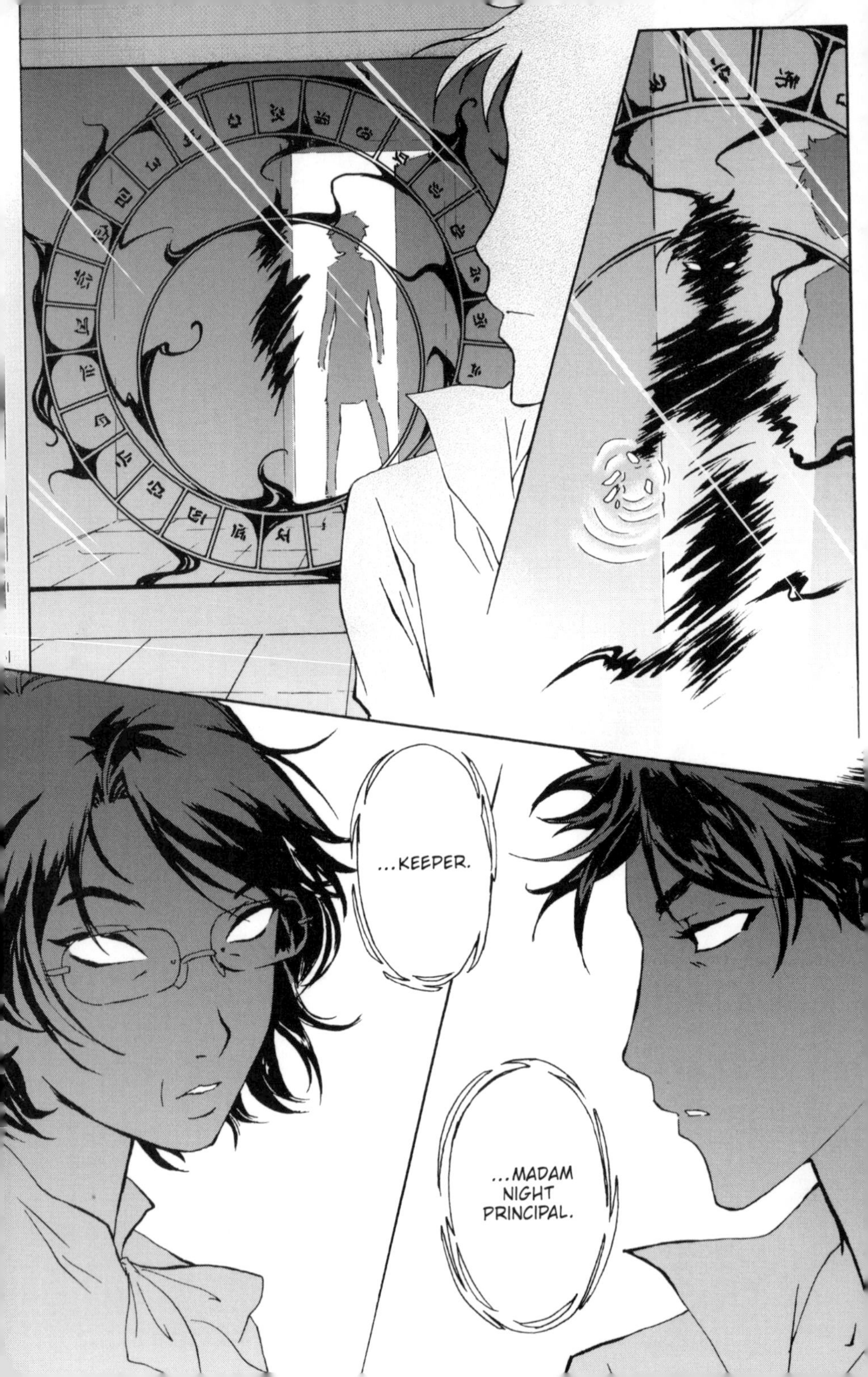
...KEEPER.
...MADAM NIGHT PRINCIPAL.

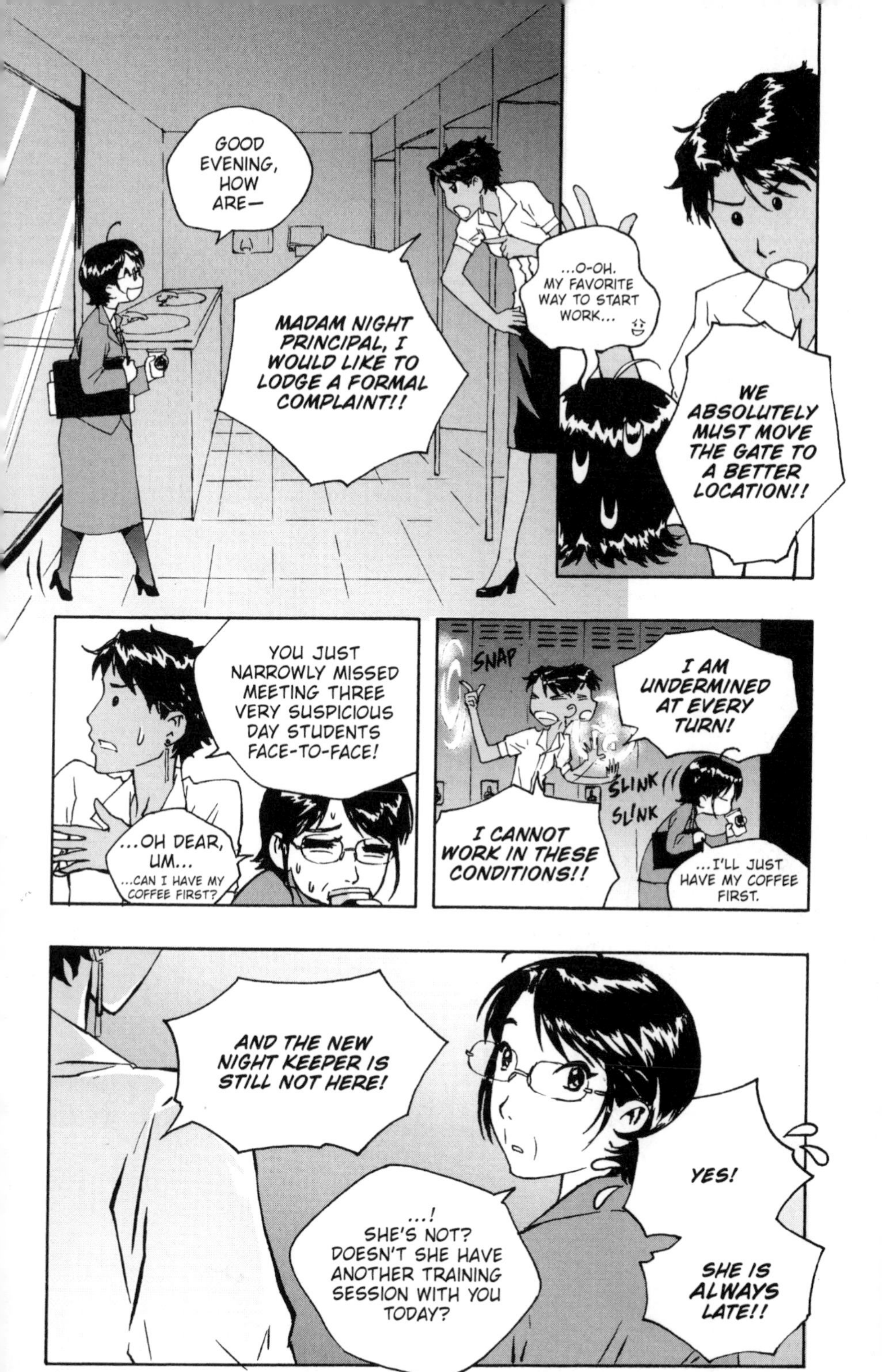
GOOD EVENING, HOW ARE—
MADAM NIGHT PRINCIPAL, I WOULD LIKE TO LODGE A FORMAL COMPLAINT!!
...O-OH. MY FAVORITE WAY TO START WORK...
WE ABSOLUTELY MUST MOVE THE GATE TO A BETTER LOCATION!!
YOU JUST NARROWLY MISSED MEETING THREE VERY SUSPICIOUS DAY STUDENTS FACE-TO-FACE!
...OH DEAR, UM...
...CAN I HAVE MY COFFEE FIRST?
SNAP
I AM UNDERMINED AT EVERY TURN!
SLINK
SLINK
I CANNOT WORK IN THESE CONDITIONS!!
...I'LL JUST HAVE MY COFFEE FIRST.
AND THE NEW NIGHT KEEPER IS STILL NOT HERE!
...! SHE'S NOT? DOESN'T SHE HAVE ANOTHER TRAINING SESSION WITH YOU TODAY?
YES!
SHE IS ALWAYS LATE!!

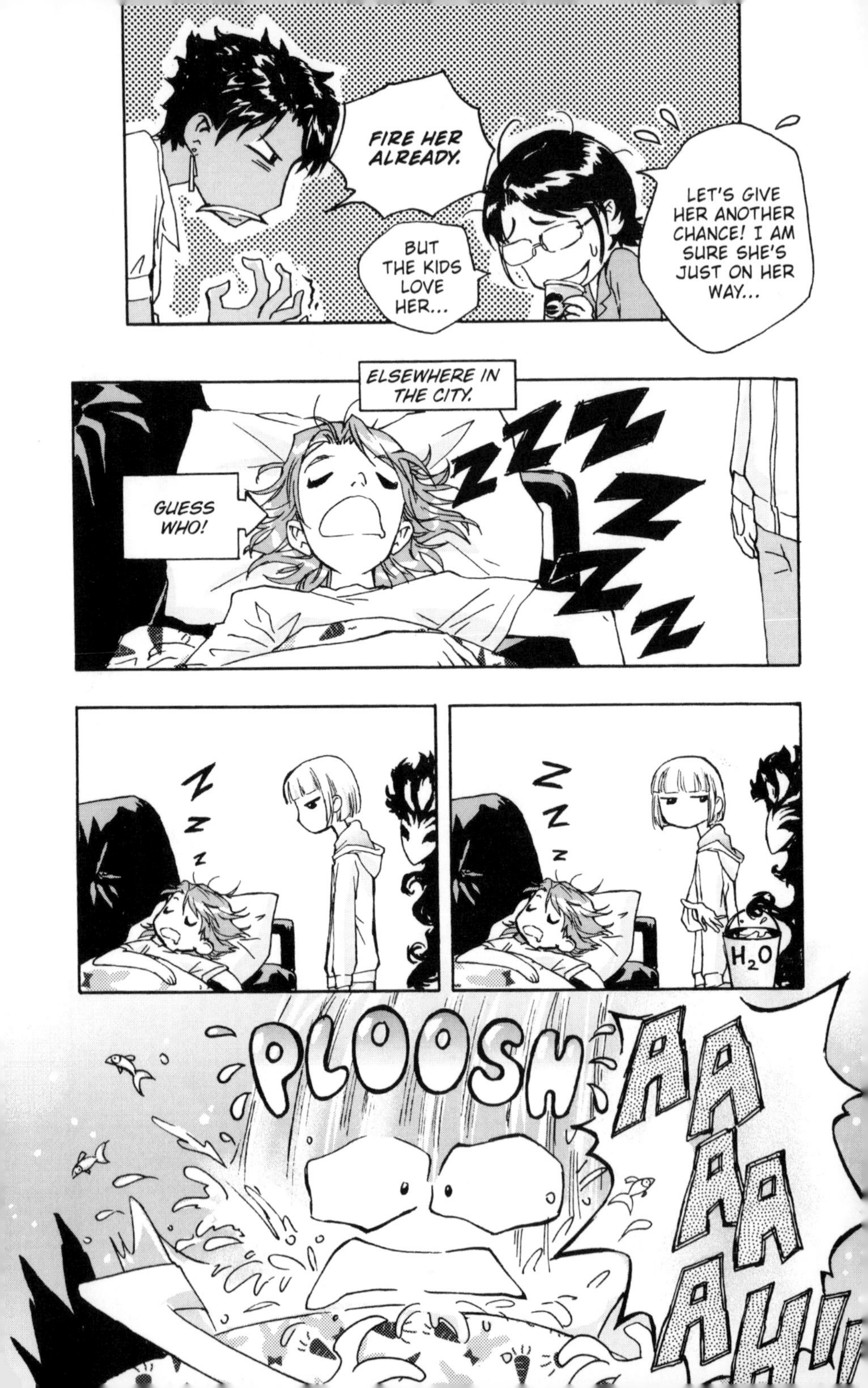
FIRE HER ALREADY.
BUT THE KIDS LOVE HER...
LET'S GIVE HER ANOTHER CHANCE! I AM SURE SHE'S JUST ON HER WAY...
ELSEWHERE IN THE CITY.
GUESS WHO!
ZZZZZZZ
Z Z Z
Z Z Z
H_2O
PLOOSH
AAAAAH!!

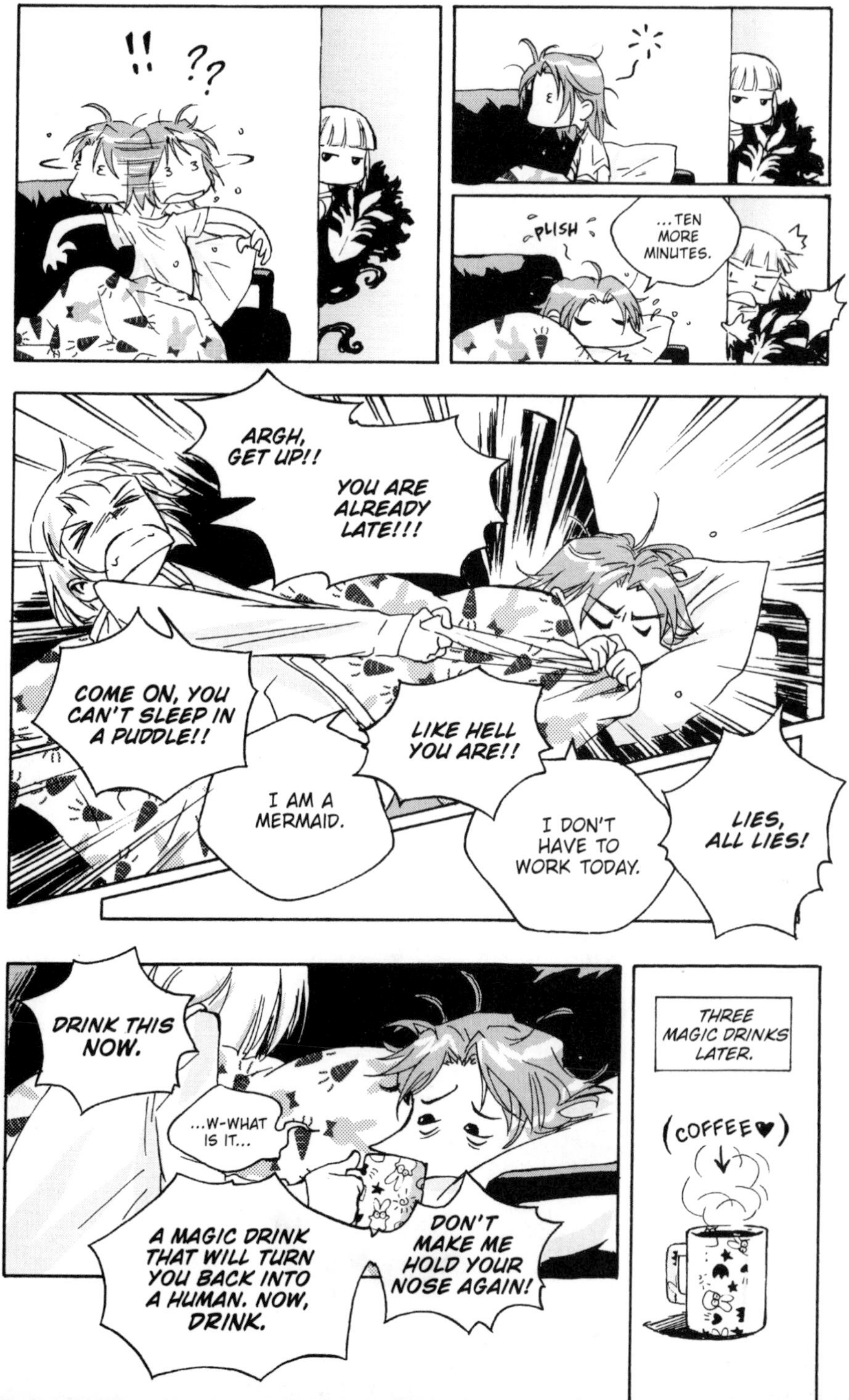
!!
??
PLISH
...TEN MORE MINUTES.
ARGH, GET UP!!
YOU ARE ALREADY LATE!!!
COME ON, YOU CAN'T SLEEP IN A PUDDLE!!
LIKE HELL YOU ARE!!
I AM A MERMAID.
I DON'T HAVE TO WORK TODAY.
LIES, ALL LIES!
DRINK THIS NOW.
...W-WHAT IS IT...
A MAGIC DRINK THAT WILL TURN YOU BACK INTO A HUMAN. NOW, DRINK.
DON'T MAKE ME HOLD YOUR NOSE AGAIN!
THREE MAGIC DRINKS LATER.
(COFFEE♥)

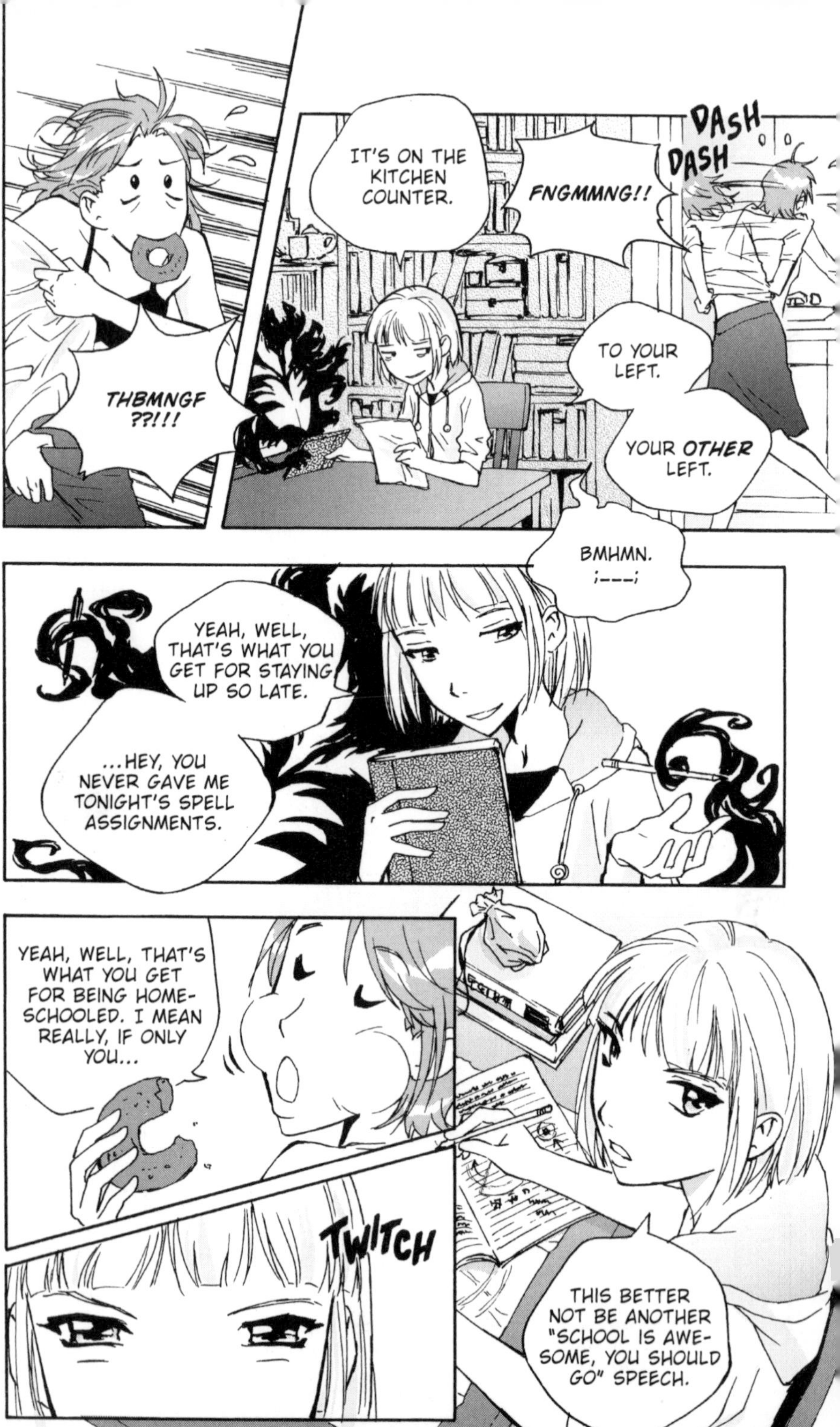
THBMNGF ??!!!
IT'S ON THE KITCHEN COUNTER.
FNGMMNG!!
DASH DASH
TO YOUR LEFT.
YOUR OTHER LEFT.
BMHMN. ;---;
YEAH, WELL, THAT'S WHAT YOU GET FOR STAYING UP SO LATE.
...HEY, YOU NEVER GAVE ME TONIGHT'S SPELL ASSIGNMENTS.
YEAH, WELL, THAT'S WHAT YOU GET FOR BEING HOME-SCHOOLED. I MEAN REALLY, IF ONLY YOU...
TWITCH
THIS BETTER NOT BE ANOTHER "SCHOOL IS AWE-SOME, YOU SHOULD GO" SPEECH.

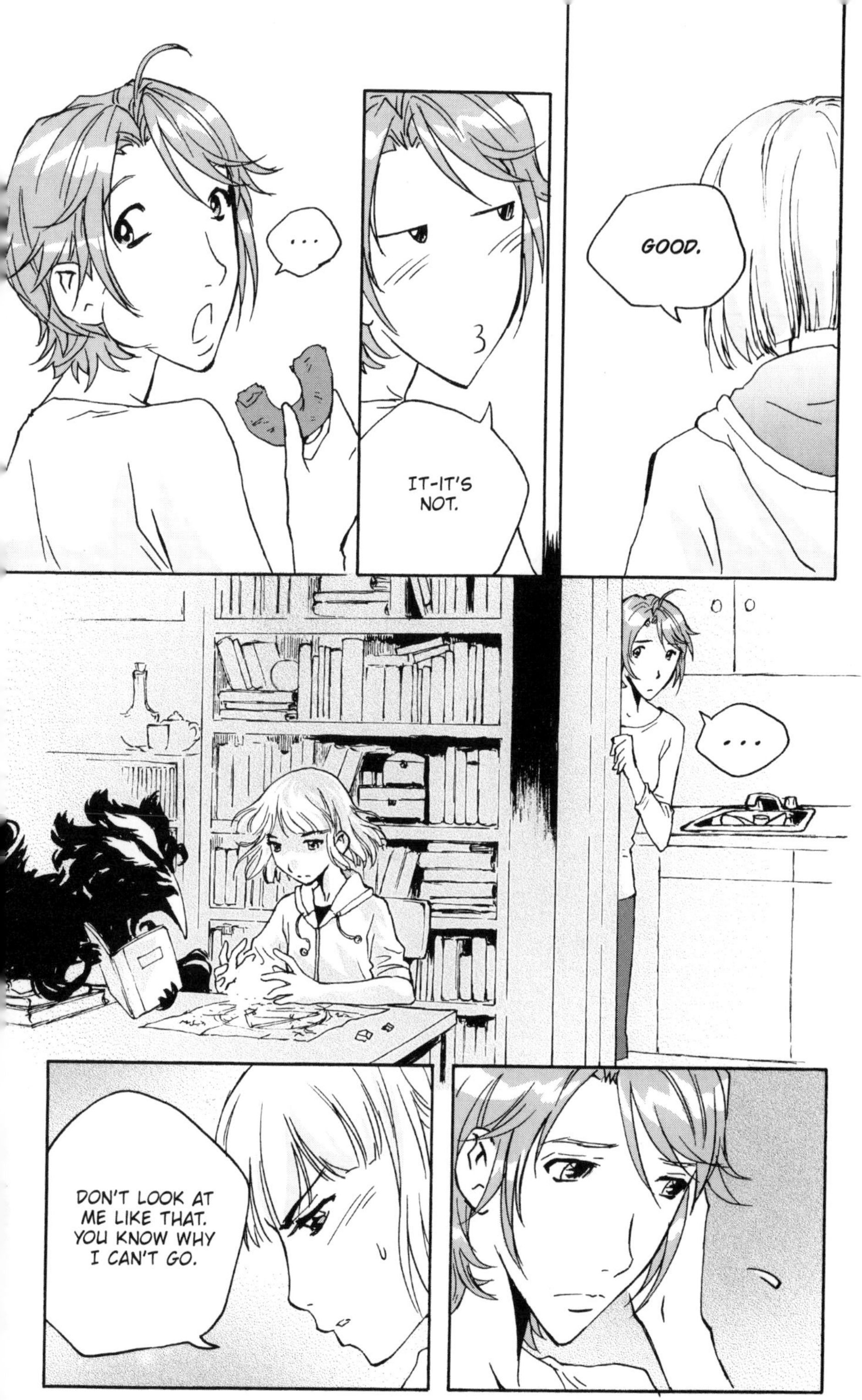

...
IT-IT'S NOT.
GOOD.
...
DON'T LOOK AT ME LIKE THAT. YOU KNOW WHY I CAN'T GO.

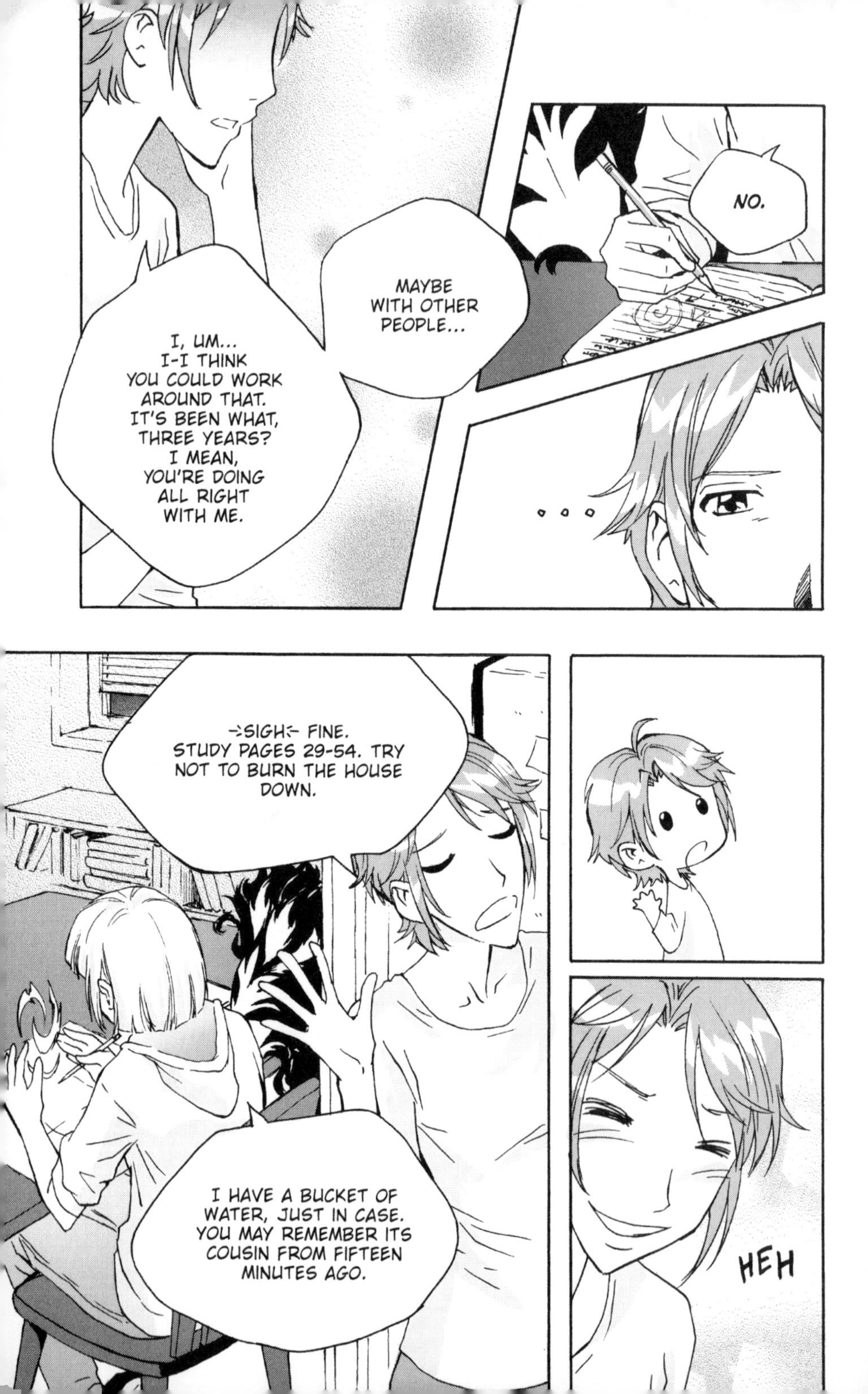
I, UM... I-I THINK YOU COULD WORK AROUND THAT. IT'S BEEN WHAT, THREE YEARS? I MEAN, YOU'RE DOING ALL RIGHT WITH ME.
MAYBE WITH OTHER PEOPLE...
NO.
...
⇢SIGH⇠ FINE. STUDY PAGES 29-54. TRY NOT TO BURN THE HOUSE DOWN.
I HAVE A BUCKET OF WATER, JUST IN CASE. YOU MAY REMEMBER ITS COUSIN FROM FIFTEEN MINUTES AGO.
HEH

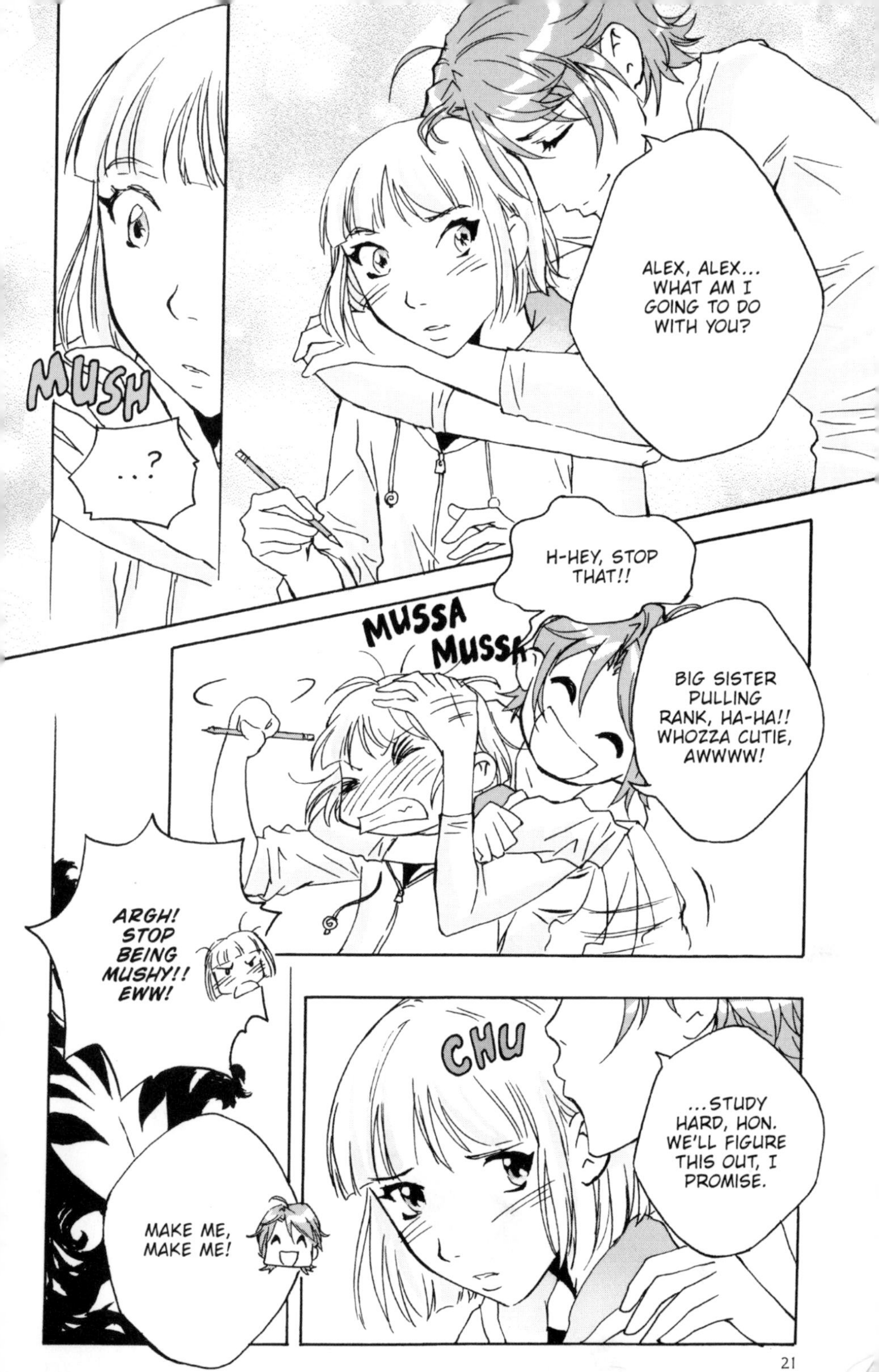
ALEX, ALEX... WHAT AM I GOING TO DO WITH YOU?
MUSH
...?
H-HEY, STOP THAT!!
MUSSA MUSSA
BIG SISTER PULLING RANK, HA-HA!! WHOZZA CUTIE, AWWWW!
ARGH! STOP BEING MUSHY!! EWW!
CHU
...STUDY HARD, HON. WE'LL FIGURE THIS OUT, I PROMISE.
MAKE ME, MAKE ME!

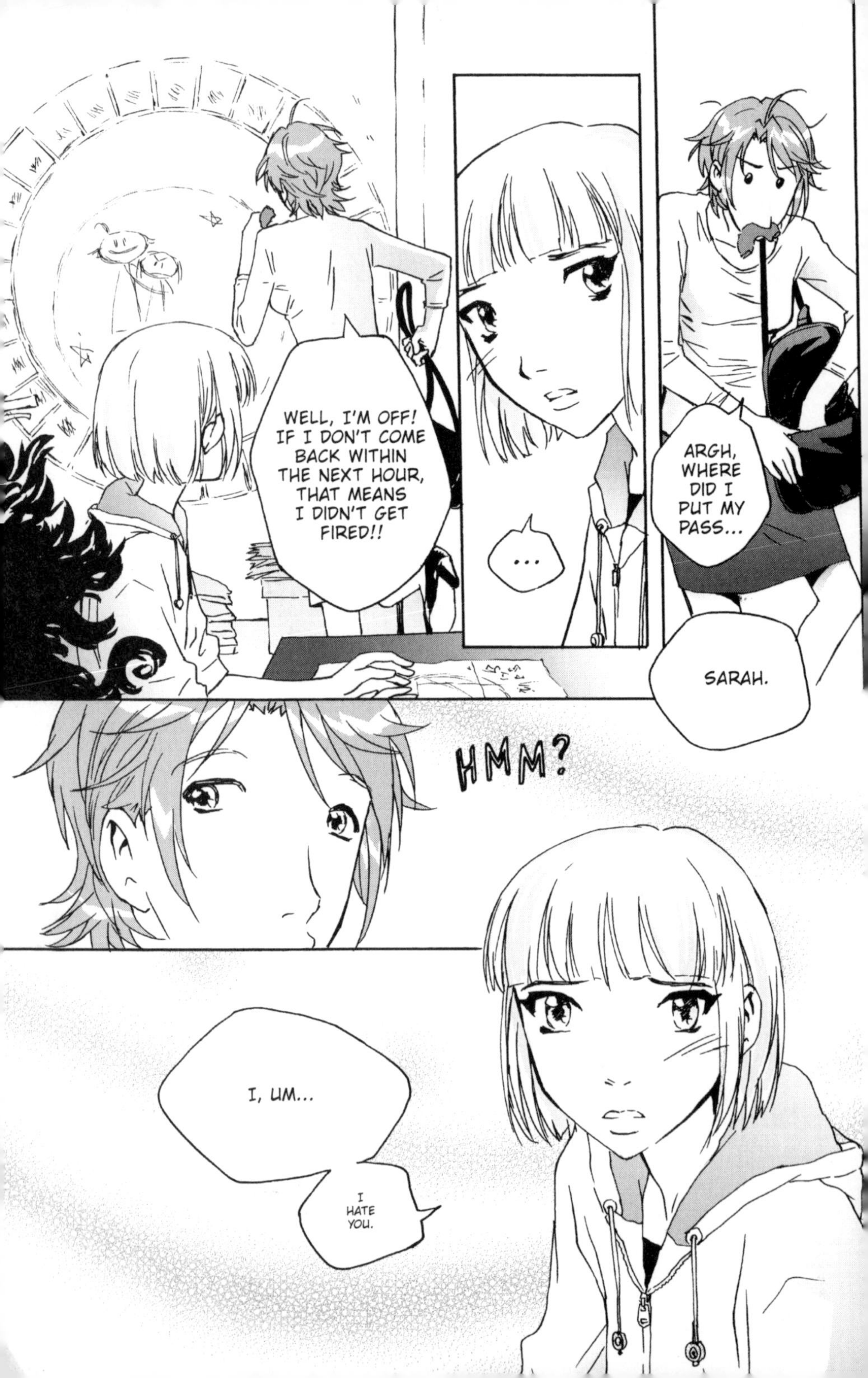
WELL, I'M OFF! IF I DON'T COME BACK WITHIN THE NEXT HOUR, THAT MEANS I DIDN'T GET FIRED!!
...
ARGH, WHERE DID I PUT MY PASS...
SARAH.
HMM?
I, UM...
I HATE YOU.

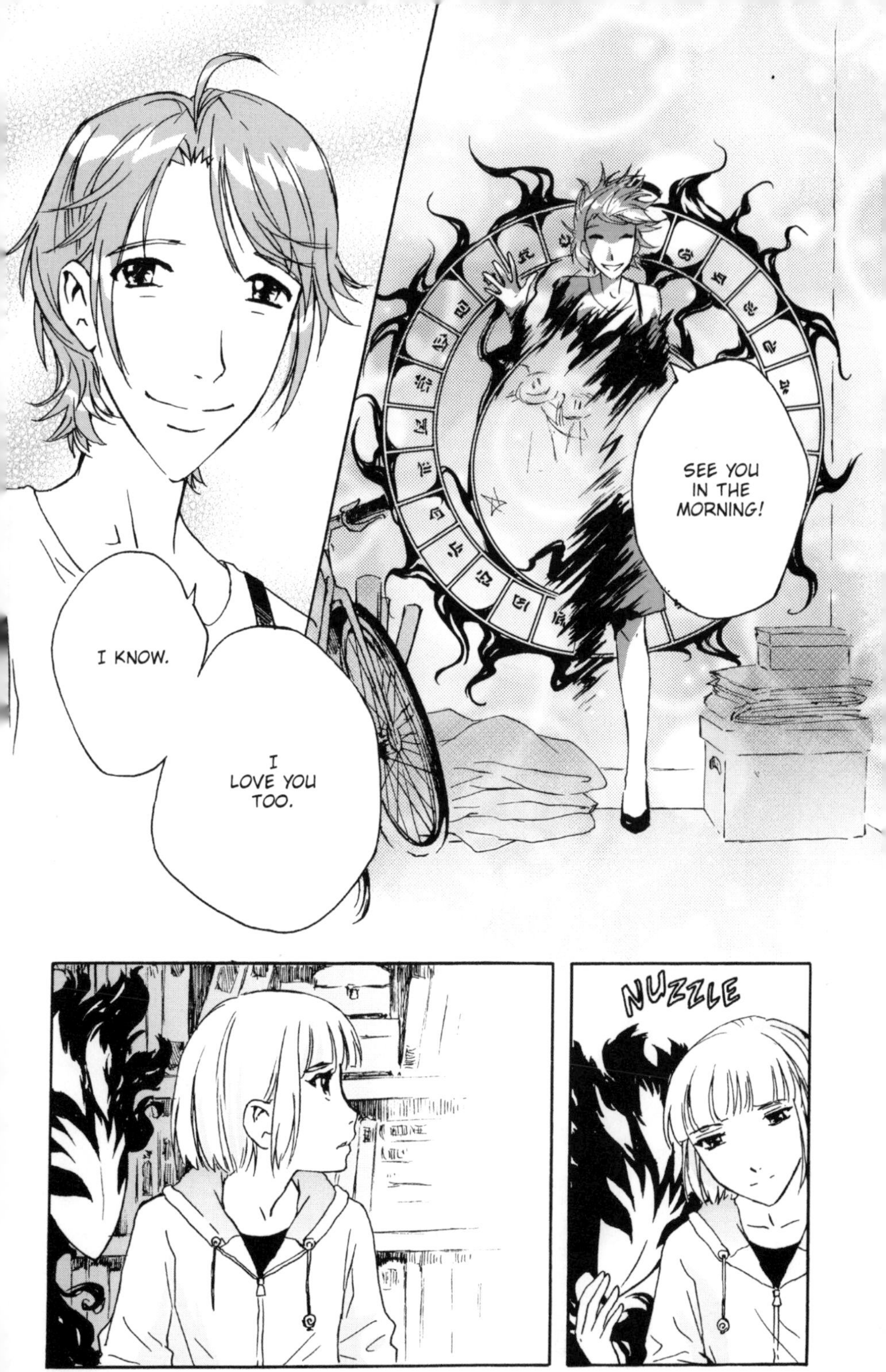
SEE YOU IN THE MORNING!
I KNOW.
I LOVE YOU TOO.
NUZZLE

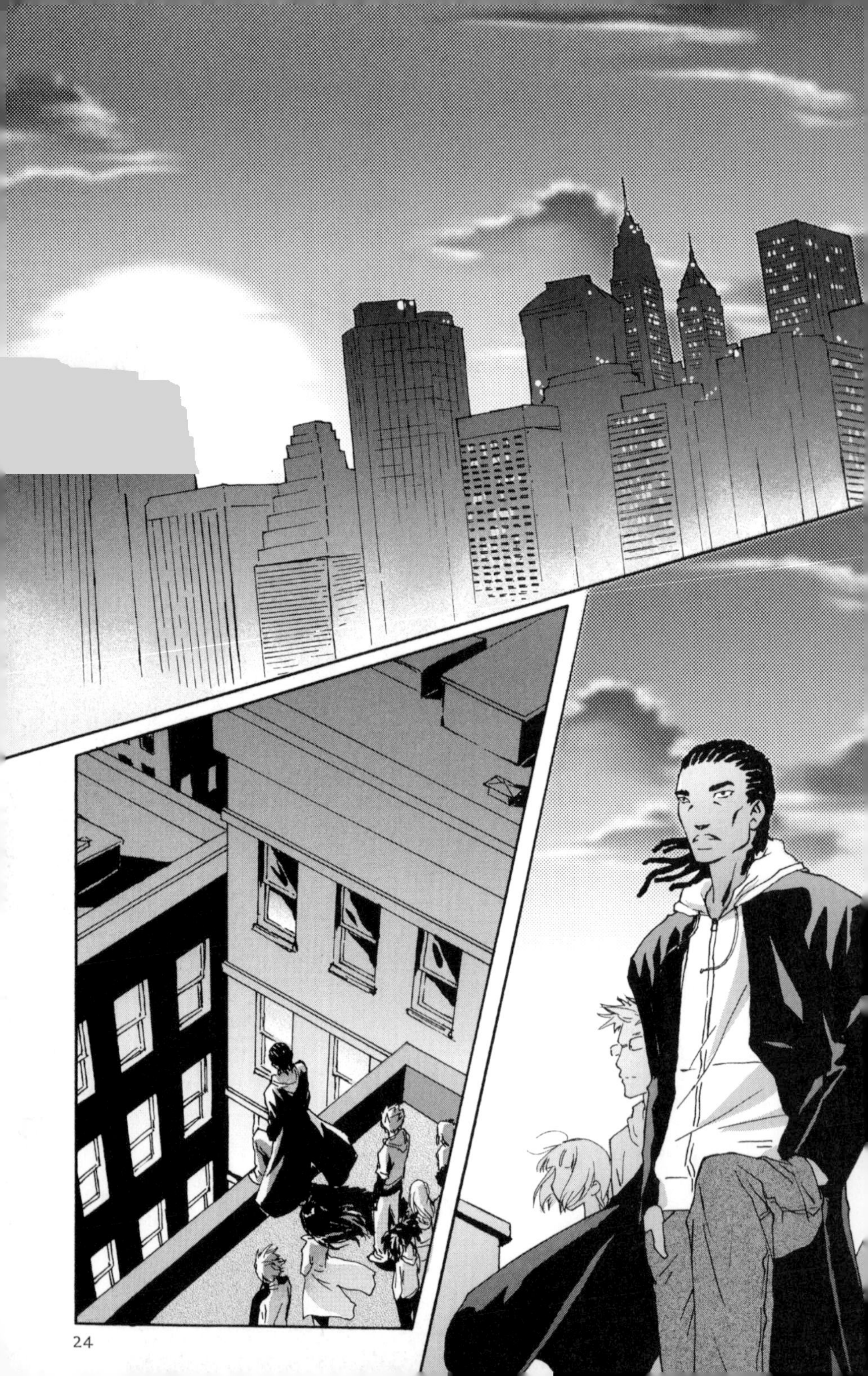

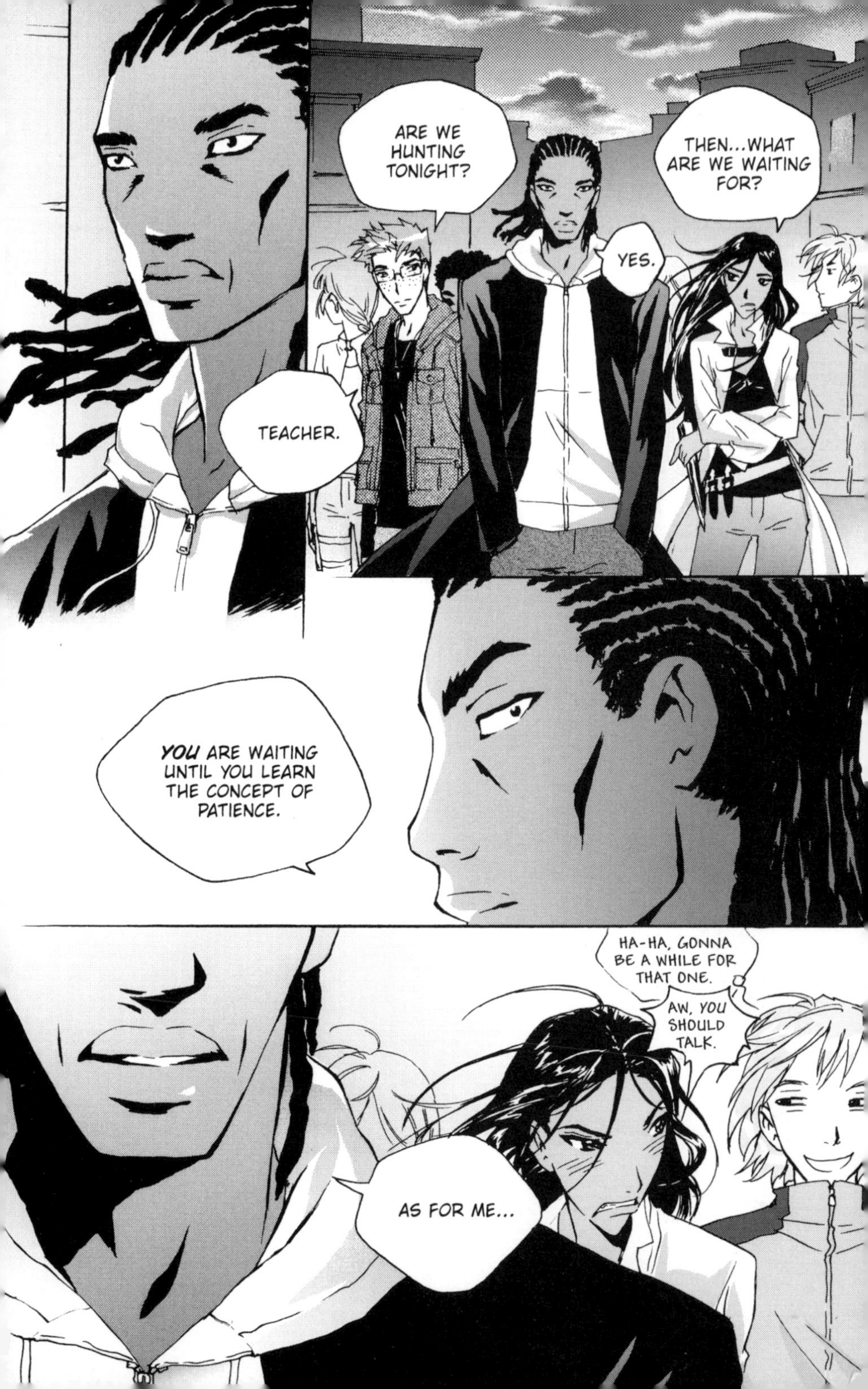
TEACHER.
ARE WE HUNTING TONIGHT?
YES.
THEN...WHAT ARE WE WAITING FOR?
YOU ARE WAITING UNTIL YOU LEARN THE CONCEPT OF PATIENCE.
HA-HA, GONNA BE A WHILE FOR THAT ONE.
AW, YOU SHOULD TALK.
AS FOR ME...

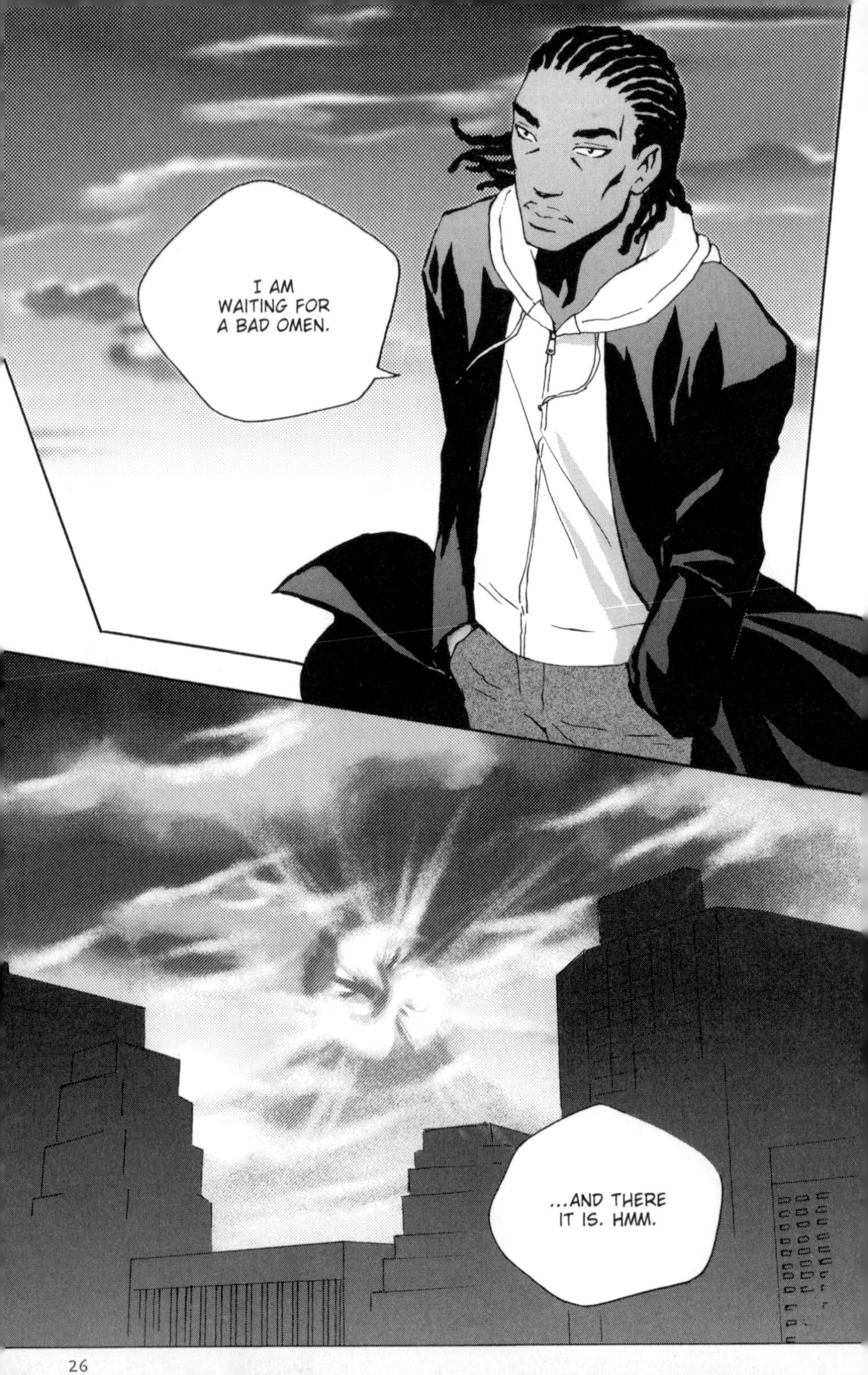
I AM WAITING FOR A BAD OMEN.
...AND THERE IT IS. HMM.

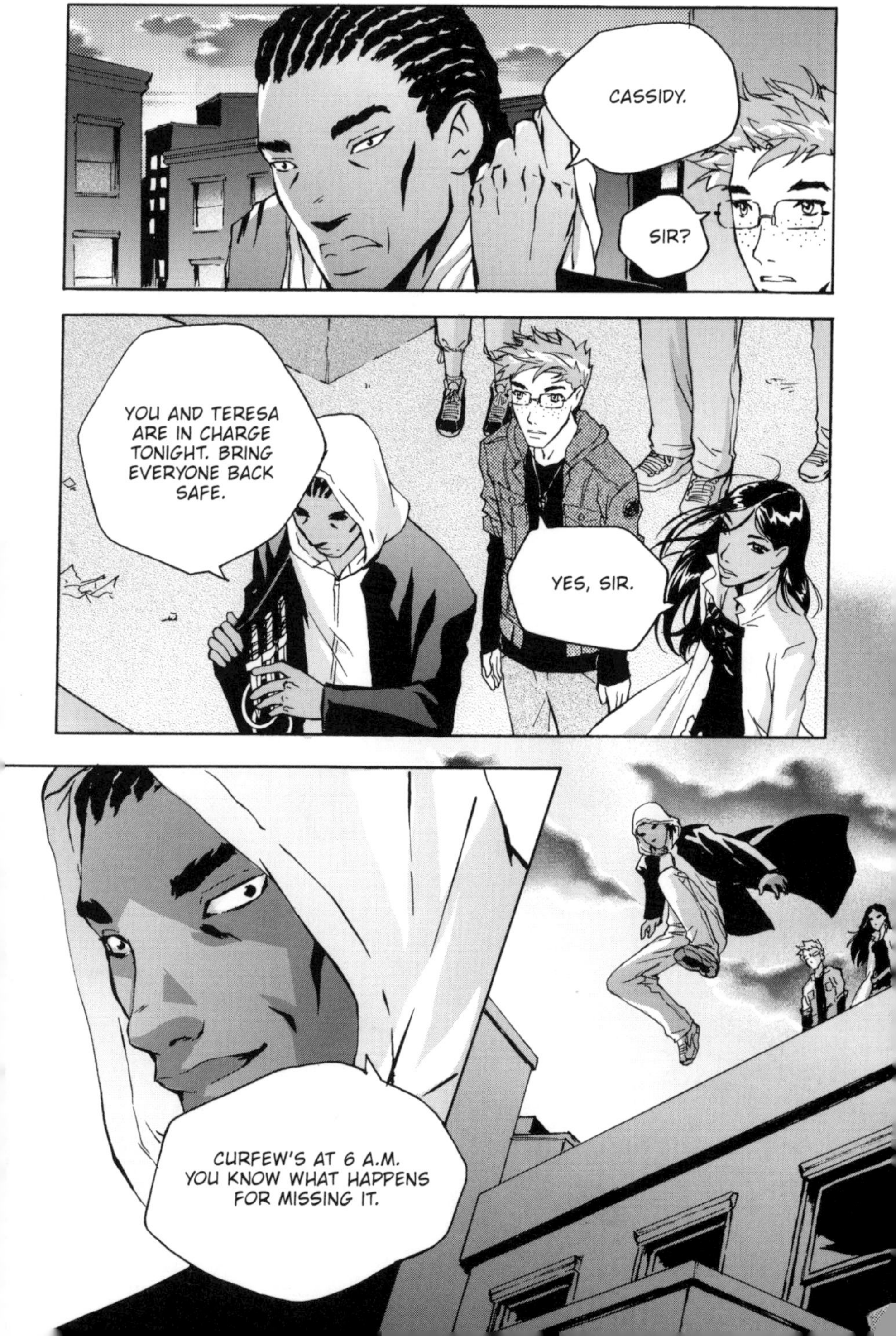
CASSIDY.
SIR?
YOU AND TERESA ARE IN CHARGE TONIGHT. BRING EVERYONE BACK SAFE.
YES, SIR.
CURFEW'S AT 6 A.M. YOU KNOW WHAT HAPPENS FOR MISSING IT.

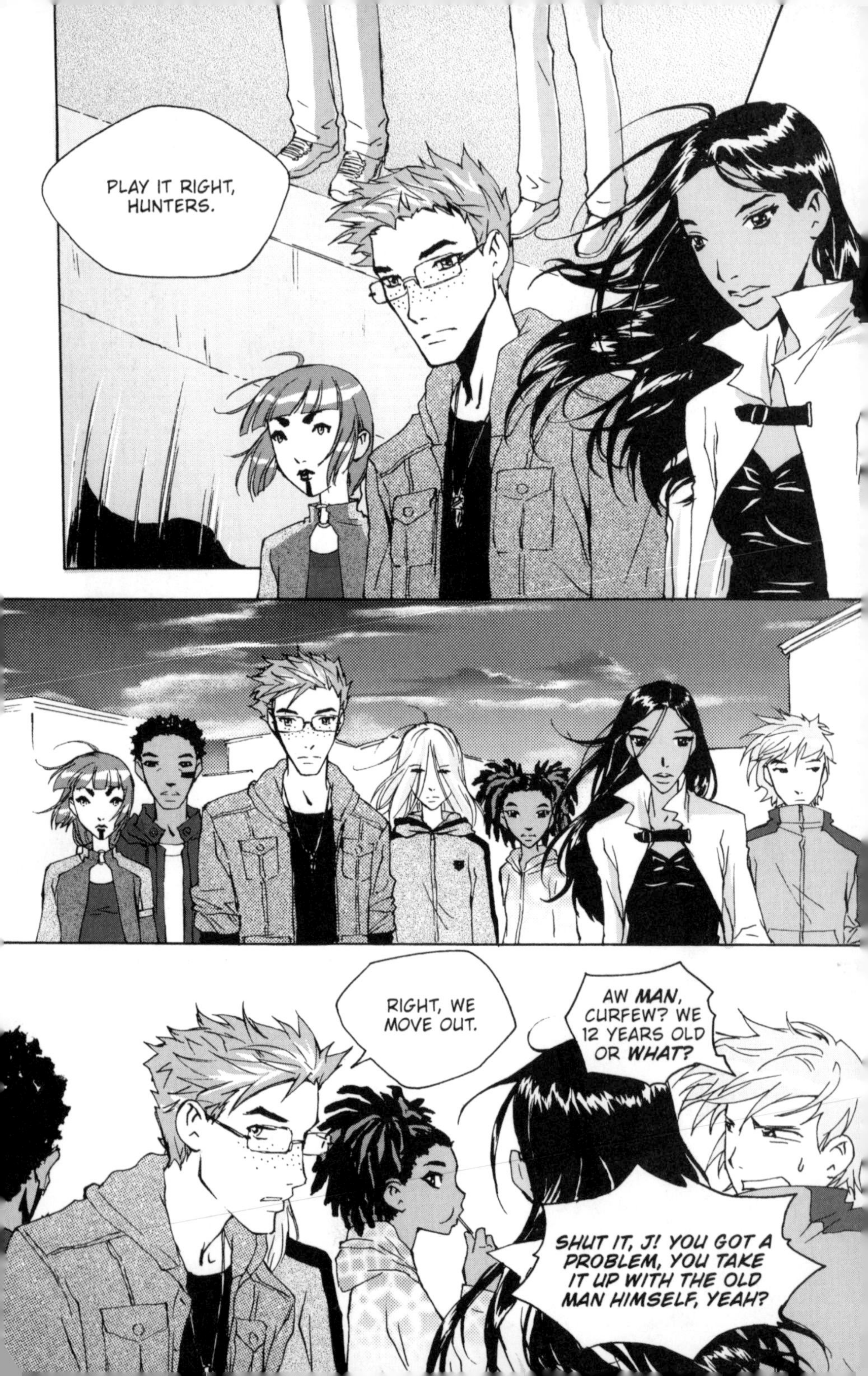
PLAY IT RIGHT, HUNTERS.
RIGHT, WE MOVE OUT.
AW MAN, CURFEW? WE 12 YEARS OLD OR WHAT?
SHUT IT, J! YOU GOT A PROBLEM, YOU TAKE IT UP WITH THE OLD MAN HIMSELF, YEAH?

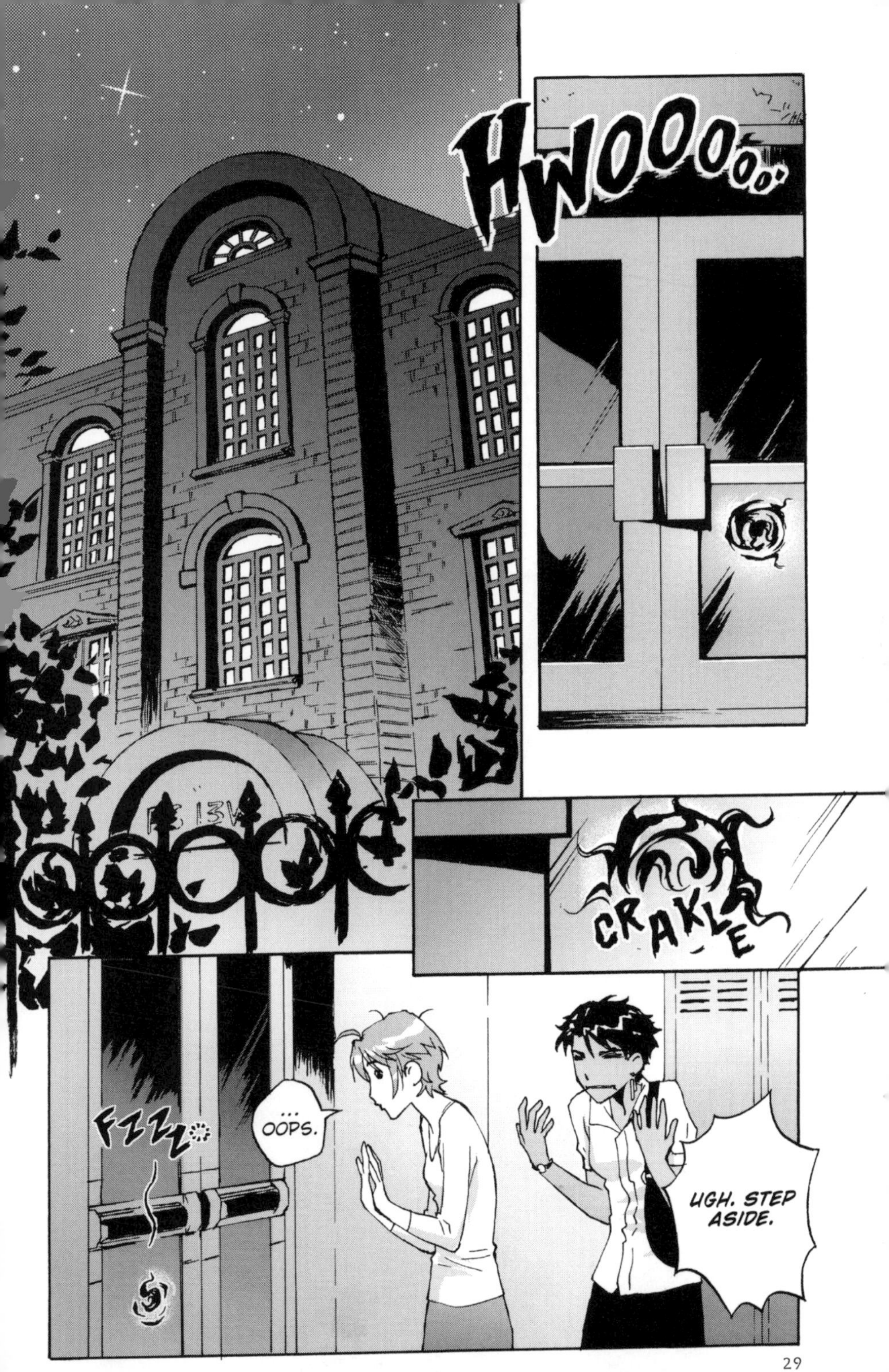
HWOOOOO
CRAKLE
FZZZ
... OOPS.
UGH. STEP ASIDE.

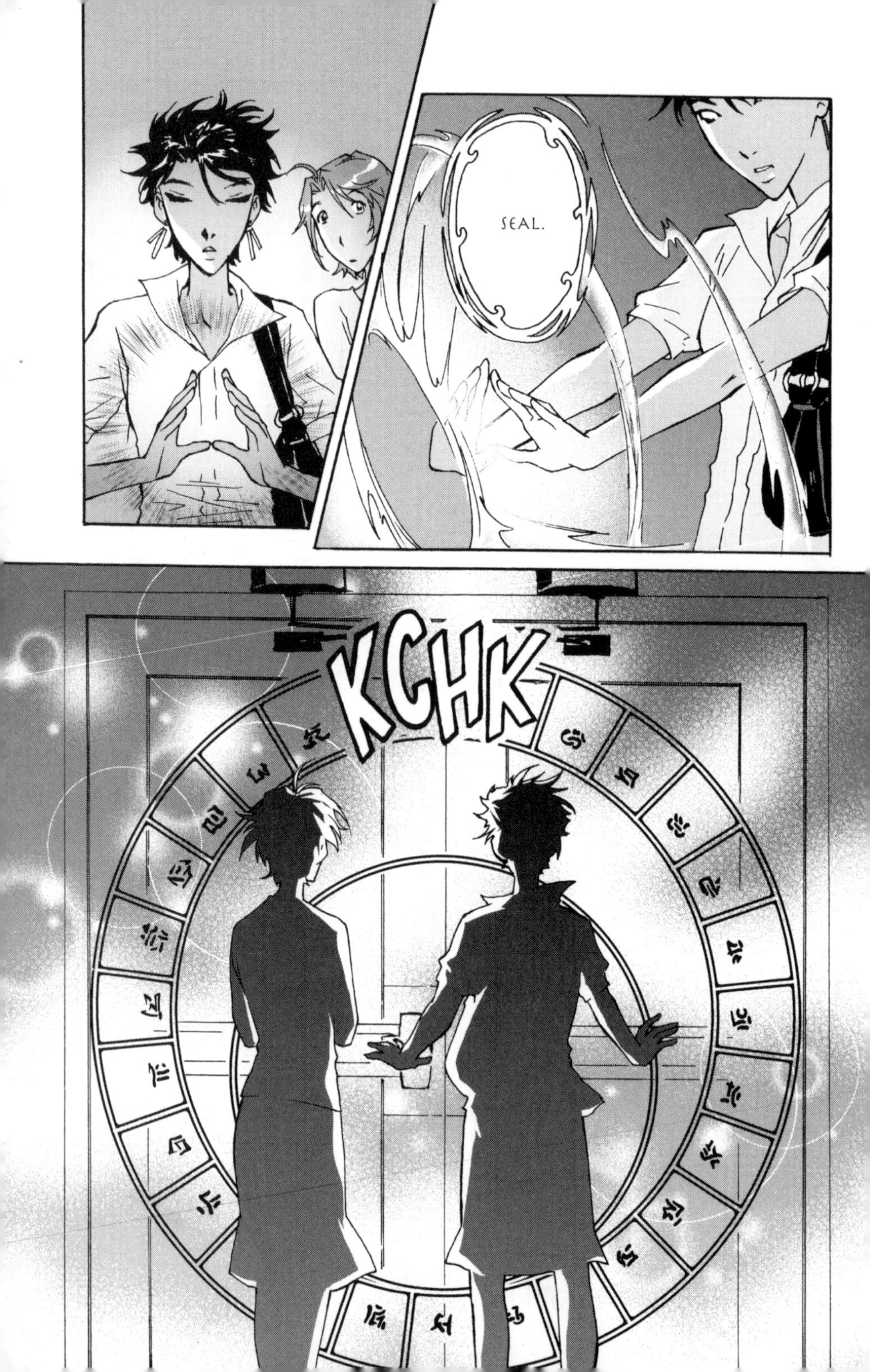
SEAL.
KCHK

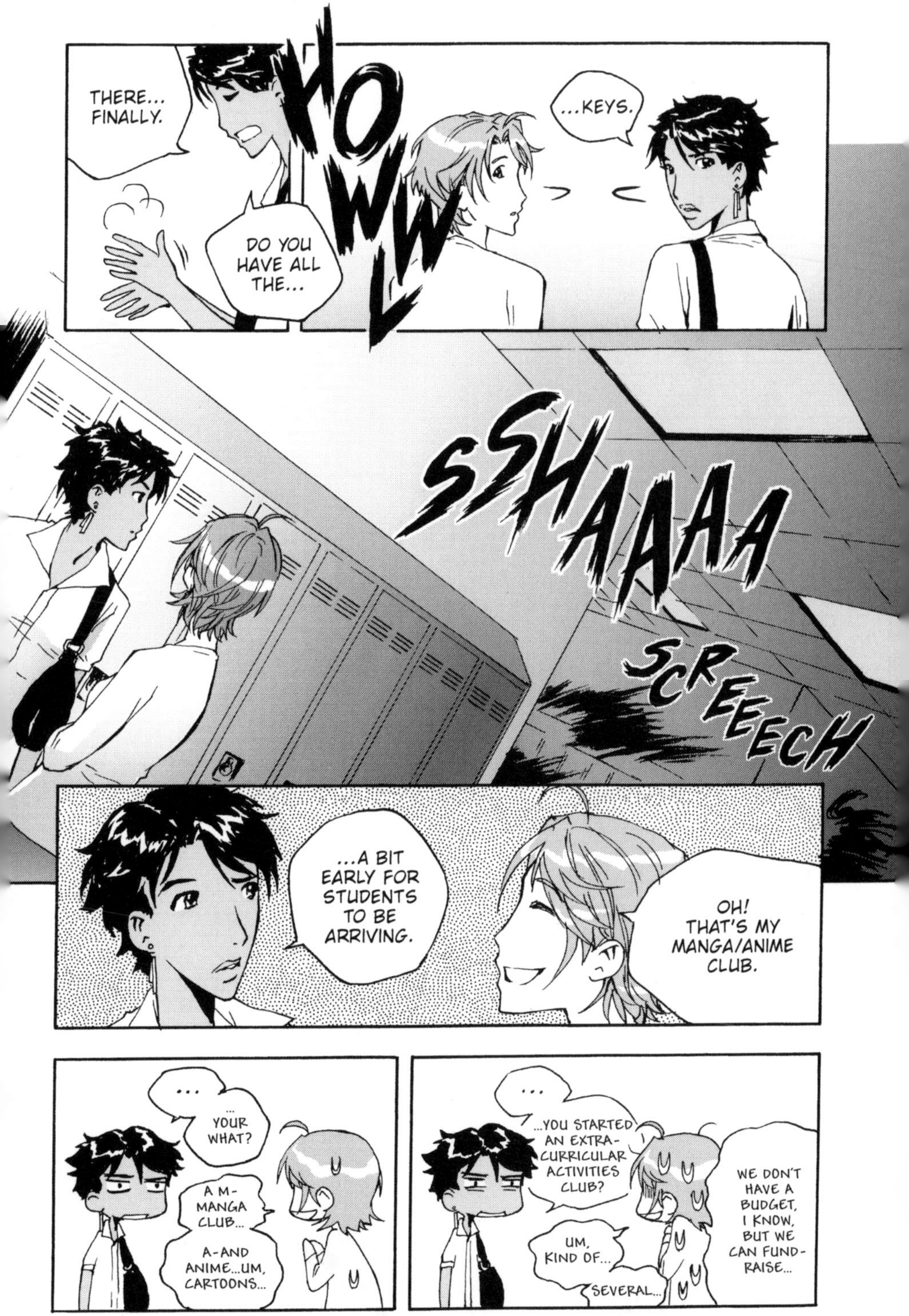

THERE... FINALLY.
HOWWWL
DO YOU HAVE ALL THE...
...KEYS.
sSHAAAAA
SCREEEECH
...A BIT EARLY FOR STUDENTS TO BE ARRIVING.
OH! THAT'S MY MANGA/ANIME CLUB.
...
... YOUR WHAT?
A M-MANGA CLUB...
A-AND ANIME...UM, CARTOONS...
...
...YOU STARTED AN EXTRA-CURRICULAR ACTIVITIES CLUB?
UM, KIND OF...
SEVERAL...
WE DON'T HAVE A BUDGET, I KNOW, BUT WE CAN FUND-RAISE...

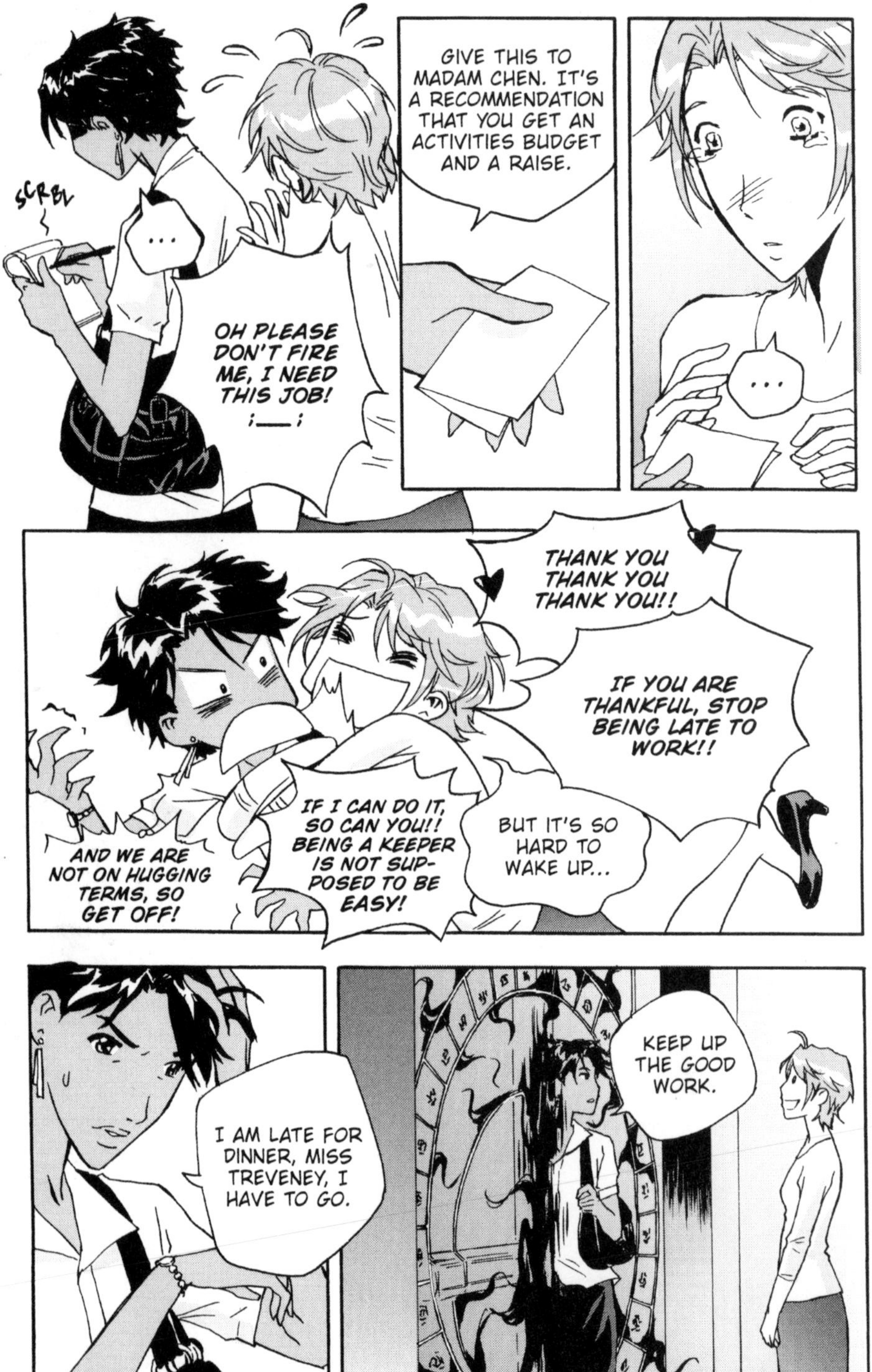
SCRBL
...
OH PLEASE DON'T FIRE ME, I NEED THIS JOB! ;___;
GIVE THIS TO MADAM CHEN. IT'S A RECOMMENDATION THAT YOU GET AN ACTIVITIES BUDGET AND A RAISE.
...
THANK YOU THANK YOU THANK YOU!!
IF YOU ARE THANKFUL, STOP BEING LATE TO WORK!!
BUT IT'S SO HARD TO WAKE UP...
IF I CAN DO IT, SO CAN YOU!! BEING A KEEPER IS NOT SUP-POSED TO BE EASY!
AND WE ARE NOT ON HUGGING TERMS, SO GET OFF!
I AM LATE FOR DINNER, MISS TREVENEY, I HAVE TO GO.
KEEP UP THE GOOD WORK.

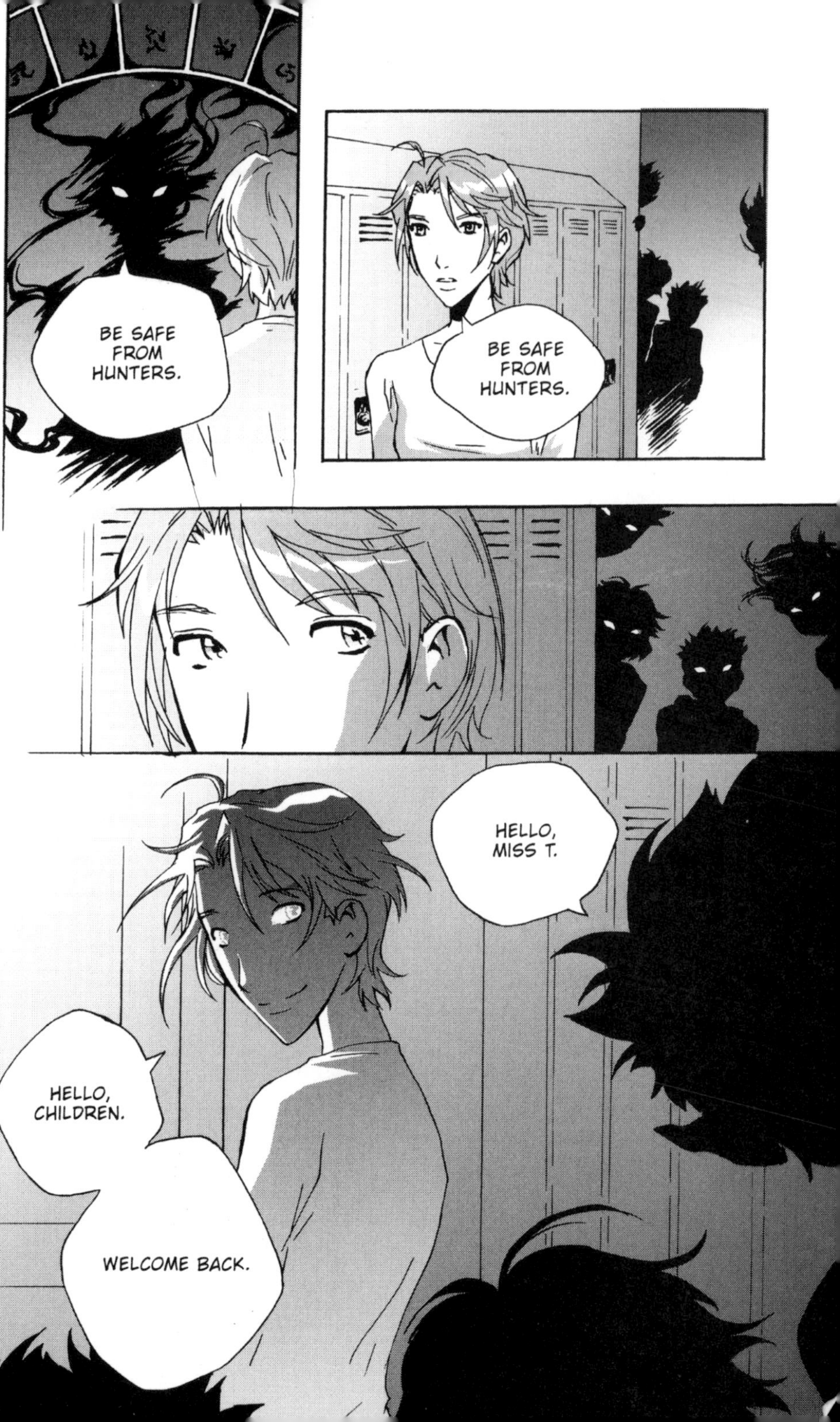
BE SAFE FROM HUNTERS.
BE SAFE FROM HUNTERS.
HELLO, MISS T.
HELLO, CHILDREN.
WELCOME BACK.

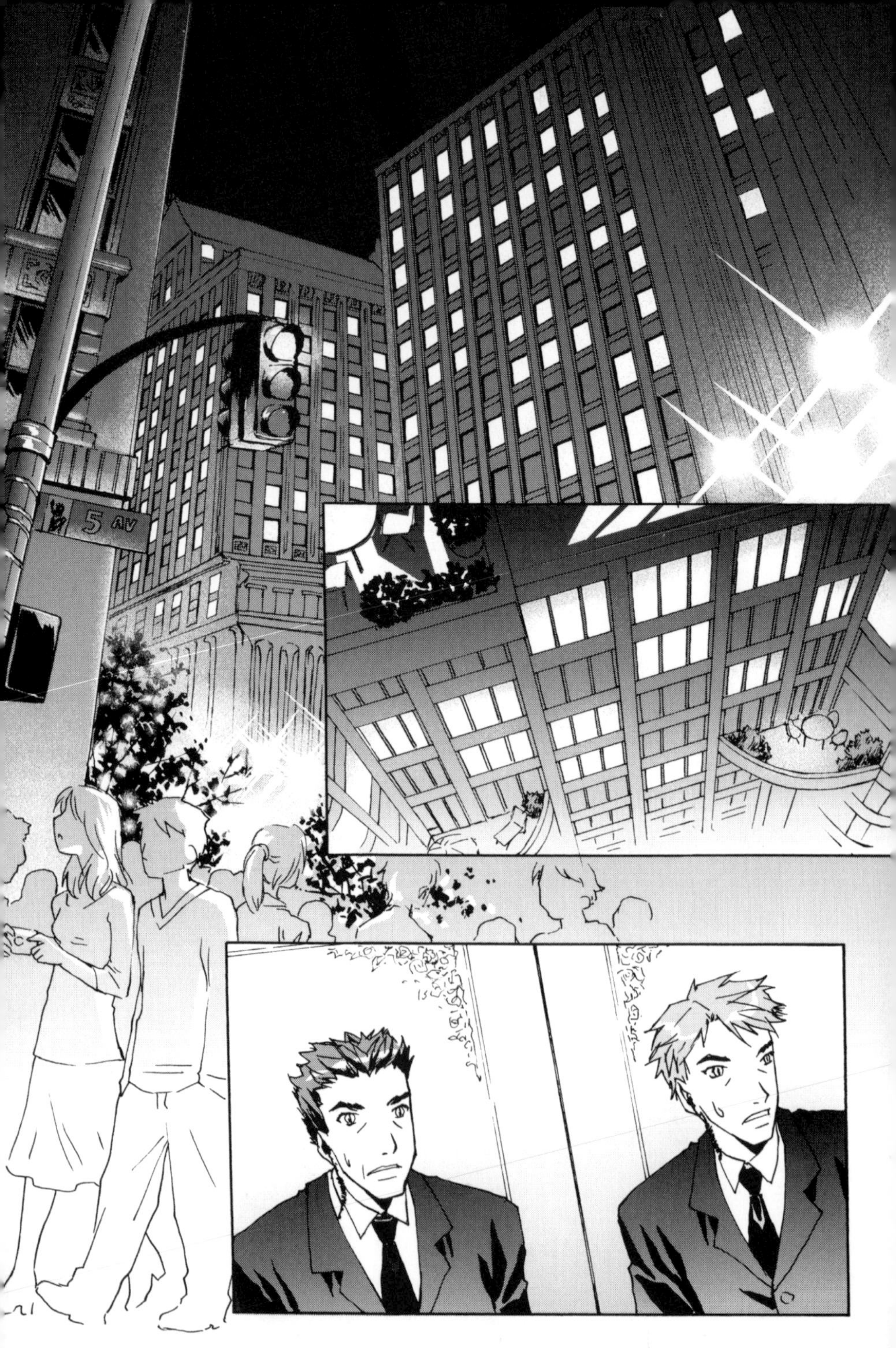
5 AV

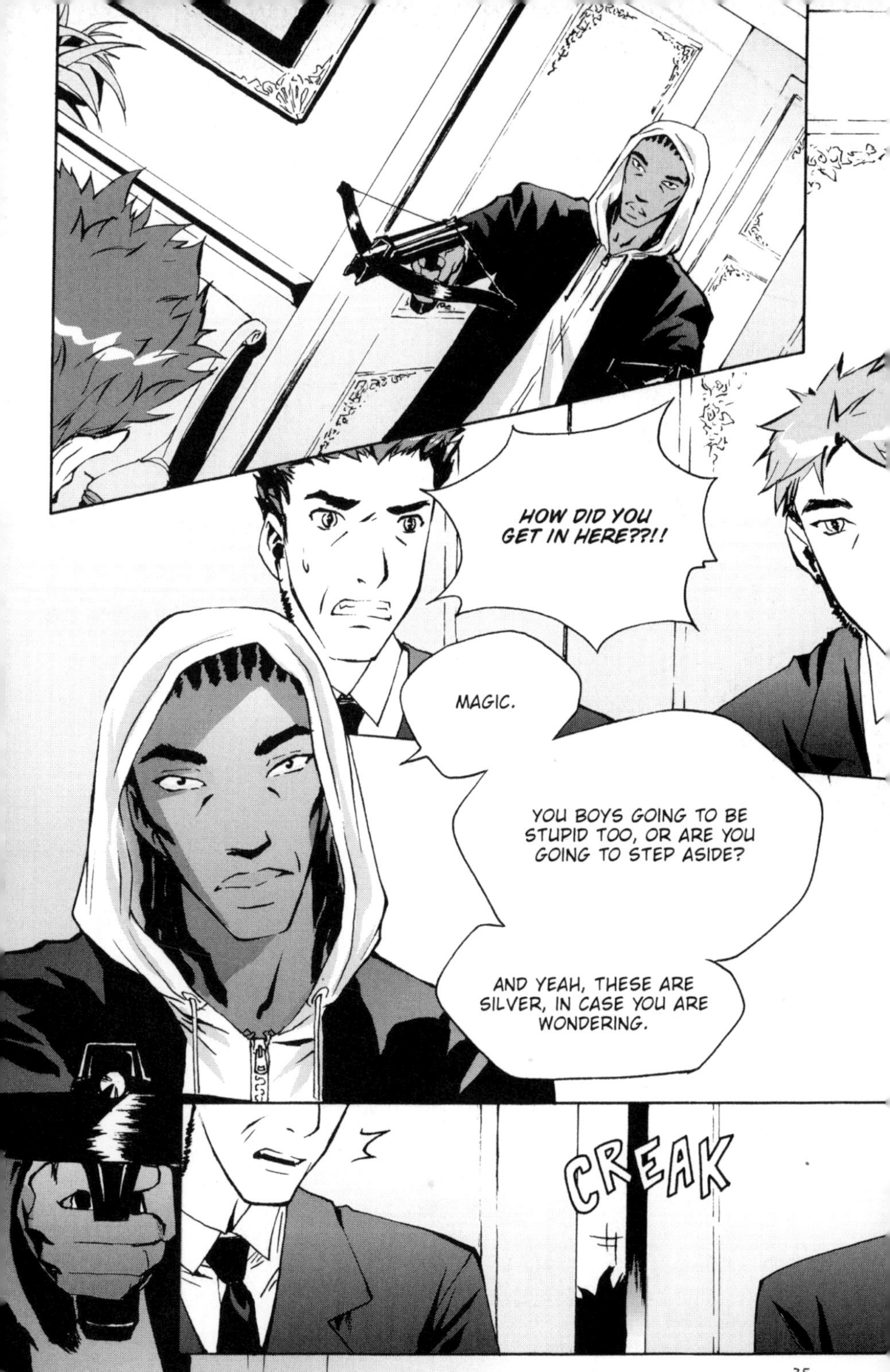
HOW DID YOU GET IN HERE??!!
MAGIC.
YOU BOYS GOING TO BE STUPID TOO, OR ARE YOU GOING TO STEP ASIDE?
AND YEAH, THESE ARE SILVER, IN CASE YOU ARE WONDERING.
CREAK

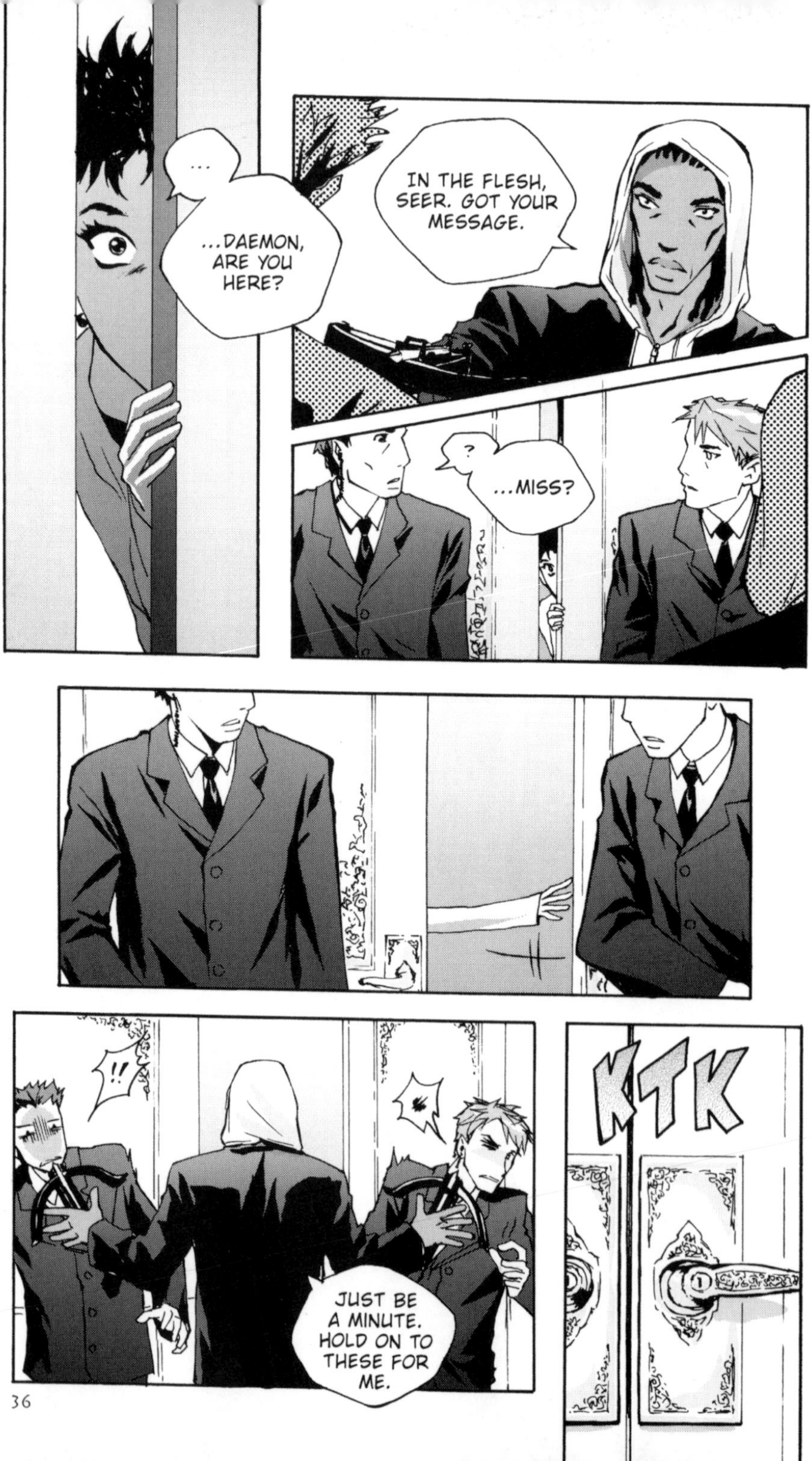
...
...DAEMON, ARE YOU HERE?
IN THE FLESH, SEER. GOT YOUR MESSAGE.
?
...MISS?
!!
JUST BE A MINUTE. HOLD ON TO THESE FOR ME.
KTK

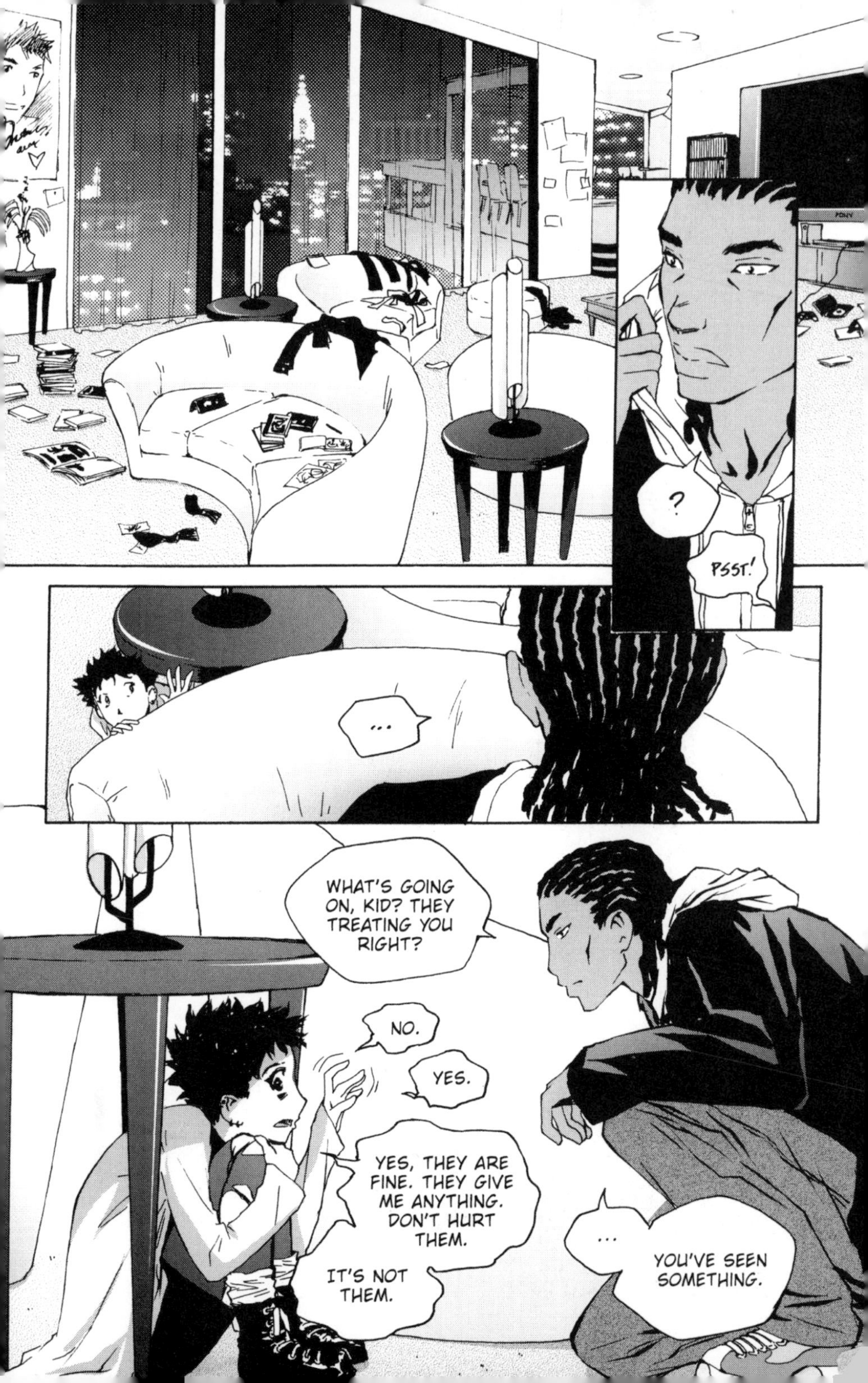
?
PSST!
...
WHAT'S GOING ON, KID? THEY TREATING YOU RIGHT?
NO.
YES.
YES, THEY ARE FINE. THEY GIVE ME ANYTHING. DON'T HURT THEM.
IT'S NOT THEM.
...
YOU'VE SEEN SOMETHING.

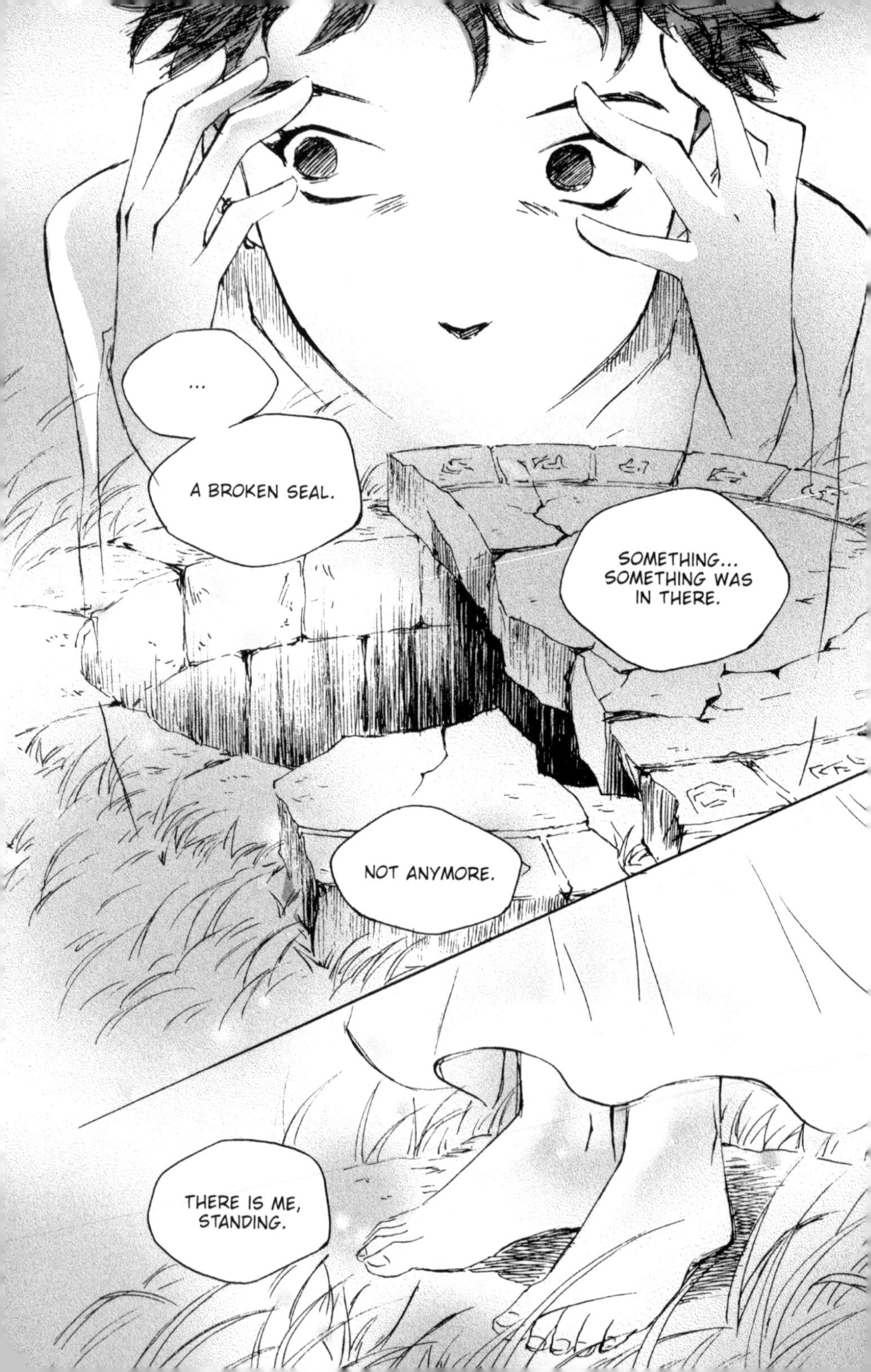
...
A BROKEN SEAL.
SOMETHING... SOMETHING WAS IN THERE.
NOT ANYMORE.
THERE IS ME, STANDING.

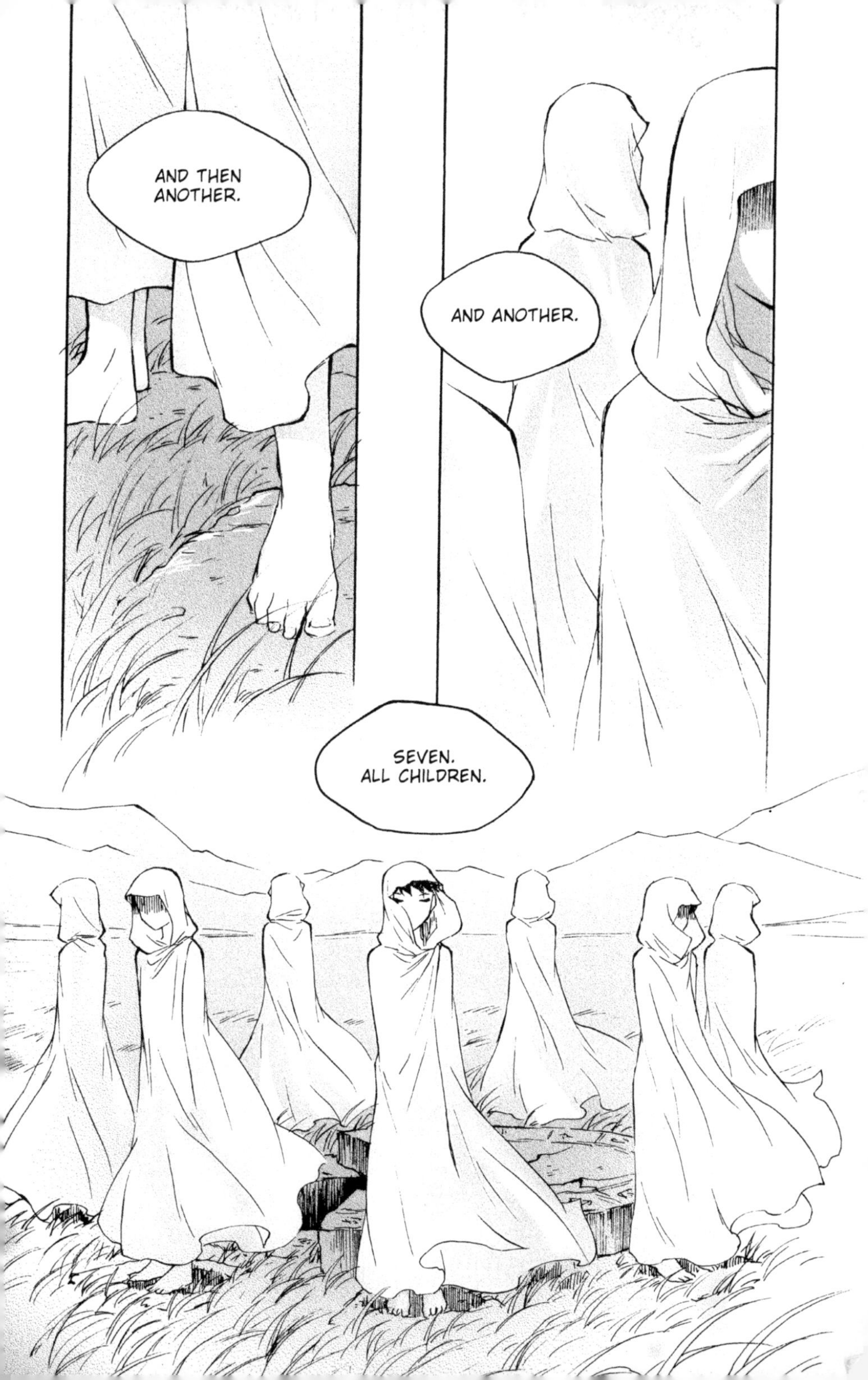
AND THEN ANOTHER.
AND ANOTHER.
SEVEN. ALL CHILDREN.

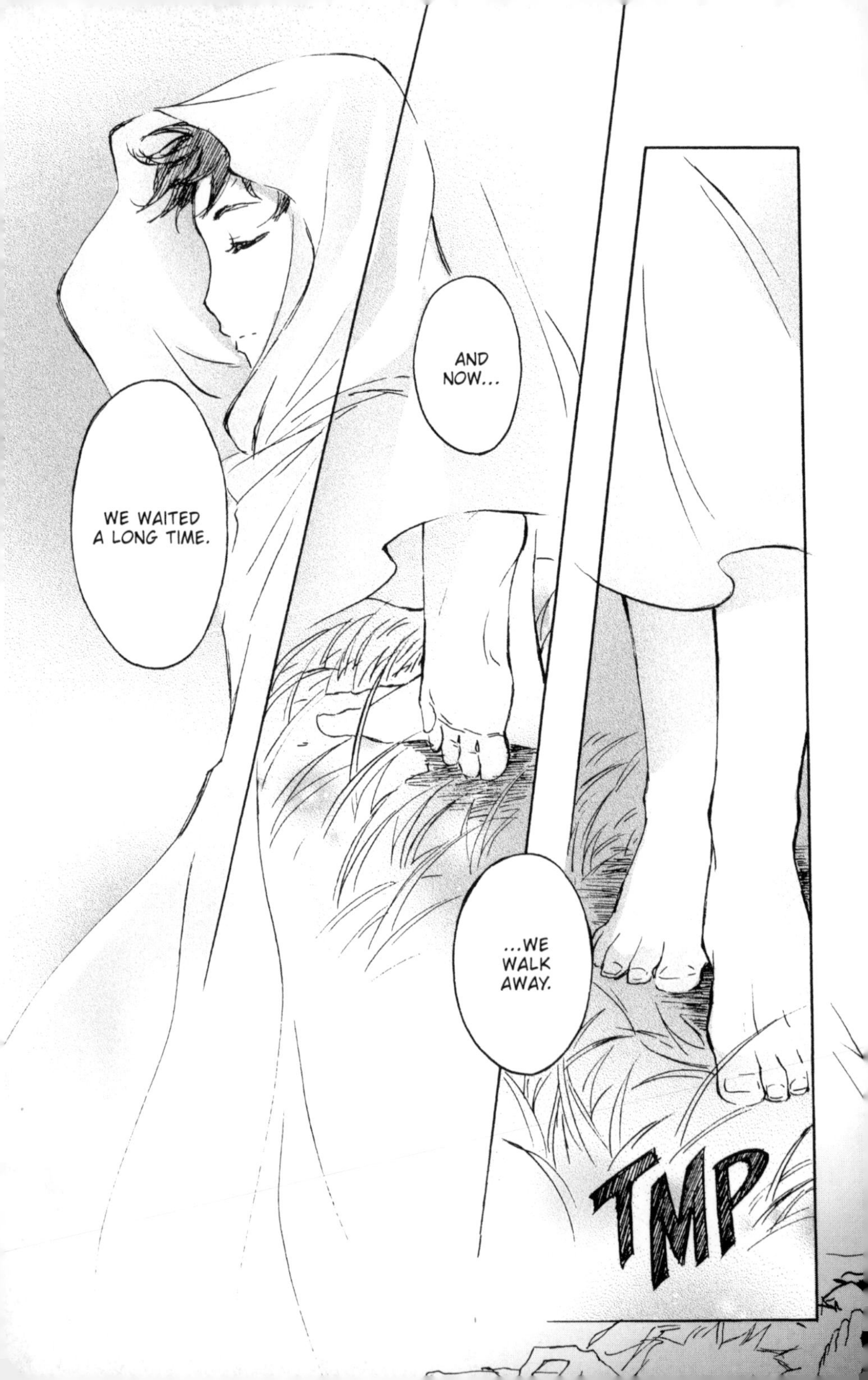
AND NOW...
...WE WALK AWAY.
TMP
WE WAITED A LONG TIME.

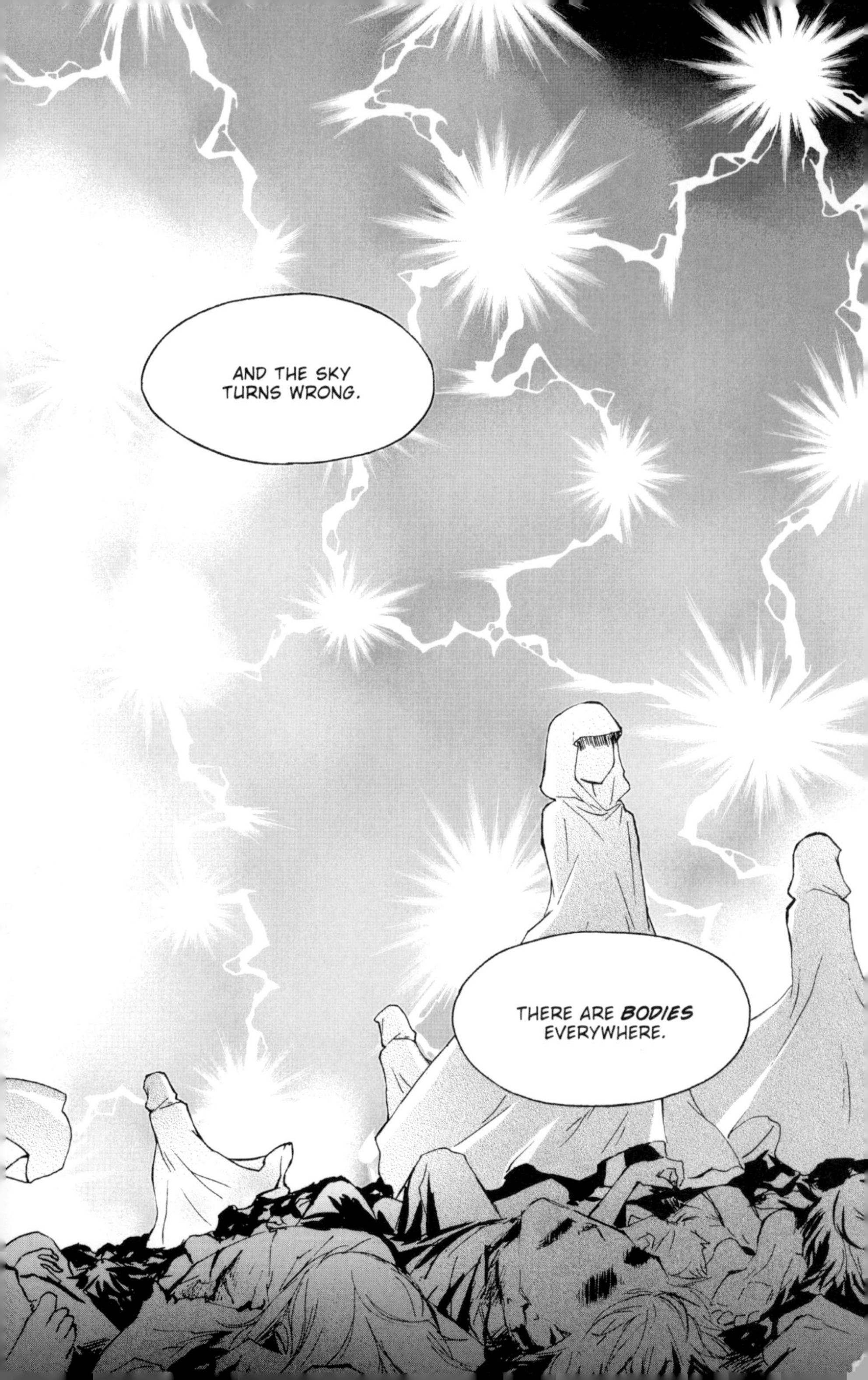
AND THE SKY TURNS WRONG.
THERE ARE BODIES EVERYWHERE.

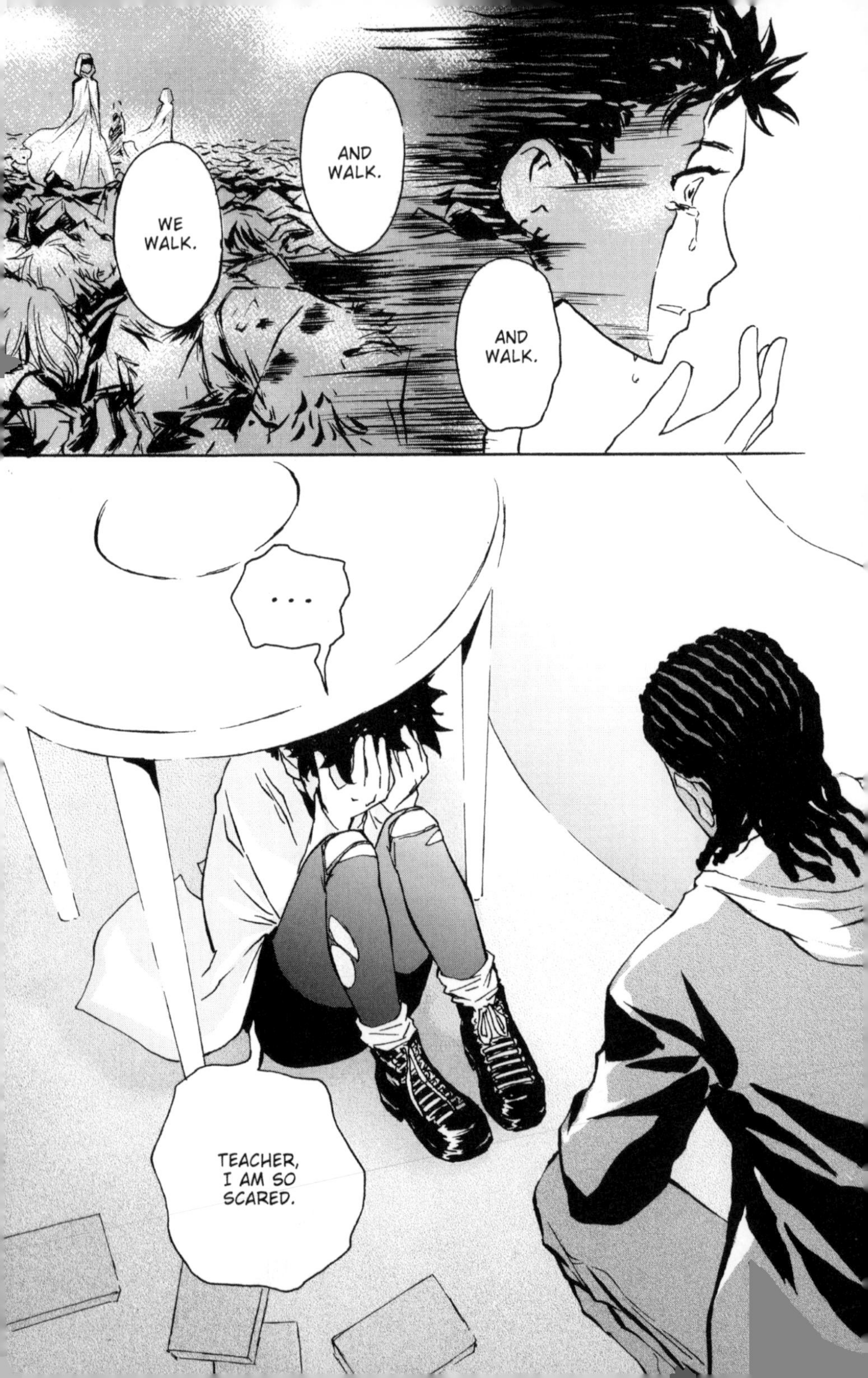
WE WALK.
AND WALK.
AND WALK.
...
TEACHER, I AM SO SCARED.

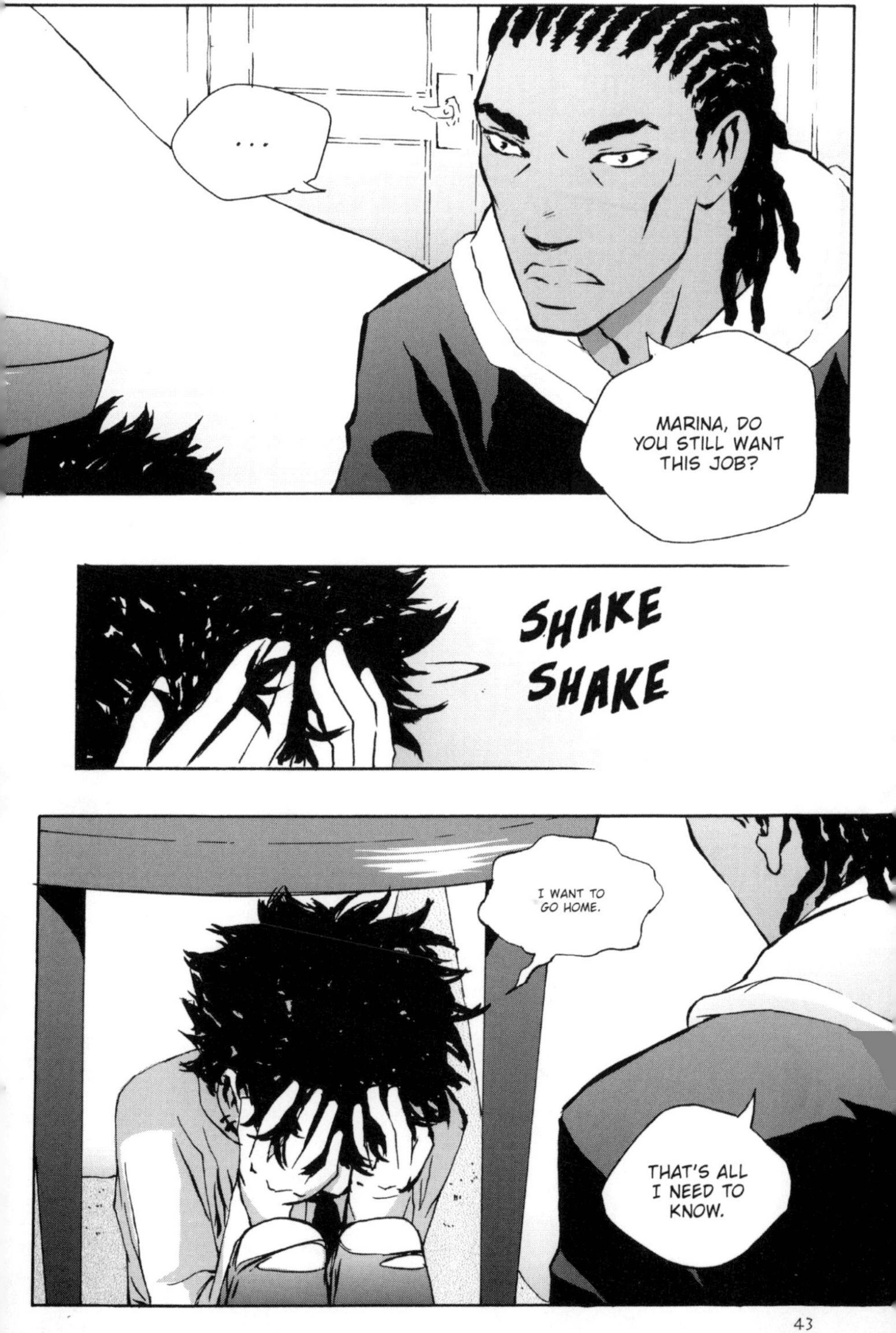
...
MARINA, DO YOU STILL WANT THIS JOB?
SHAKE
SHAKE
I WANT TO GO HOME.
THAT'S ALL I NEED TO KNOW.

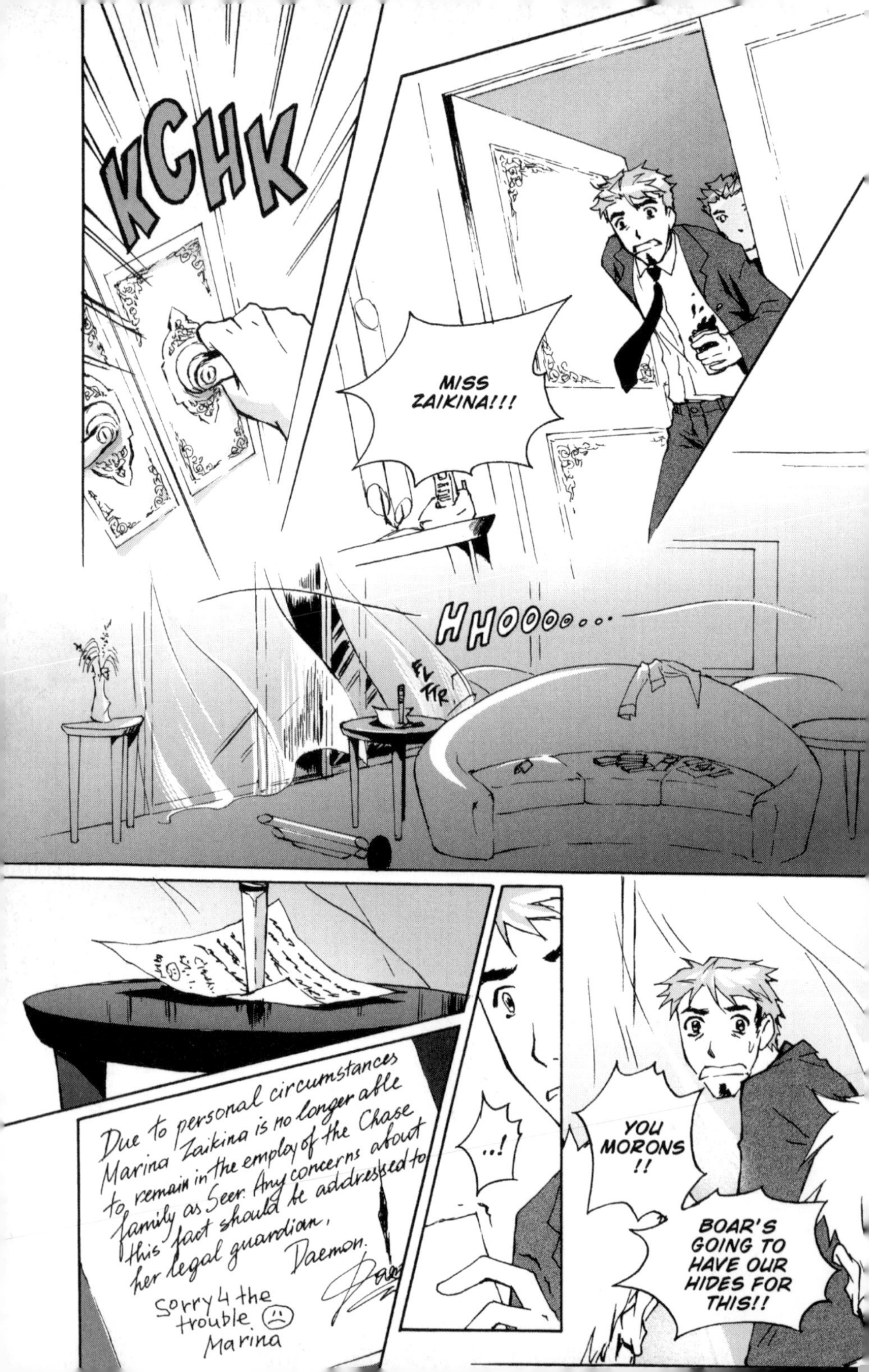
KCHK
MISS ZAIKINA!!!
HHOOooo...
FLTTR
Due to personal circumstances Marina Zaikina is no longer able to remain in the employ of the Chase family as Seer. Any concerns about this fact should be addressed to her legal guardian,
Daemon.
Sorry 4 the trouble ☹ Marina
YOU MORONS !!
..!
BOAR'S GOING TO HAVE OUR HIDES FOR THIS!!

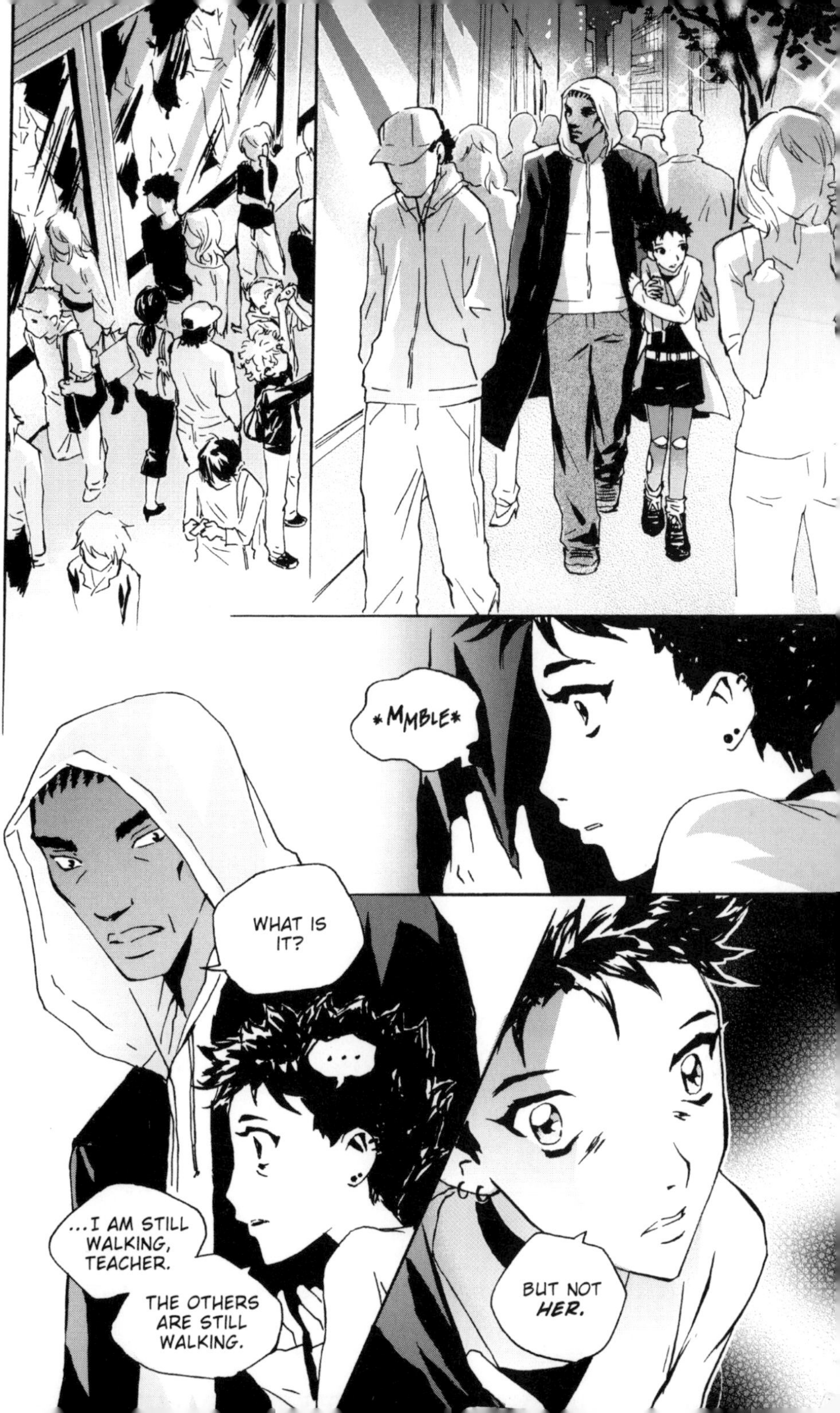
MMBLE
WHAT IS IT?
...
...I AM STILL WALKING, TEACHER.
THE OTHERS ARE STILL WALKING.
BUT NOT *HER.*

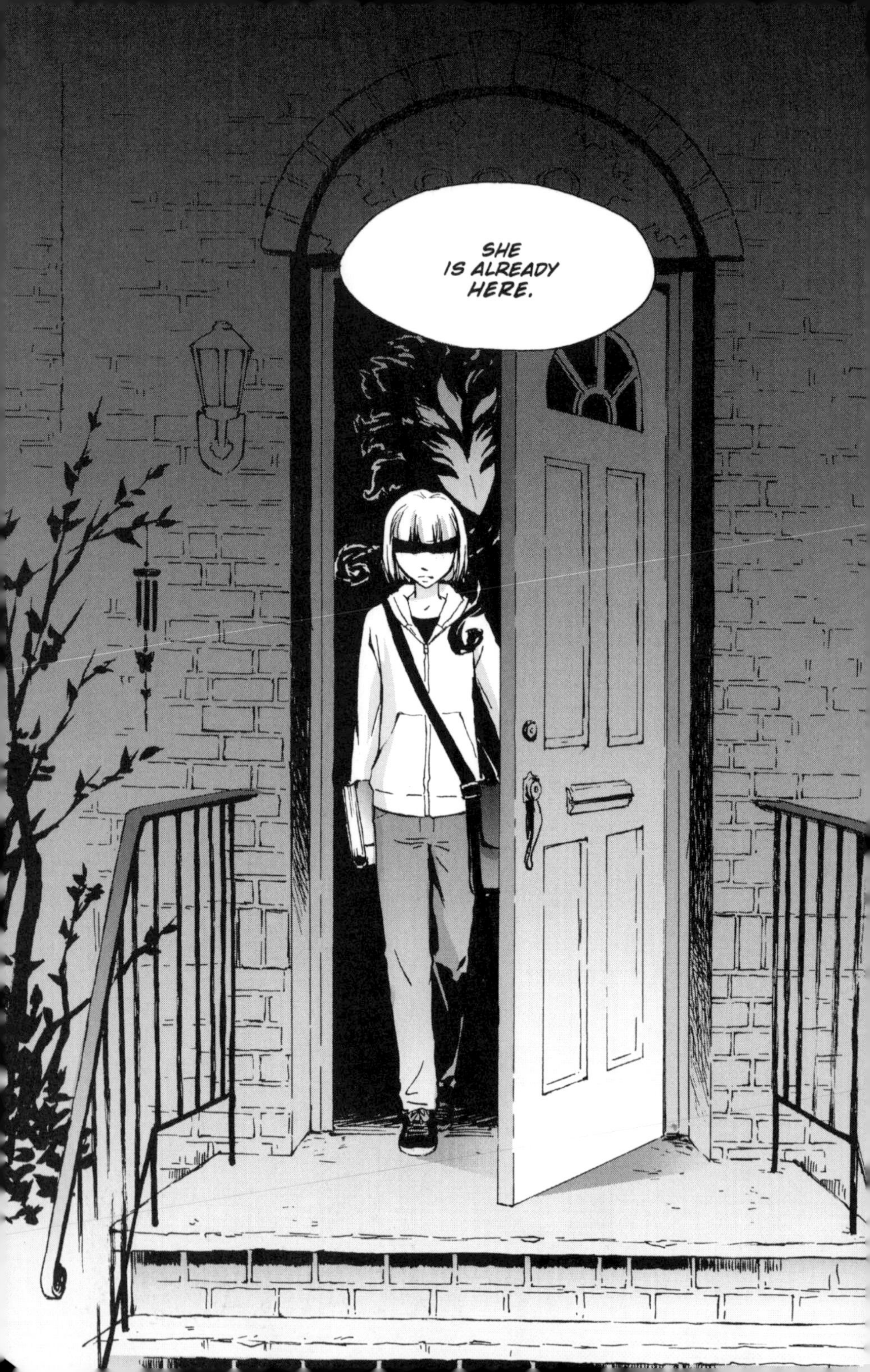
SHE IS ALREADY HERE.

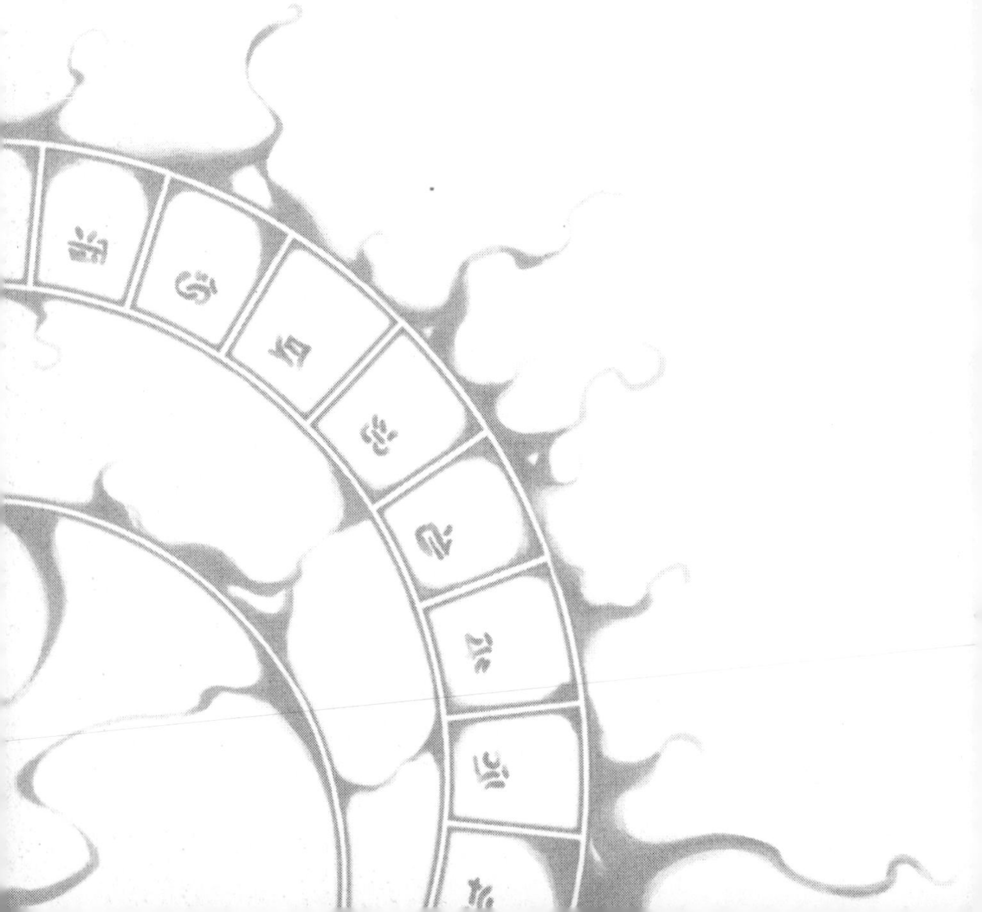

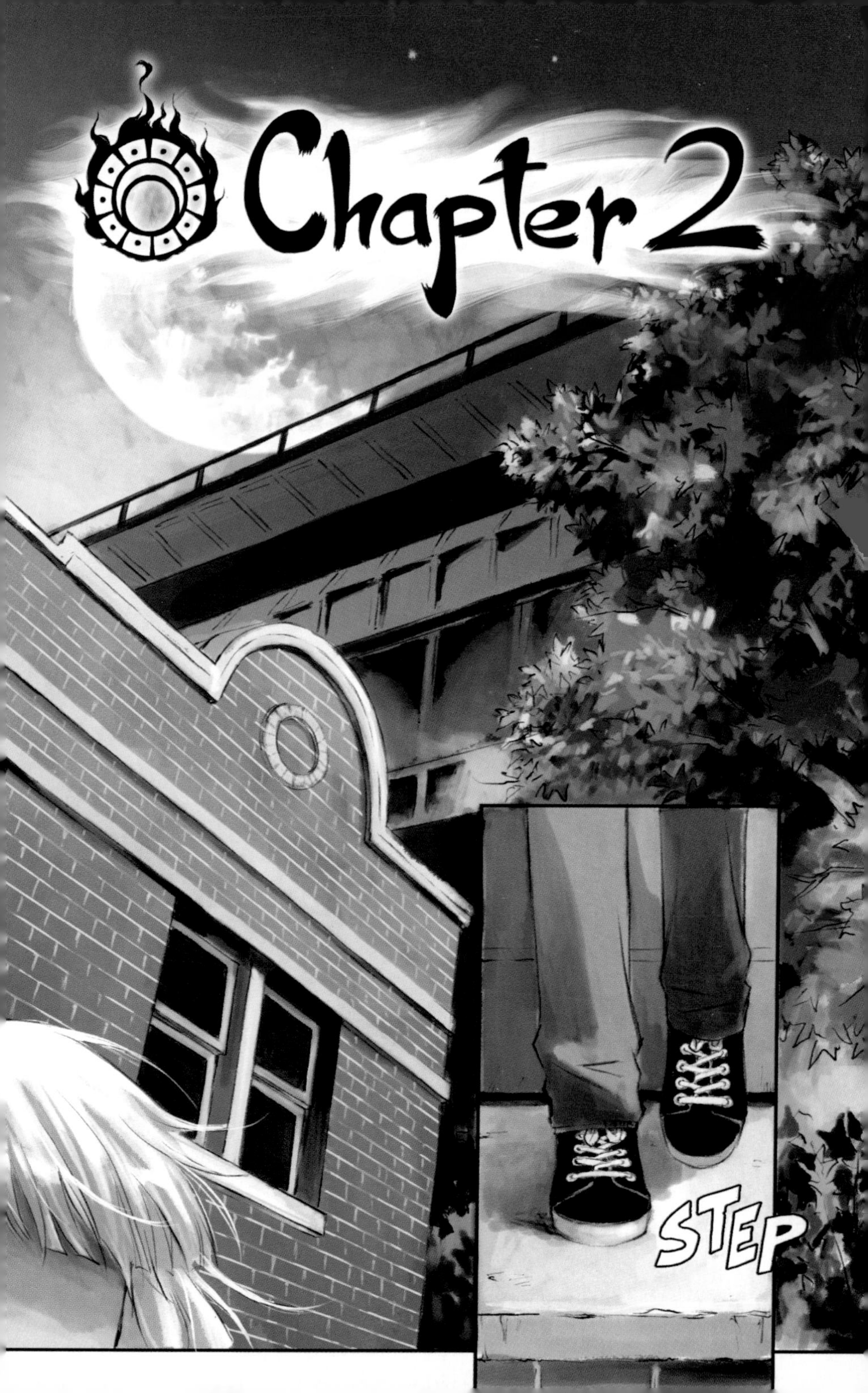
Chapter 2
STEP

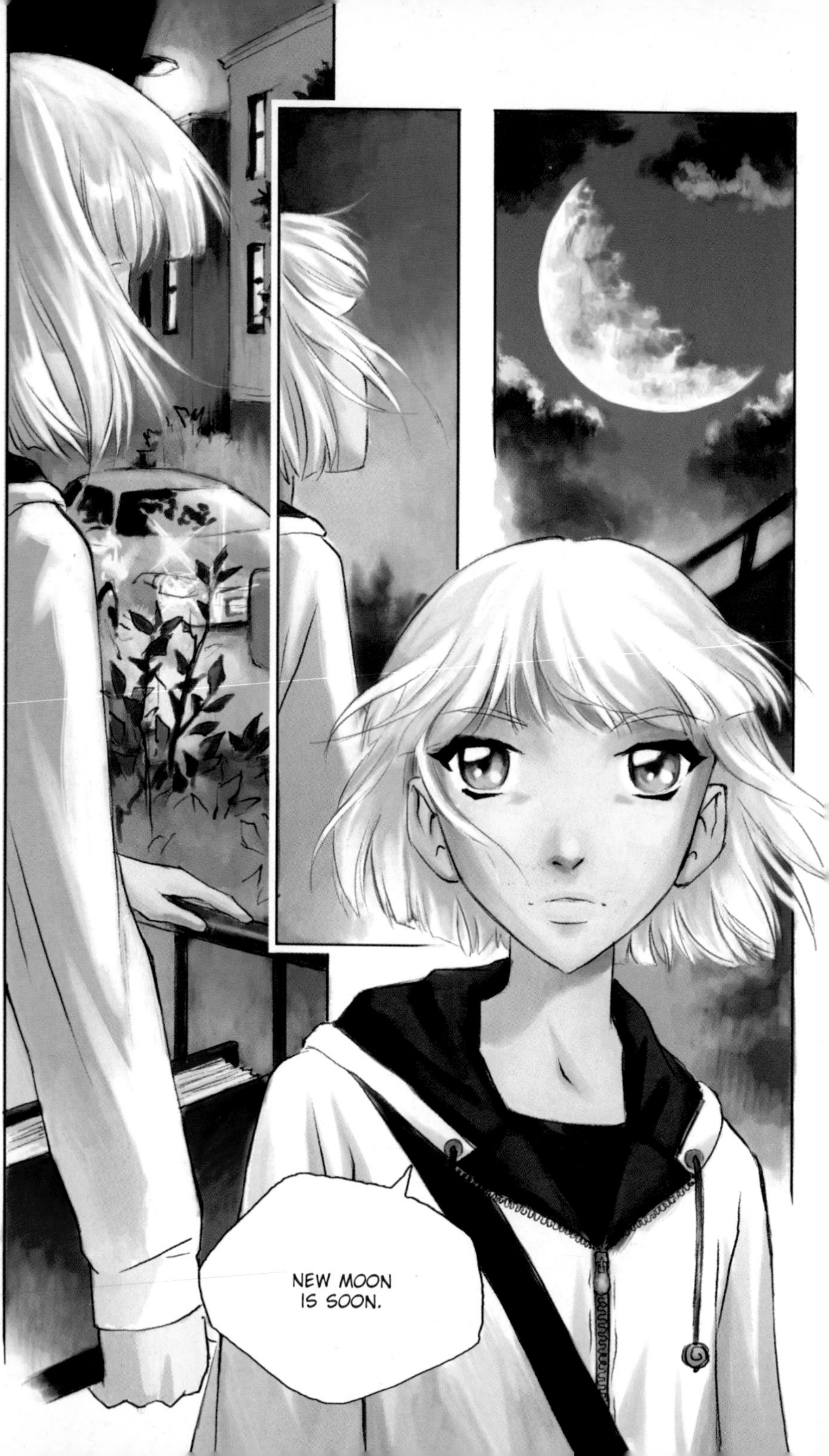
NEW MOON IS SOON.

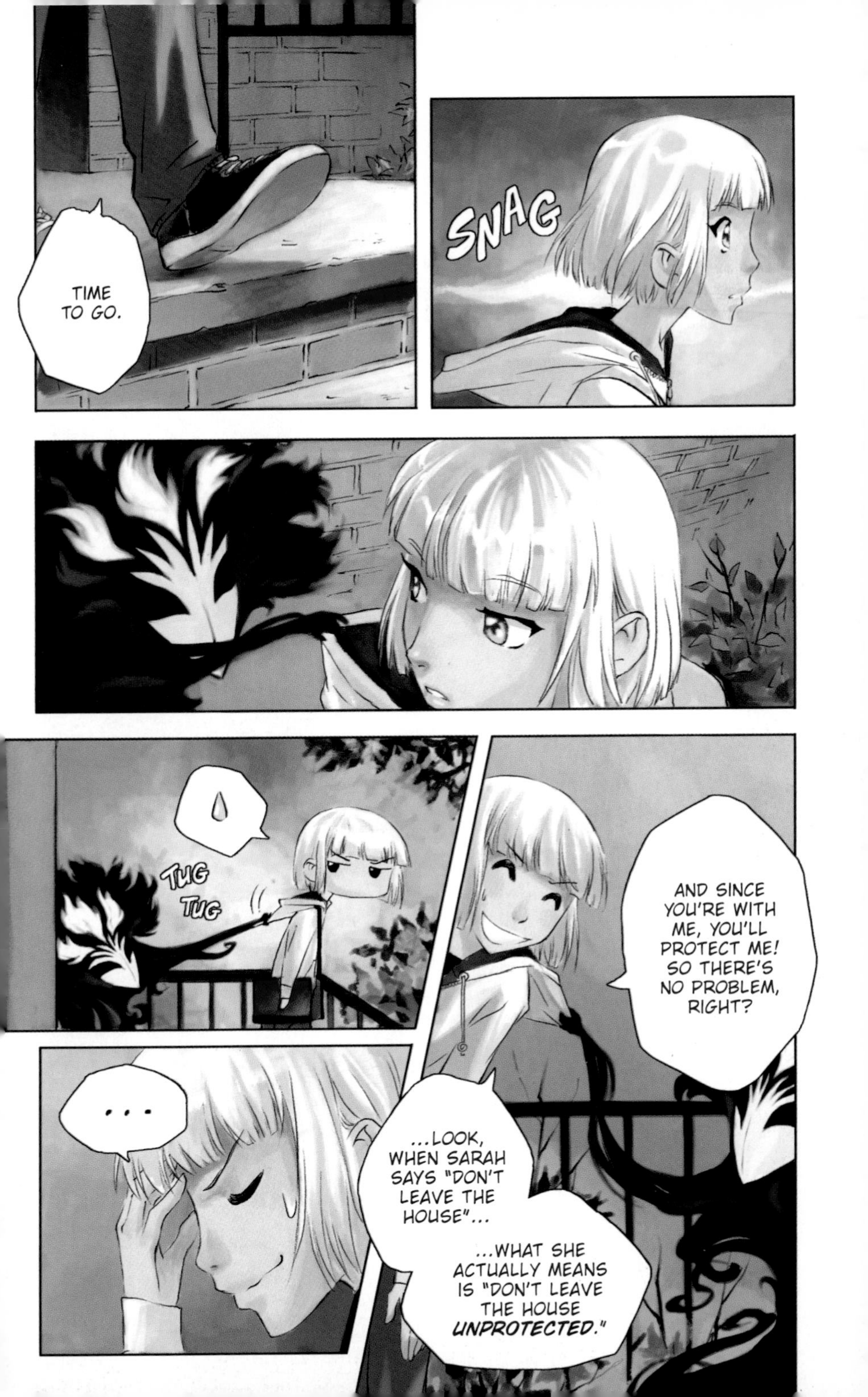
TIME TO GO.
SNAG
TUG TUG
AND SINCE YOU'RE WITH ME, YOU'LL PROTECT ME! SO THERE'S NO PROBLEM, RIGHT?
...
...LOOK, WHEN SARAH SAYS "DON'T LEAVE THE HOUSE"...
...WHAT SHE ACTUALLY MEANS IS "DON'T LEAVE THE HOUSE UNPROTECTED."

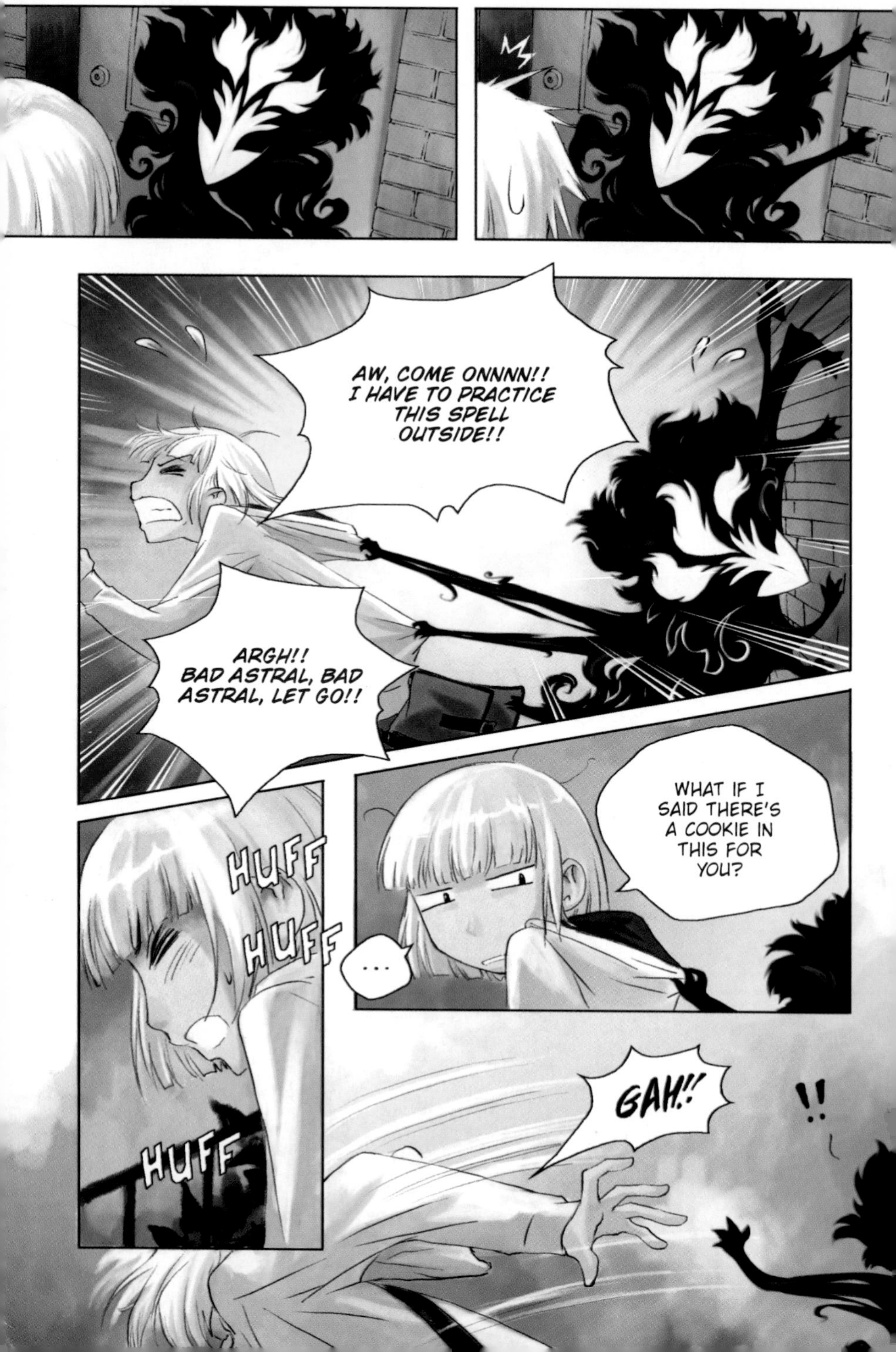
AW, COME ONNNN!! I HAVE TO PRACTICE THIS SPELL OUTSIDE!!
ARGH!! BAD ASTRAL, BAD ASTRAL, LET GO!!
WHAT IF I SAID THERE'S A COOKIE IN THIS FOR YOU?
HUFF
HUFF
...
HUFF
GAH!!
!!

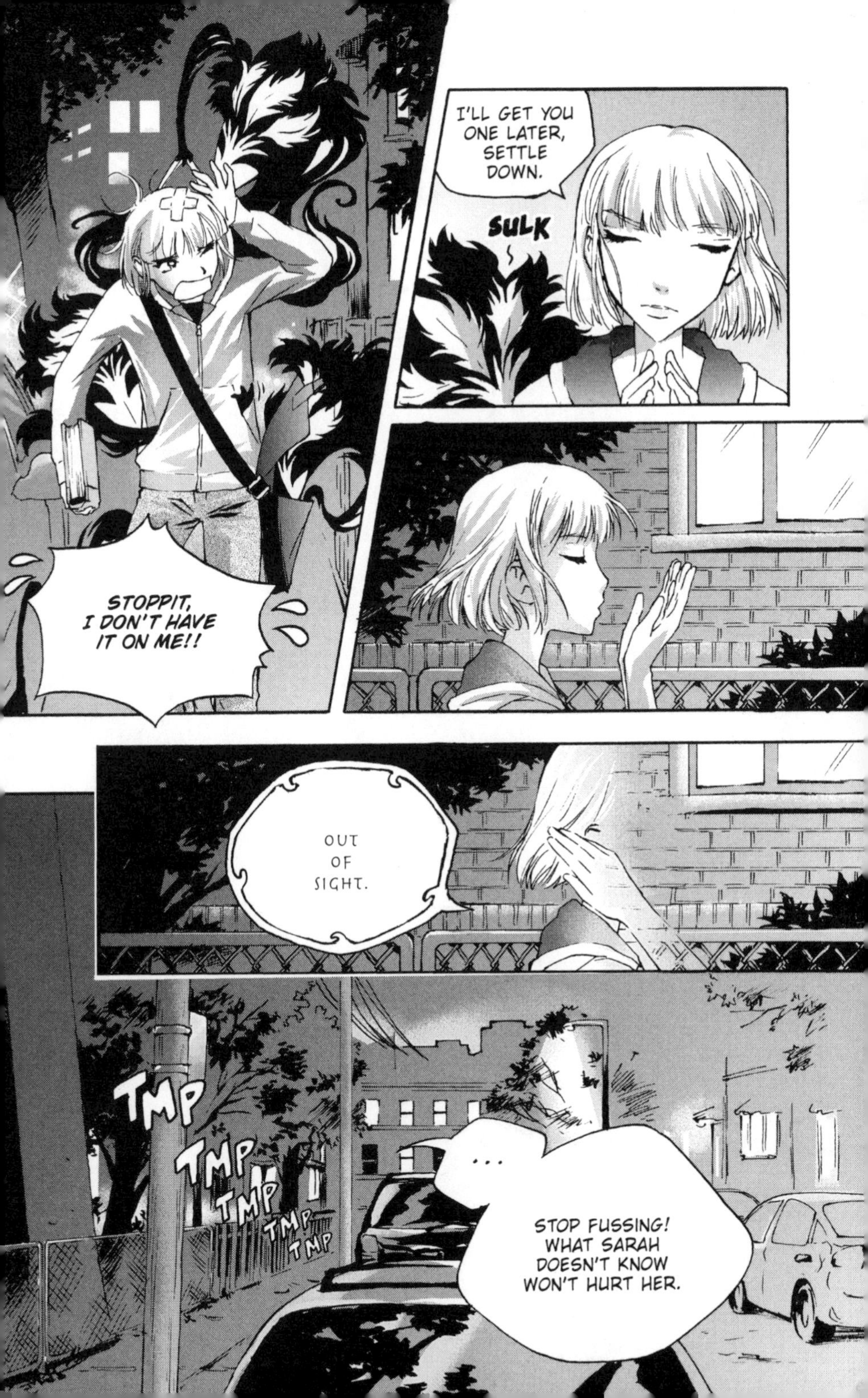
STOPPIT, I DON'T HAVE IT ON ME!!
I'LL GET YOU ONE LATER, SETTLE DOWN.
SULK
OUT OF SIGHT.
TMP TMP TMP TMP TMP
...
STOP FUSSING! WHAT SARAH DOESN'T KNOW WON'T HURT HER.

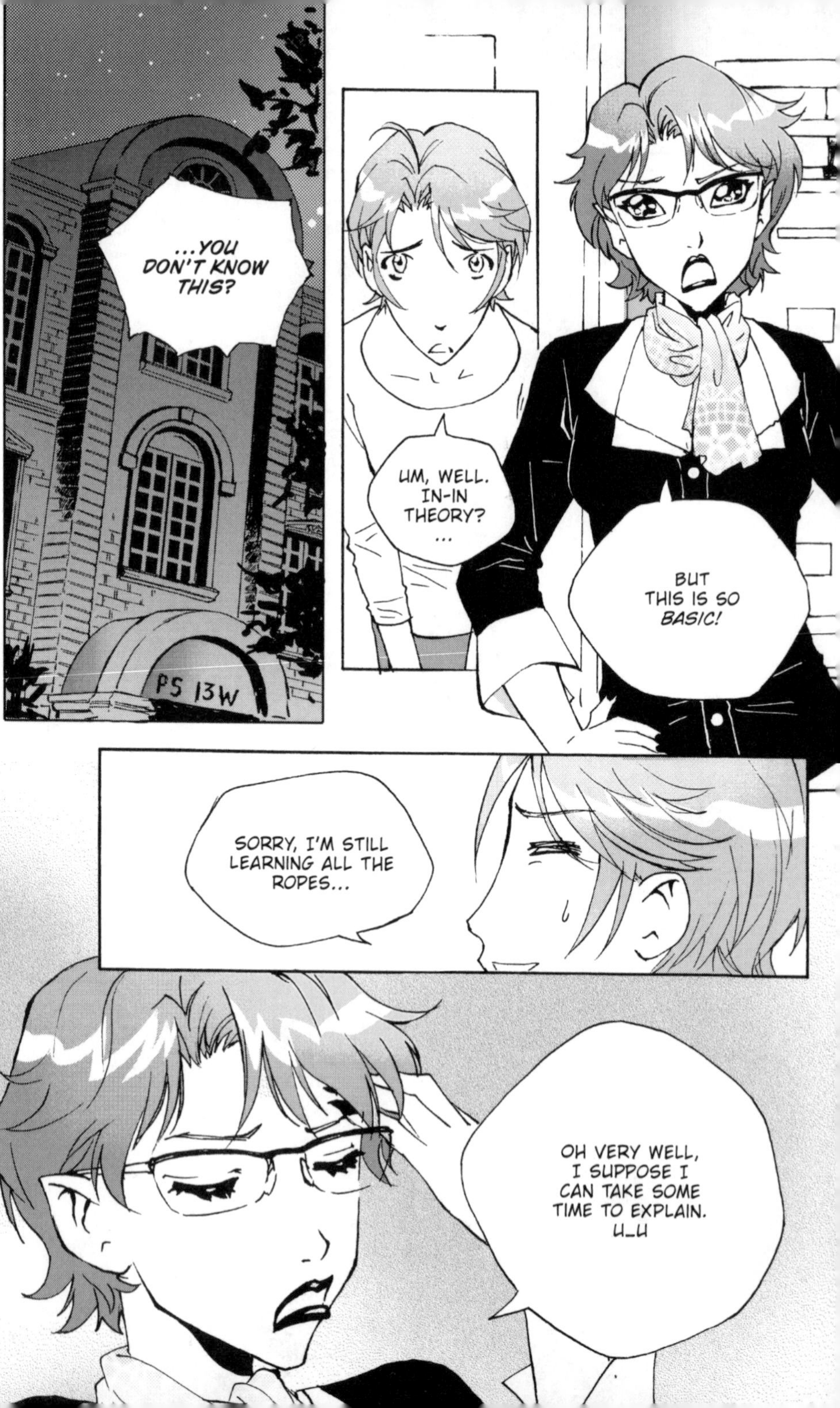
...YOU DON'T KNOW THIS?
PS 13W
UM, WELL. IN-IN THEORY? ...
BUT THIS IS SO *BASIC!*
SORRY, I'M STILL LEARNING ALL THE ROPES...
OH VERY WELL, I SUPPOSE I CAN TAKE SOME TIME TO EXPLAIN. u_u

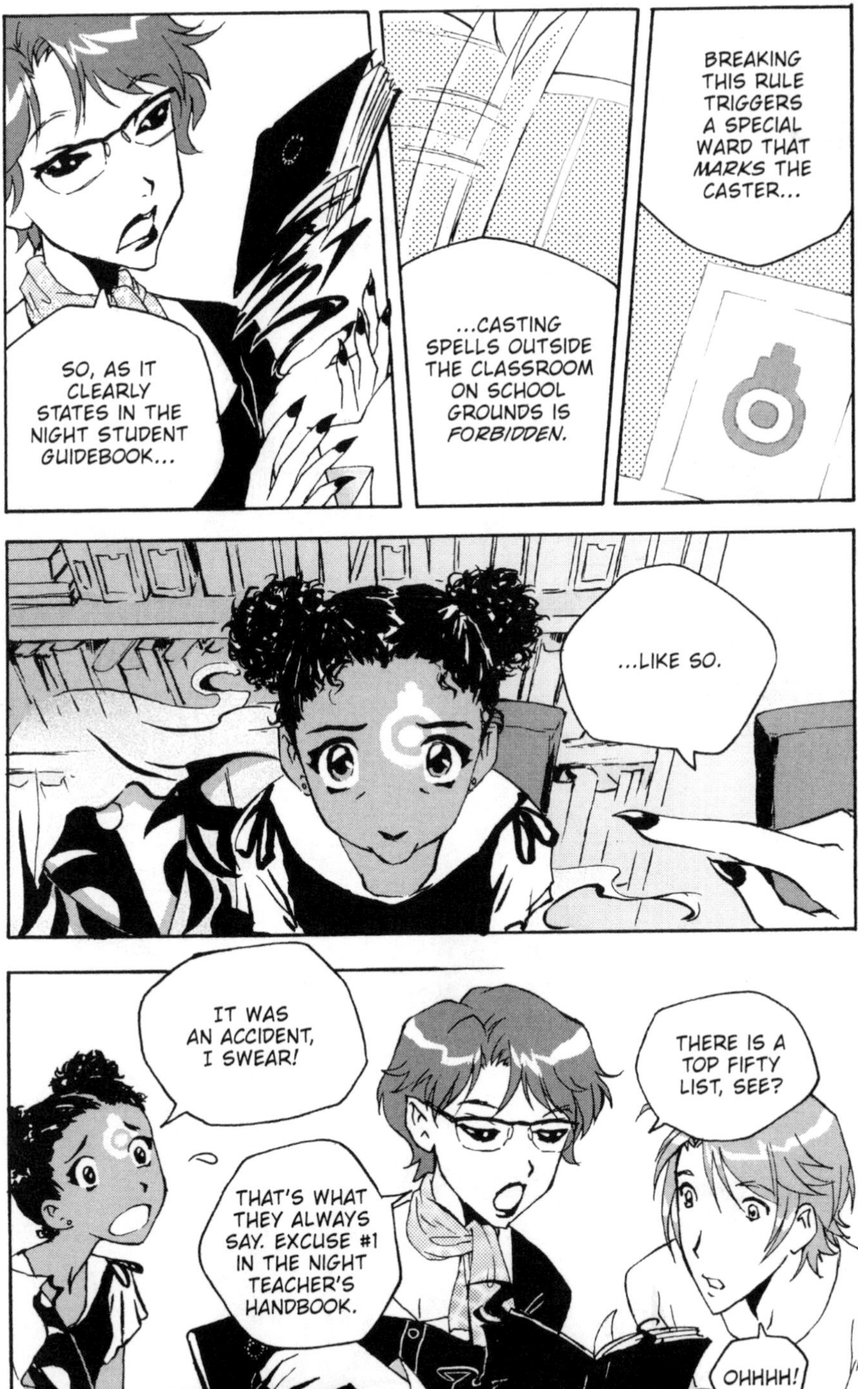
SO, AS IT CLEARLY STATES IN THE NIGHT STUDENT GUIDEBOOK...
...CASTING SPELLS OUTSIDE THE CLASSROOM ON SCHOOL GROUNDS IS *FORBIDDEN*.
BREAKING THIS RULE TRIGGERS A SPECIAL WARD THAT *MARKS* THE CASTER...
...LIKE SO.
IT WAS AN ACCIDENT, I SWEAR!
THAT'S WHAT THEY ALWAYS SAY. EXCUSE #1 IN THE NIGHT TEACHER'S HANDBOOK.
THERE IS A TOP FIFTY LIST, SEE?
OHHHH!

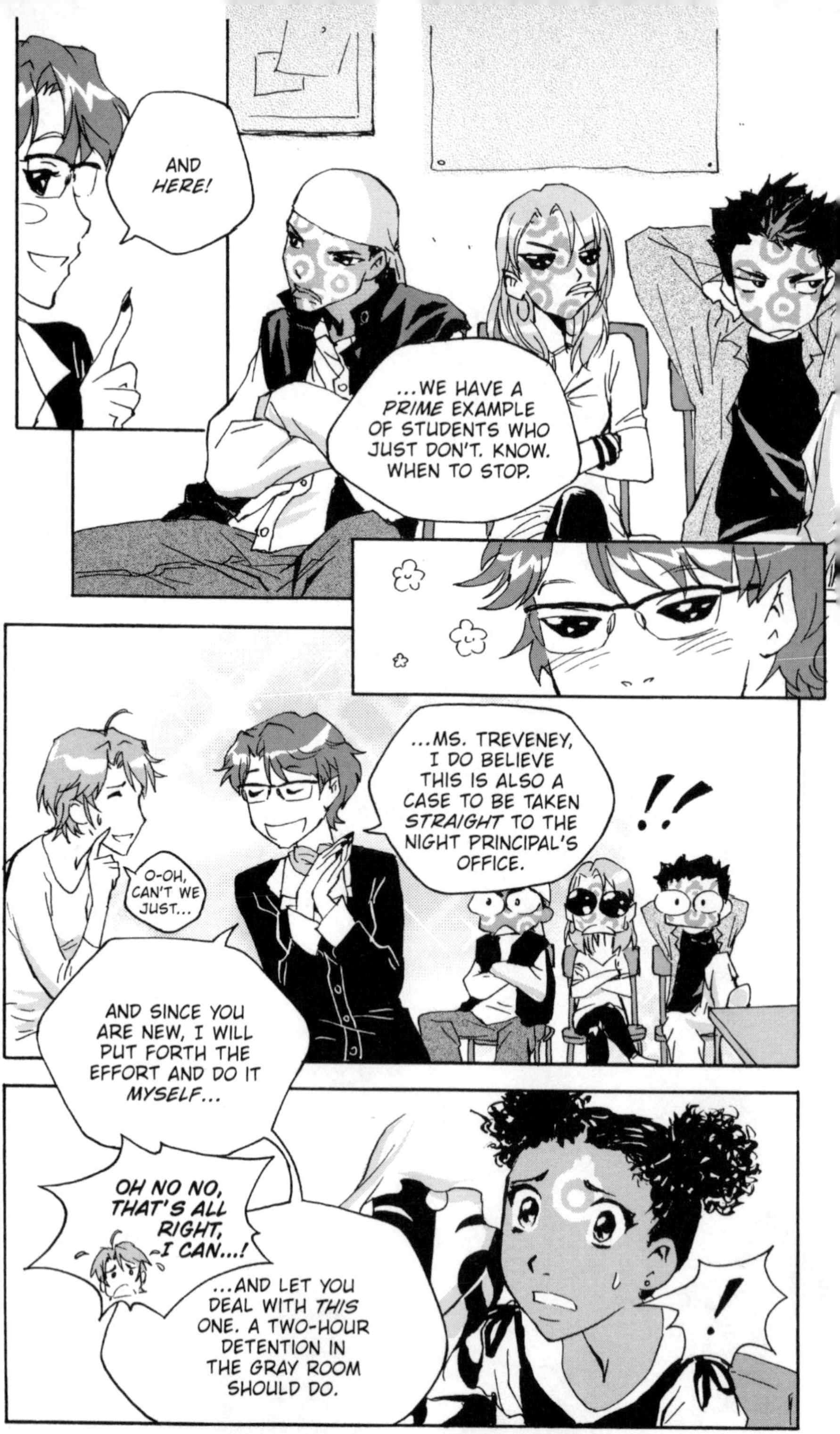
AND HERE!
...WE HAVE A PRIME EXAMPLE OF STUDENTS WHO JUST DON'T. KNOW. WHEN TO STOP.
...MS. TREVENEY, I DO BELIEVE THIS IS ALSO A CASE TO BE TAKEN STRAIGHT TO THE NIGHT PRINCIPAL'S OFFICE.
!!
O-OH, CAN'T WE JUST...
AND SINCE YOU ARE NEW, I WILL PUT FORTH THE EFFORT AND DO IT MYSELF...
OH NO NO, THAT'S ALL RIGHT, I CAN...!
...AND LET YOU DEAL WITH THIS ONE. A TWO-HOUR DETENTION IN THE GRAY ROOM SHOULD DO.
!

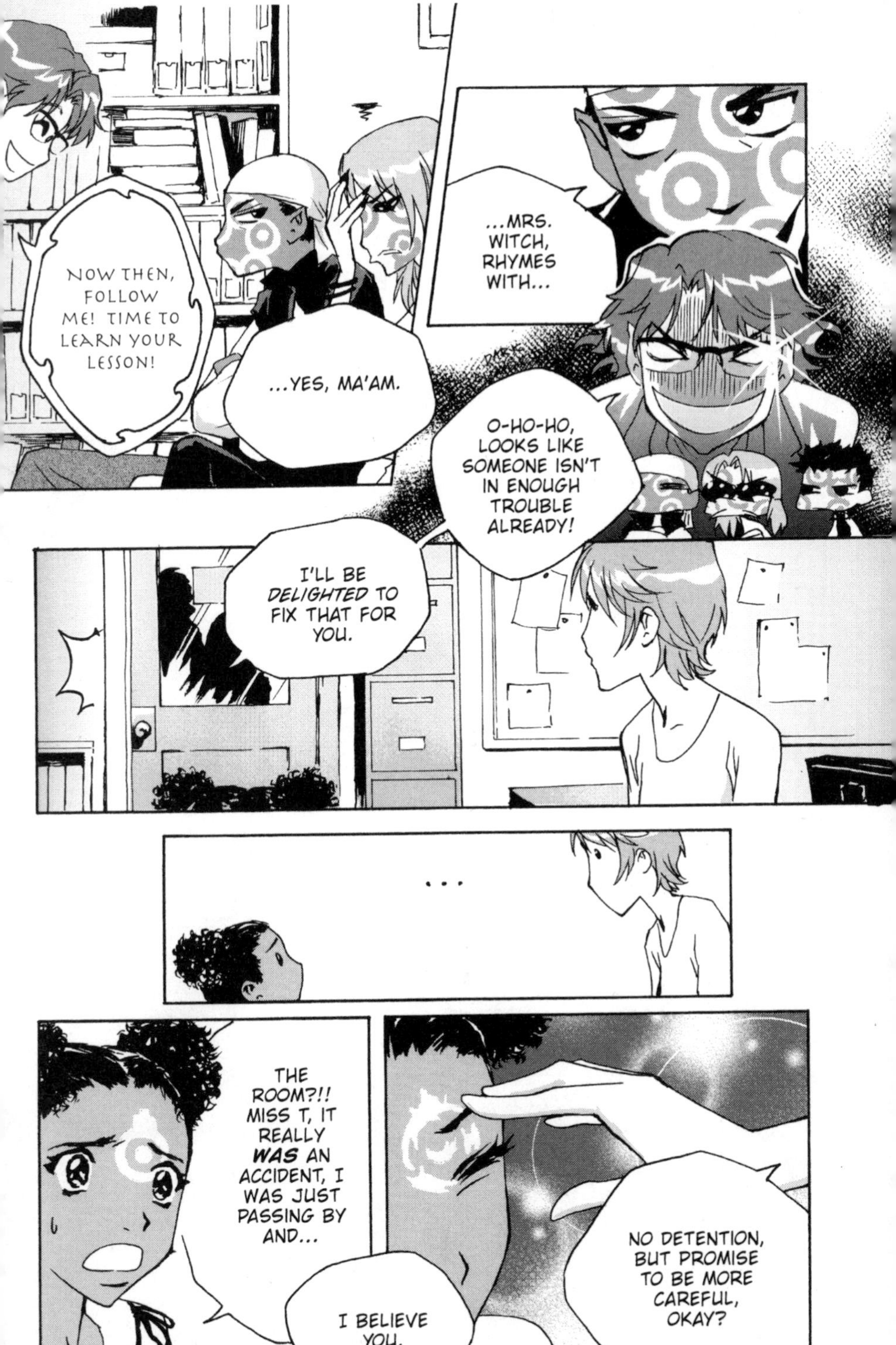
NOW THEN, FOLLOW ME! TIME TO LEARN YOUR LESSON!
...YES, MA'AM.
...MRS. WITCH, RHYMES WITH...
O-HO-HO, LOOKS LIKE SOMEONE ISN'T IN ENOUGH TROUBLE ALREADY!
I'LL BE DELIGHTED TO FIX THAT FOR YOU.
...
THE ROOM?!! MISS T, IT REALLY WAS AN ACCIDENT, I WAS JUST PASSING BY AND...
I BELIEVE YOU.
NO DETENTION, BUT PROMISE TO BE MORE CAREFUL, OKAY?

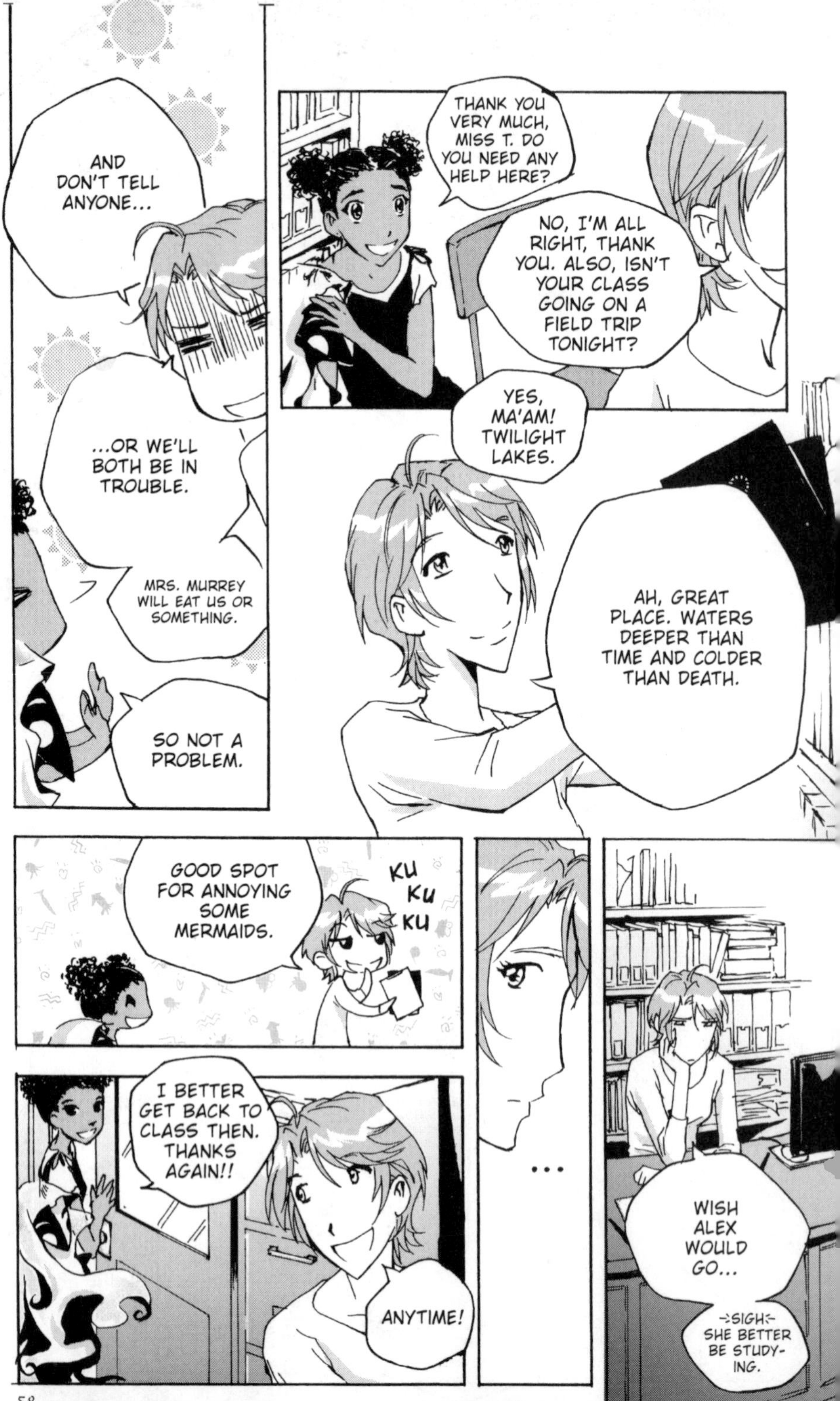
AND DON'T TELL ANYONE...
...OR WE'LL BOTH BE IN TROUBLE.
MRS. MURREY WILL EAT US OR SOMETHING.
SO NOT A PROBLEM.
THANK YOU VERY MUCH, MISS T. DO YOU NEED ANY HELP HERE?
NO, I'M ALL RIGHT, THANK YOU. ALSO, ISN'T YOUR CLASS GOING ON A FIELD TRIP TONIGHT?
YES, MA'AM! TWILIGHT LAKES.
AH, GREAT PLACE. WATERS DEEPER THAN TIME AND COLDER THAN DEATH.
GOOD SPOT FOR ANNOYING SOME MERMAIDS.
KU KU KU
I BETTER GET BACK TO CLASS THEN. THANKS AGAIN!!
ANYTIME!
...
WISH ALEX WOULD GO...
SIGH
SHE BETTER BE STUDY-ING.

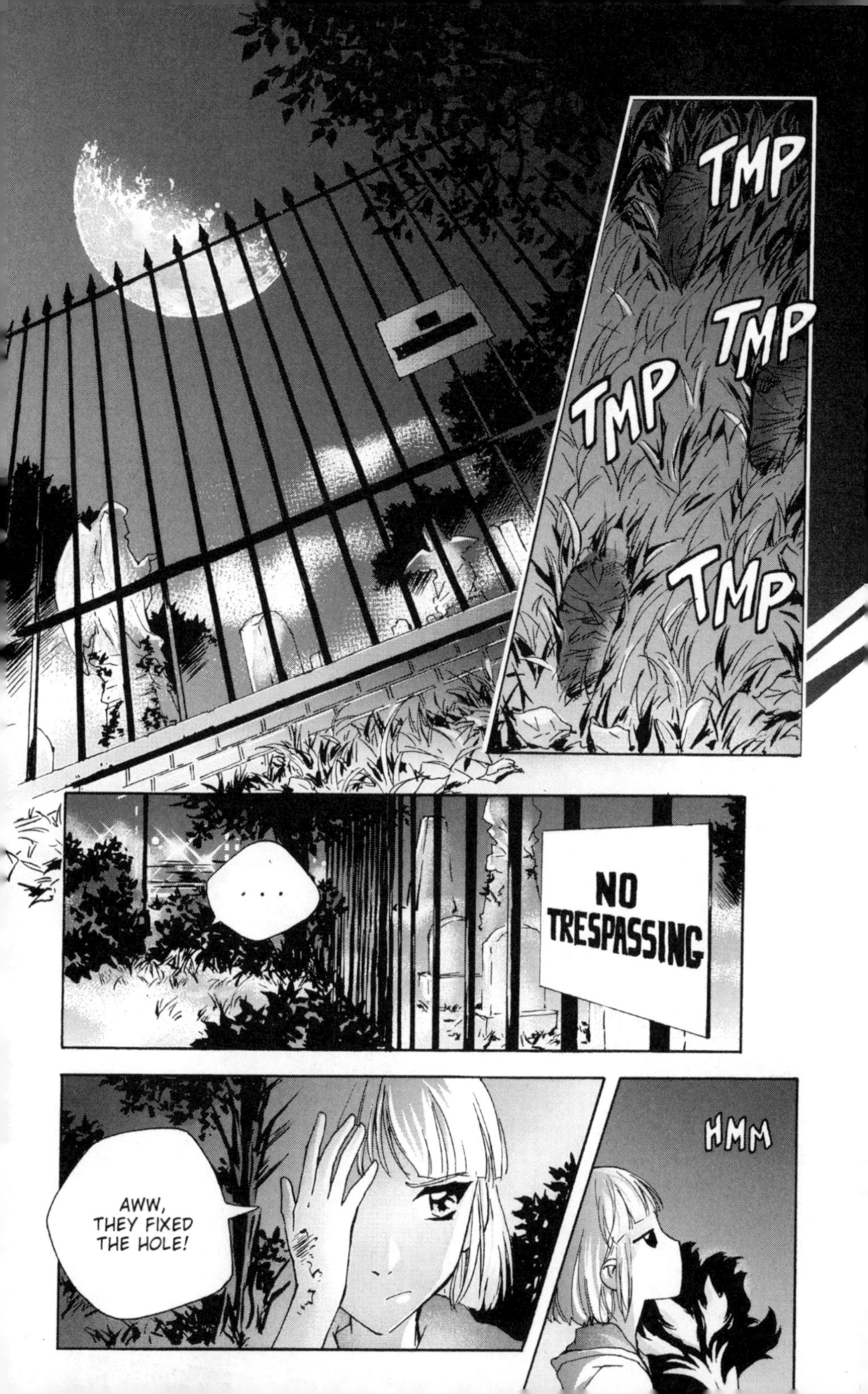
TMP
TMP
TMP
TMP
NO TRESPASSING
...
HMM
AWW, THEY FIXED THE HOLE!

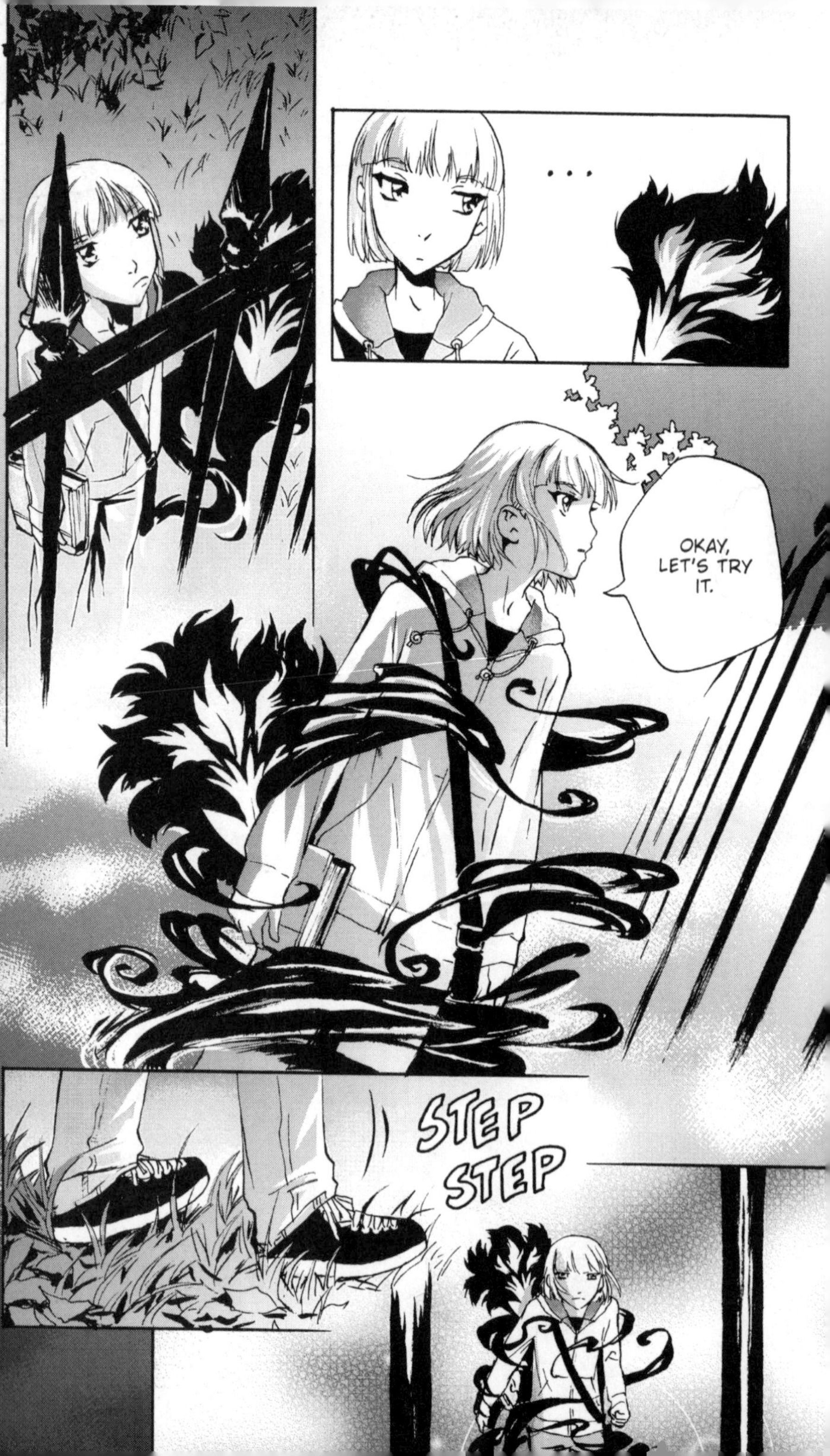
. . .
OKAY, LET'S TRY IT.
STEP STEP

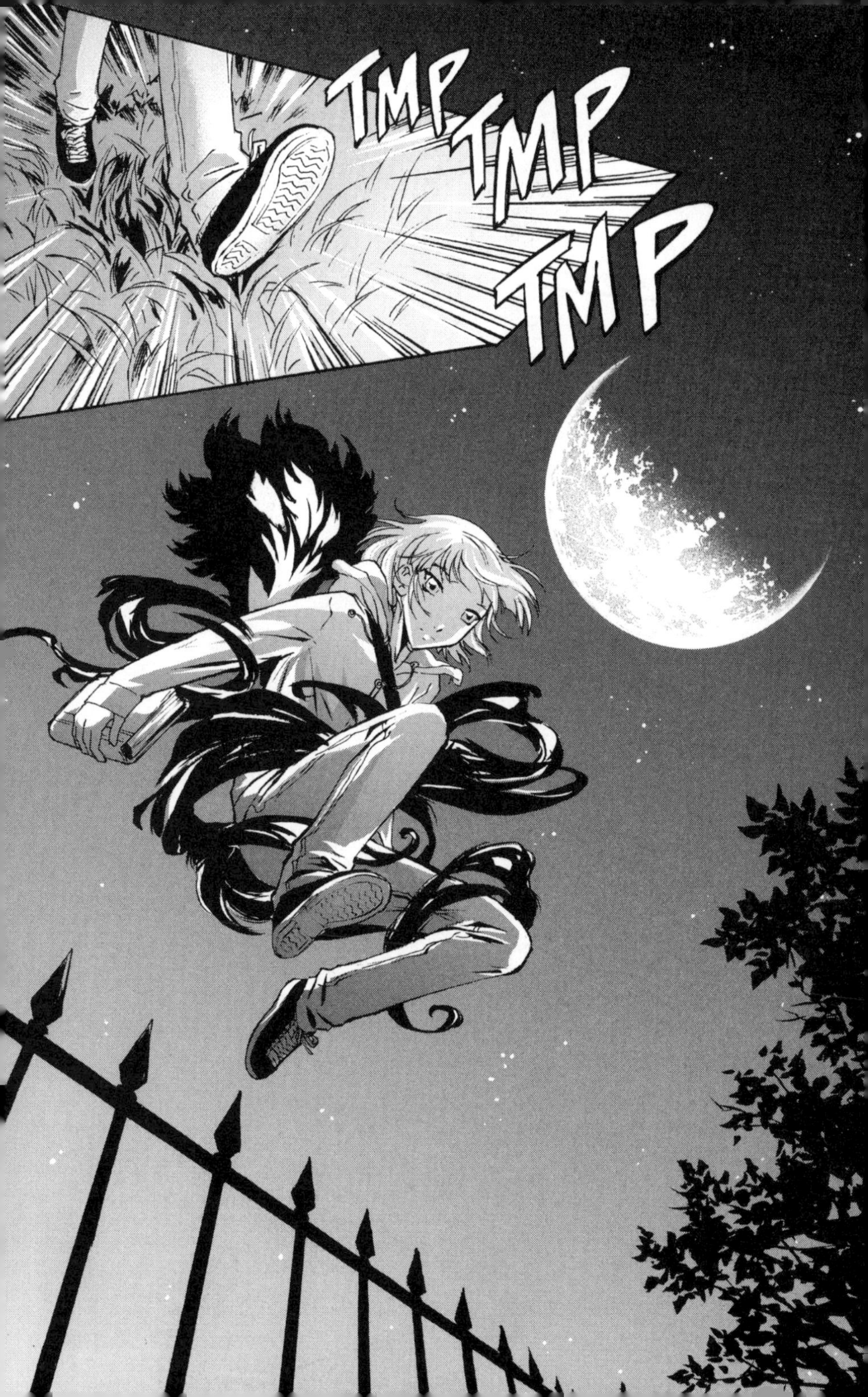
TMP TMP TMP

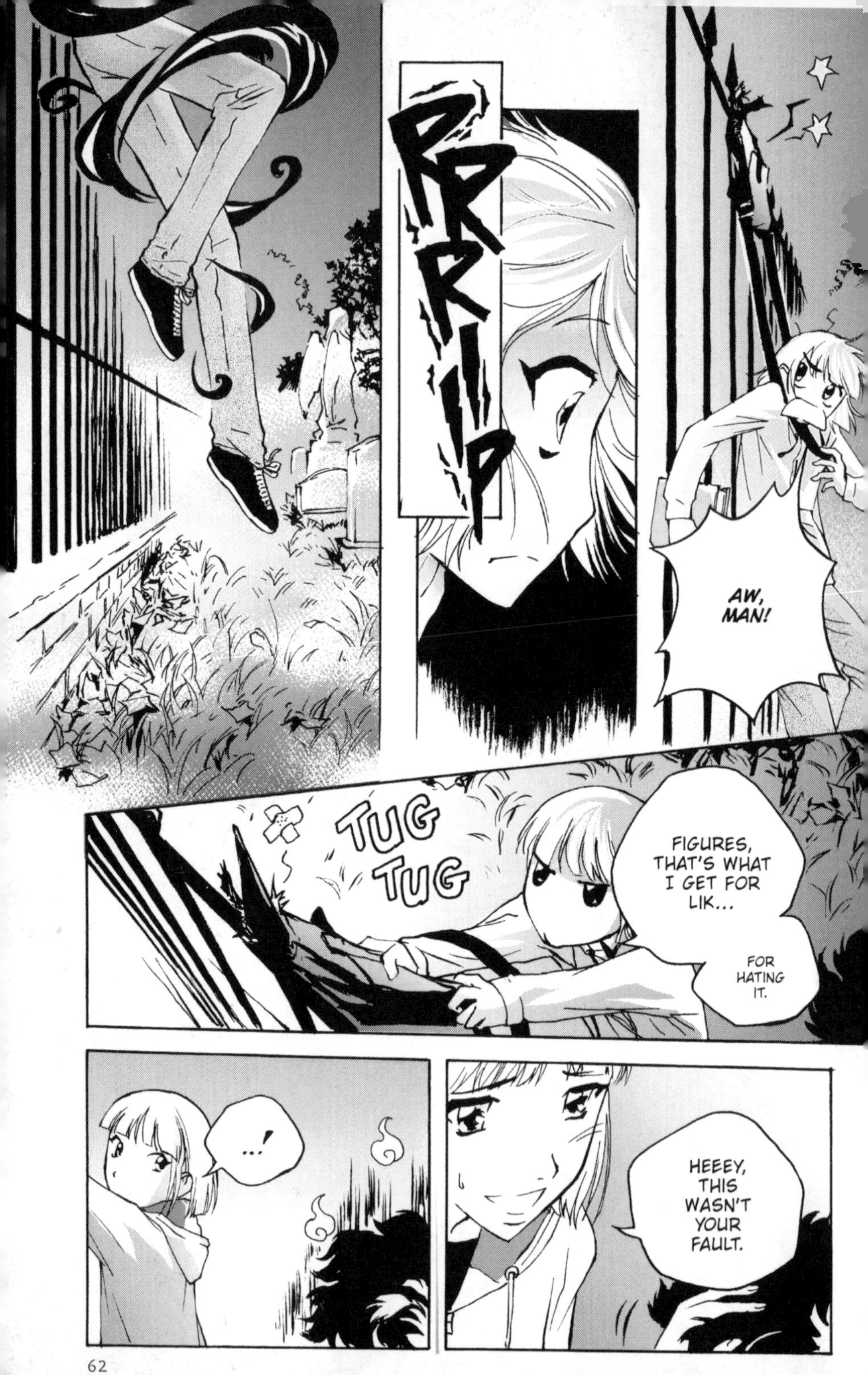

RRRIIP
AW, MAN!
TUG TUG
FIGURES, THAT'S WHAT I GET FOR LIK...
FOR HATING IT.
...!
HEEEY, THIS WASN'T YOUR FAULT.

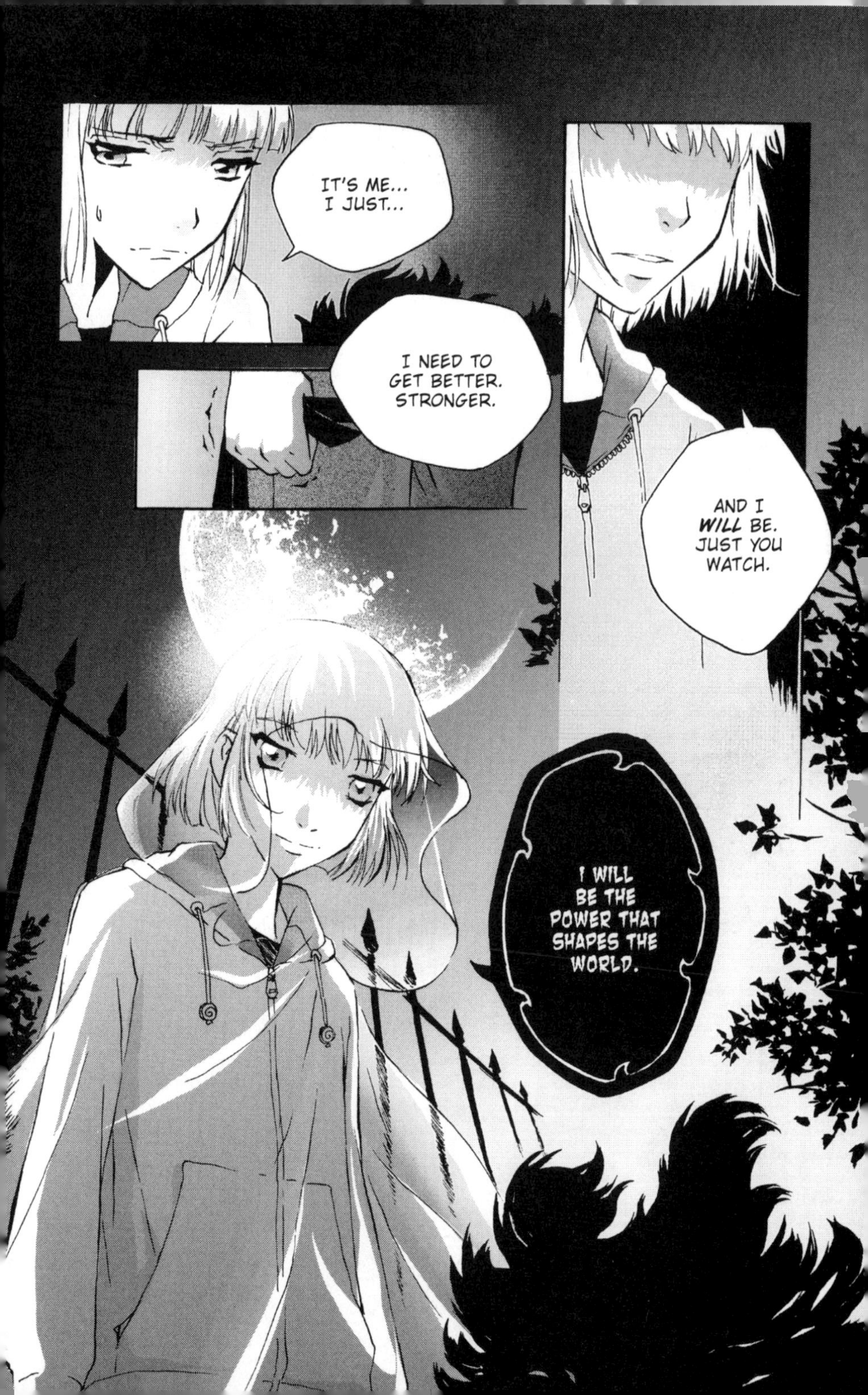
IT'S ME... I JUST...
I NEED TO GET BETTER. STRONGER.
AND I WILL BE. JUST YOU WATCH.
I WILL BE THE POWER THAT SHAPES THE WORLD.

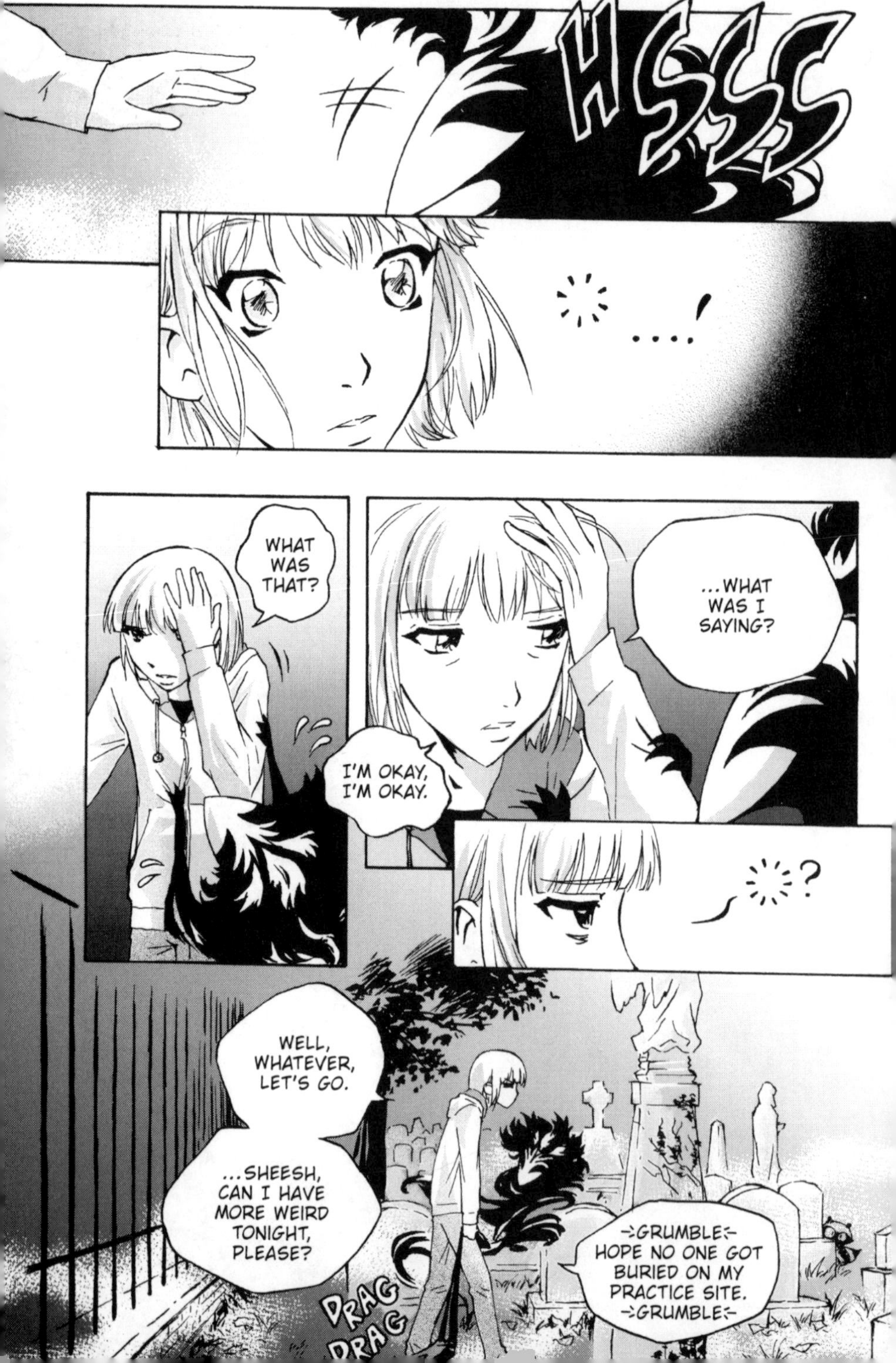
HSSS
...!
WHAT WAS THAT?
...WHAT WAS I SAYING?
I'M OKAY, I'M OKAY.
?
WELL, WHATEVER, LET'S GO.
...SHEESH, CAN I HAVE MORE WEIRD TONIGHT, PLEASE?
GRUMBLE HOPE NO ONE GOT BURIED ON MY PRACTICE SITE. GRUMBLE
DRAG DRAG

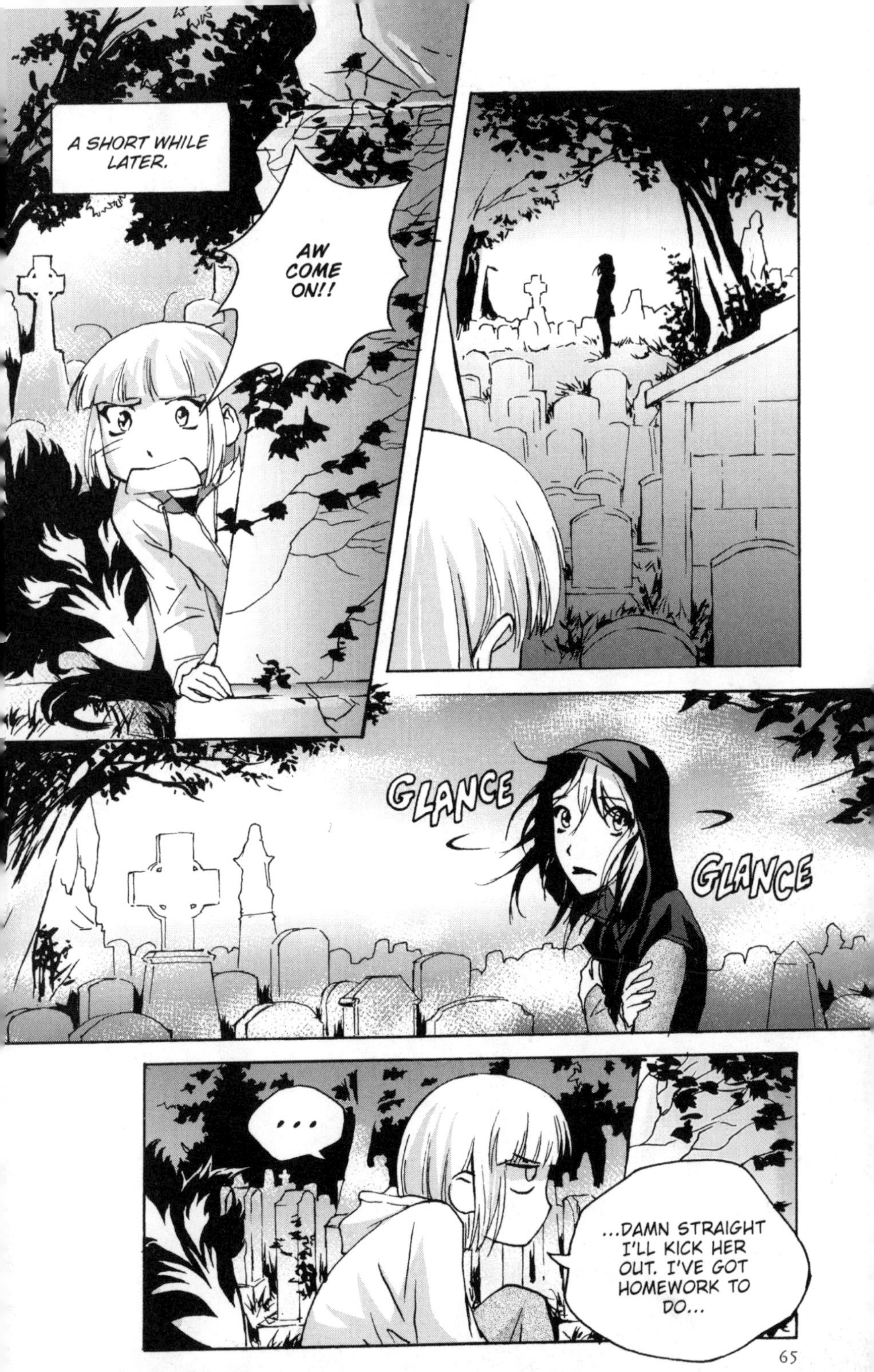
A SHORT WHILE LATER.
AW COME ON!!
GLANCE
GLANCE
...
...DAMN STRAIGHT I'LL KICK HER OUT. I'VE GOT HOMEWORK TO DO...

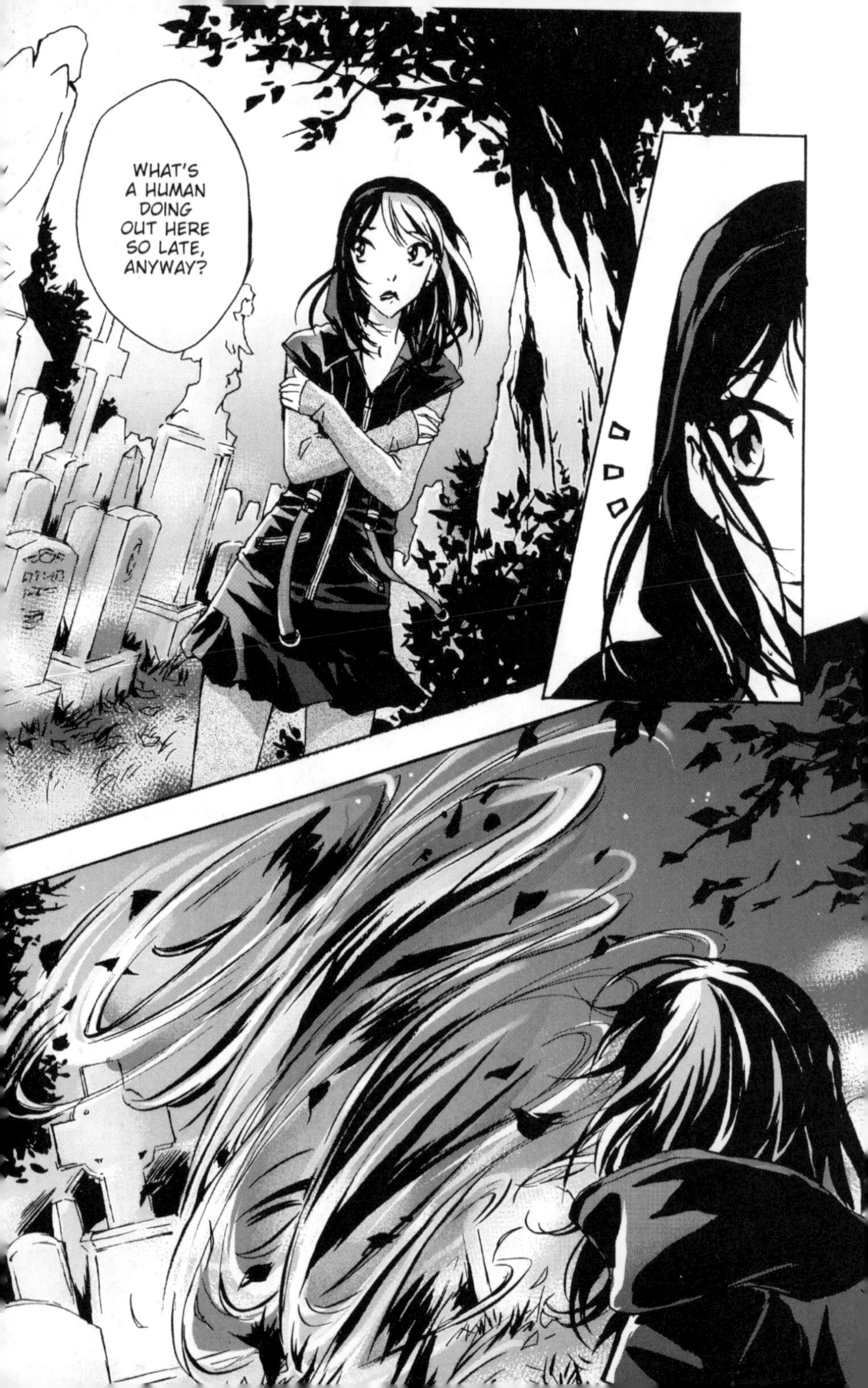
WHAT'S A HUMAN DOING OUT HERE SO LATE, ANYWAY?

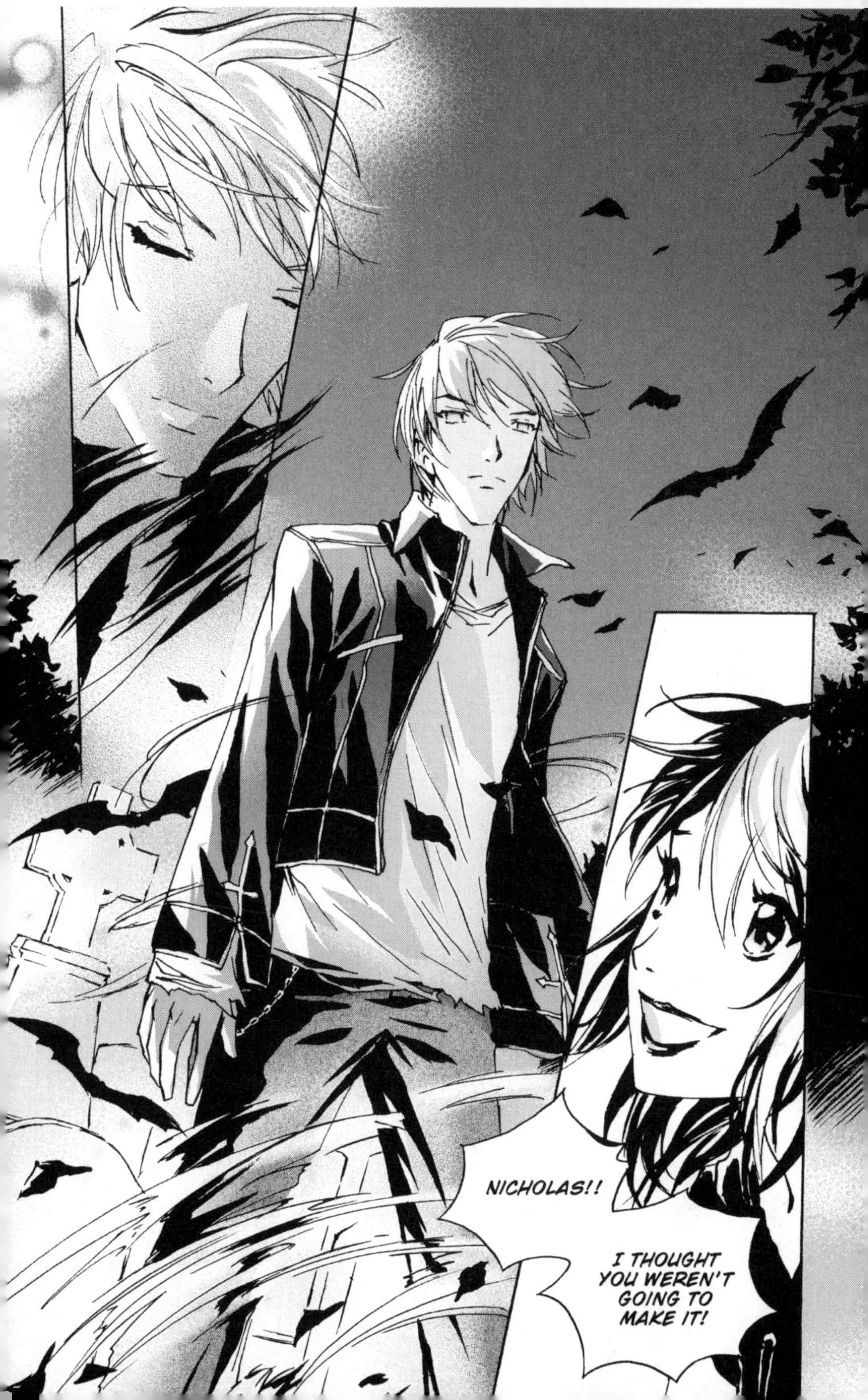
NICHOLAS!!
I THOUGHT YOU WEREN'T GOING TO MAKE IT!

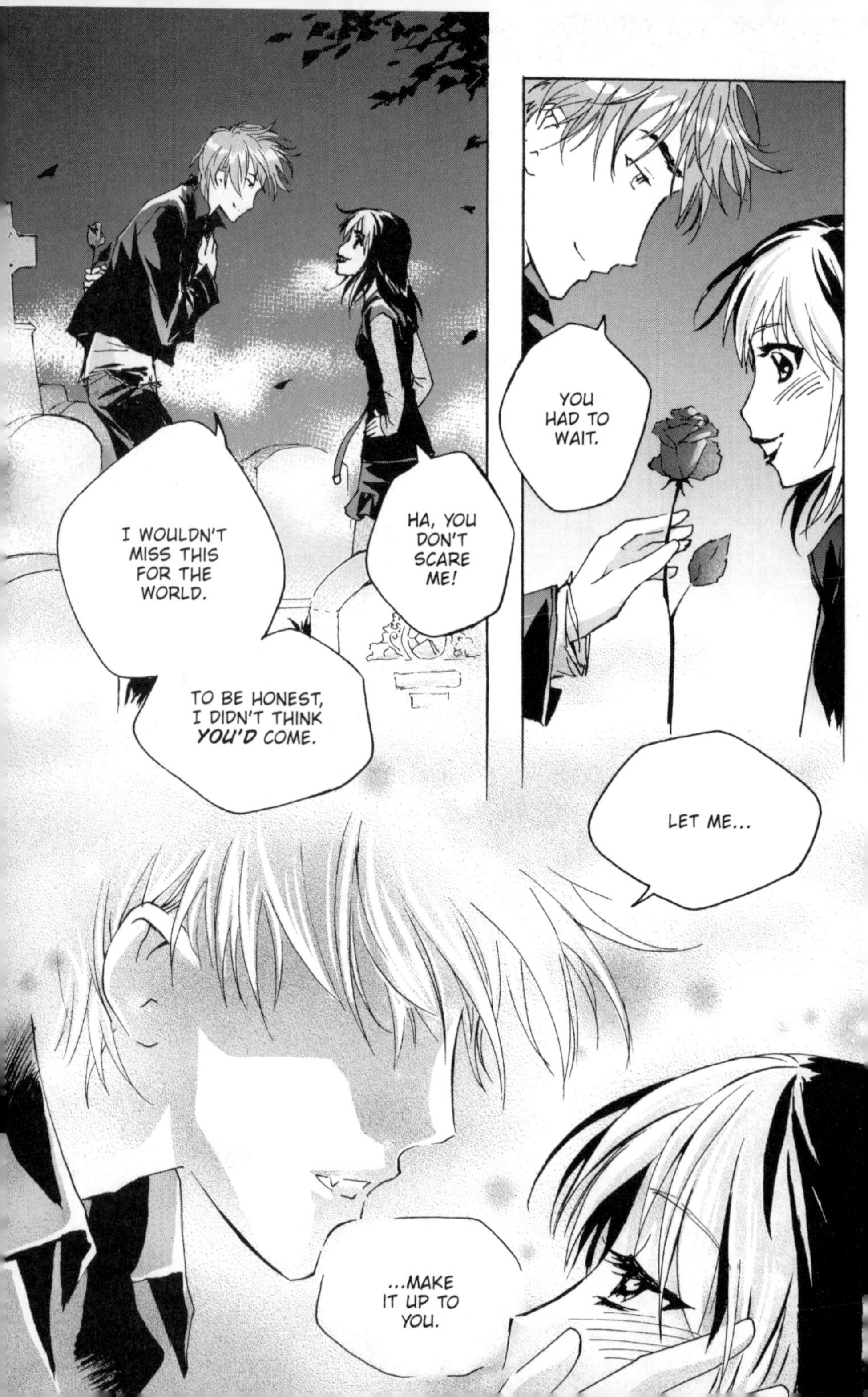
I WOULDN'T MISS THIS FOR THE WORLD.
HA, YOU DON'T SCARE ME!
TO BE HONEST, I DIDN'T THINK *YOU'D* COME.
YOU HAD TO WAIT.
LET ME...
...MAKE IT UP TO YOU.

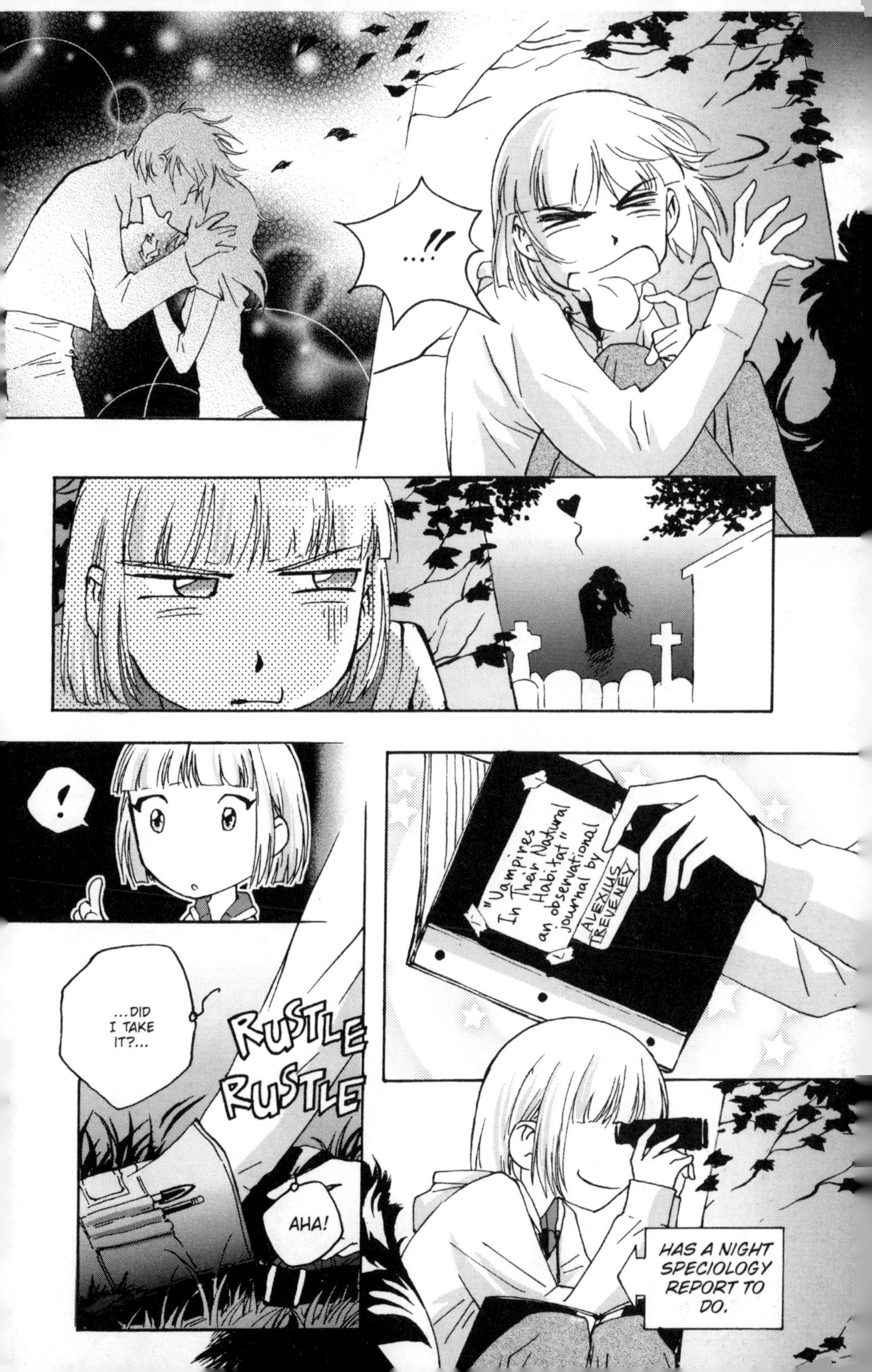

...!!
!
"Vampires In Their Natural Habitat" an observational journal by ALEXIUS TREVENEY
...DID I TAKE IT?...
RUSTLE RUSTLE
AHA!
HAS A NIGHT SPECIOLOGY REPORT TO DO.

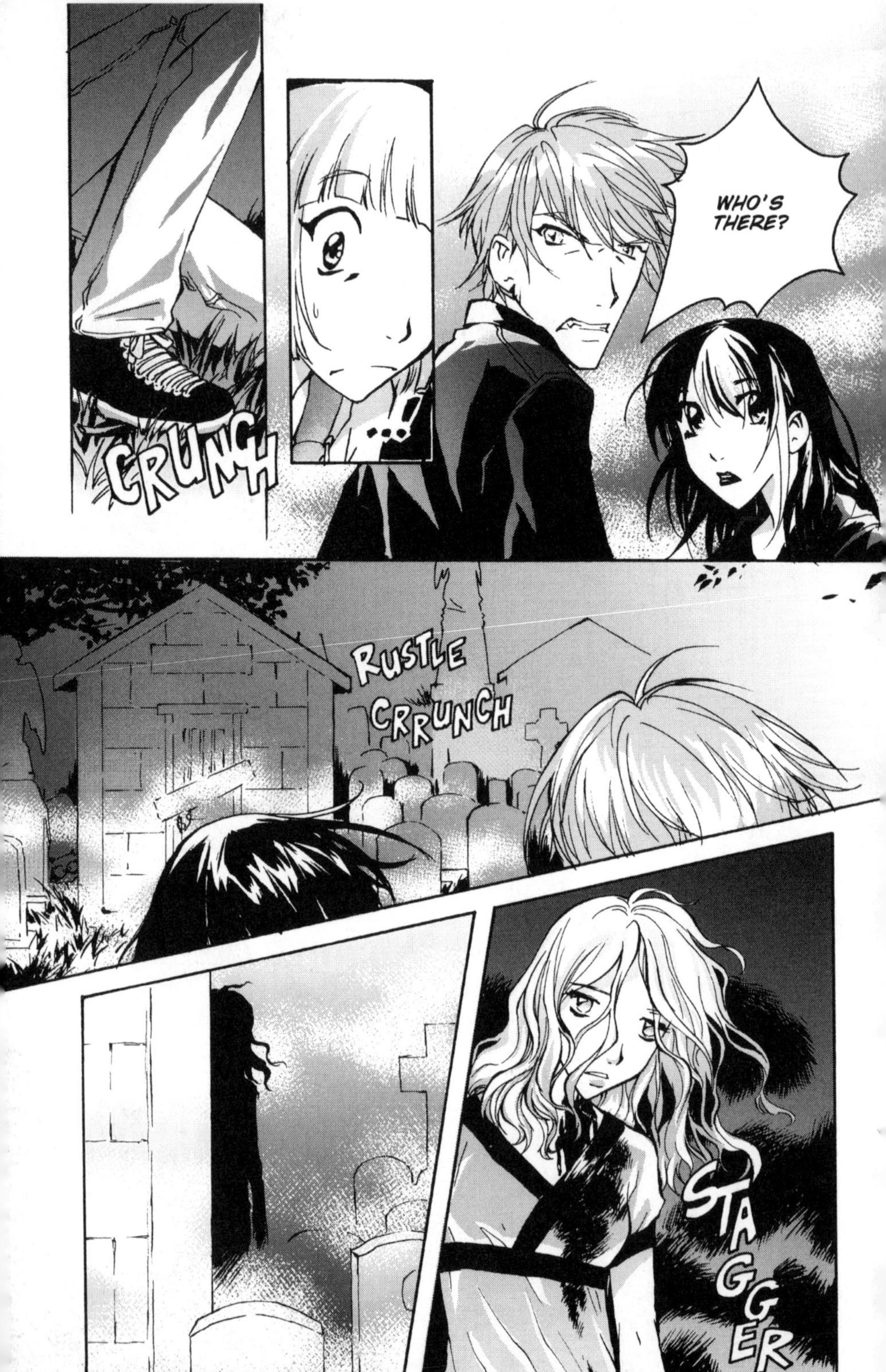

WHO'S THERE?
...!
CRUNCH
RUSTLE
CRRUNCH
STAGGER

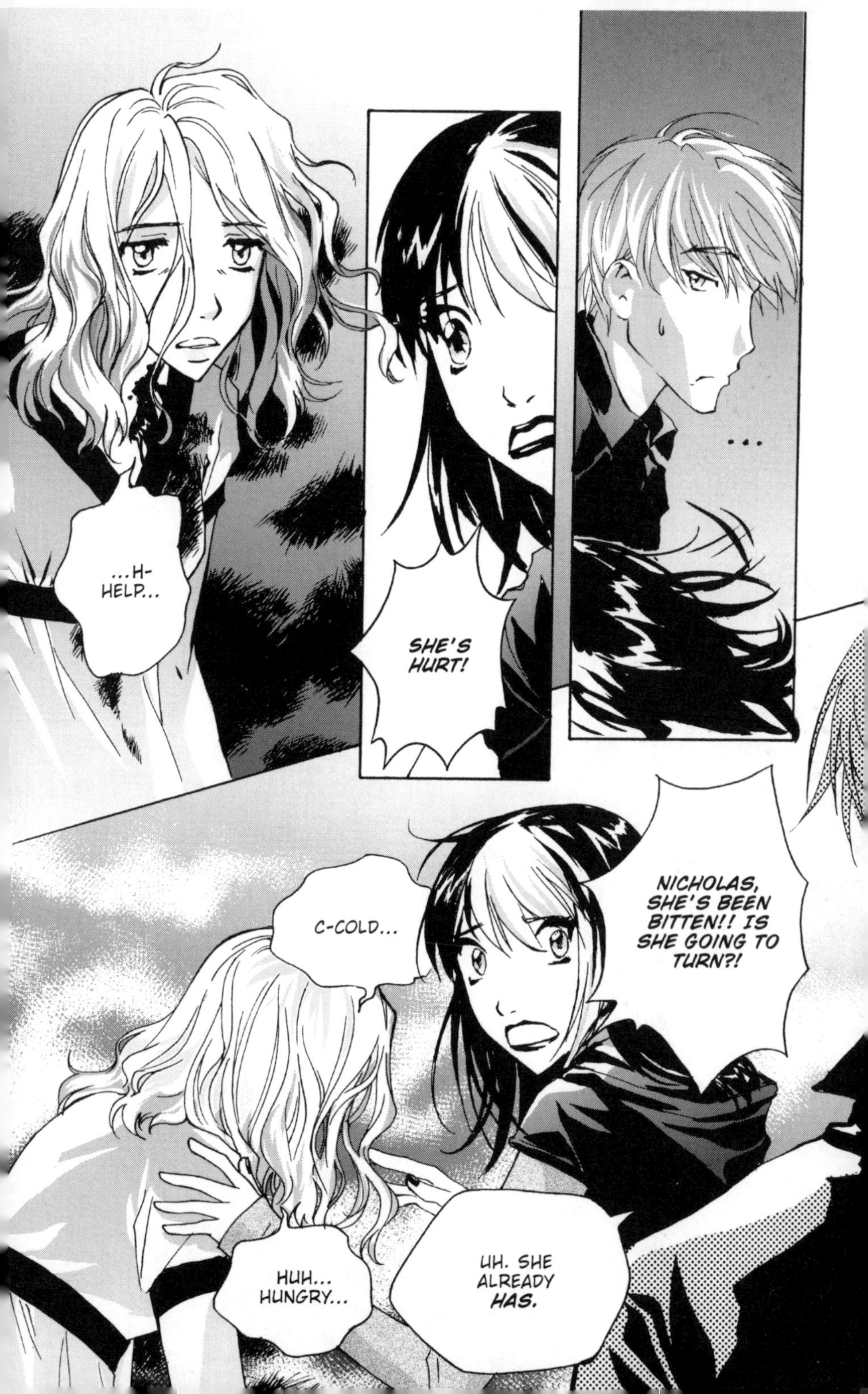

...H-
HELP...
SHE'S
HURT!
...
C-COLD...
NICHOLAS, SHE'S BEEN BITTEN!! IS SHE GOING TO TURN?!
HUH... HUNGRY...
UH. SHE ALREADY **HAS.**

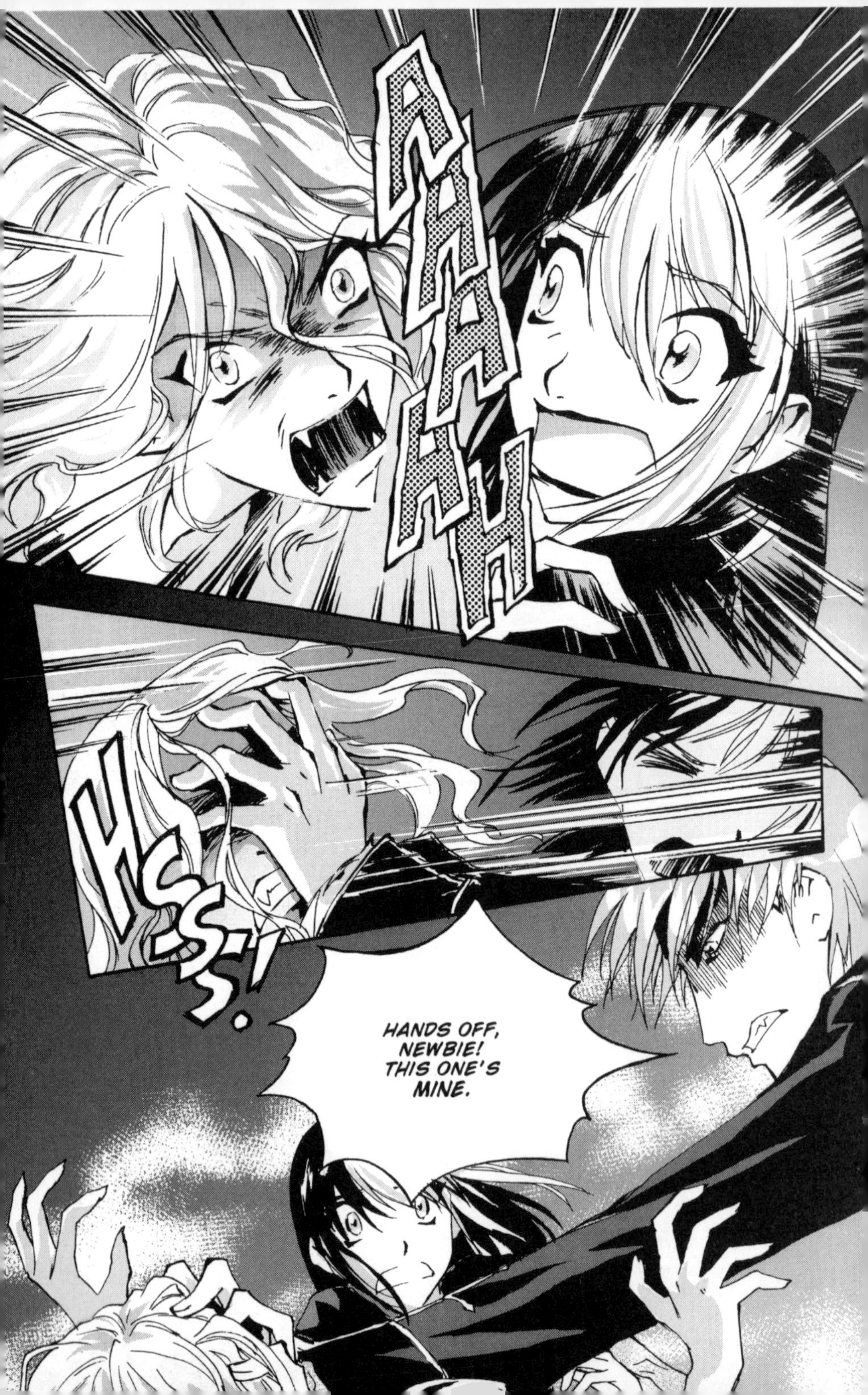
AAAAHH
HSSS!
HANDS OFF, NEWBIE! THIS ONE'S MINE.

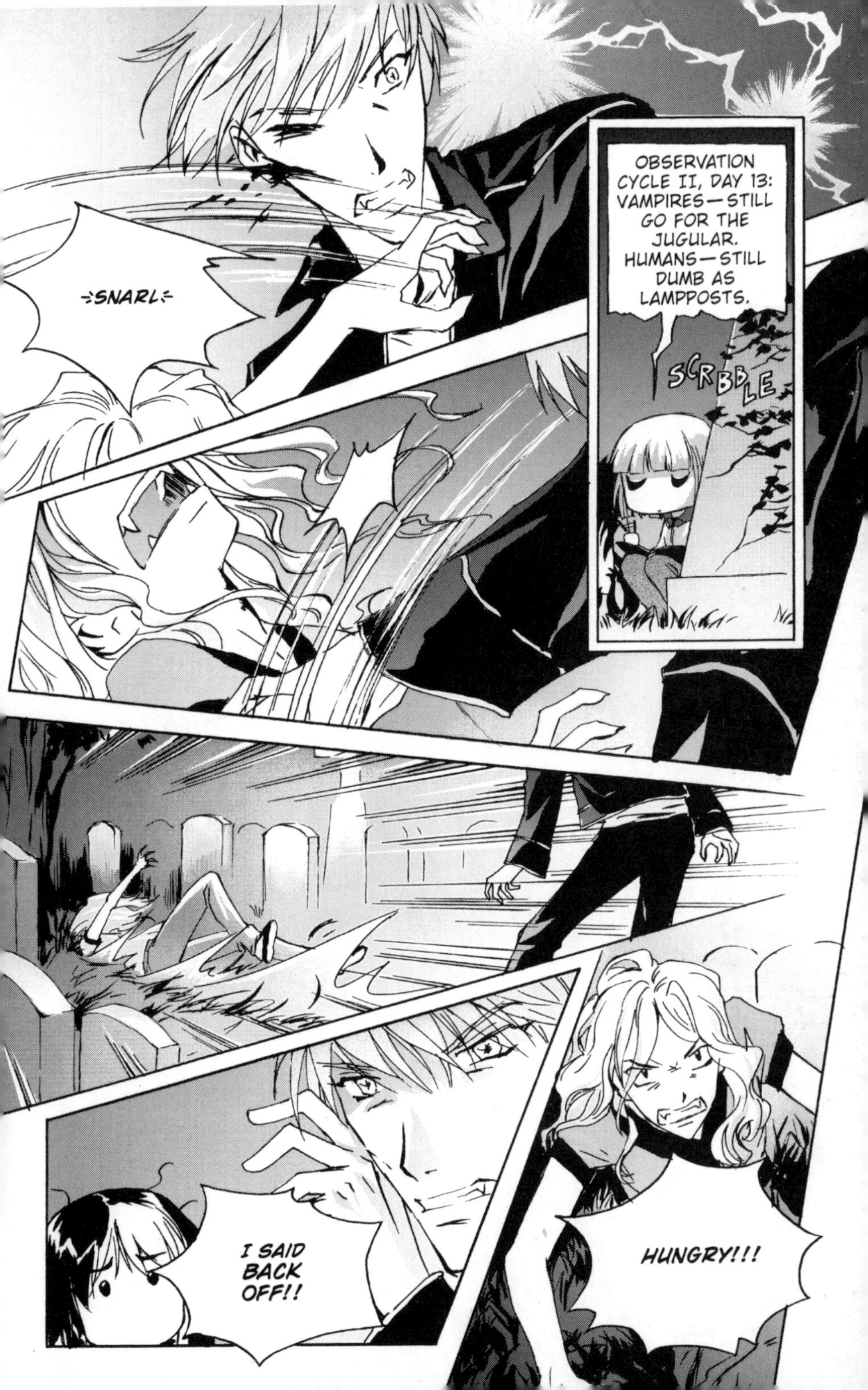
OBSERVATION CYCLE II, DAY 13: VAMPIRES—STILL GO FOR THE JUGULAR. HUMANS—STILL DUMB AS LAMPPOSTS.
SCRBBLE
SNARL
HUNGRY!!!
I SAID BACK OFF!!

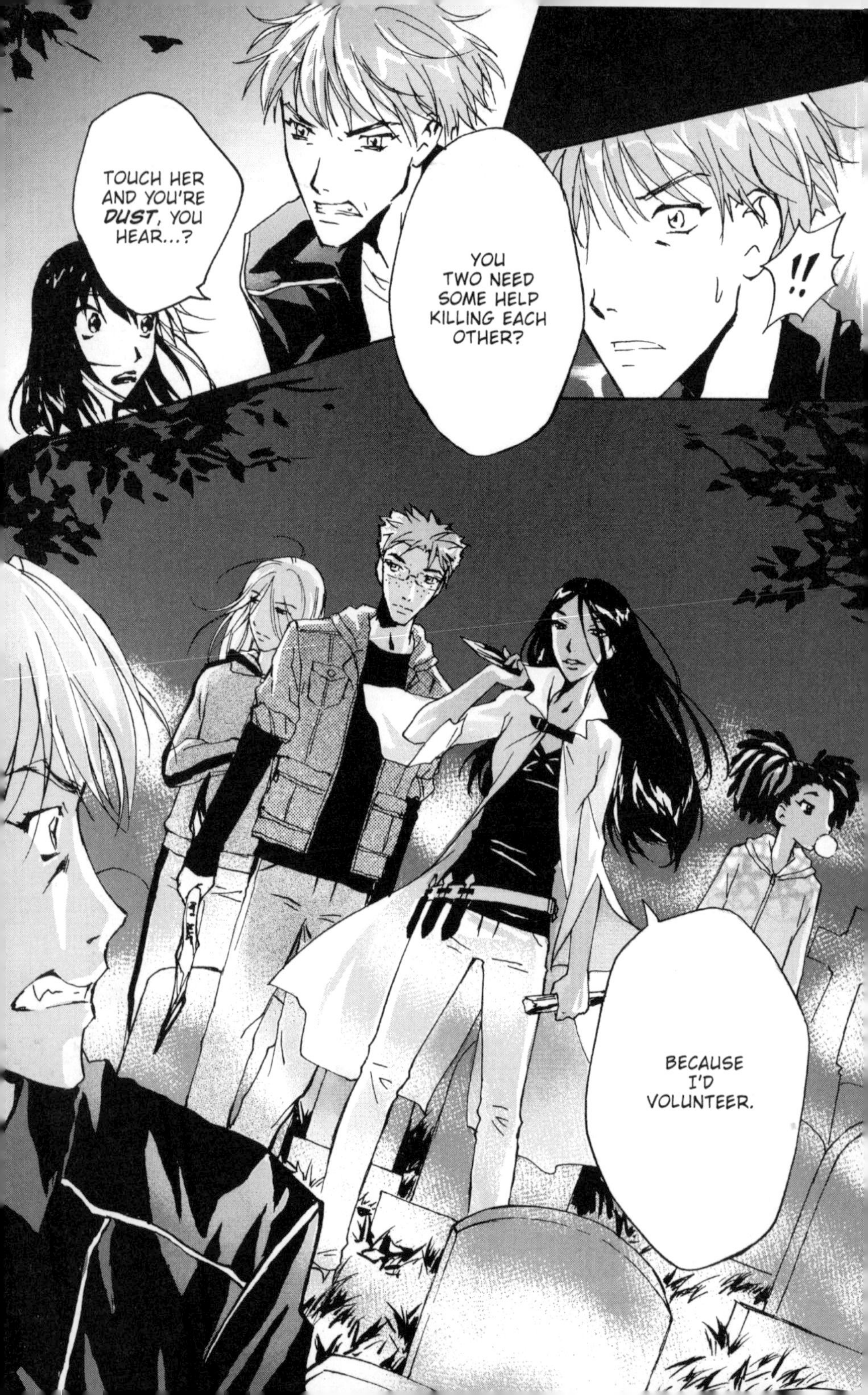
TOUCH HER AND YOU'RE DUST, YOU HEAR...?
YOU TWO NEED SOME HELP KILLING EACH OTHER?
!!
BECAUSE I'D VOLUNTEER.

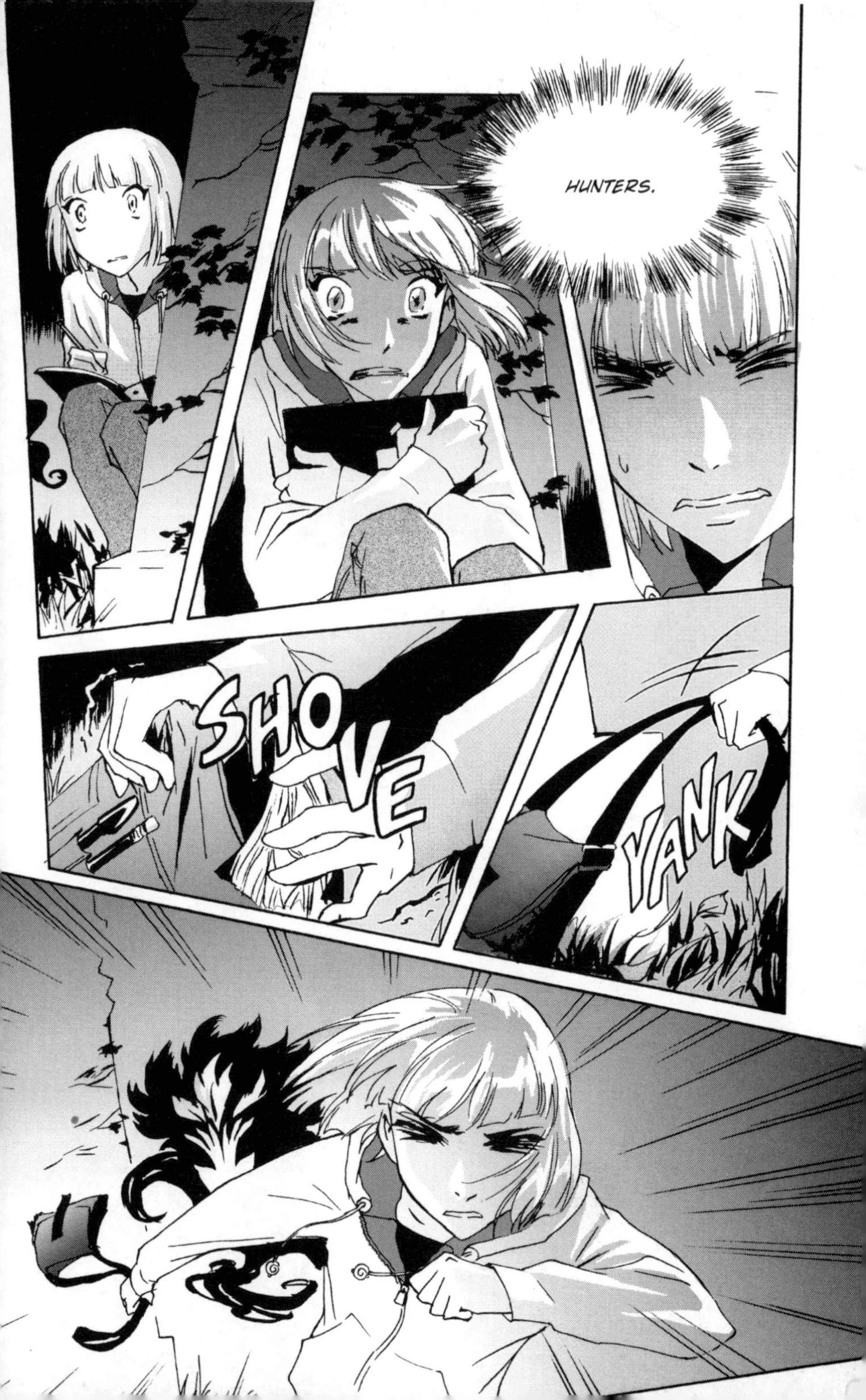
HUNTERS.
SHOVE
YANK

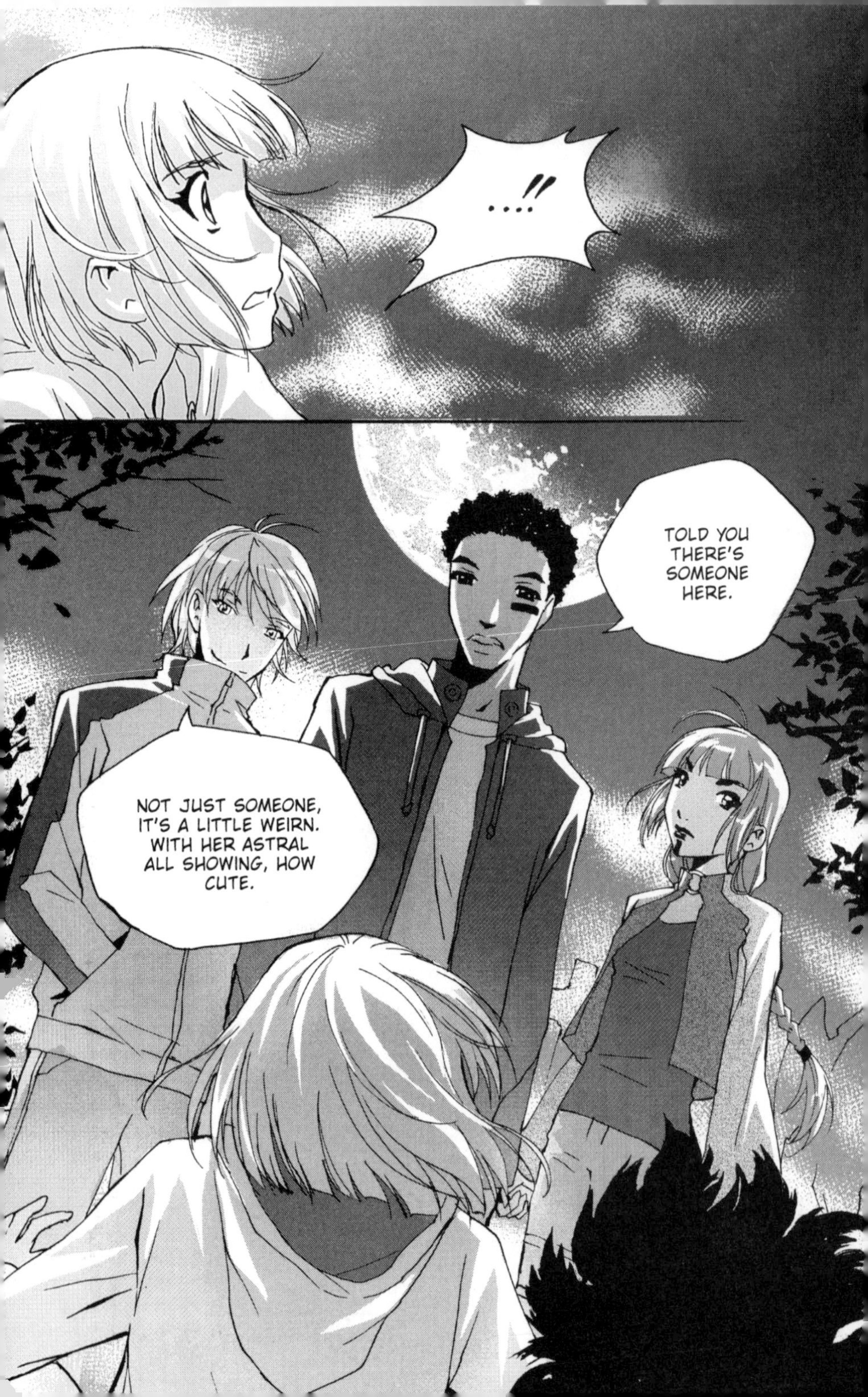
...!!
TOLD YOU THERE'S SOMEONE HERE.
NOT JUST SOMEONE, IT'S A LITTLE WEIRN. WITH HER ASTRAL ALL SHOWING, HOW CUTE.

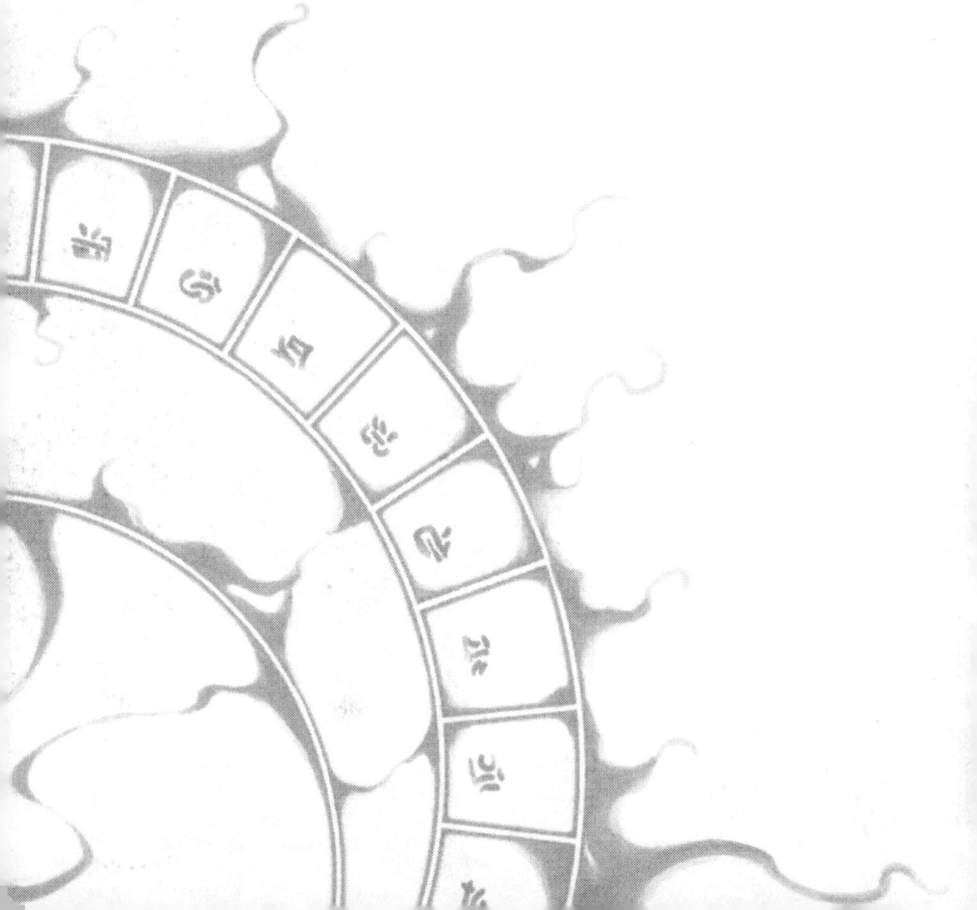

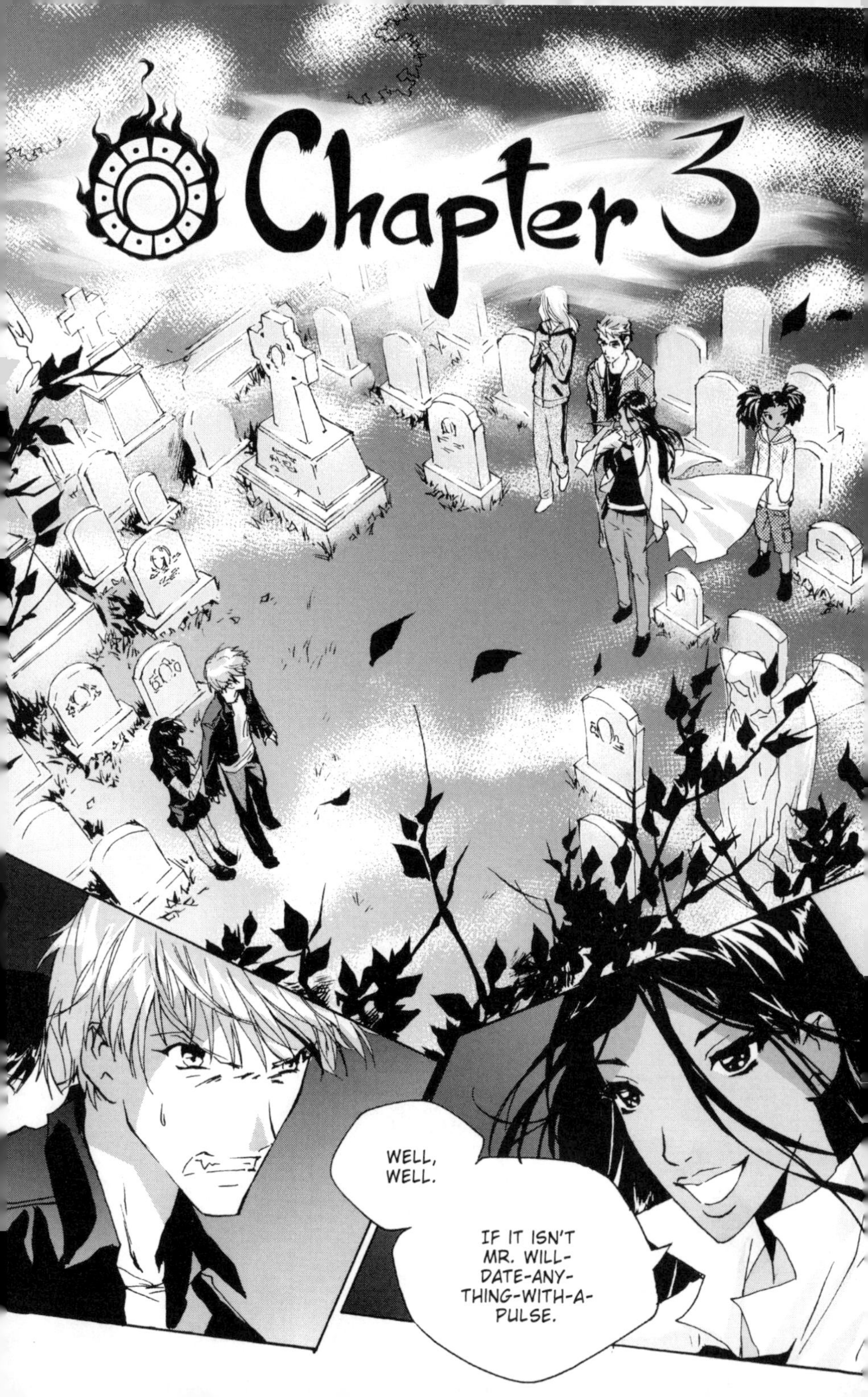
Chapter 3
WELL, WELL.
IF IT ISN'T MR. WILL-DATE-ANY-THING-WITH-A-PULSE.

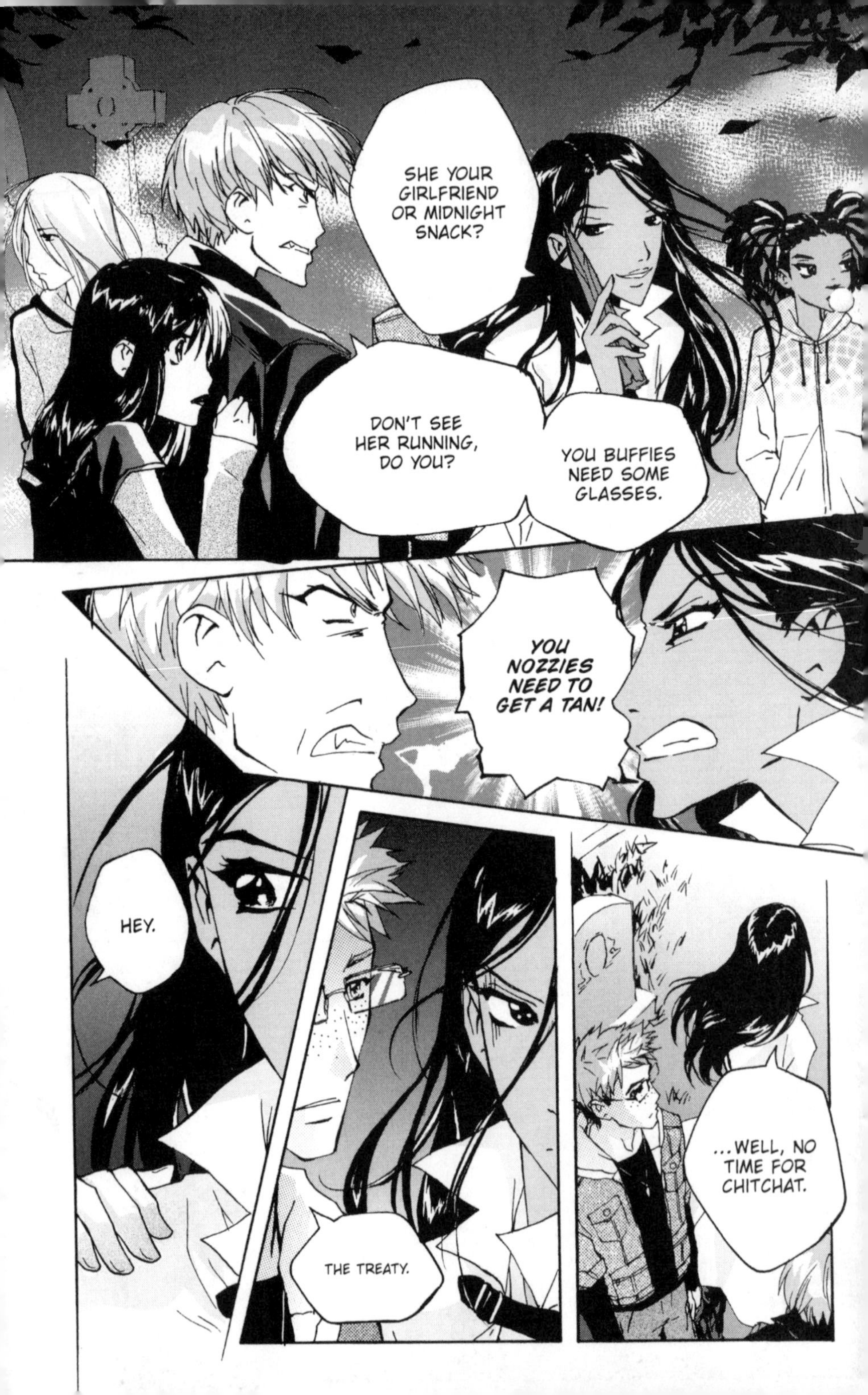
SHE YOUR GIRLFRIEND OR MIDNIGHT SNACK?
DON'T SEE HER RUNNING, DO YOU?
YOU BUFFIES NEED SOME GLASSES.
YOU NOZZIES NEED TO GET A TAN!
HEY.
THE TREATY.
...WELL, NO TIME FOR CHITCHAT.

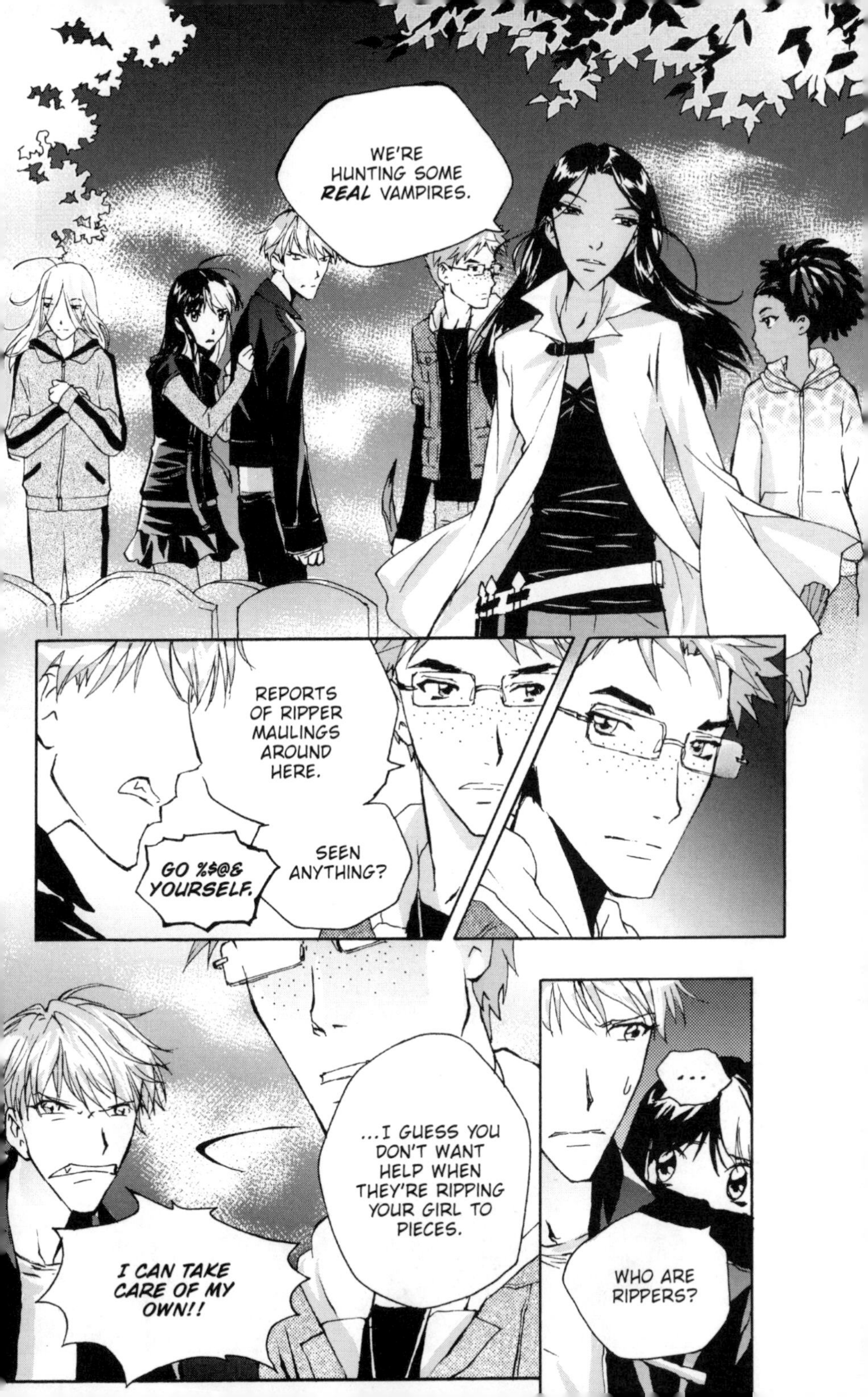

WE'RE HUNTING SOME *REAL* VAMPIRES.
REPORTS OF RIPPER MAULINGS AROUND HERE.
SEEN ANYTHING?
GO %$@& YOURSELF.
...I GUESS YOU DON'T WANT HELP WHEN THEY'RE RIPPING YOUR GIRL TO PIECES.
I CAN TAKE CARE OF MY OWN!!
...
WHO ARE RIPPERS?

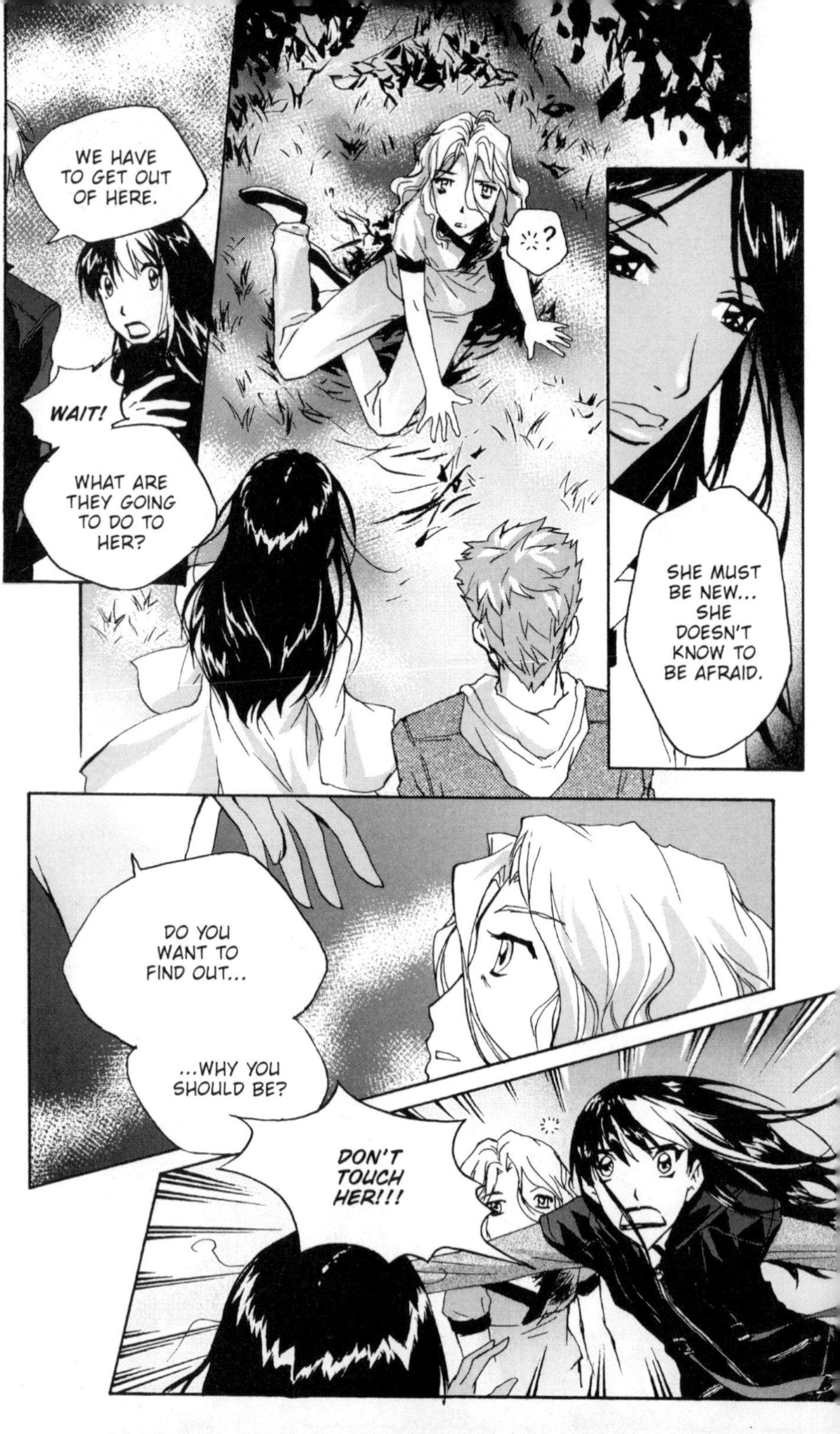
WE HAVE TO GET OUT OF HERE.
?
SHE MUST BE NEW... SHE DOESN'T KNOW TO BE AFRAID.
WAIT!
WHAT ARE THEY GOING TO DO TO HER?
DO YOU WANT TO FIND OUT...
...WHY YOU SHOULD BE?
DON'T TOUCH HER!!!

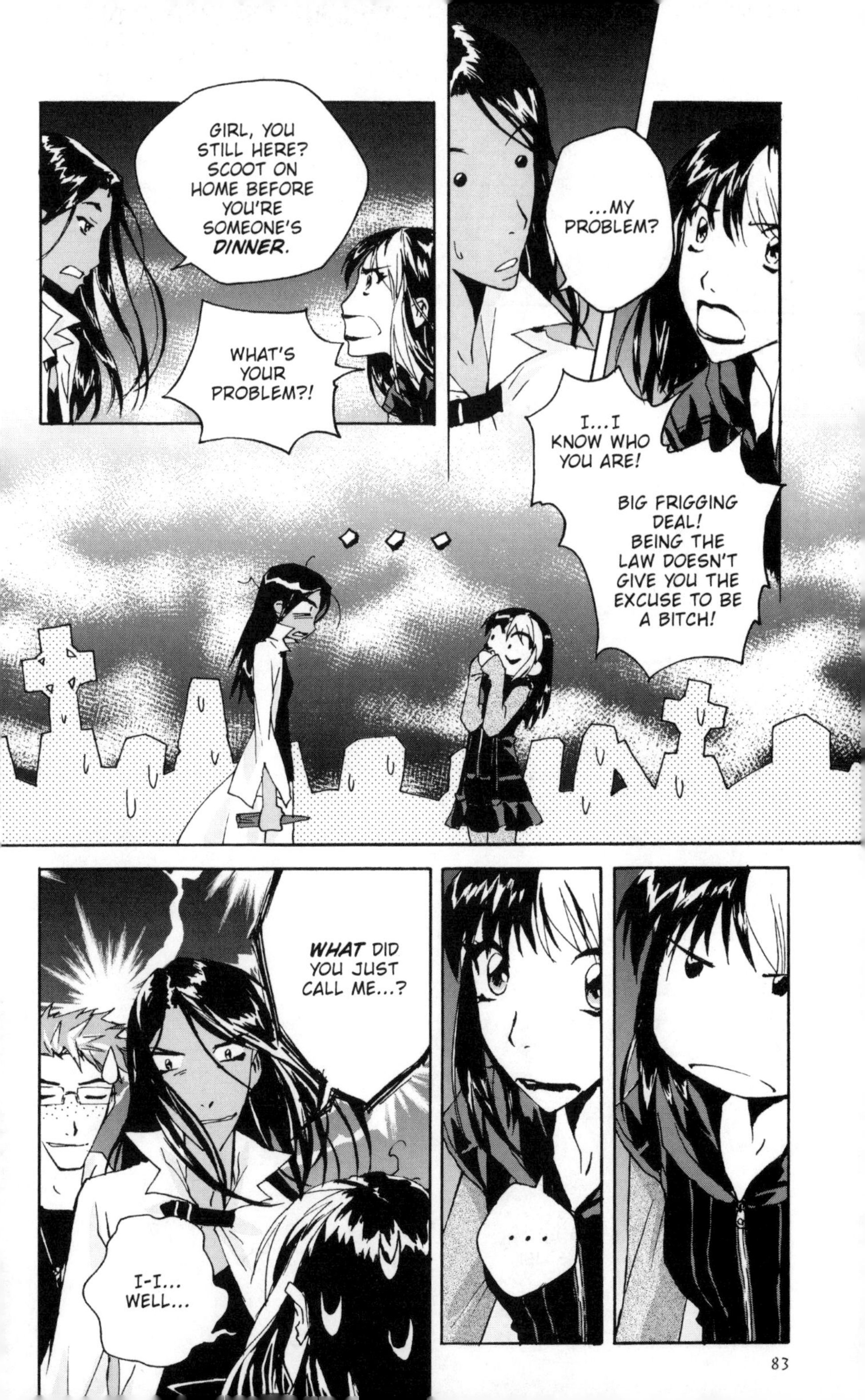
GIRL, YOU STILL HERE? SCOOT ON HOME BEFORE YOU'RE SOMEONE'S *DINNER*.
WHAT'S YOUR PROBLEM?!
...MY PROBLEM?
I...I KNOW WHO YOU ARE!
BIG FRIGGING DEAL! BEING THE LAW DOESN'T GIVE YOU THE EXCUSE TO BE A BITCH!
WHAT DID YOU JUST CALL ME...?
I-I... WELL...
...

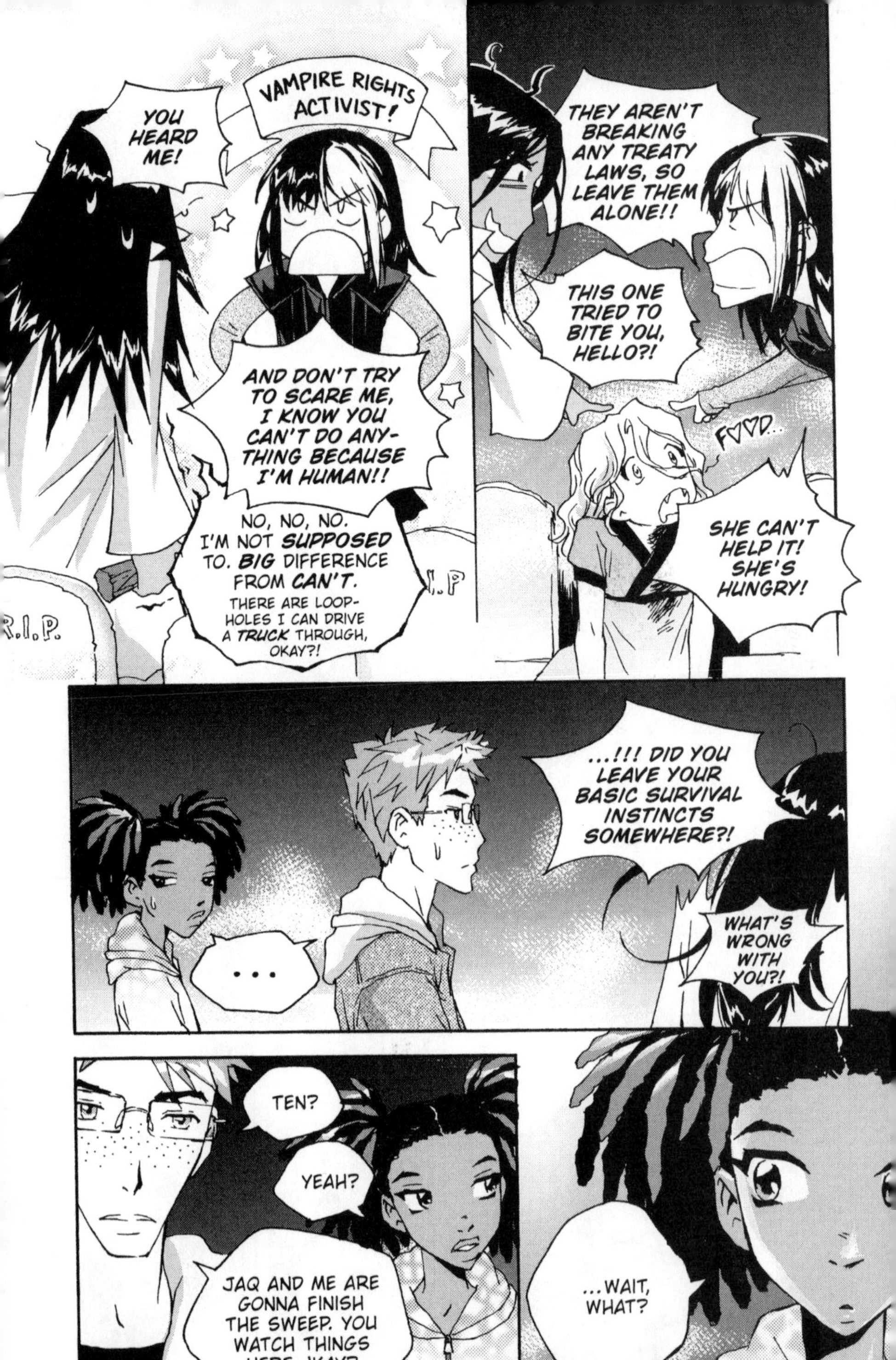
YOU HEARD ME!
VAMPIRE RIGHTS ACTIVIST!
AND DON'T TRY TO SCARE ME, I KNOW YOU CAN'T DO ANY-THING BECAUSE I'M HUMAN!!
NO, NO, NO. I'M NOT SUPPOSED TO. BIG DIFFERENCE FROM CAN'T. THERE ARE LOOP-HOLES I CAN DRIVE A TRUCK THROUGH, OKAY?!
R.I.P.
THEY AREN'T BREAKING ANY TREATY LAWS, SO LEAVE THEM ALONE!!
THIS ONE TRIED TO BITE YOU, HELLO?!
FOOD..
SHE CAN'T HELP IT! SHE'S HUNGRY!
...!!! DID YOU LEAVE YOUR BASIC SURVIVAL INSTINCTS SOMEWHERE?!
WHAT'S WRONG WITH YOU?!
...
TEN?
YEAH?
JAQ AND ME ARE GONNA FINISH THE SWEEP. YOU WATCH THINGS HERE, 'KAY?
...WAIT, WHAT?

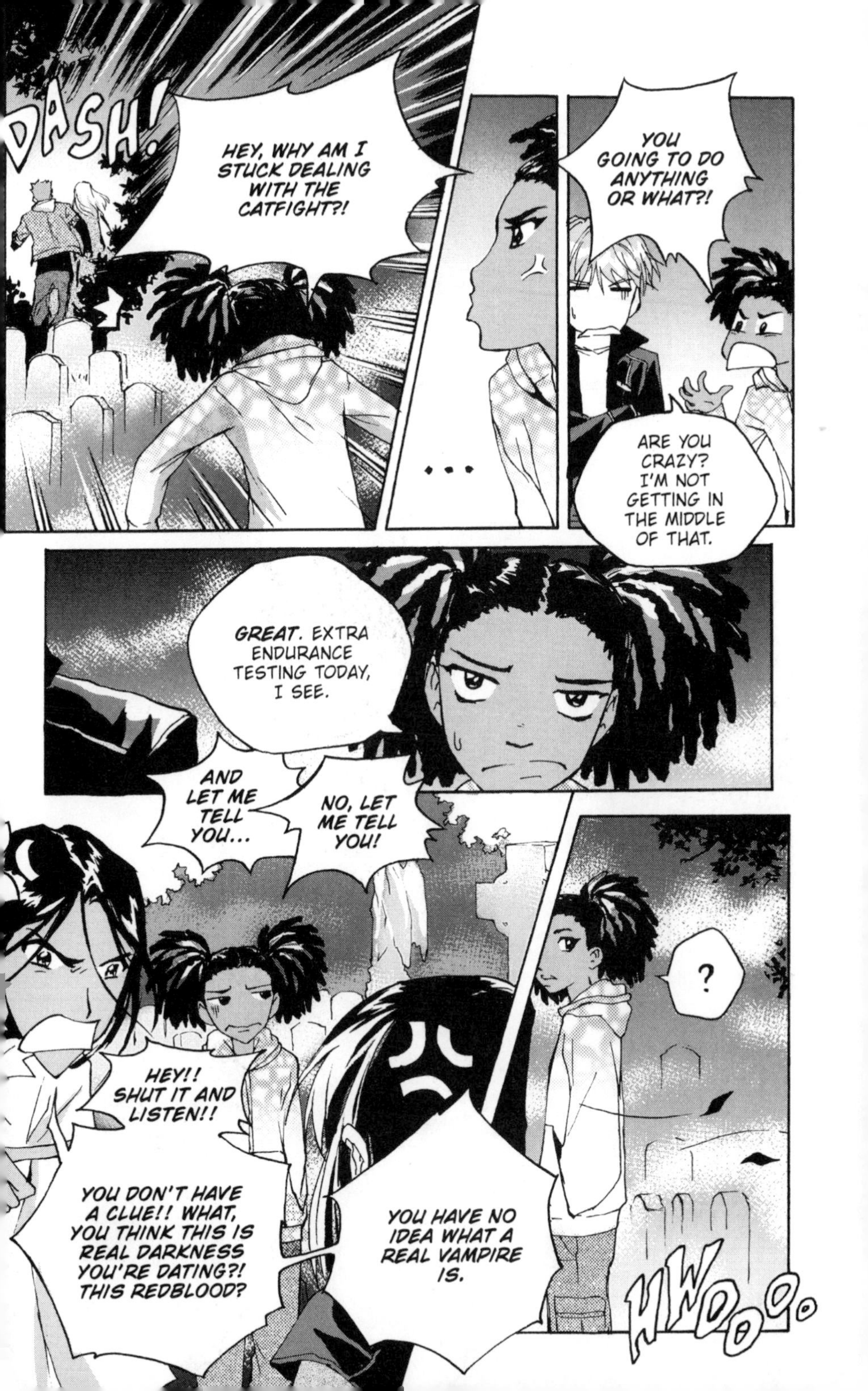
DASH!
HEY, WHY AM I STUCK DEALING WITH THE CATFIGHT?!
...
YOU GOING TO DO ANYTHING OR WHAT?!
ARE YOU CRAZY? I'M NOT GETTING IN THE MIDDLE OF THAT.
GREAT. EXTRA ENDURANCE TESTING TODAY, I SEE.
AND LET ME TELL YOU...
NO, LET ME TELL YOU!
?
HEY!! SHUT IT AND LISTEN!!
YOU DON'T HAVE A CLUE!! WHAT, YOU THINK THIS IS REAL DARKNESS YOU'RE DATING?! THIS REDBLOOD?
YOU HAVE NO IDEA WHAT A REAL VAMPIRE IS.
HWOOoo

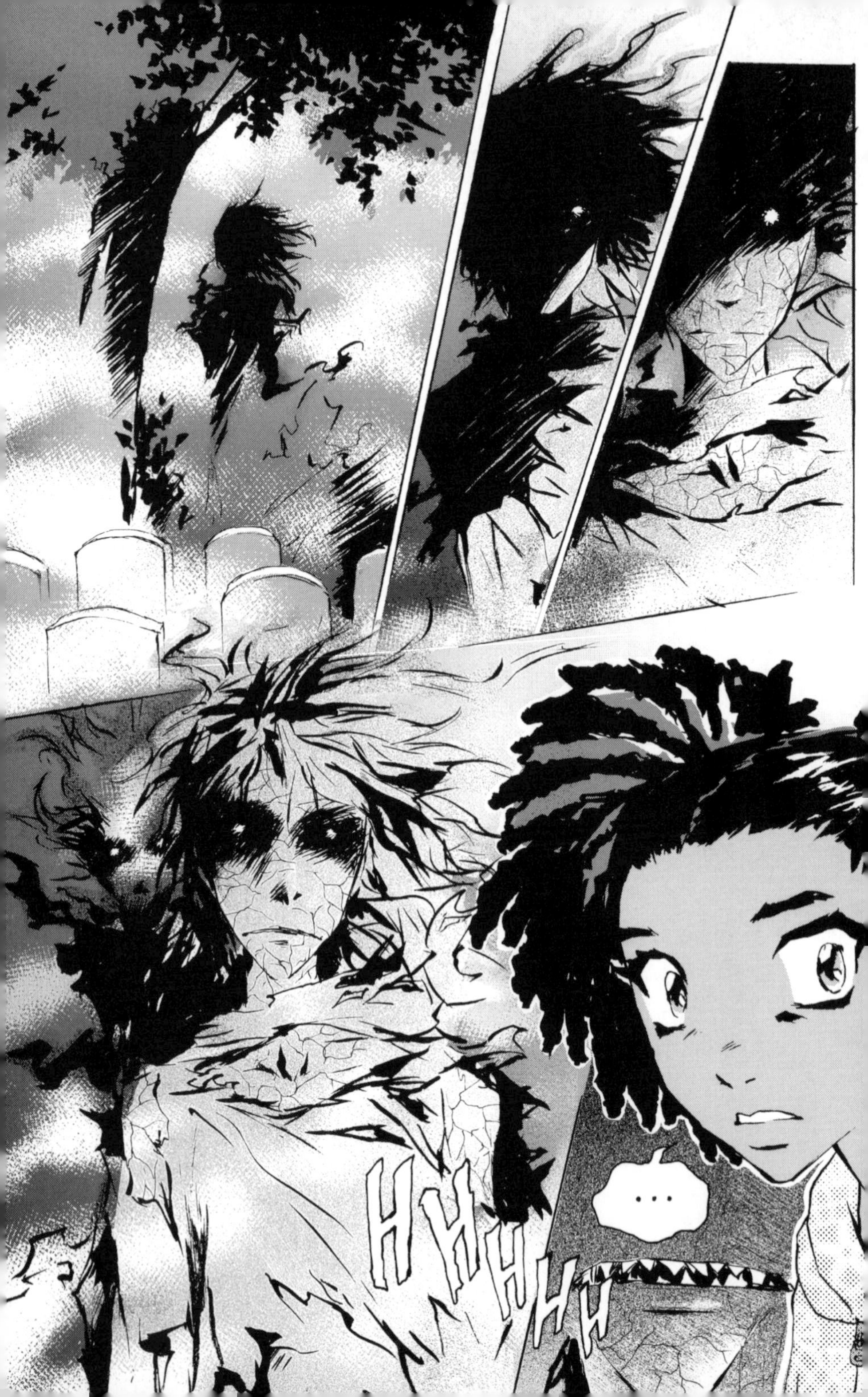
HHHHHH
...

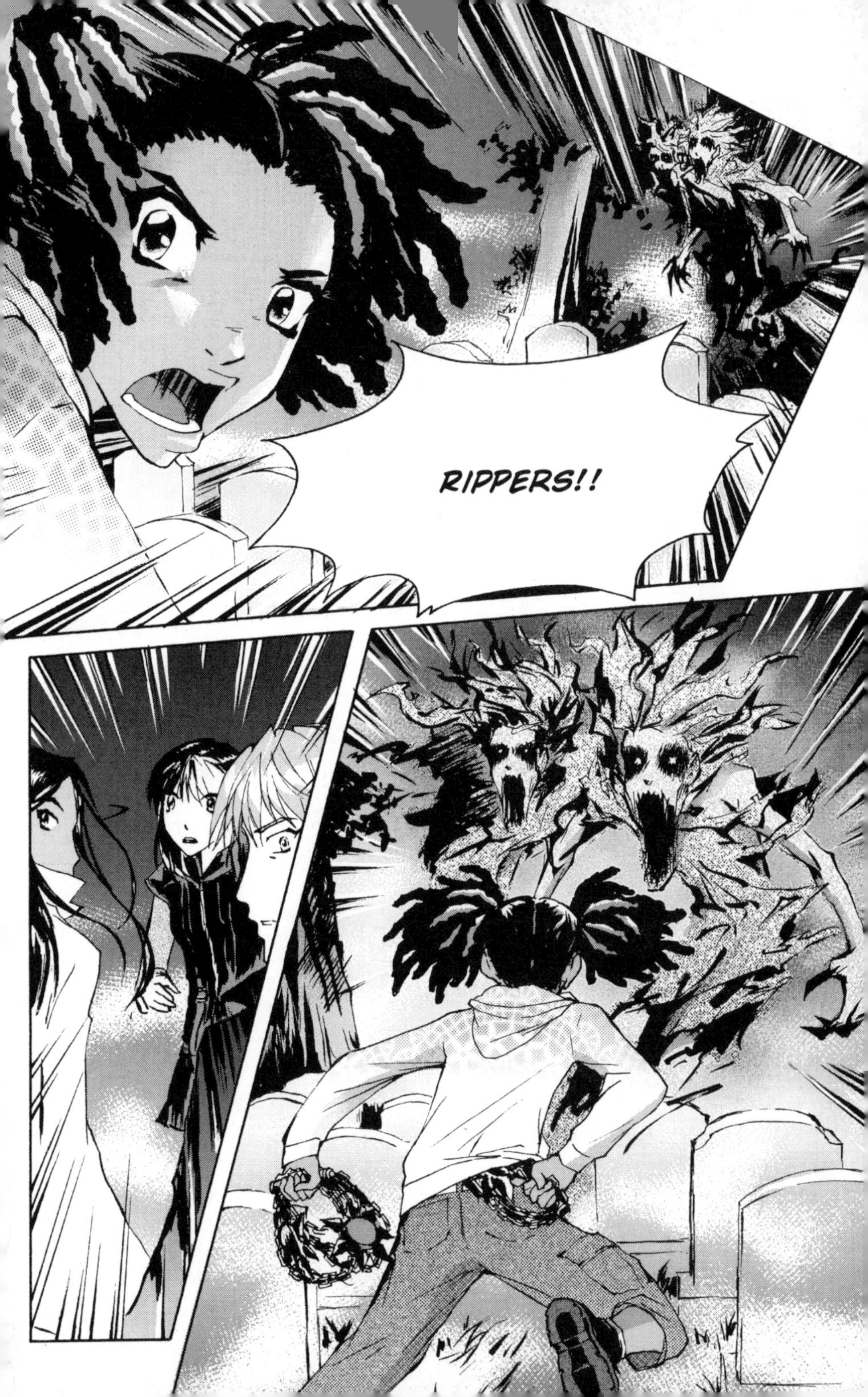
RIPPERS!!

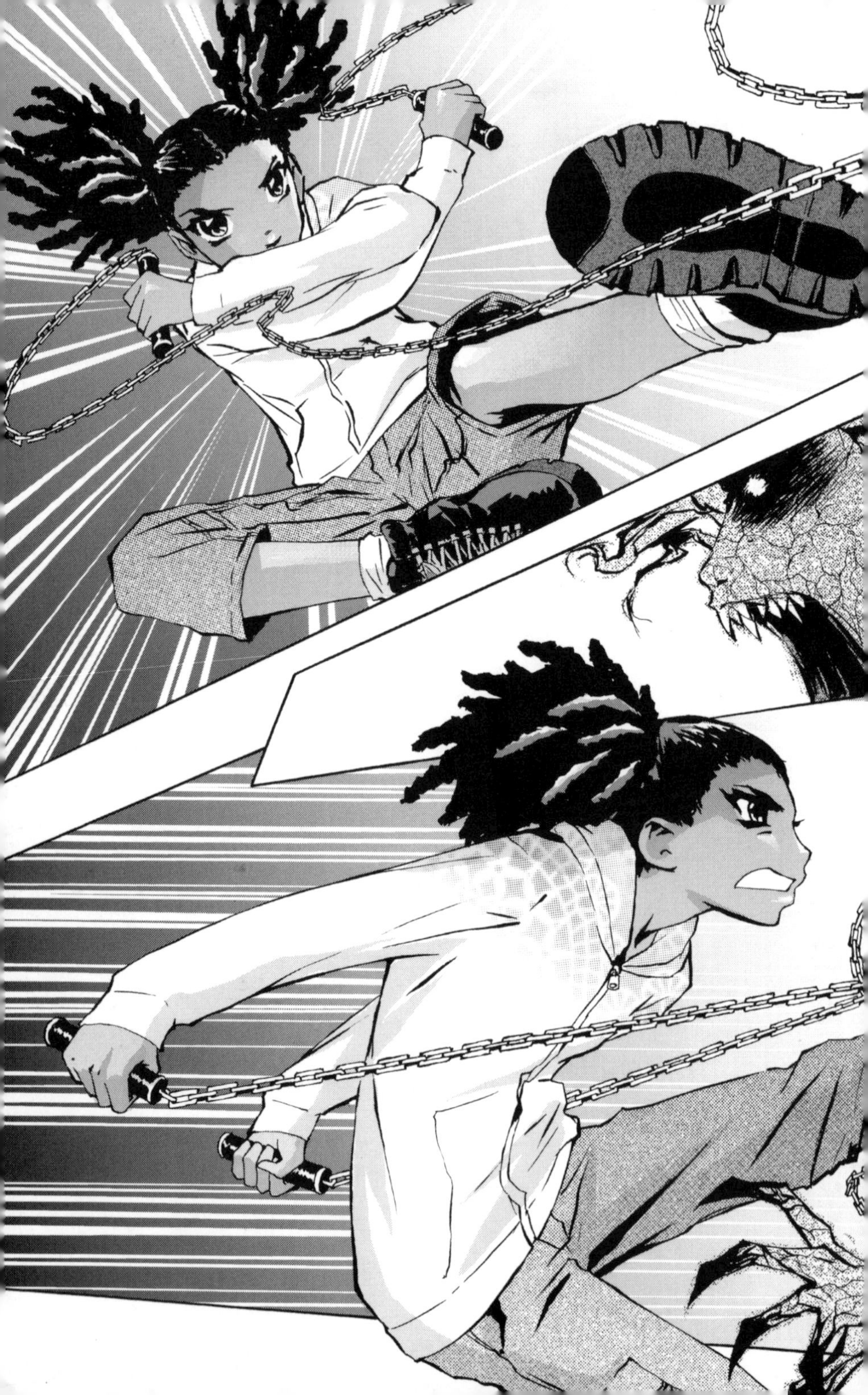

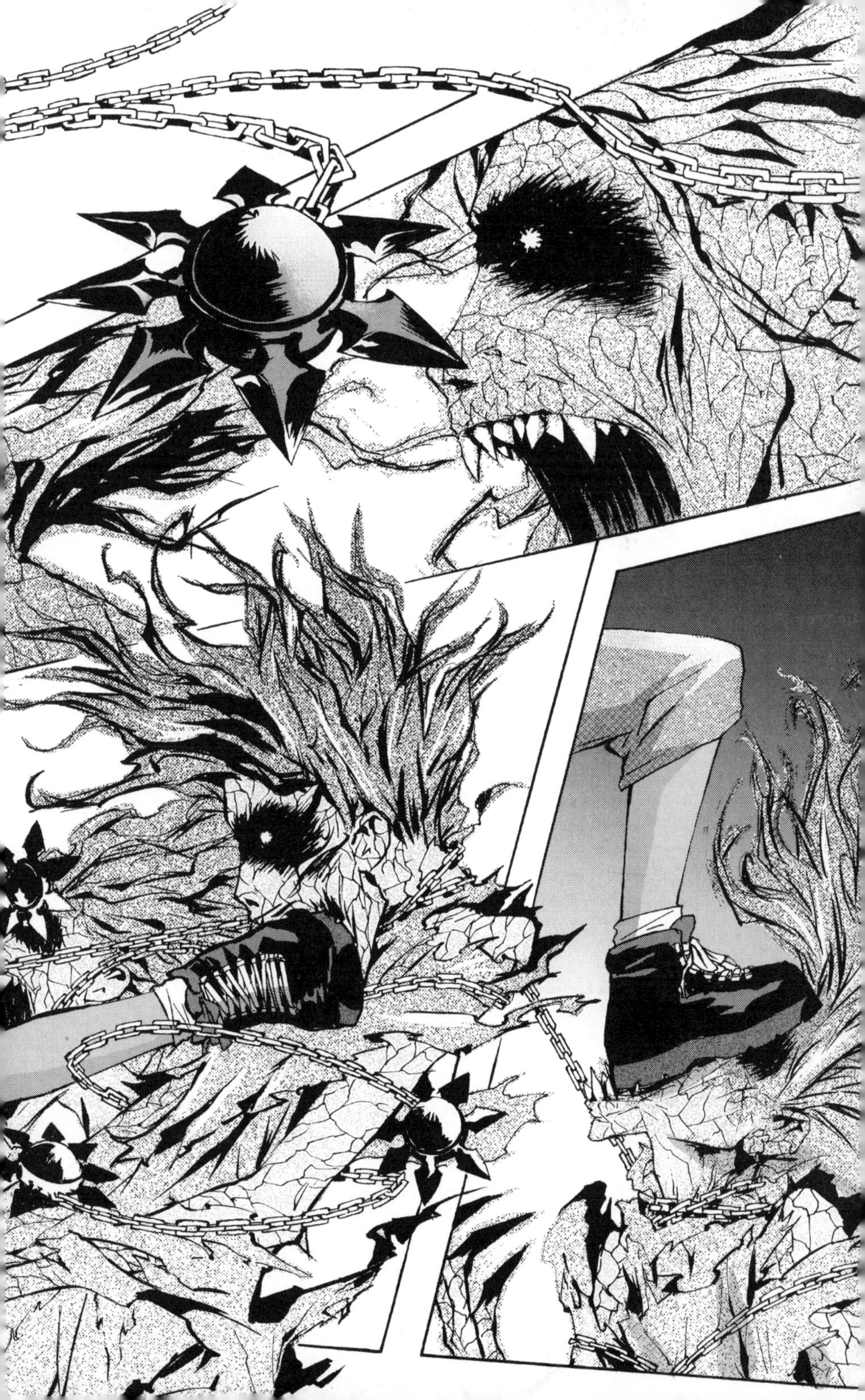

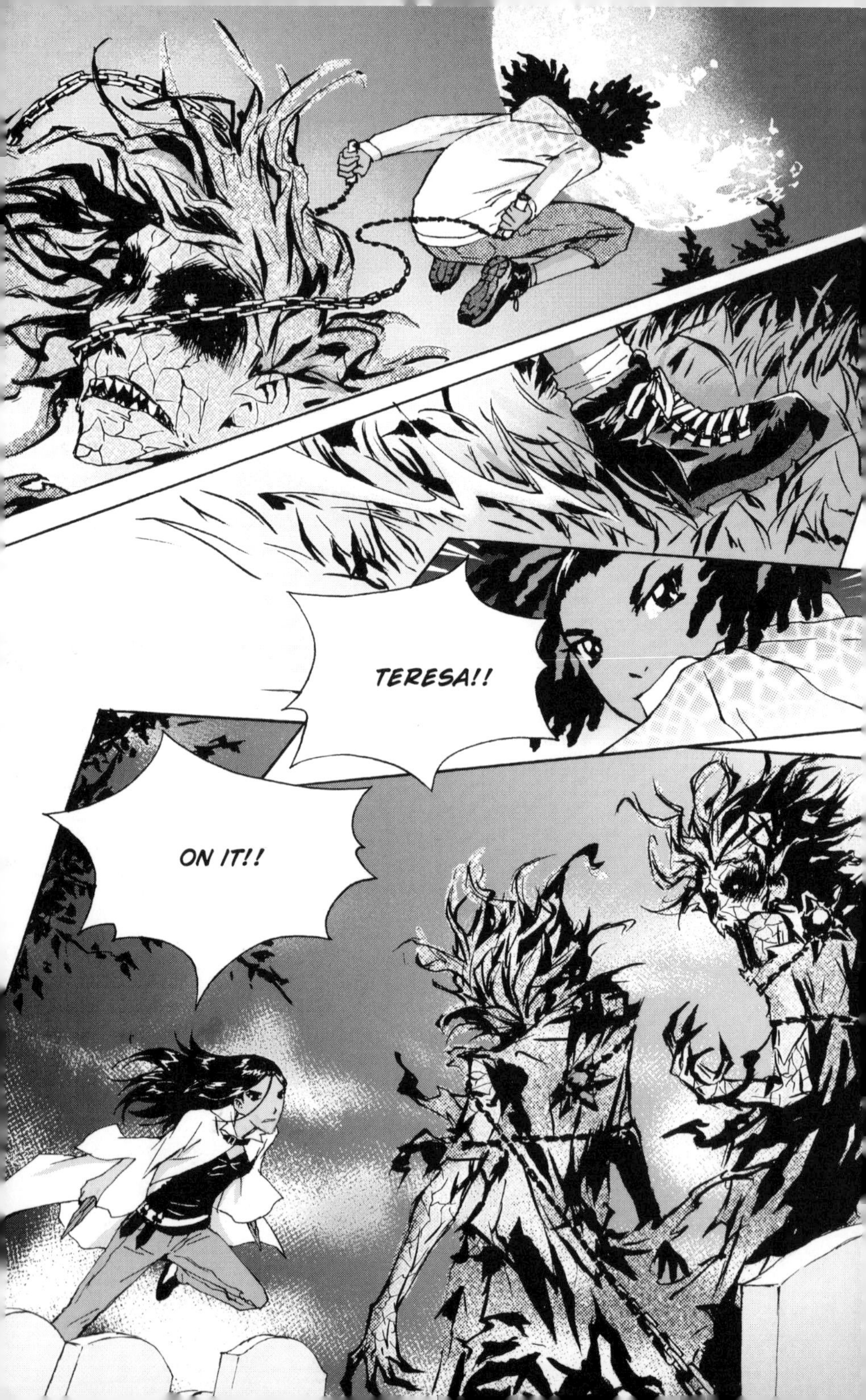
TERESA!!
ON IT!!

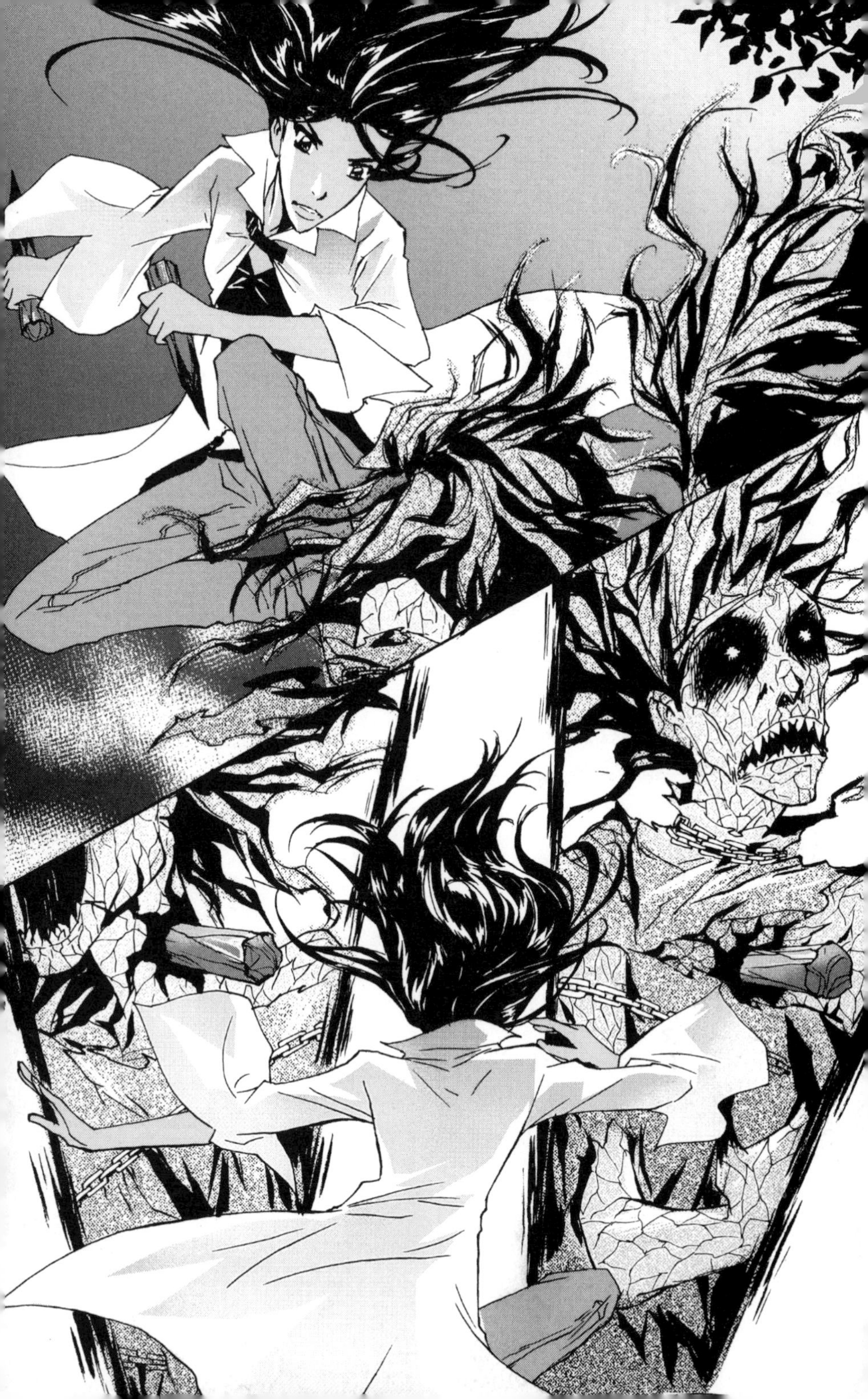

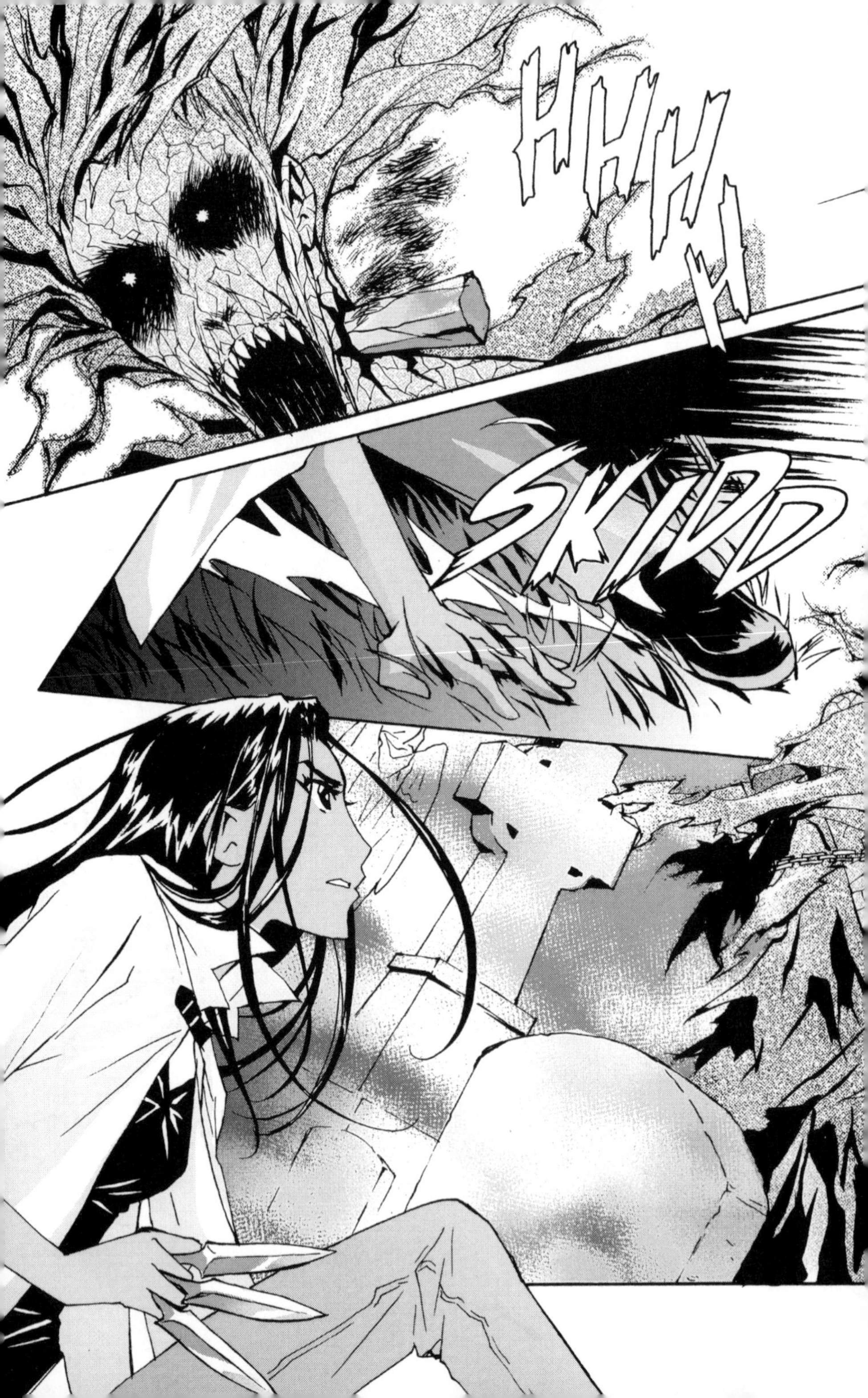
HHHHH
SKIDD

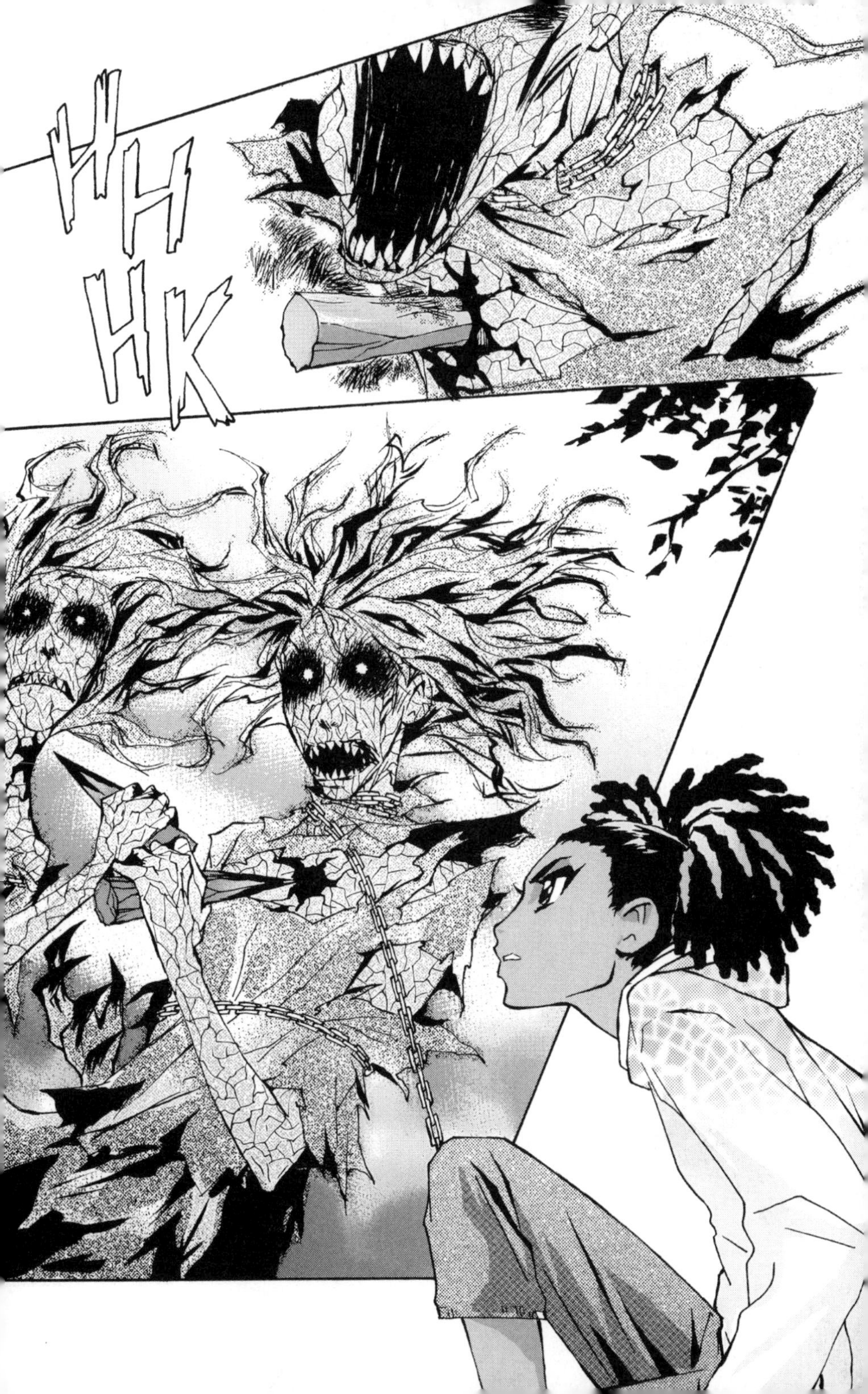
HHHK

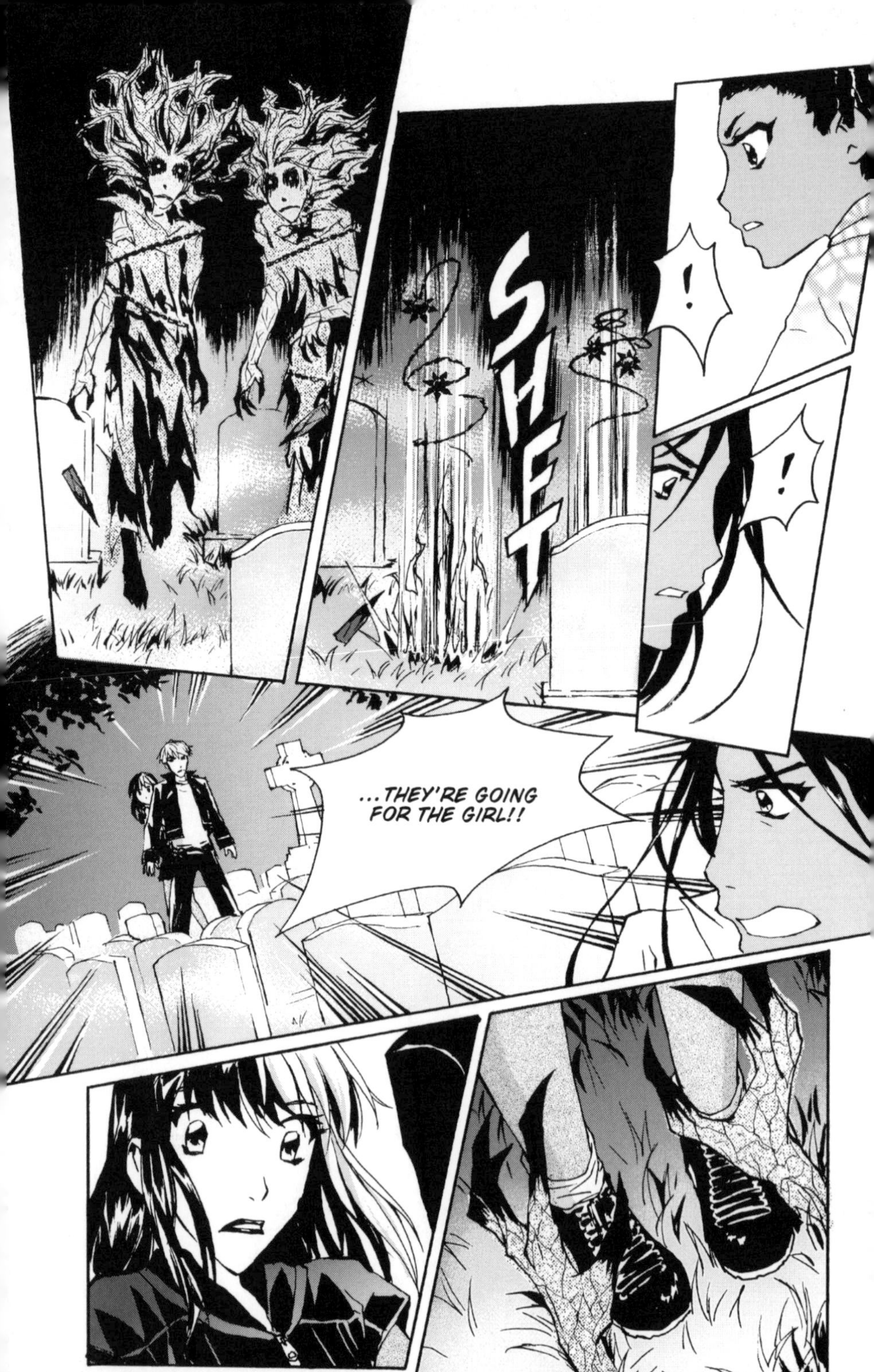

SHFT
!
!
...THEY'RE GOING FOR THE GIRL!!

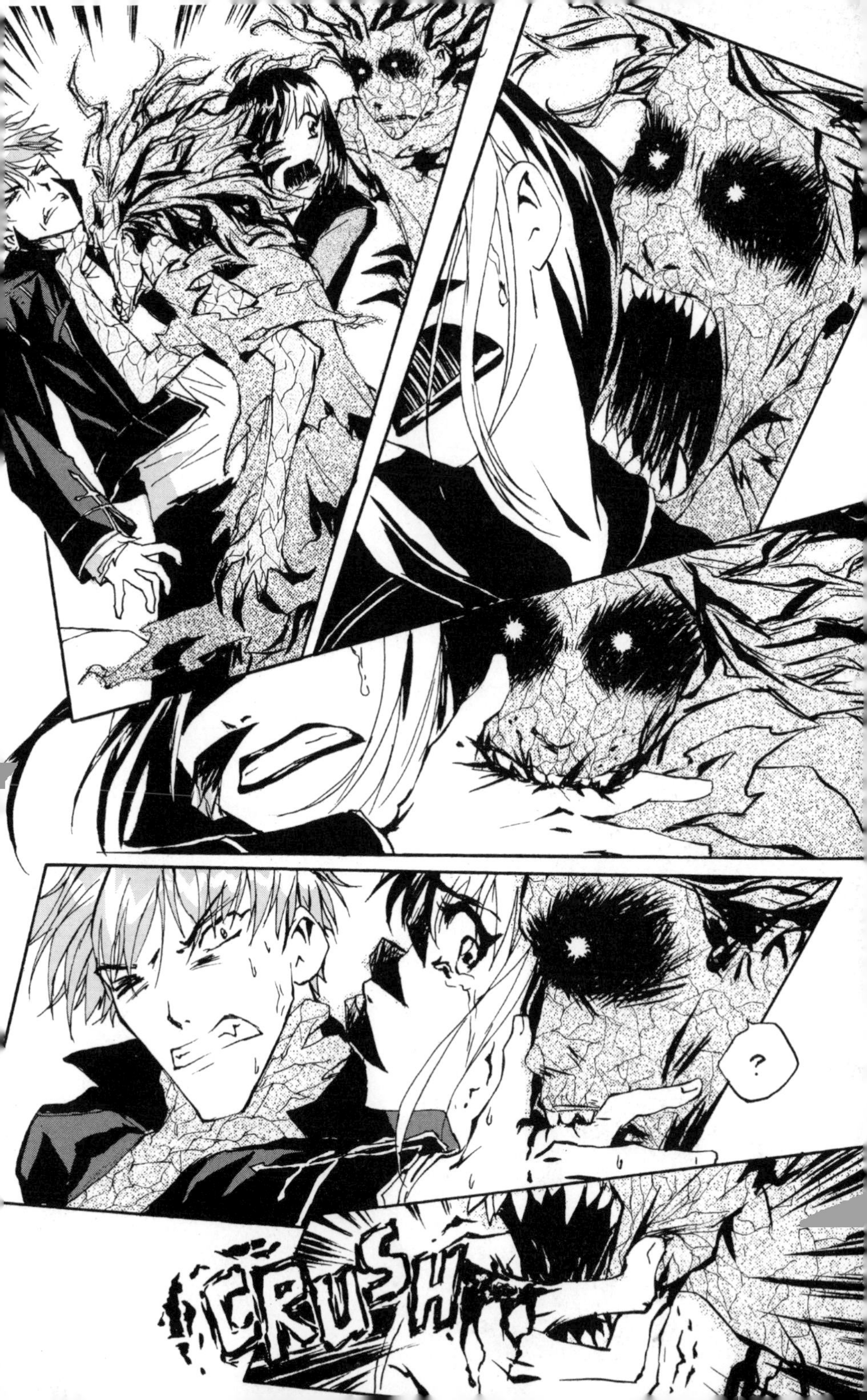
?
CRUSH

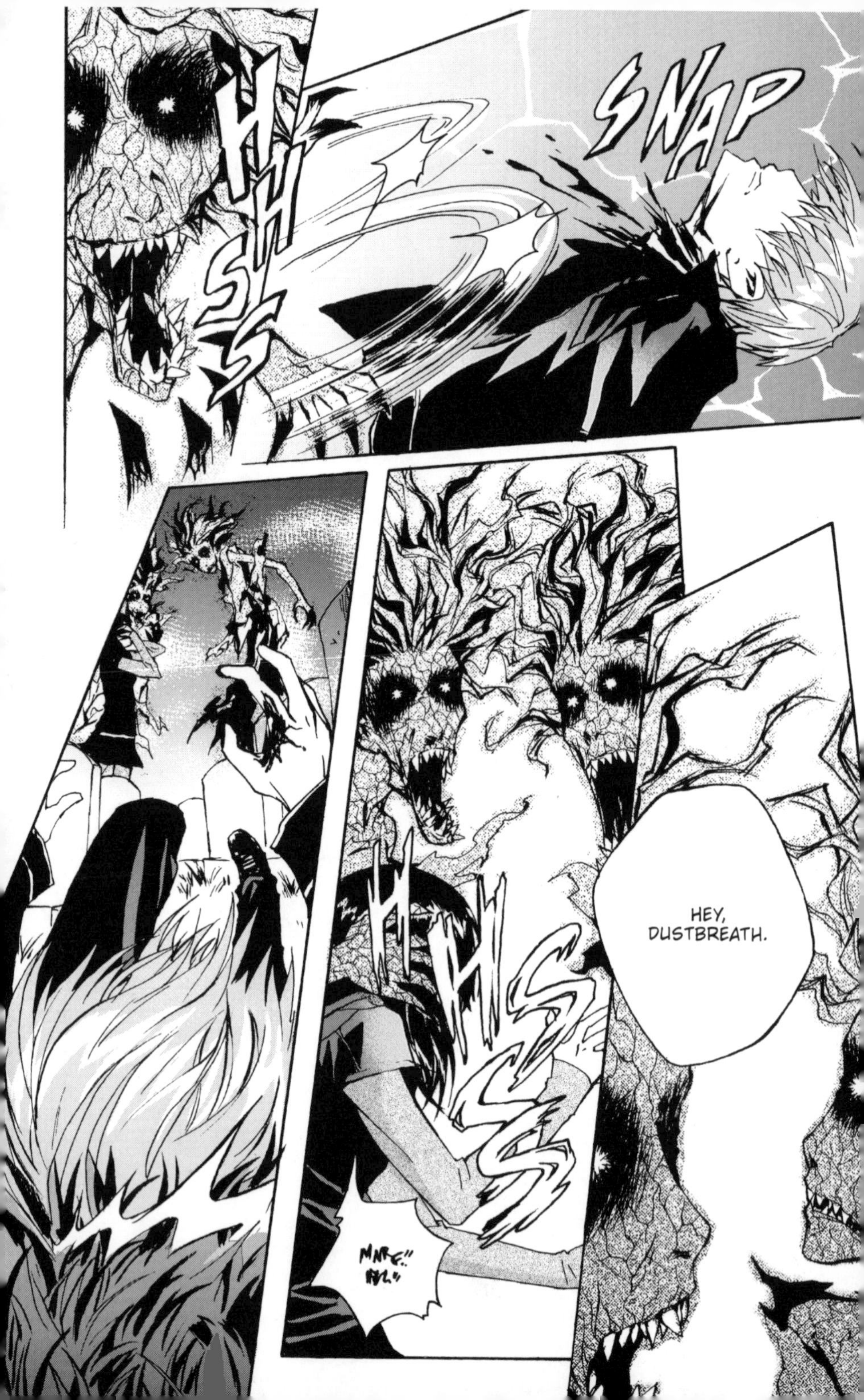
SNAP
HEY, DUSTBREATH.

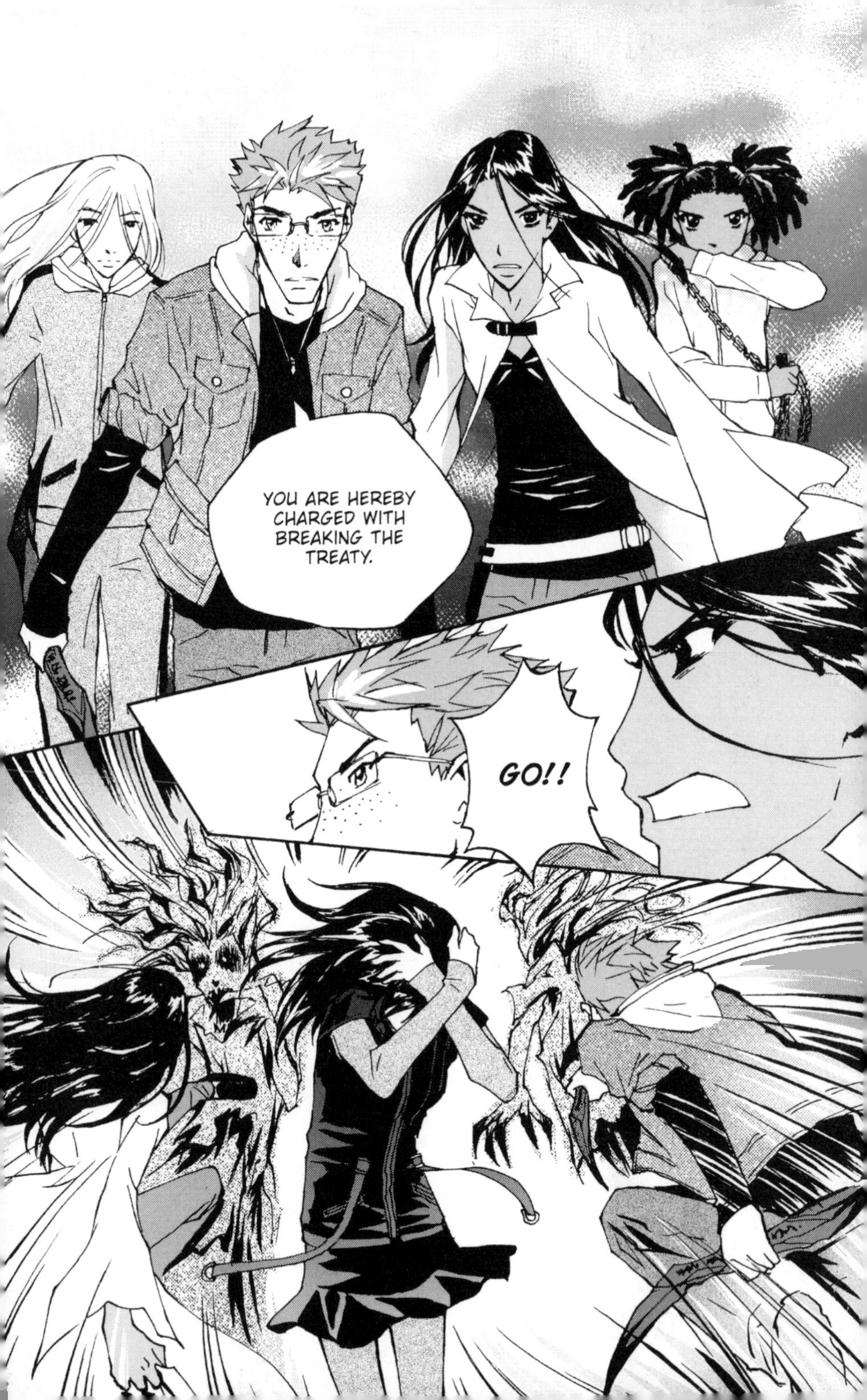
YOU ARE HEREBY CHARGED WITH BREAKING THE TREATY.
GO!!

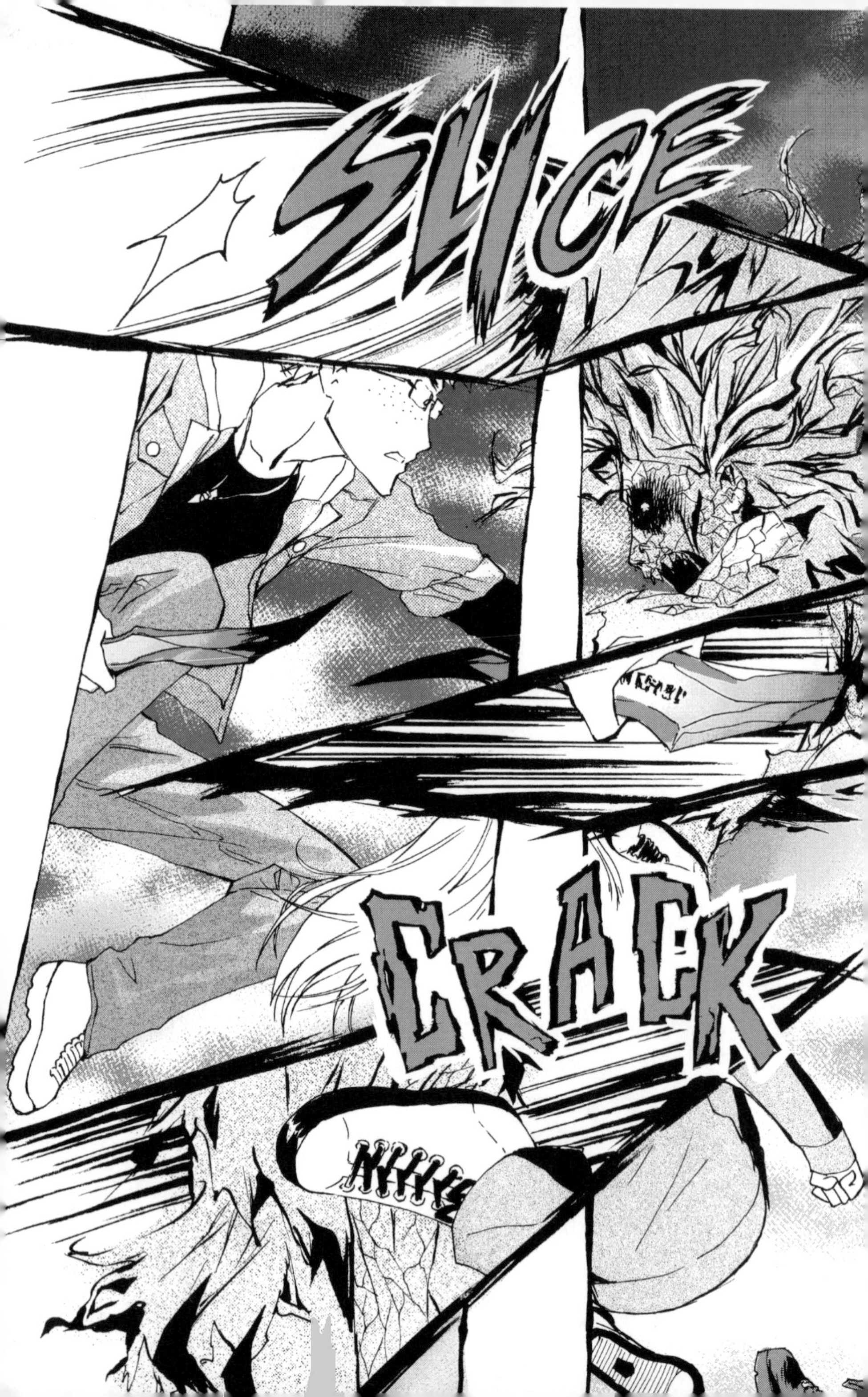
SLICE
CRACK

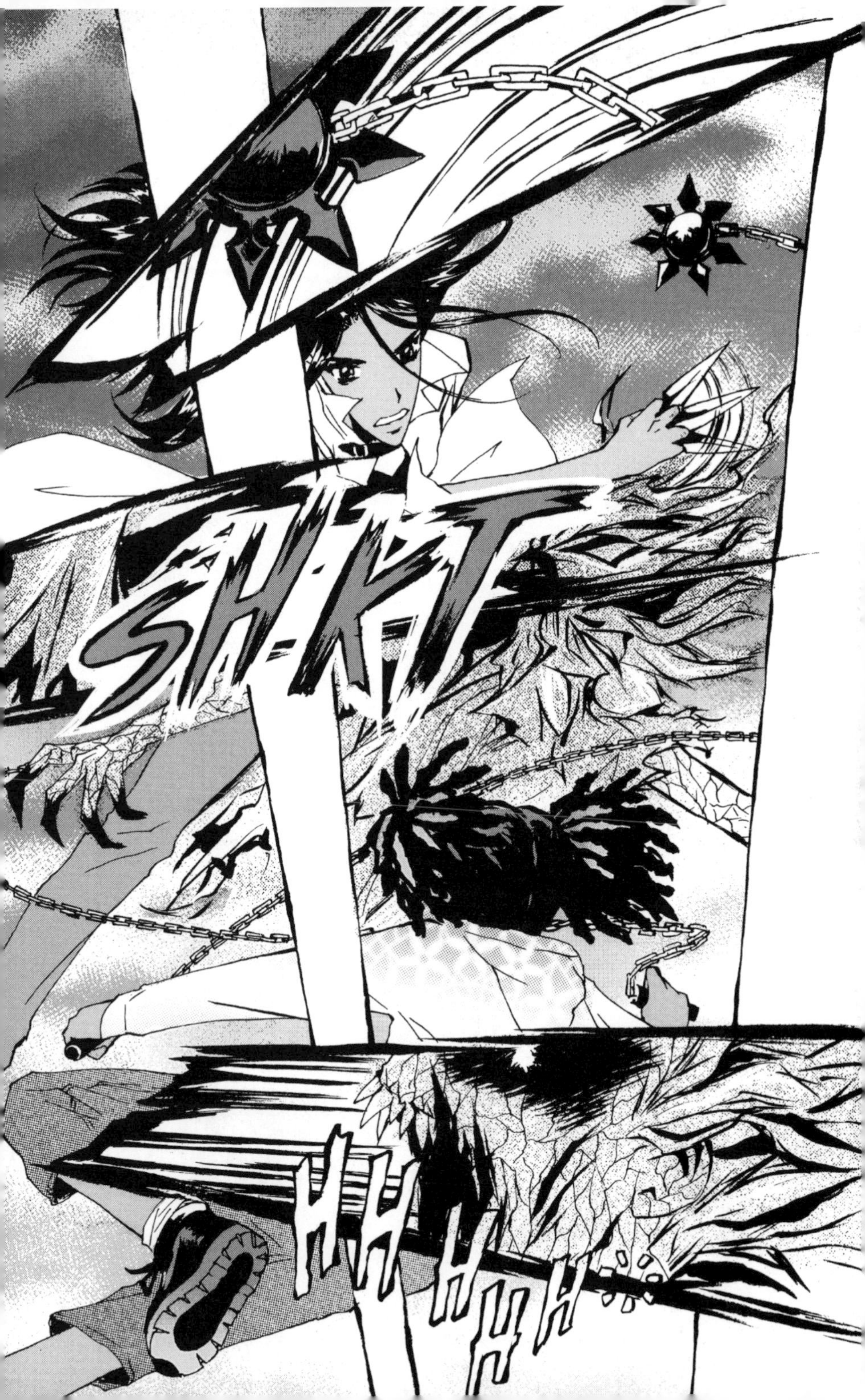
SH-KT
HHHHH...

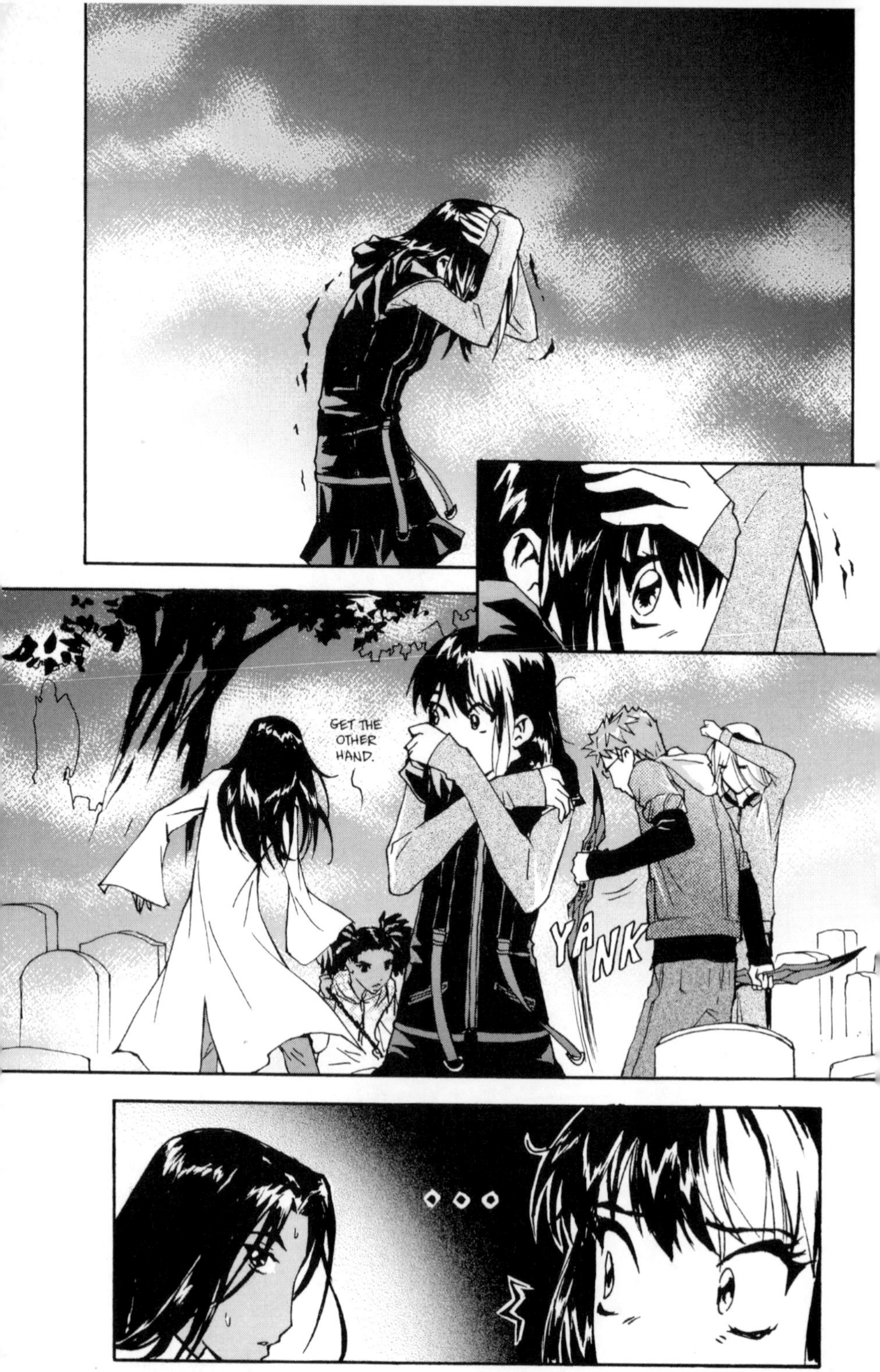
GET THE OTHER HAND.
YANK

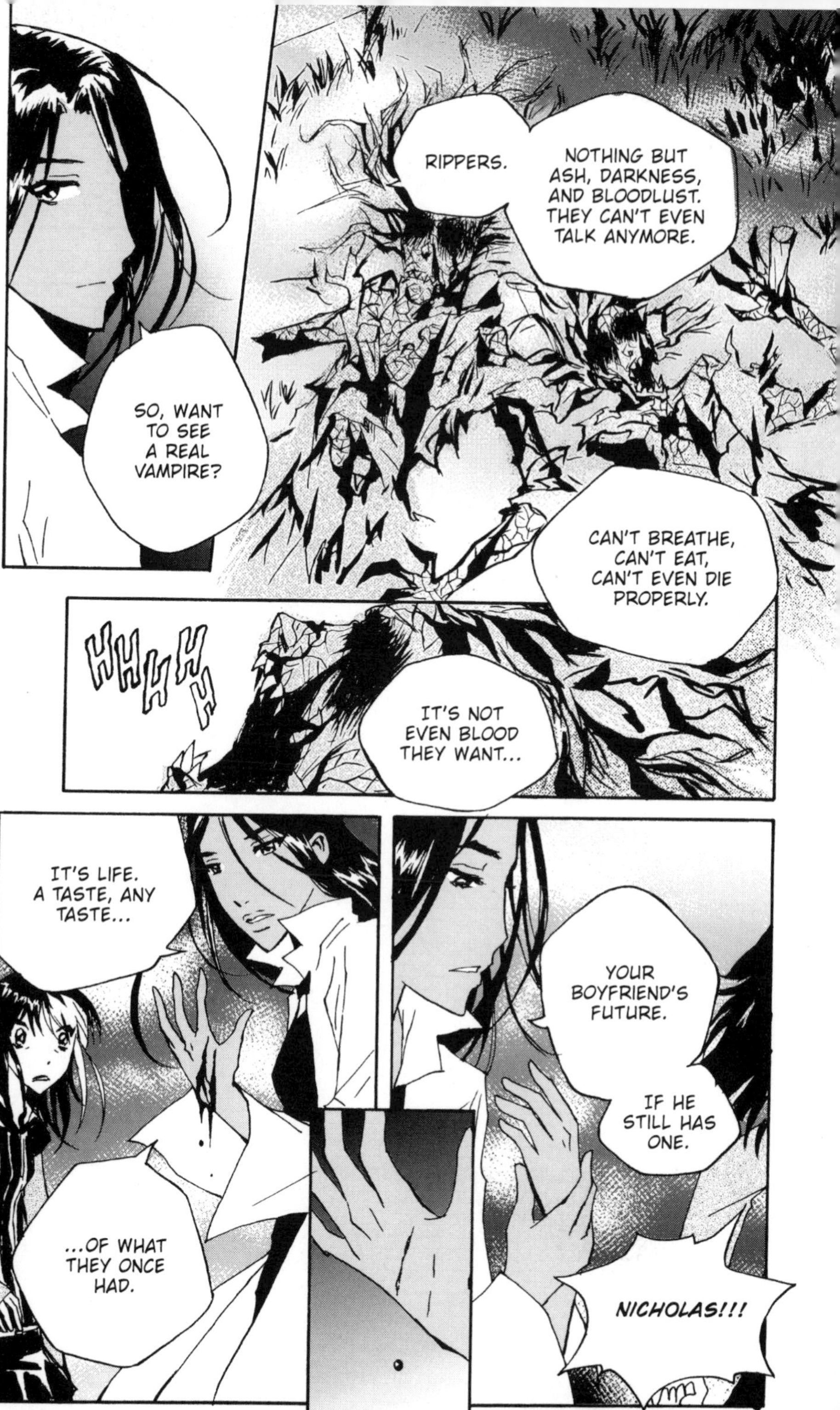
SO, WANT TO SEE A REAL VAMPIRE?
RIPPERS.
NOTHING BUT ASH, DARKNESS, AND BLOODLUST. THEY CAN'T EVEN TALK ANYMORE.
CAN'T BREATHE, CAN'T EAT, CAN'T EVEN DIE PROPERLY.
HHHHHH
IT'S NOT EVEN BLOOD THEY WANT...
IT'S LIFE. A TASTE, ANY TASTE...
...OF WHAT THEY ONCE HAD.
YOUR BOYFRIEND'S FUTURE.
IF HE STILL HAS ONE.
NICHOLAS!!!

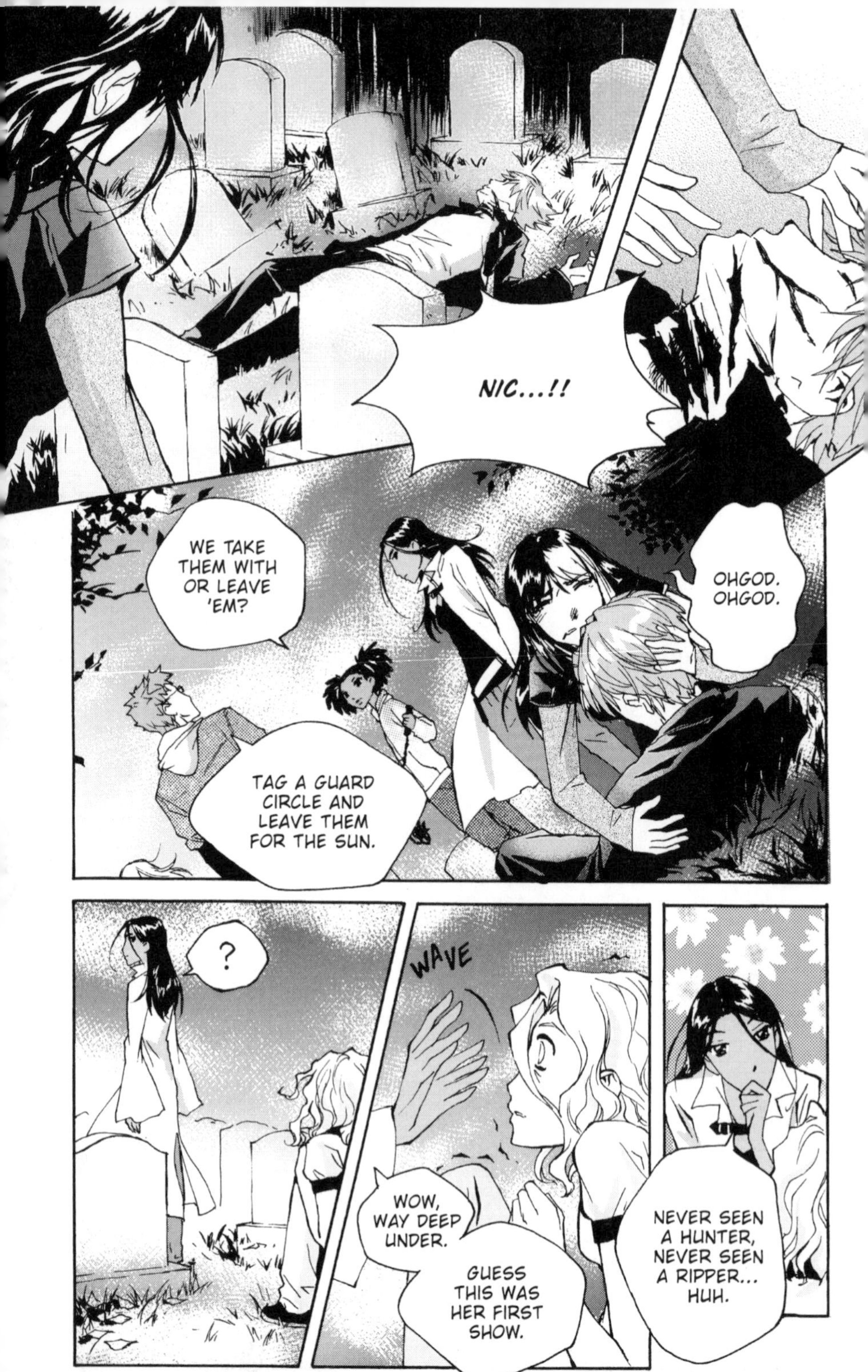
NIC...!!
WE TAKE THEM WITH OR LEAVE 'EM?
OHGOD. OHGOD.
TAG A GUARD CIRCLE AND LEAVE THEM FOR THE SUN.
?
WAVE
WOW, WAY DEEP UNDER.
GUESS THIS WAS HER FIRST SHOW.
NEVER SEEN A HUNTER, NEVER SEEN A RIPPER... HUH.

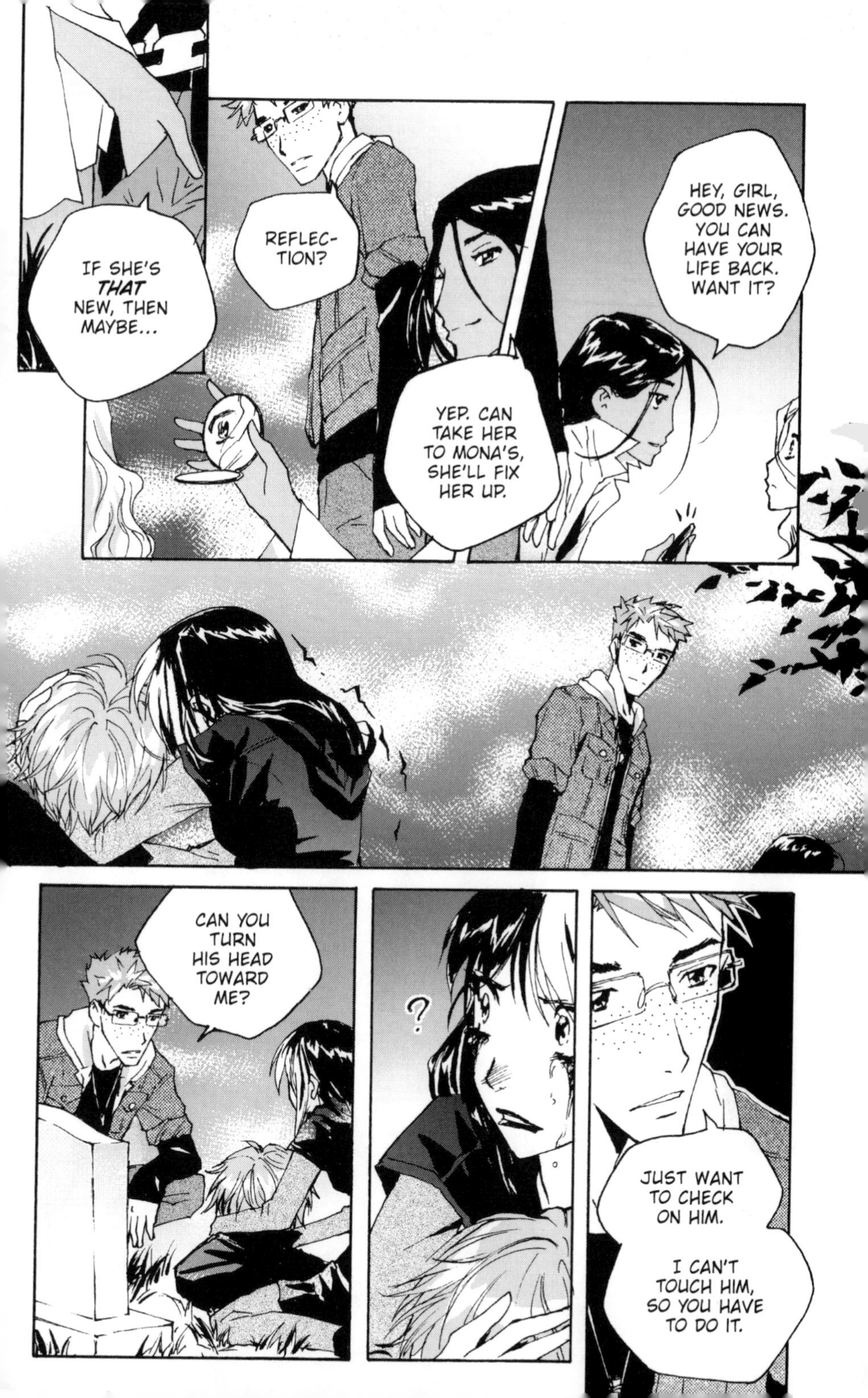
IF SHE'S *THAT* NEW, THEN MAYBE...
REFLEC-TION?
YEP. CAN TAKE HER TO MONA'S, SHE'LL FIX HER UP.
HEY, GIRL, GOOD NEWS. YOU CAN HAVE YOUR LIFE BACK. WANT IT?
CAN YOU TURN HIS HEAD TOWARD ME?
?
JUST WANT TO CHECK ON HIM.
I CAN'T TOUCH HIM, SO YOU HAVE TO DO IT.

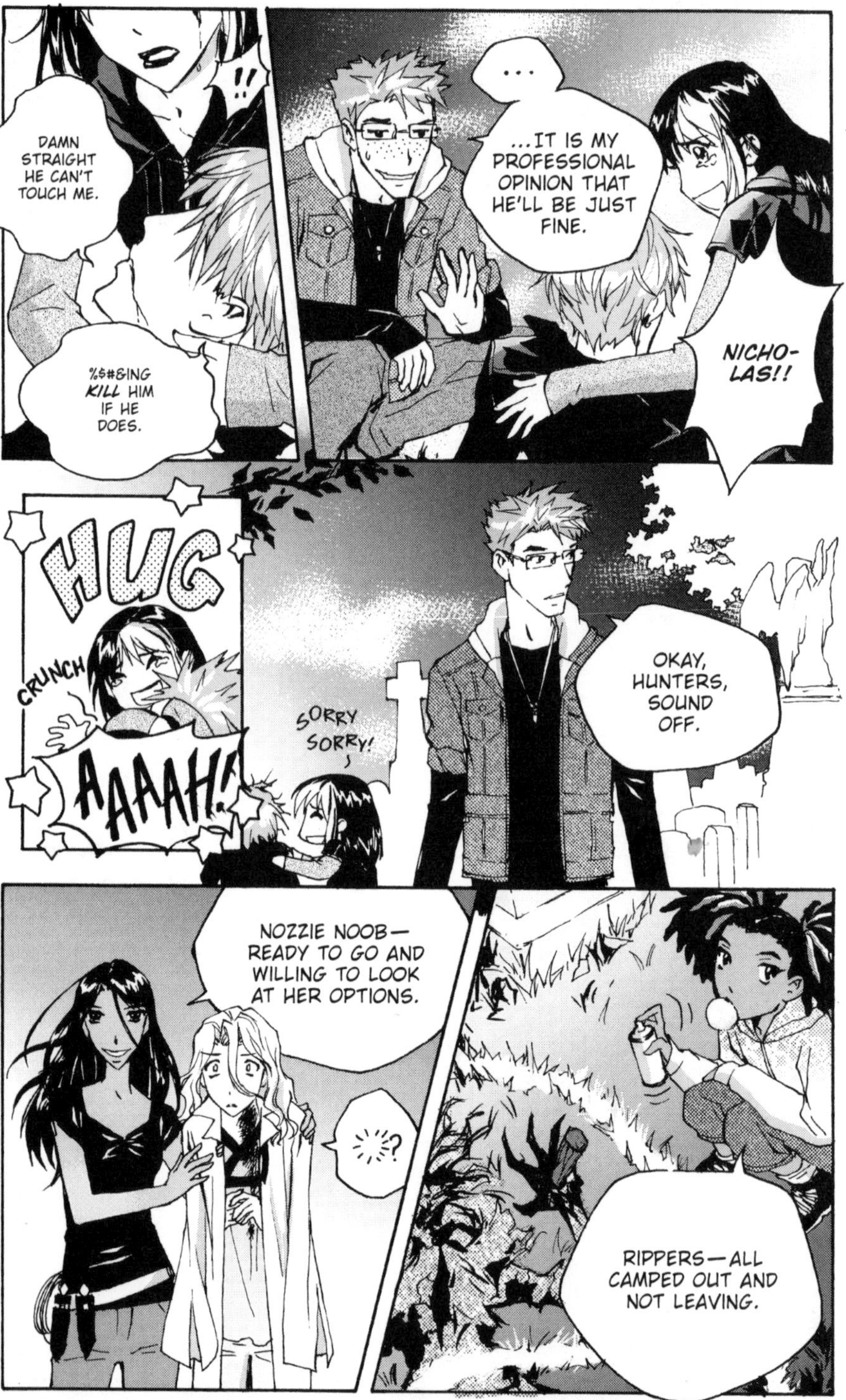
DAMN STRAIGHT HE CAN'T TOUCH ME.
%$#&ING KILL HIM IF HE DOES.
!!
...
...IT IS MY PROFESSIONAL OPINION THAT HE'LL BE JUST FINE.
NICHO-LAS!!
HUG
CRUNCH
AAAAH!
SORRY SORRY!
OKAY, HUNTERS, SOUND OFF.
NOZZIE NOOB—READY TO GO AND WILLING TO LOOK AT HER OPTIONS.
?
RIPPERS—ALL CAMPED OUT AND NOT LEAVING.

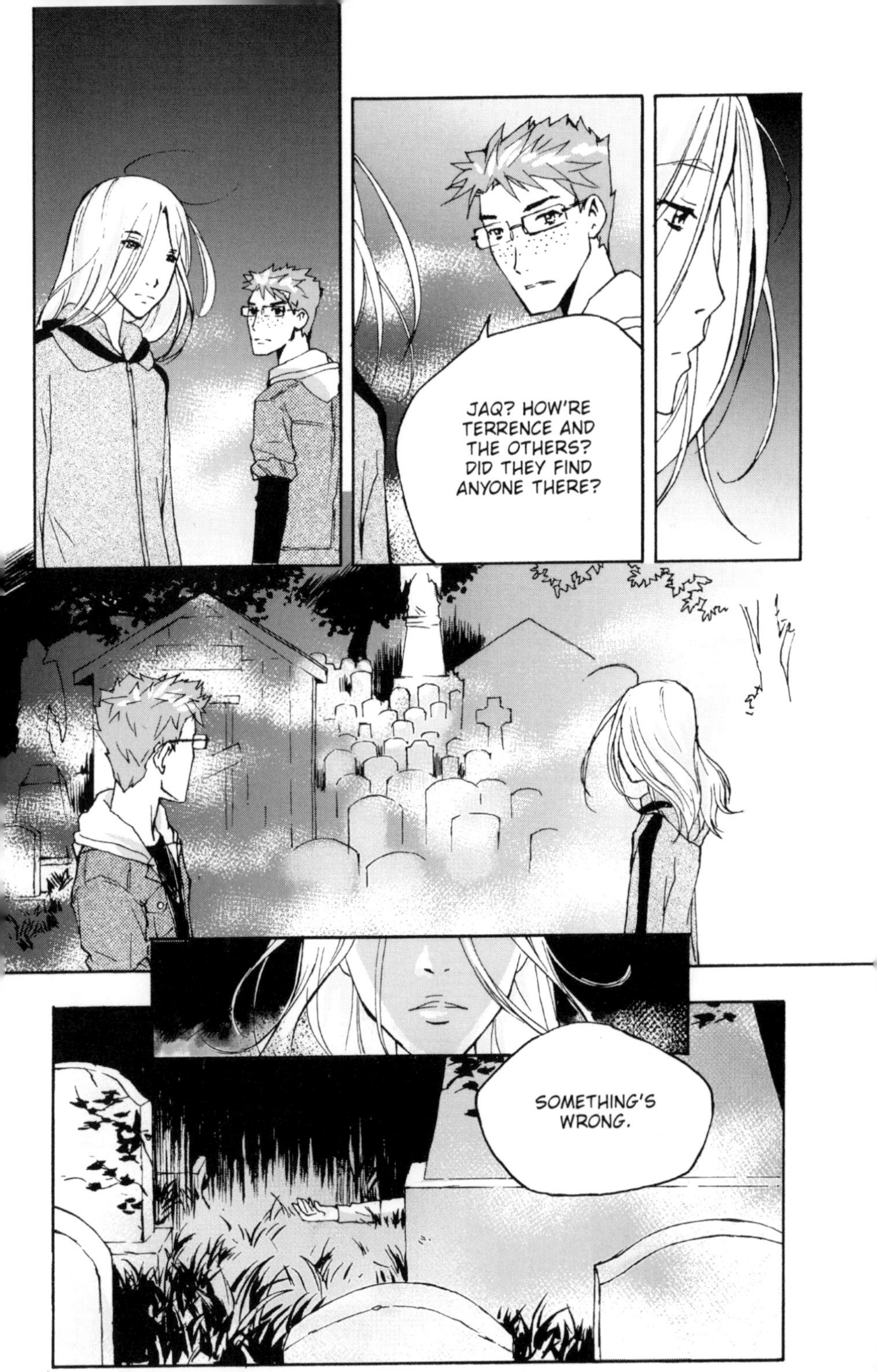
JAQ? HOW'RE TERRENCE AND THE OTHERS? DID THEY FIND ANYONE THERE?
SOMETHING'S WRONG.

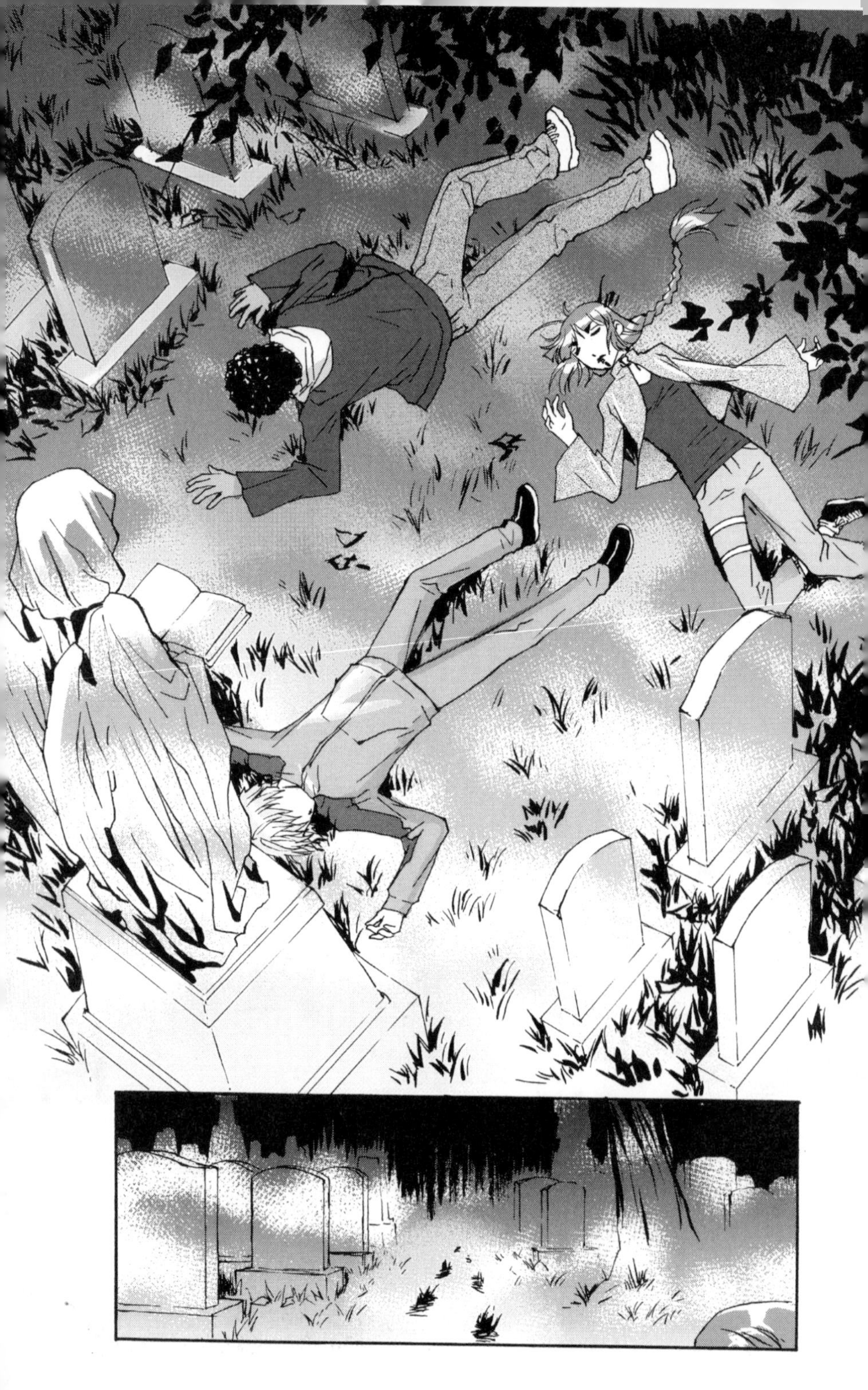

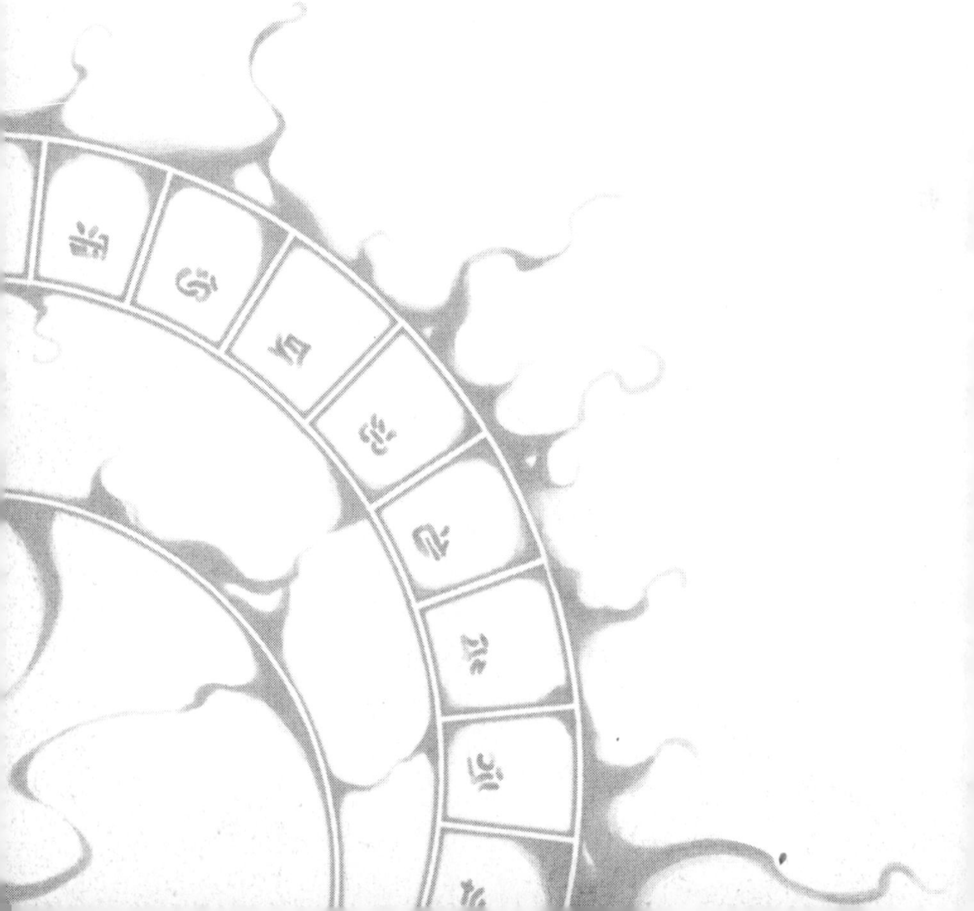

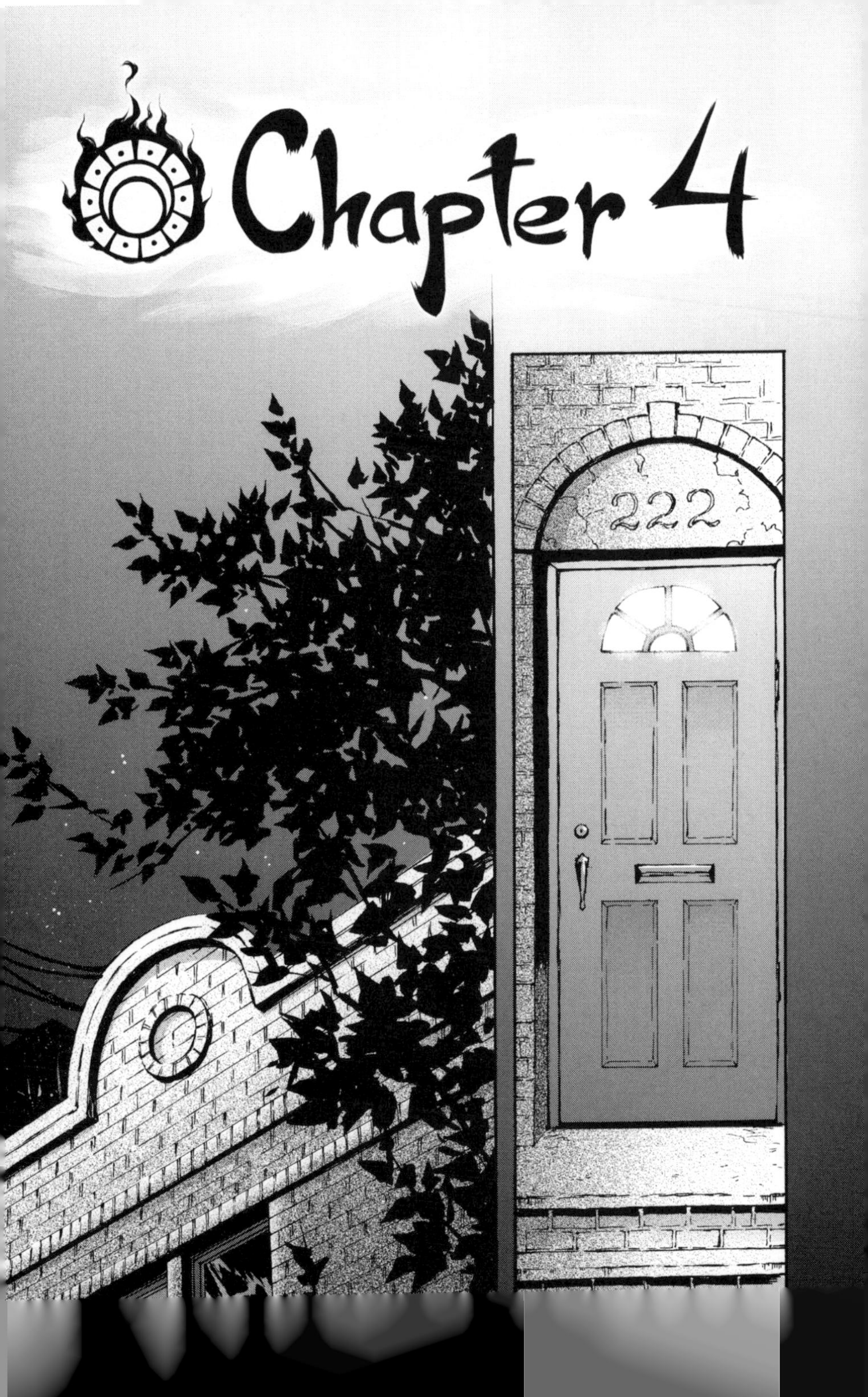
Chapter 4
222

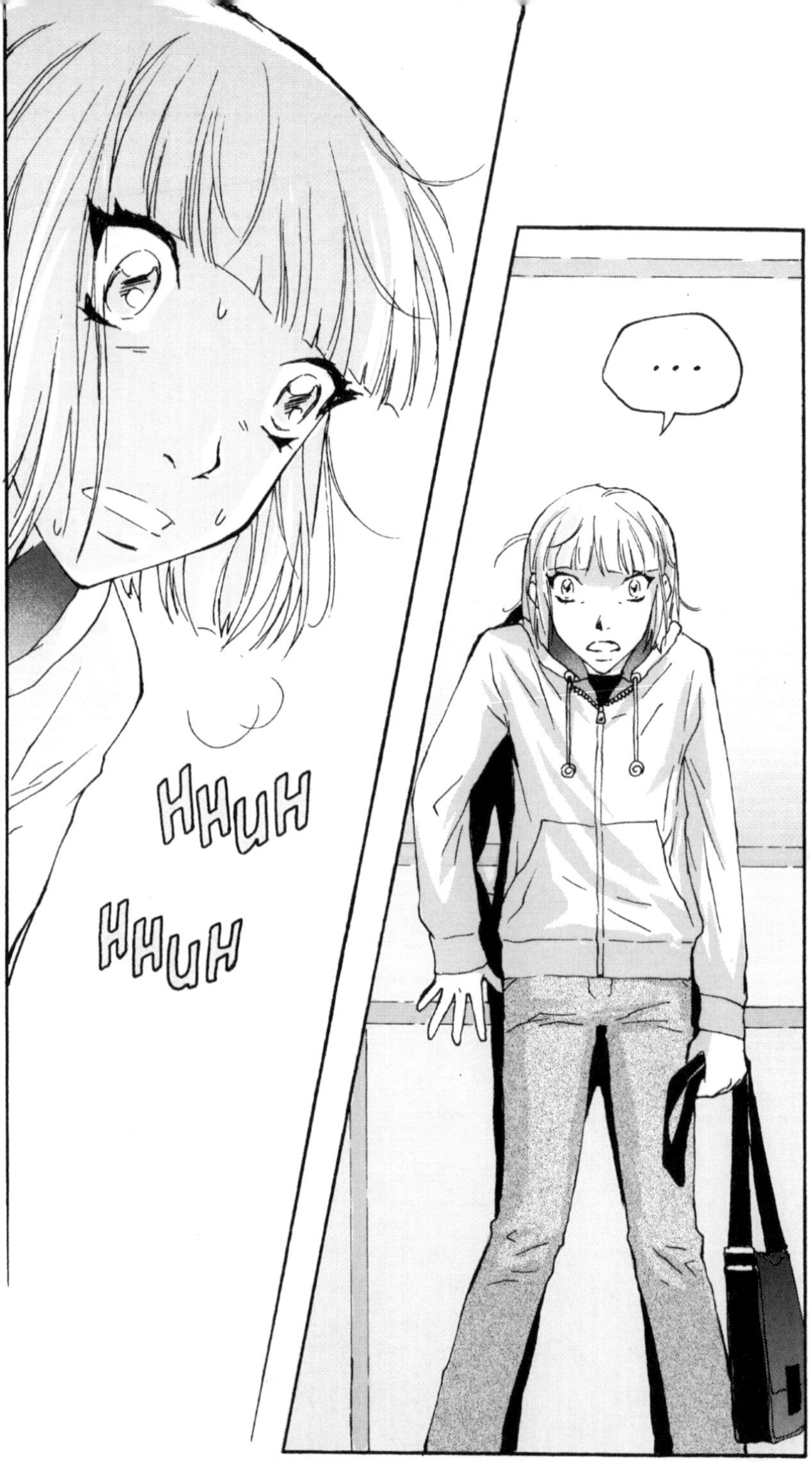
HHUH
HHUH
...

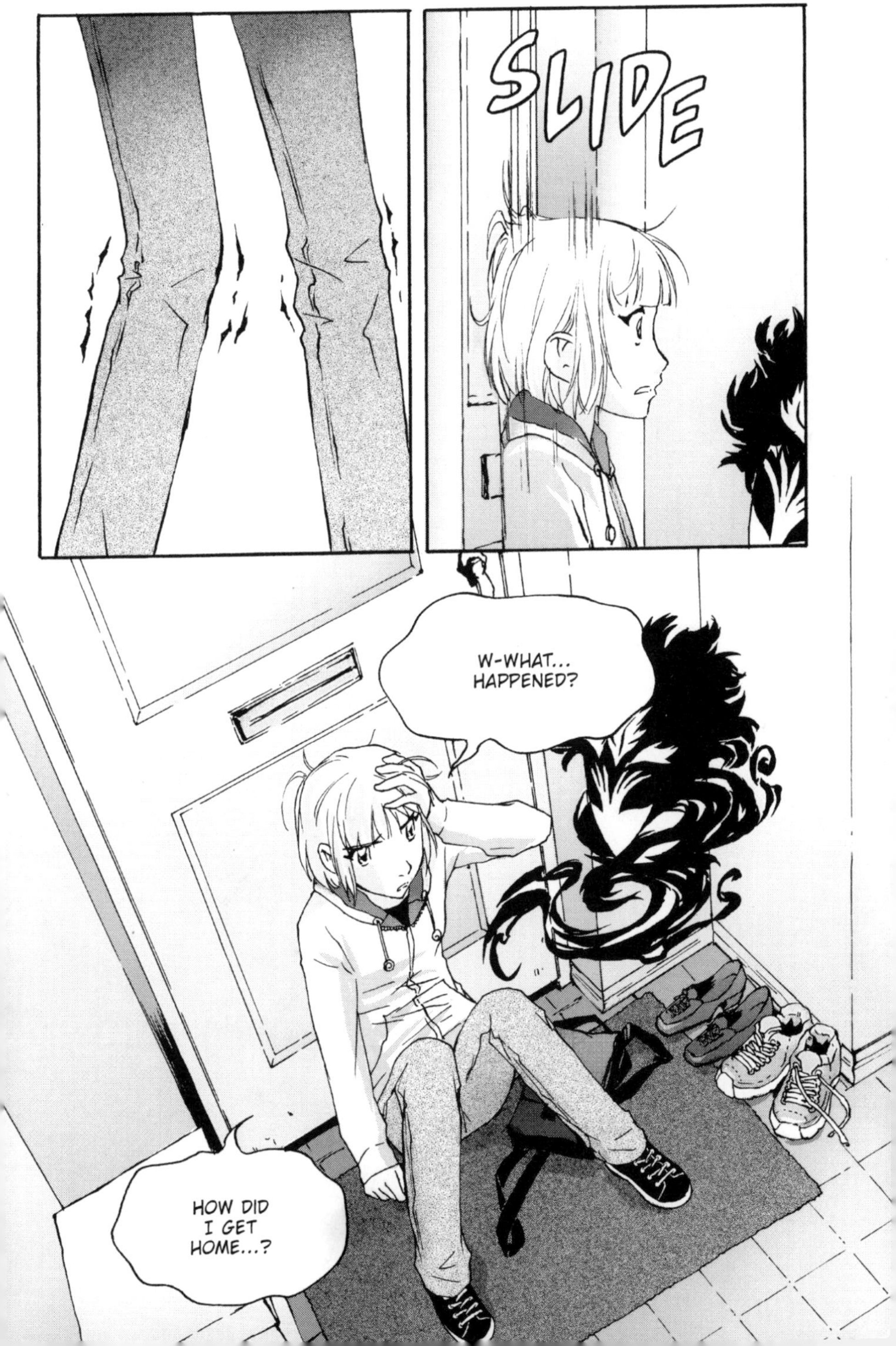
SLIDE
W-WHAT... HAPPENED?
HOW DID I GET HOME...?

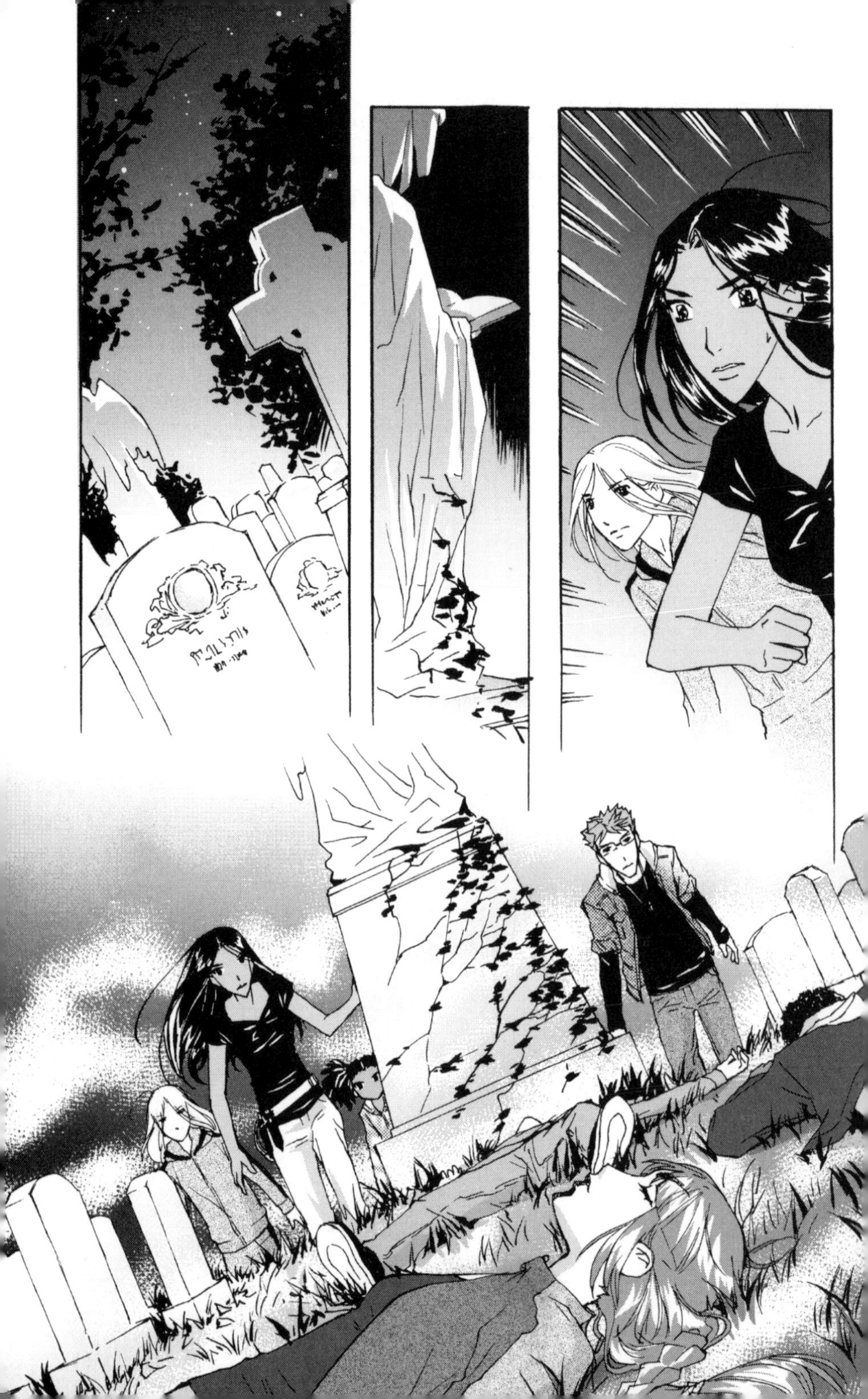

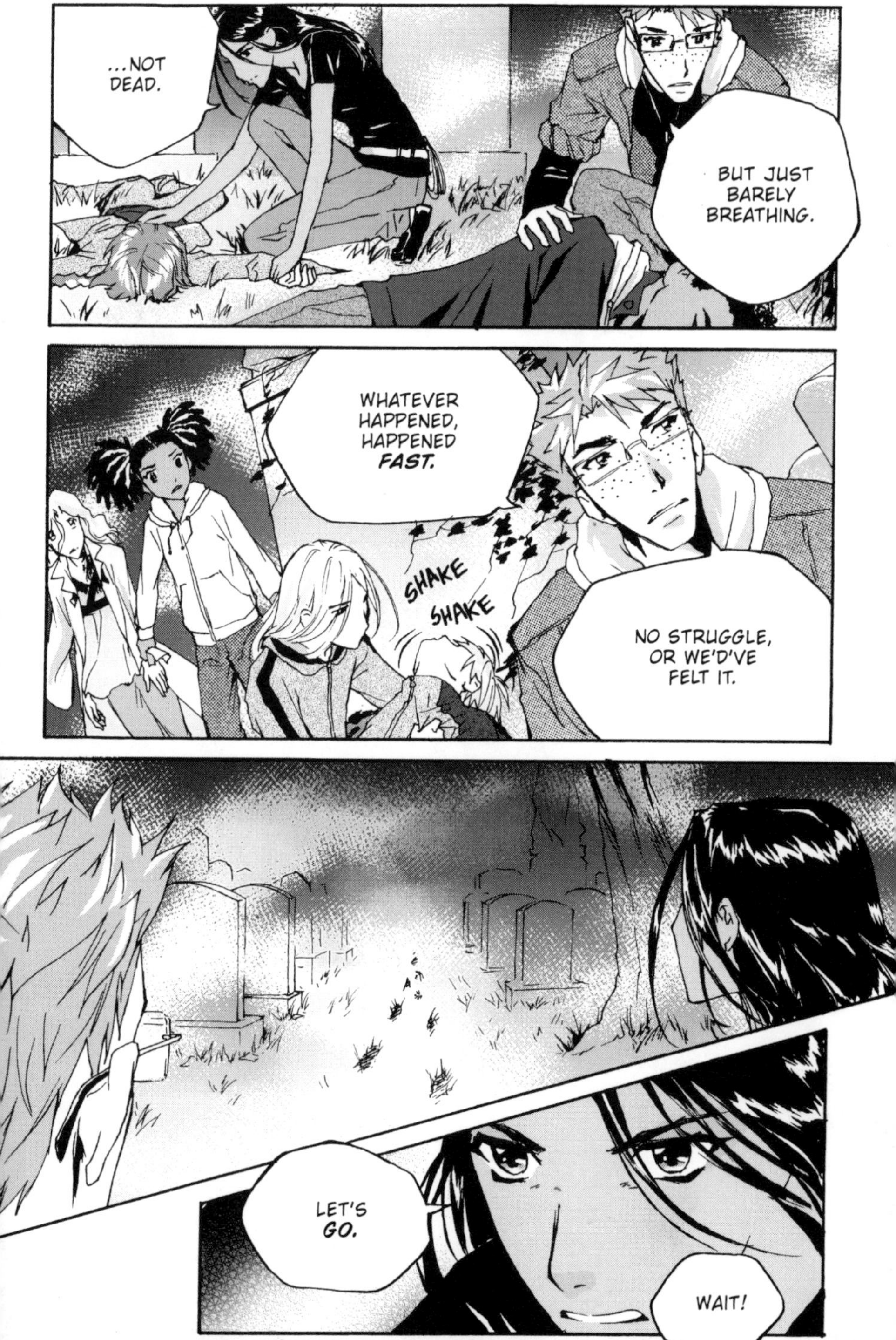
...NOT DEAD.
BUT JUST BARELY BREATHING.
WHATEVER HAPPENED, HAPPENED FAST.
SHAKE
SHAKE
NO STRUGGLE, OR WE'D'VE FELT IT.
LET'S GO.
WAIT!

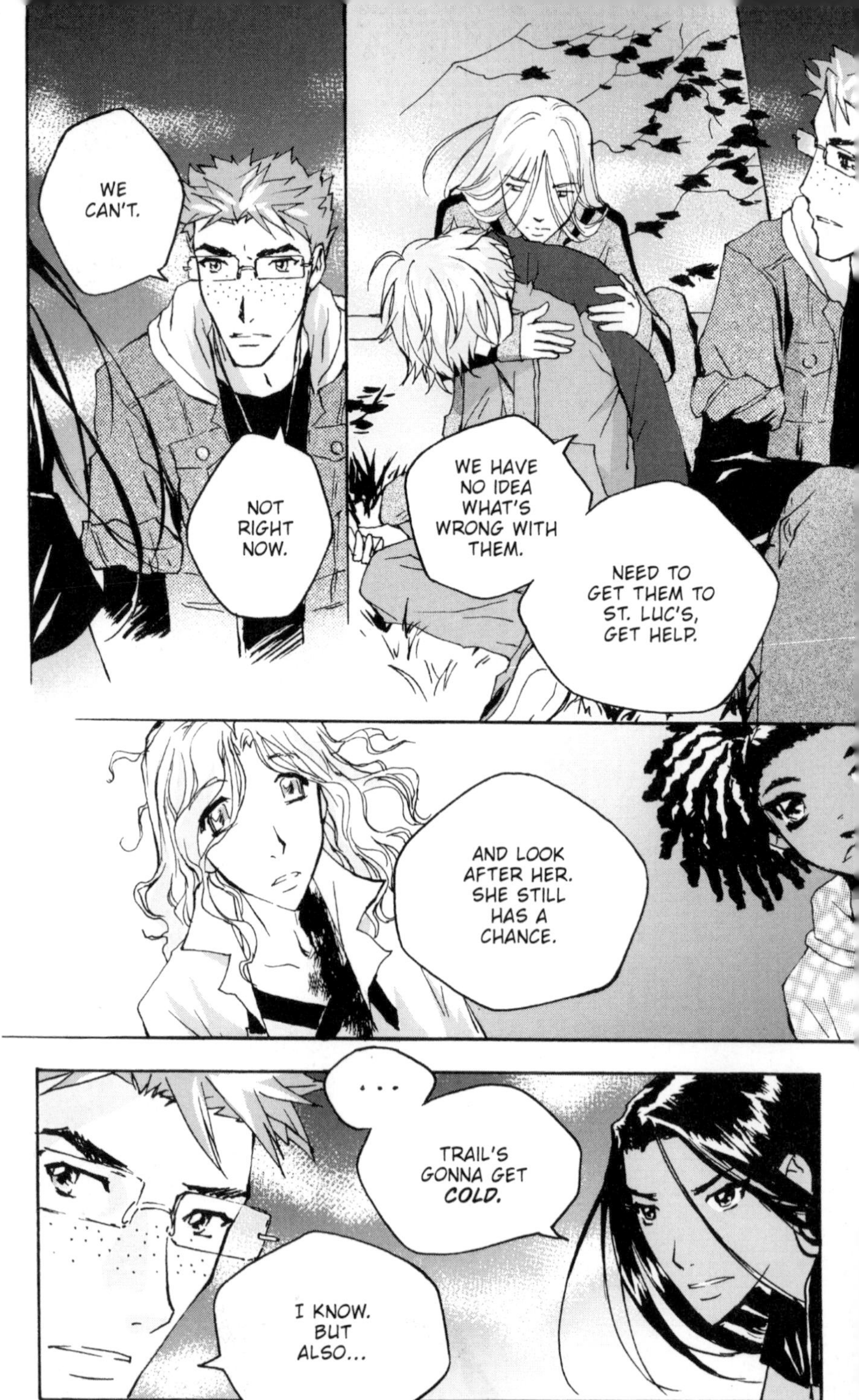
WE CAN'T.
NOT RIGHT NOW.
WE HAVE NO IDEA WHAT'S WRONG WITH THEM.
NEED TO GET THEM TO ST. LUC'S, GET HELP.
AND LOOK AFTER HER. SHE STILL HAS A CHANCE.
...
TRAIL'S GONNA GET *COLD.*
I KNOW. BUT ALSO...

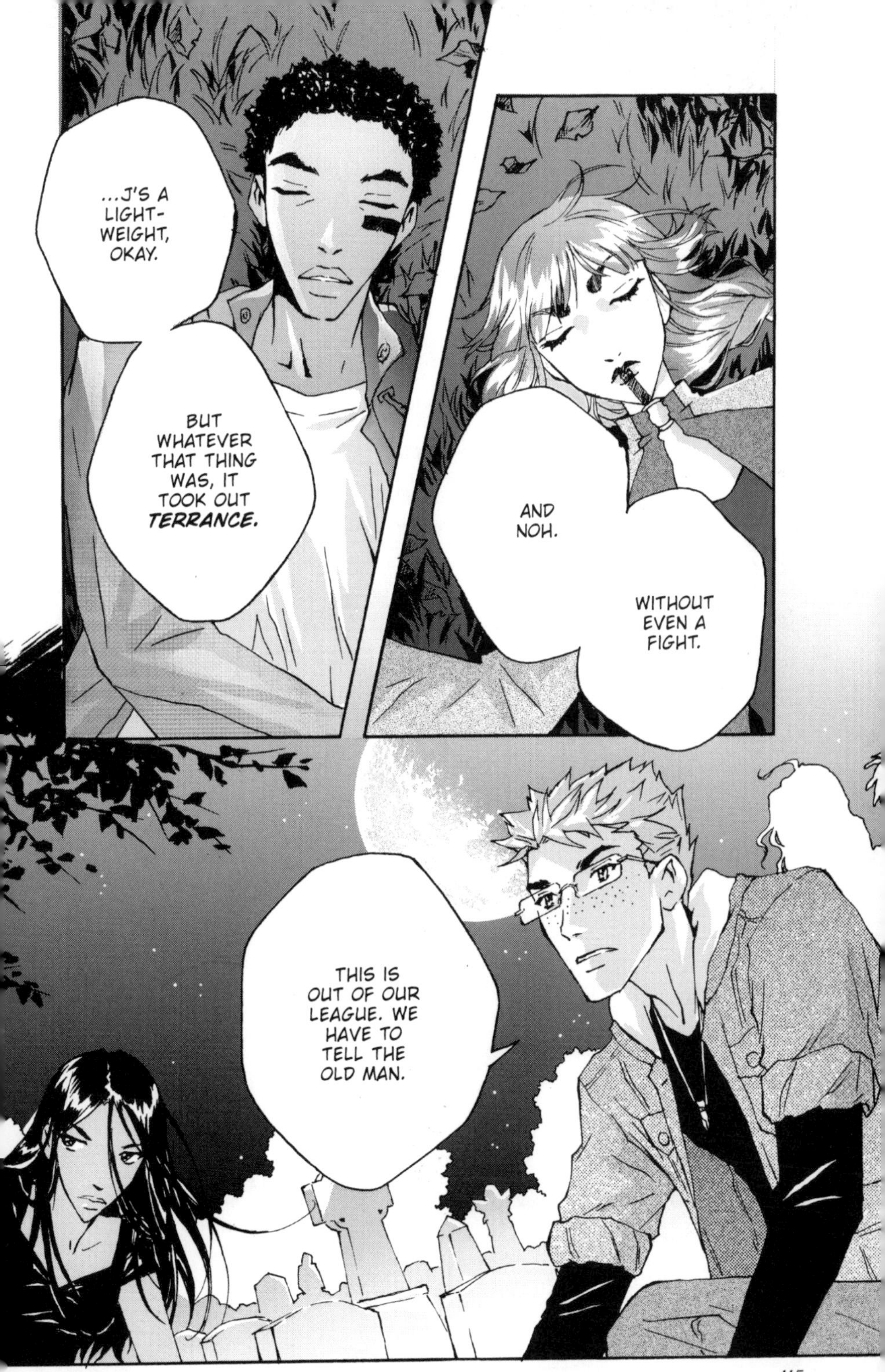
...J'S A LIGHT-WEIGHT, OKAY.
BUT WHATEVER THAT THING WAS, IT TOOK OUT TERRANCE.
AND NOH.
WITHOUT EVEN A FIGHT.
THIS IS OUT OF OUR LEAGUE. WE HAVE TO TELL THE OLD MAN.

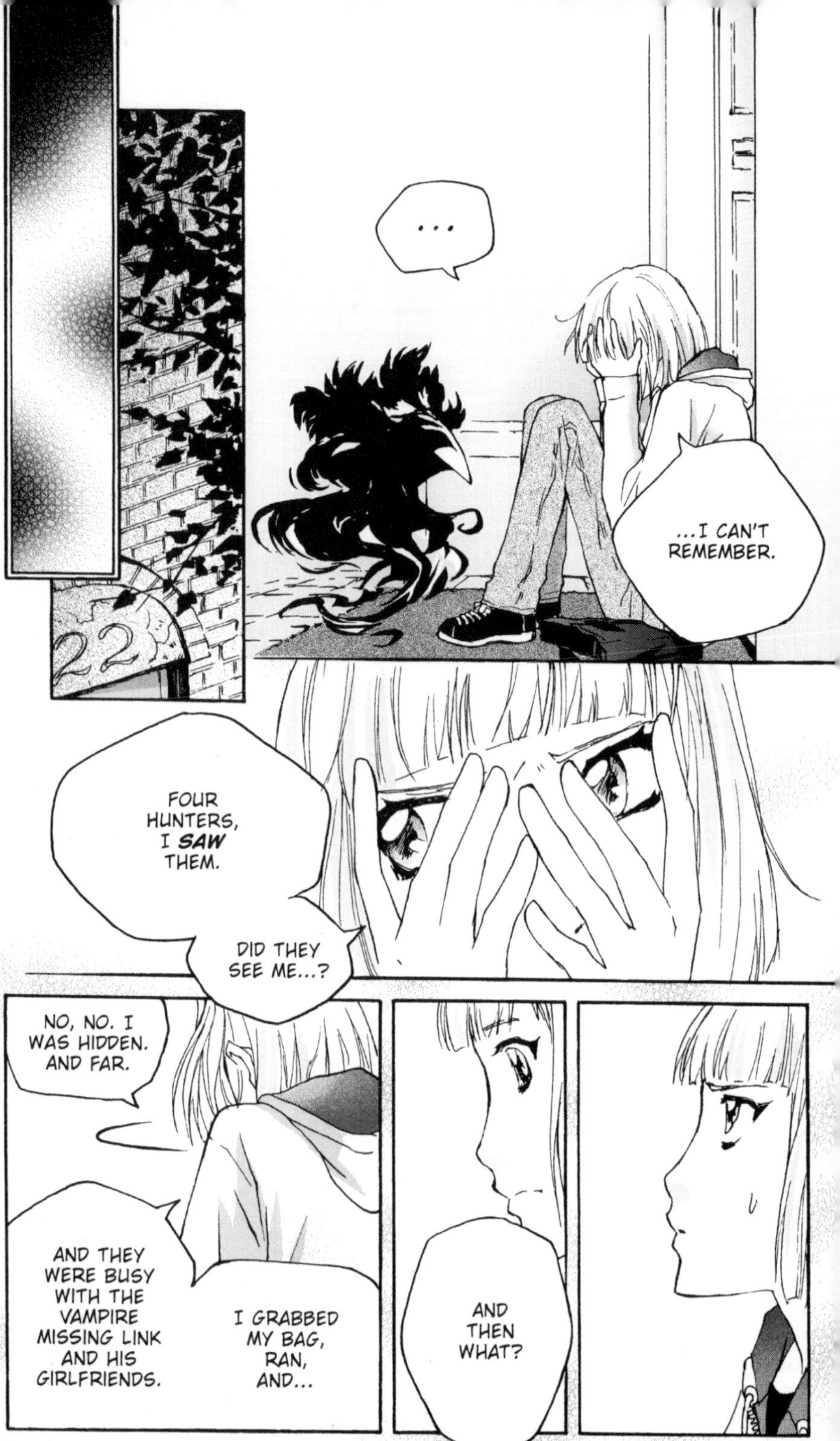
...
...I CAN'T REMEMBER.
FOUR HUNTERS, I SAW THEM.
DID THEY SEE ME...?
NO, NO. I WAS HIDDEN. AND FAR.
AND THEY WERE BUSY WITH THE VAMPIRE MISSING LINK AND HIS GIRLFRIENDS.
I GRABBED MY BAG, RAN, AND...
AND THEN WHAT?

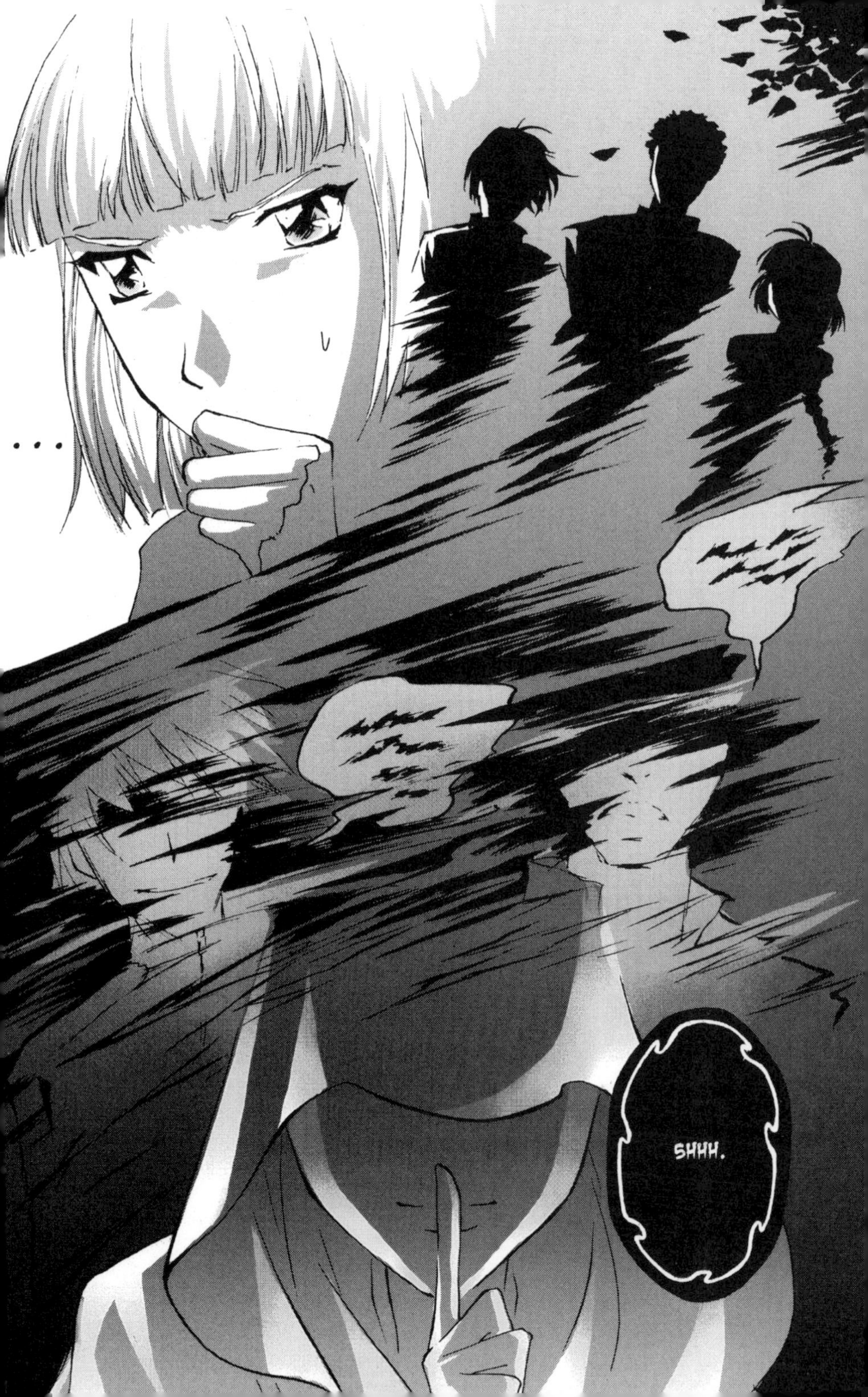
...
SHHH.

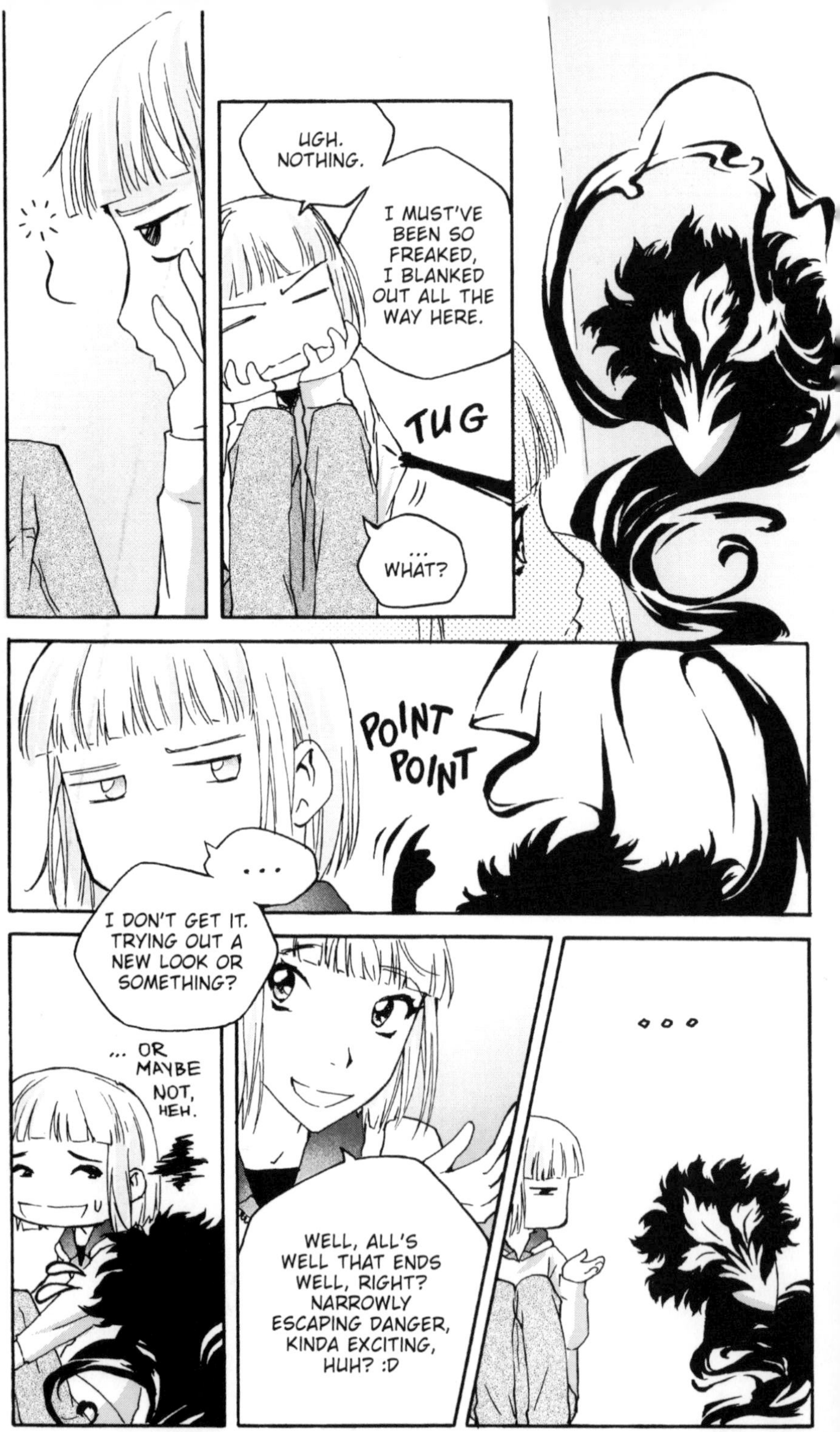
UGH. NOTHING.
I MUST'VE BEEN SO FREAKED, I BLANKED OUT ALL THE WAY HERE.
TUG
... WHAT?
POINT POINT
...
I DON'T GET IT. TRYING OUT A NEW LOOK OR SOMETHING?
... OR MAYBE NOT, HEH.
WELL, ALL'S WELL THAT ENDS WELL, RIGHT? NARROWLY ESCAPING DANGER, KINDA EXCITING, HUH? :D
...

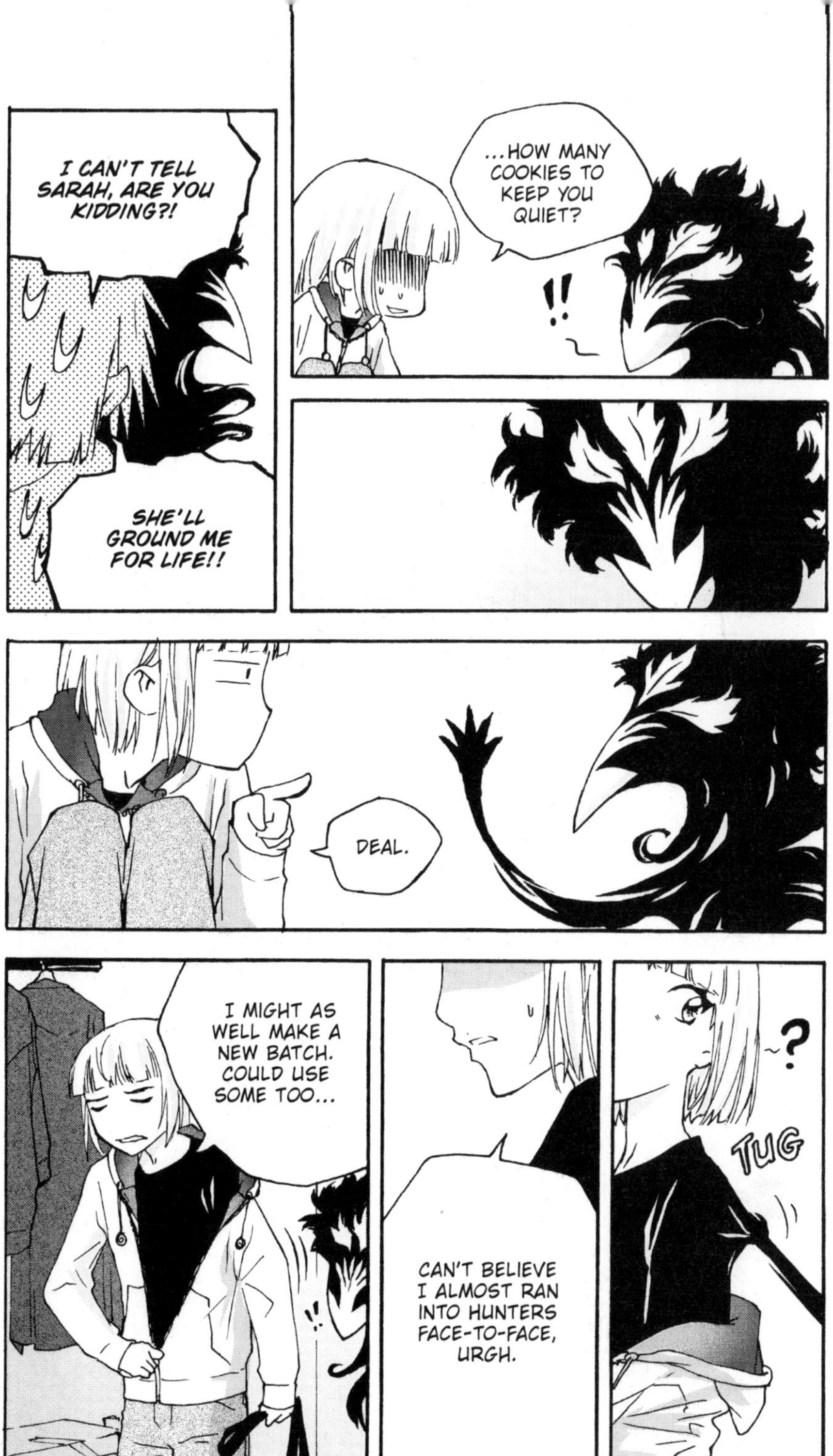

...HOW MANY COOKIES TO KEEP YOU QUIET?
!!
I CAN'T TELL SARAH, ARE YOU KIDDING?!
SHE'LL GROUND ME FOR LIFE!!
DEAL.
?
TUG
CAN'T BELIEVE I ALMOST RAN INTO HUNTERS FACE-TO-FACE, URGH.
I MIGHT AS WELL MAKE A NEW BATCH. COULD USE SOME TOO...
!!

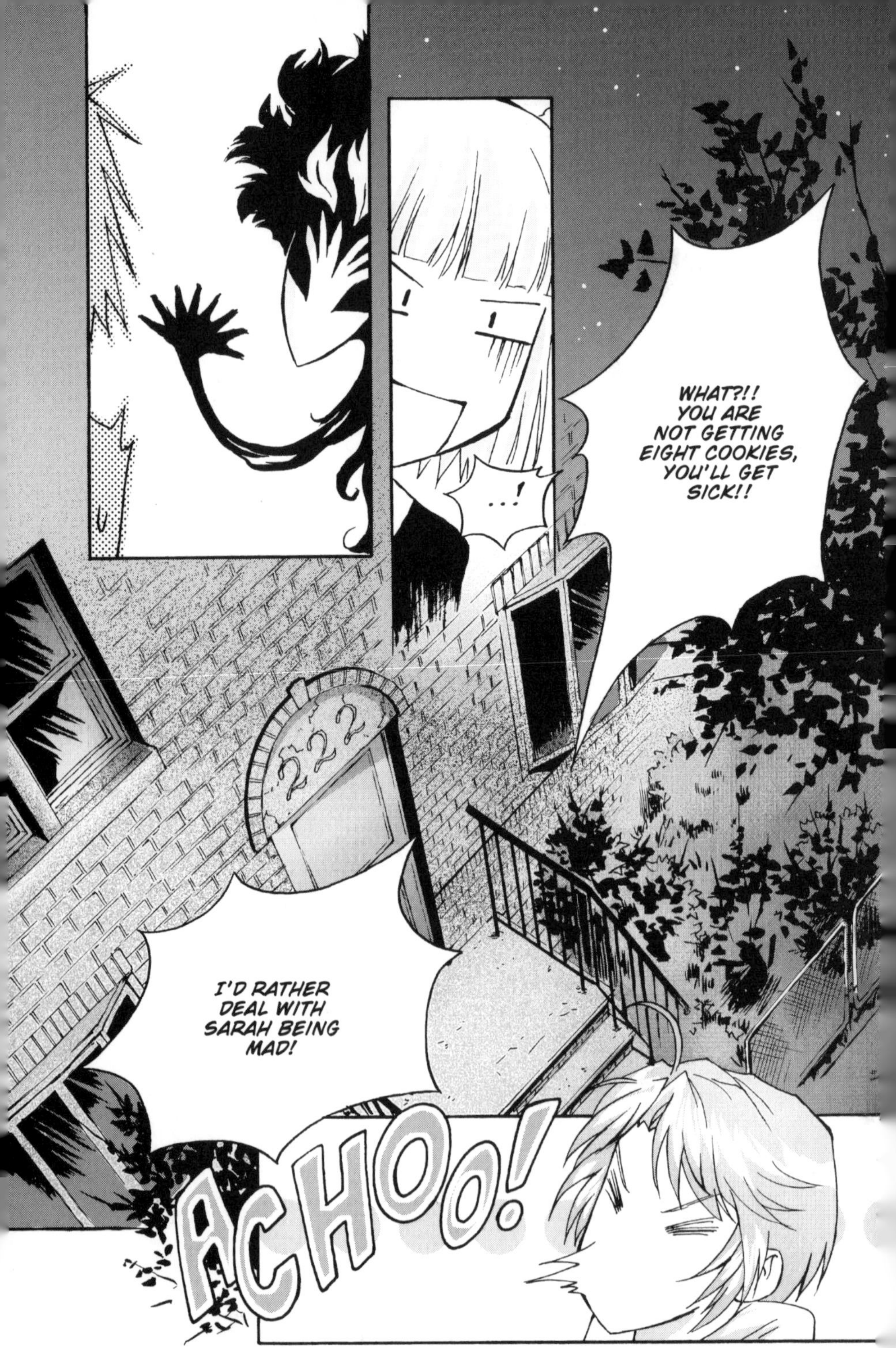
WHAT?!! YOU ARE NOT GETTING EIGHT COOKIES, YOU'LL GET SICK!!
...!
222
I'D RATHER DEAL WITH SARAH BEING MAD!
ACHOO!

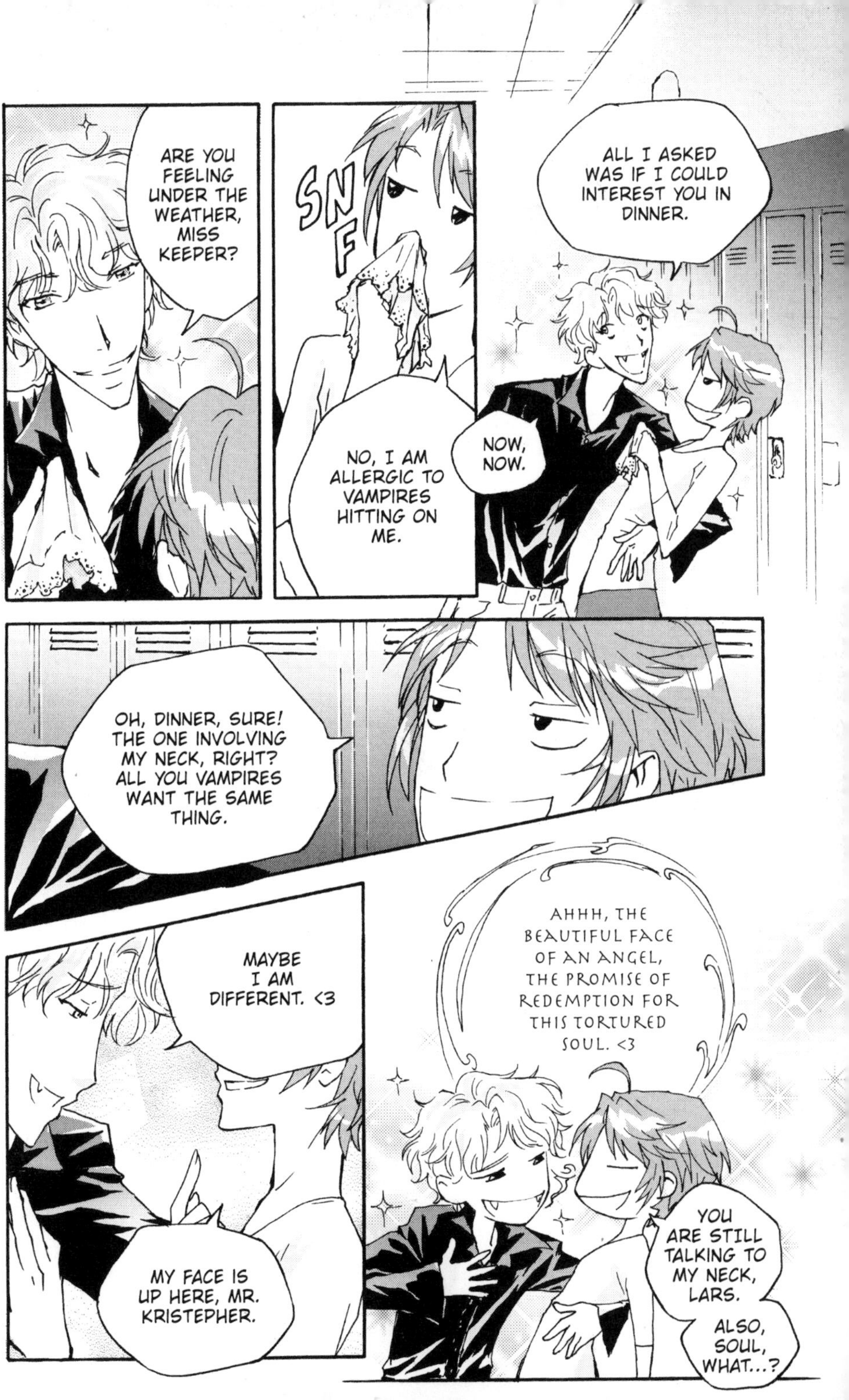
ARE YOU FEELING UNDER THE WEATHER, MISS KEEPER?
SNF
NO, I AM ALLERGIC TO VAMPIRES HITTING ON ME.
ALL I ASKED WAS IF I COULD INTEREST YOU IN DINNER.
NOW, NOW.
OH, DINNER, SURE! THE ONE INVOLVING MY NECK, RIGHT? ALL YOU VAMPIRES WANT THE SAME THING.
MAYBE I AM DIFFERENT. <3
MY FACE IS UP HERE, MR. KRISTEPHER.
AHHH, THE BEAUTIFUL FACE OF AN ANGEL, THE PROMISE OF REDEMPTION FOR THIS TORTURED SOUL. <3
YOU ARE STILL TALKING TO MY NECK, LARS.
ALSO, SOUL, WHAT...?

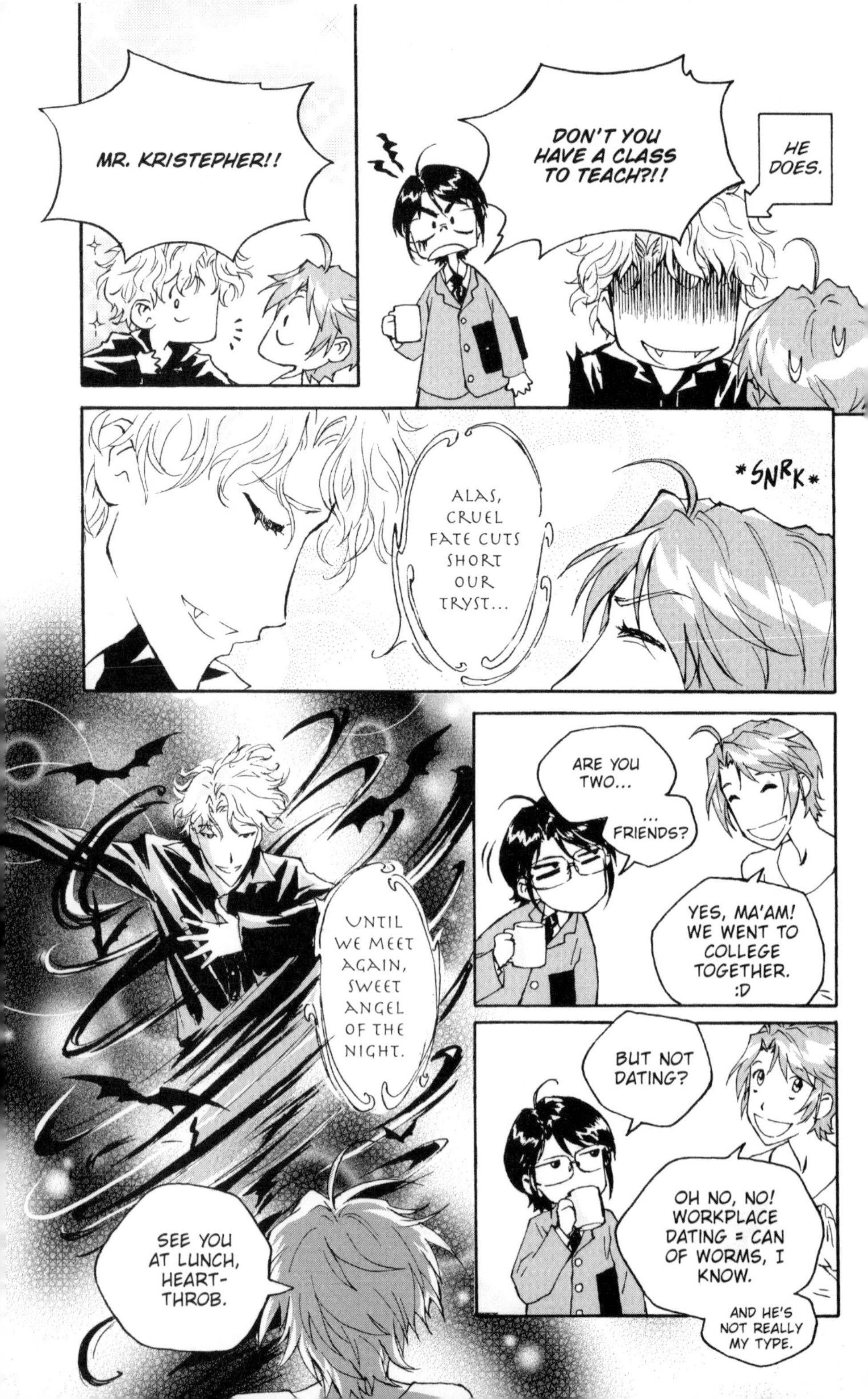
MR. KRISTEPHER!!
DON'T YOU HAVE A CLASS TO TEACH?!!
HE DOES.
ALAS, CRUEL FATE CUTS SHORT OUR TRYST...
SNRK
UNTIL WE MEET AGAIN, SWEET ANGEL OF THE NIGHT.
SEE YOU AT LUNCH, HEART-THROB.
ARE YOU TWO...
... FRIENDS?
YES, MA'AM! WE WENT TO COLLEGE TOGETHER. :D
BUT NOT DATING?
OH NO, NO! WORKPLACE DATING = CAN OF WORMS, I KNOW.
AND HE'S NOT REALLY MY TYPE.

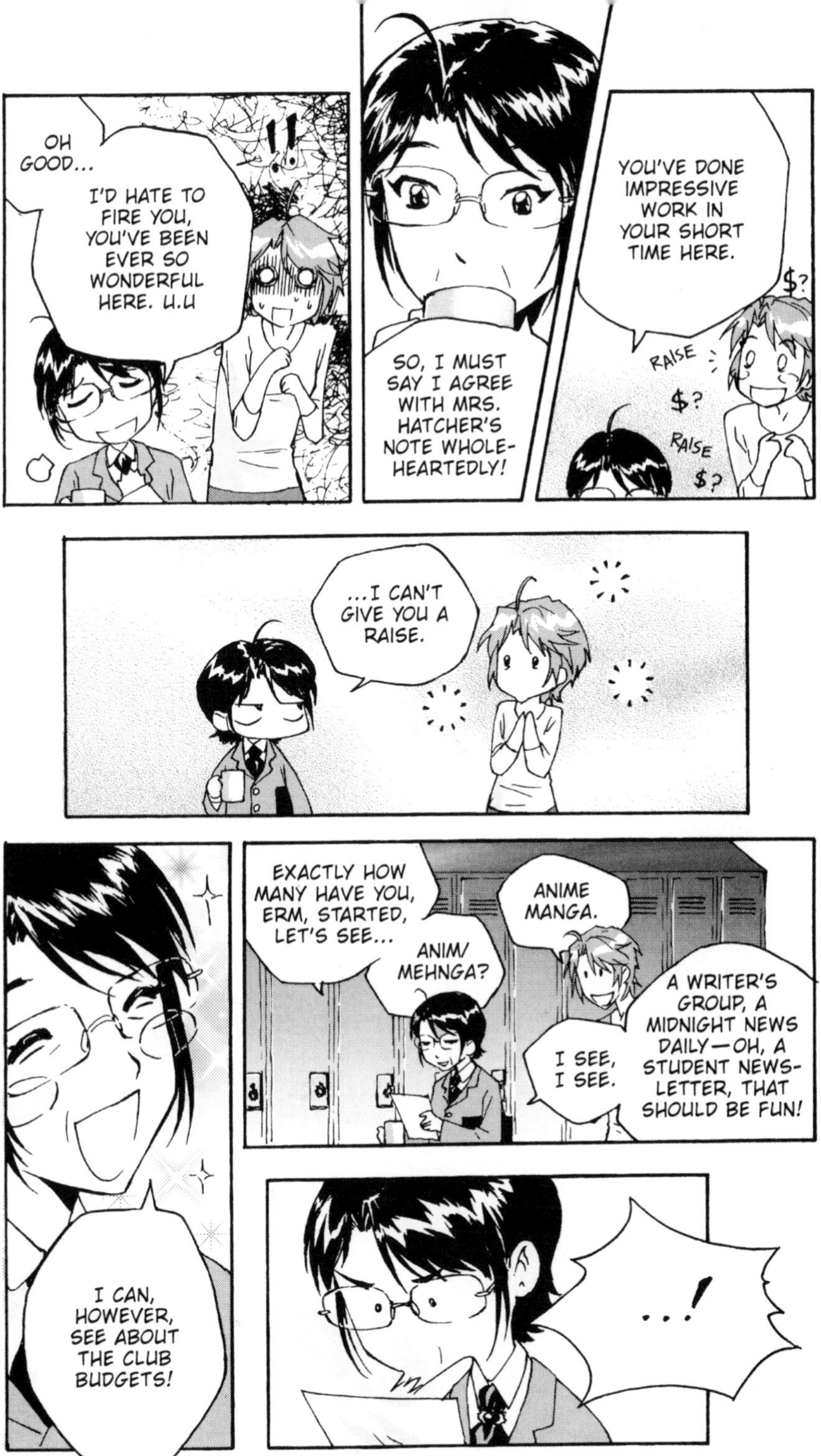
OH GOOD...
I'D HATE TO FIRE YOU, YOU'VE BEEN EVER SO WONDERFUL HERE. u.u
!!
SO, I MUST SAY I AGREE WITH MRS. HATCHER'S NOTE WHOLE-HEARTEDLY!
YOU'VE DONE IMPRESSIVE WORK IN YOUR SHORT TIME HERE.
$?
RAISE
$?
RAISE
$?
...I CAN'T GIVE YOU A RAISE.
I CAN, HOWEVER, SEE ABOUT THE CLUB BUDGETS!
EXACTLY HOW MANY HAVE YOU, ERM, STARTED, LET'S SEE...
ANIME MANGA.
ANIM/MEHNGA?
A WRITER'S GROUP, A MIDNIGHT NEWS DAILY—OH, A STUDENT NEWS-LETTER, THAT SHOULD BE FUN!
I SEE, I SEE.
...!

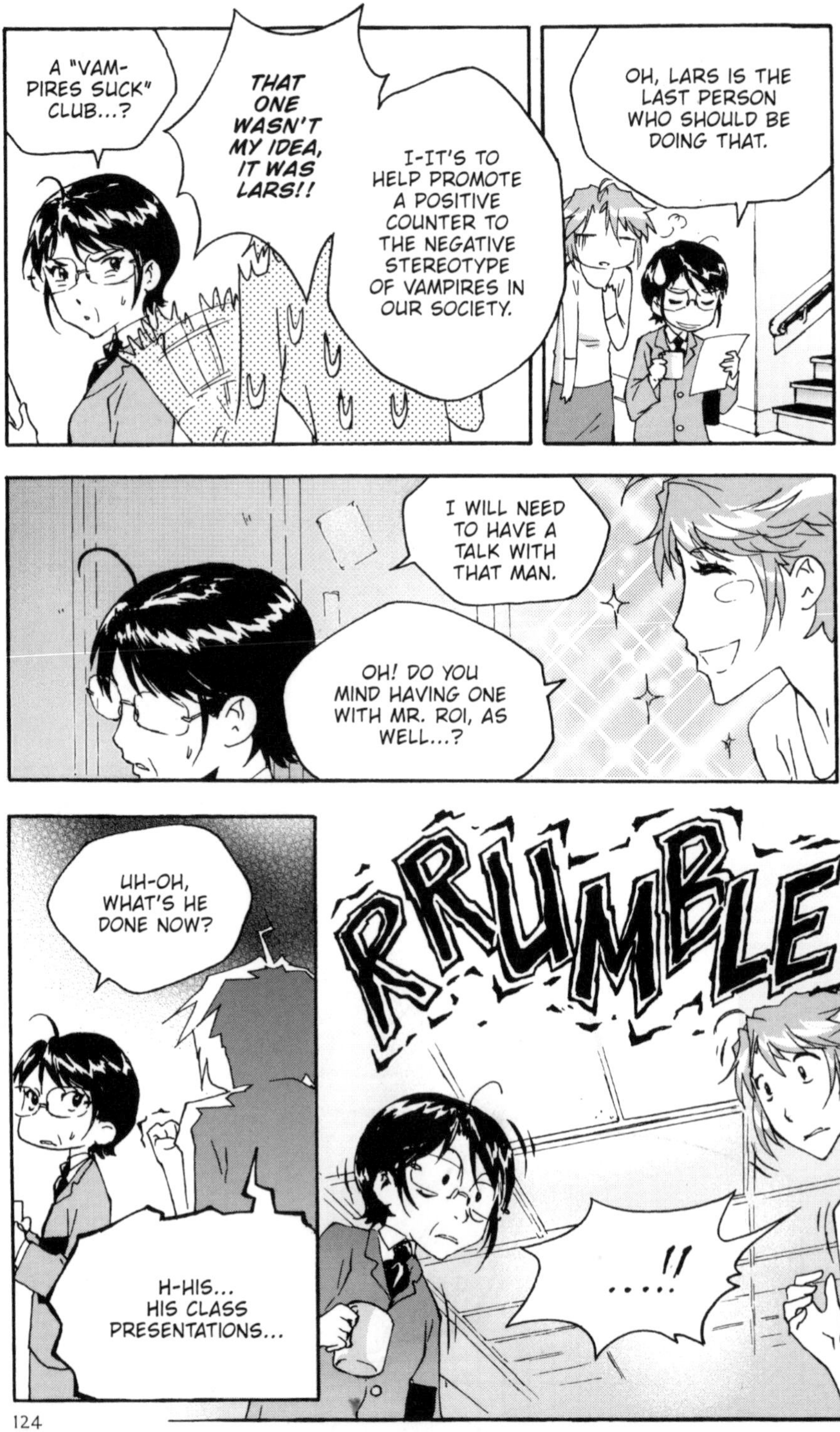

A "VAMPIRES SUCK" CLUB...?
THAT ONE WASN'T MY IDEA, IT WAS LARS!!
I-IT'S TO HELP PROMOTE A POSITIVE COUNTER TO THE NEGATIVE STEREOTYPE OF VAMPIRES IN OUR SOCIETY.
OH, LARS IS THE LAST PERSON WHO SHOULD BE DOING THAT.
I WILL NEED TO HAVE A TALK WITH THAT MAN.
OH! DO YOU MIND HAVING ONE WITH MR. ROI, AS WELL...?
UH-OH, WHAT'S HE DONE NOW?
RRUMBLE
H-HIS... HIS CLASS PRESENTATIONS...
....!!

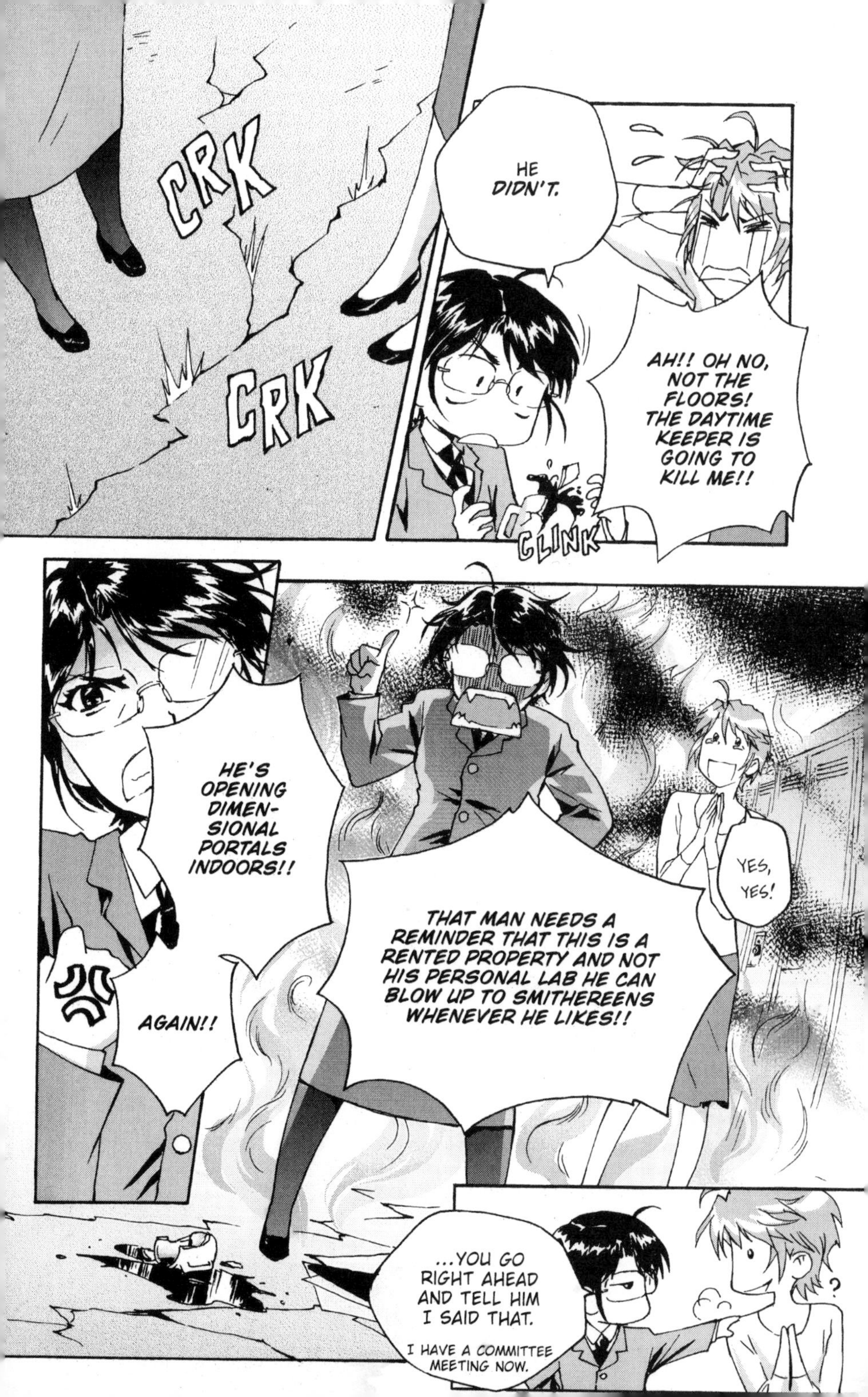
CRK
CRK
HE DIDN'T.
AH!! OH NO, NOT THE FLOORS! THE DAYTIME KEEPER IS GOING TO KILL ME!!
CLINK
HE'S OPENING DIMENSIONAL PORTALS INDOORS!!
AGAIN!!
THAT MAN NEEDS A REMINDER THAT THIS IS A RENTED PROPERTY AND NOT HIS PERSONAL LAB HE CAN BLOW UP TO SMITHEREENS WHENEVER HE LIKES!!
YES, YES!
...YOU GO RIGHT AHEAD AND TELL HIM I SAID THAT.
I HAVE A COMMITTEE MEETING NOW.
?

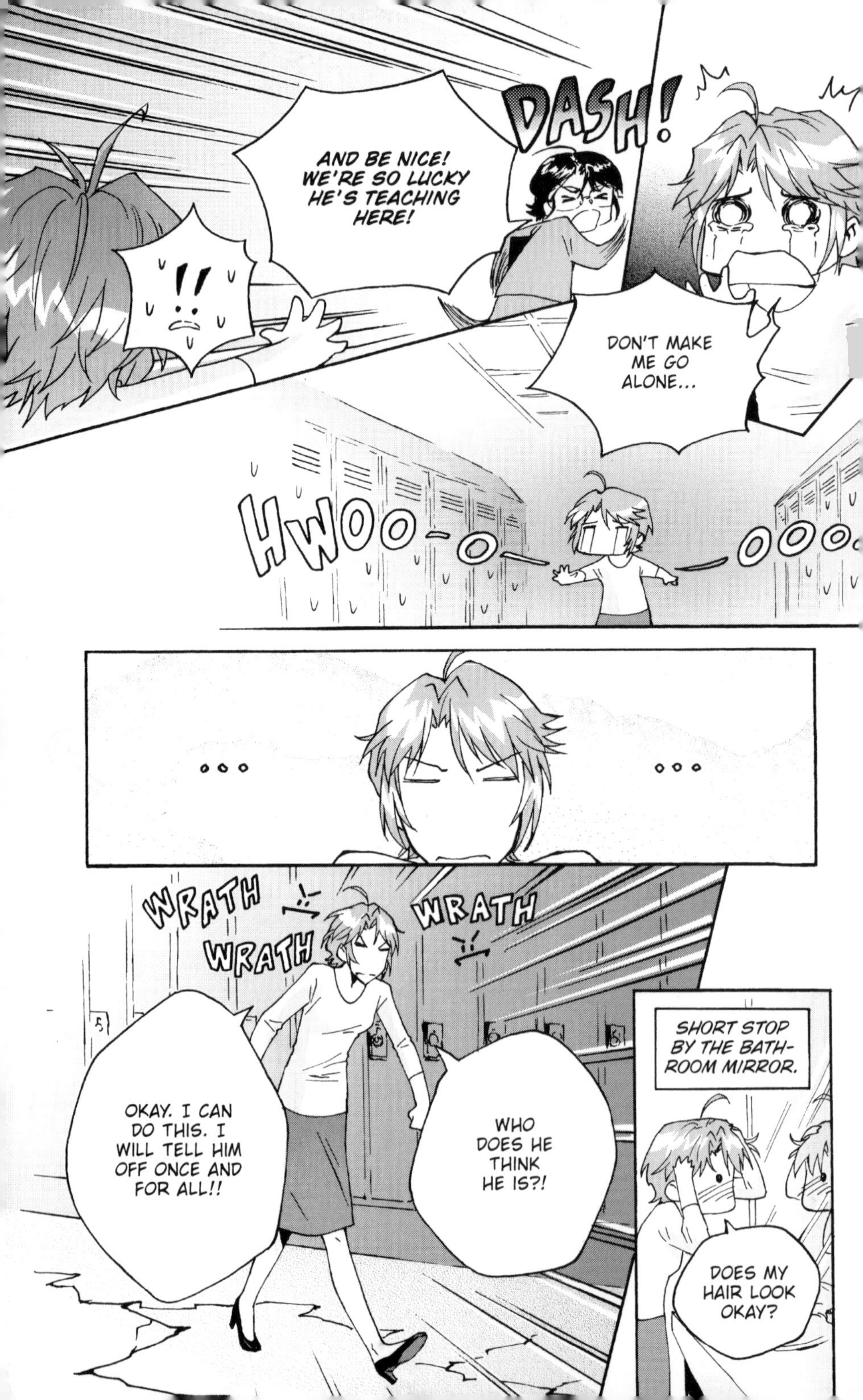
DASH!
AND BE NICE! WE'RE SO LUCKY HE'S TEACHING HERE!
!!
DON'T MAKE ME GO ALONE...
HWOO-O-OOO
...
...
WRATH
WRATH
WRATH
OKAY. I CAN DO THIS. I WILL TELL HIM OFF ONCE AND FOR ALL!!
WHO DOES HE THINK HE IS?!
SHORT STOP BY THE BATH-ROOM MIRROR.
DOES MY HAIR LOOK OKAY?

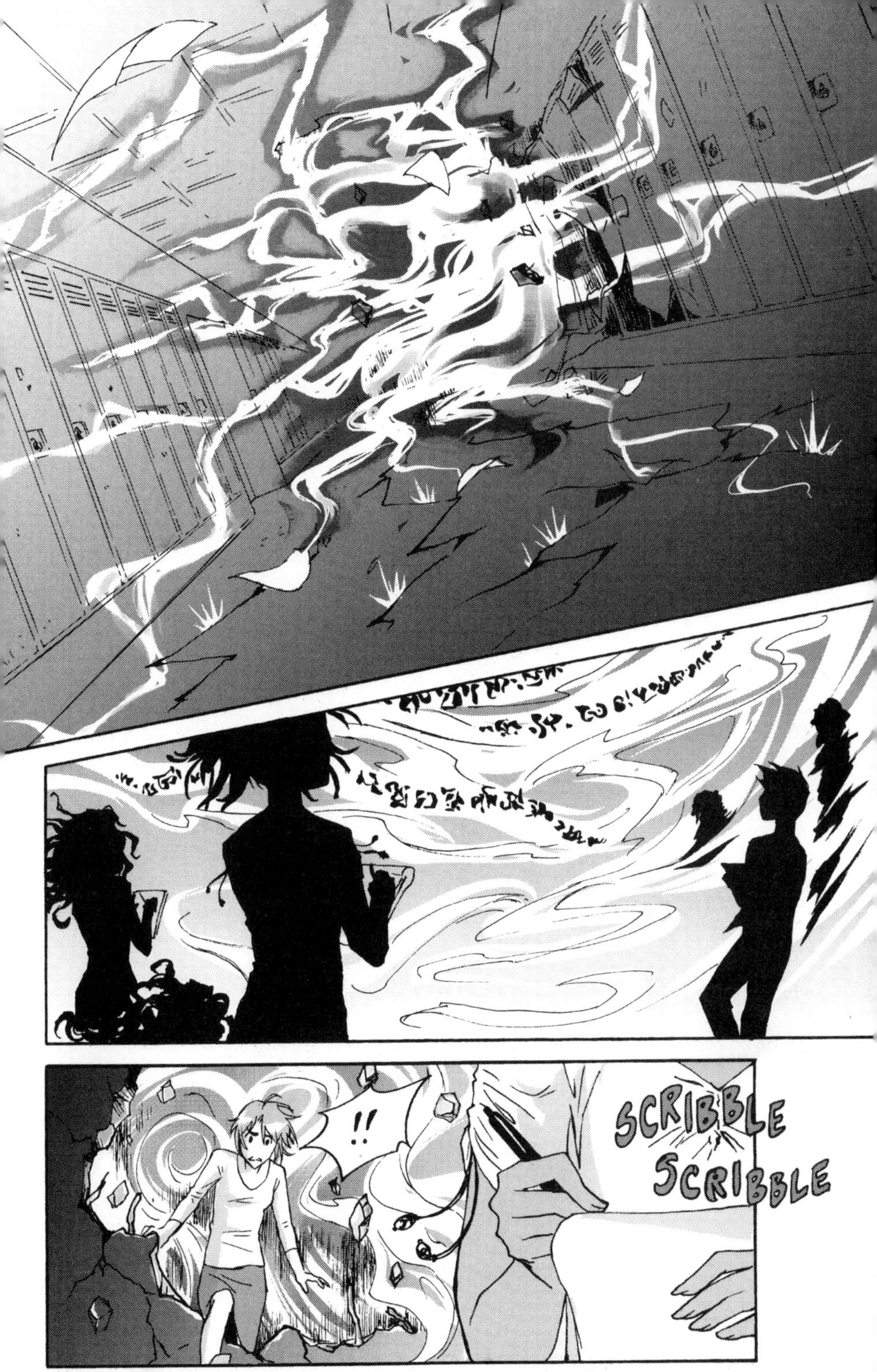
!!
SCRIBBLE
SCRIBBLE

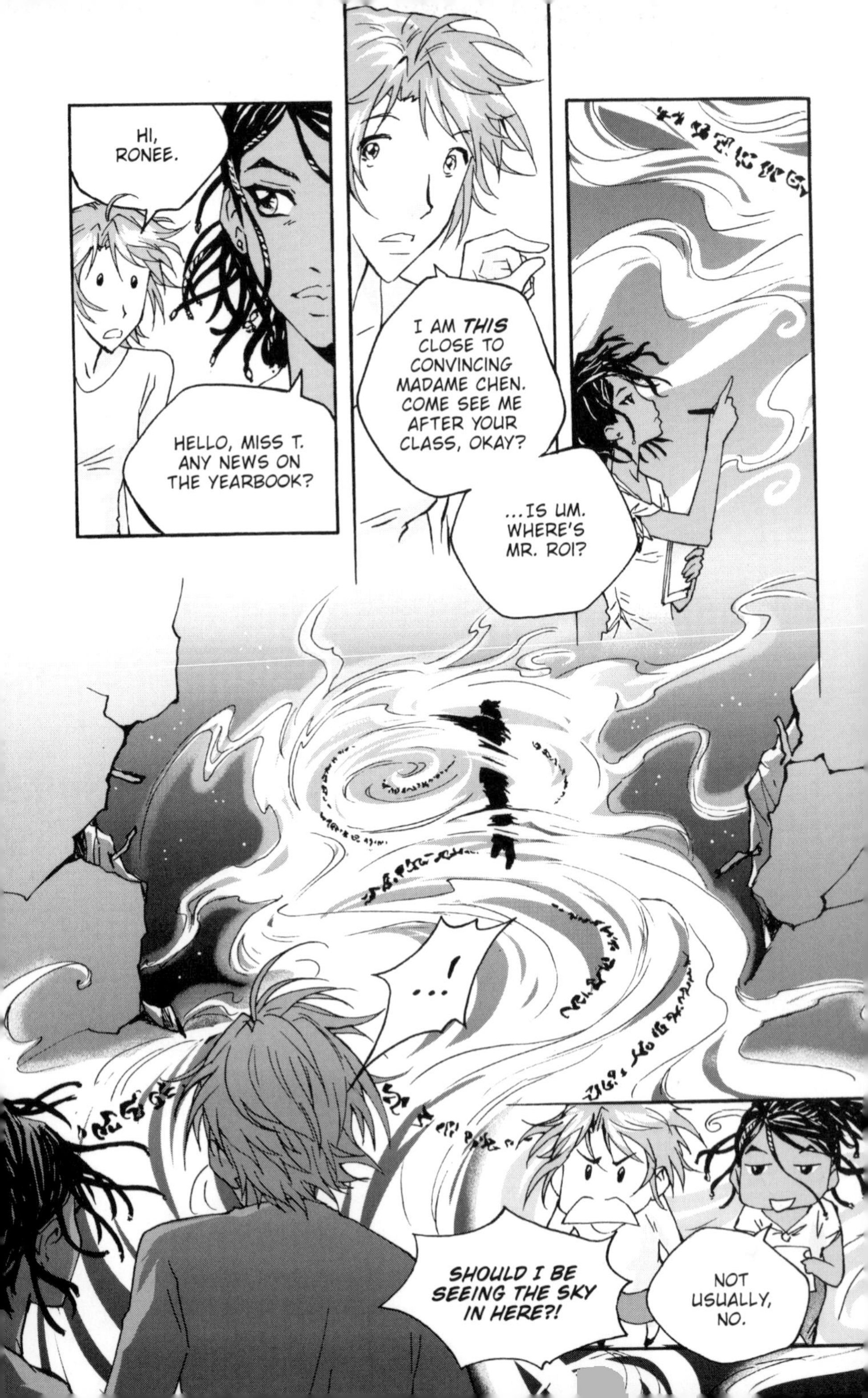
HI, RONEE.
HELLO, MISS T. ANY NEWS ON THE YEARBOOK?
I AM *THIS* CLOSE TO CONVINCING MADAME CHEN. COME SEE ME AFTER YOUR CLASS, OKAY?
...IS UM. WHERE'S MR. ROI?
...!
SHOULD I BE SEEING THE SKY IN HERE?!
NOT USUALLY, NO.

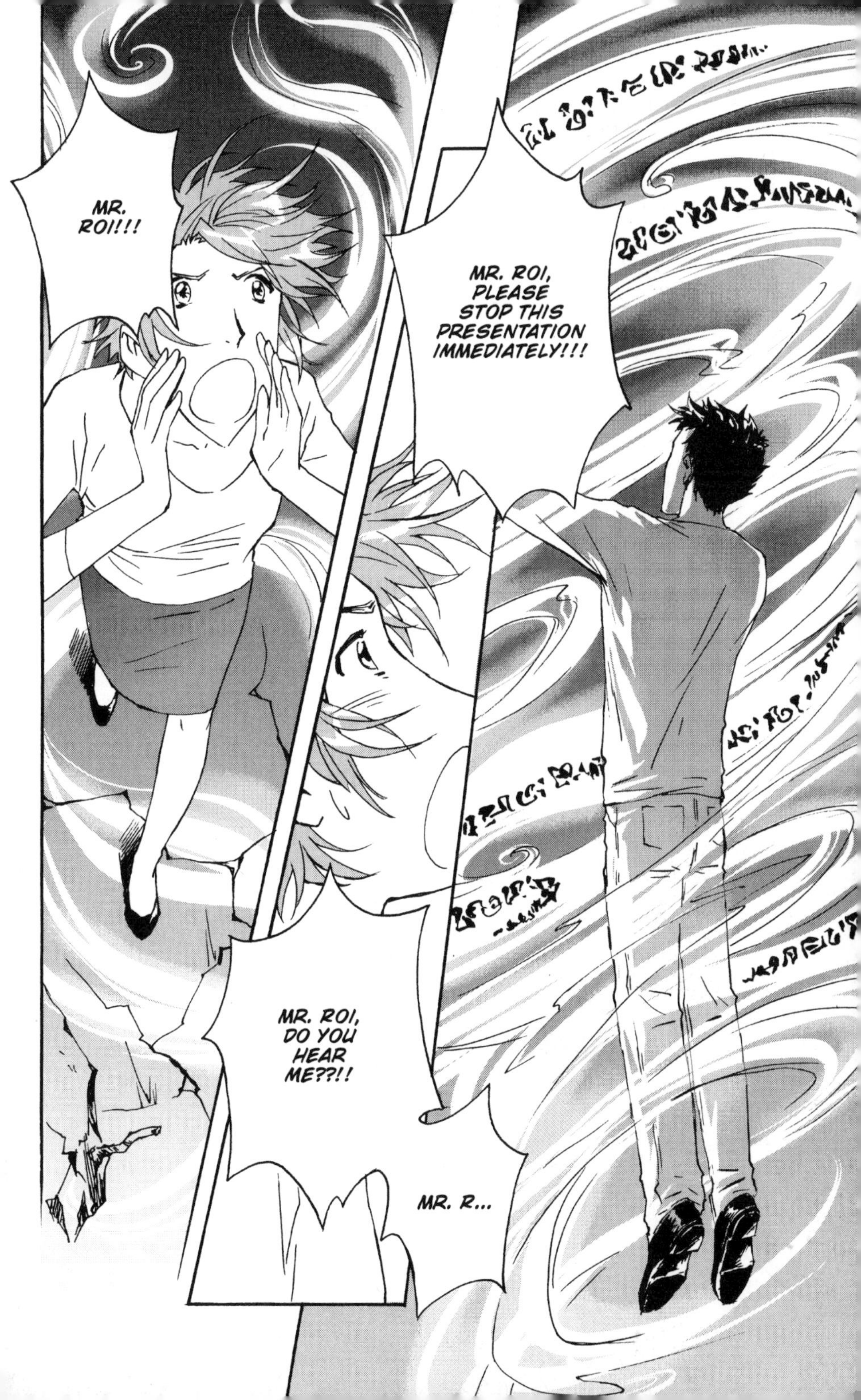
MR. ROI, PLEASE STOP THIS PRESENTATION IMMEDIATELY!!!
MR. ROI!!!
MR. ROI, DO YOU HEAR ME??!!
MR. R...

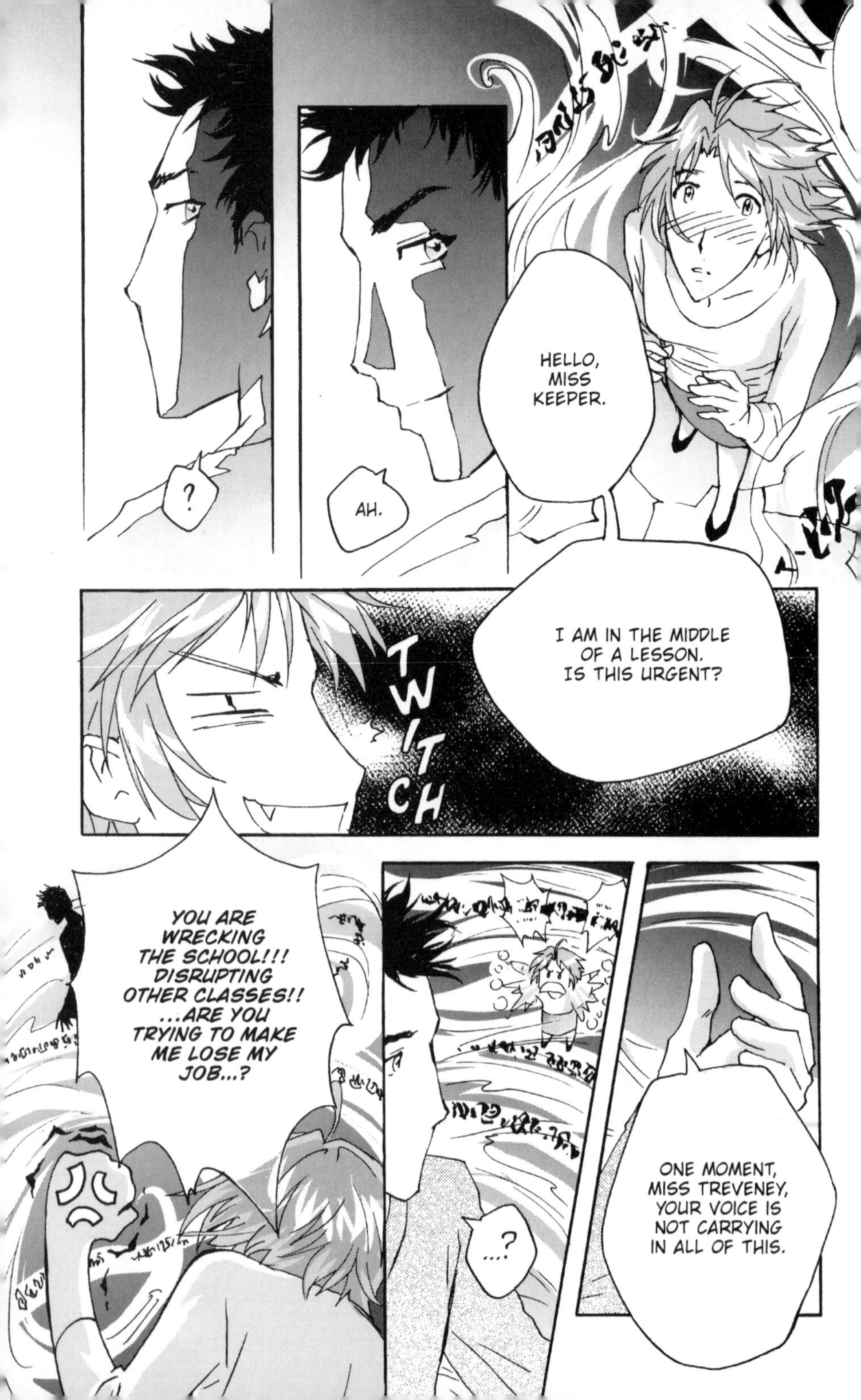
?
AH.
HELLO, MISS KEEPER.
I AM IN THE MIDDLE OF A LESSON. IS THIS URGENT?
TWITCH
YOU ARE WRECKING THE SCHOOL!!! DISRUPTING OTHER CLASSES!! ...ARE YOU TRYING TO MAKE ME LOSE MY JOB...?
ONE MOMENT, MISS TREVENEY, YOUR VOICE IS NOT CARRYING IN ALL OF THIS.
....?

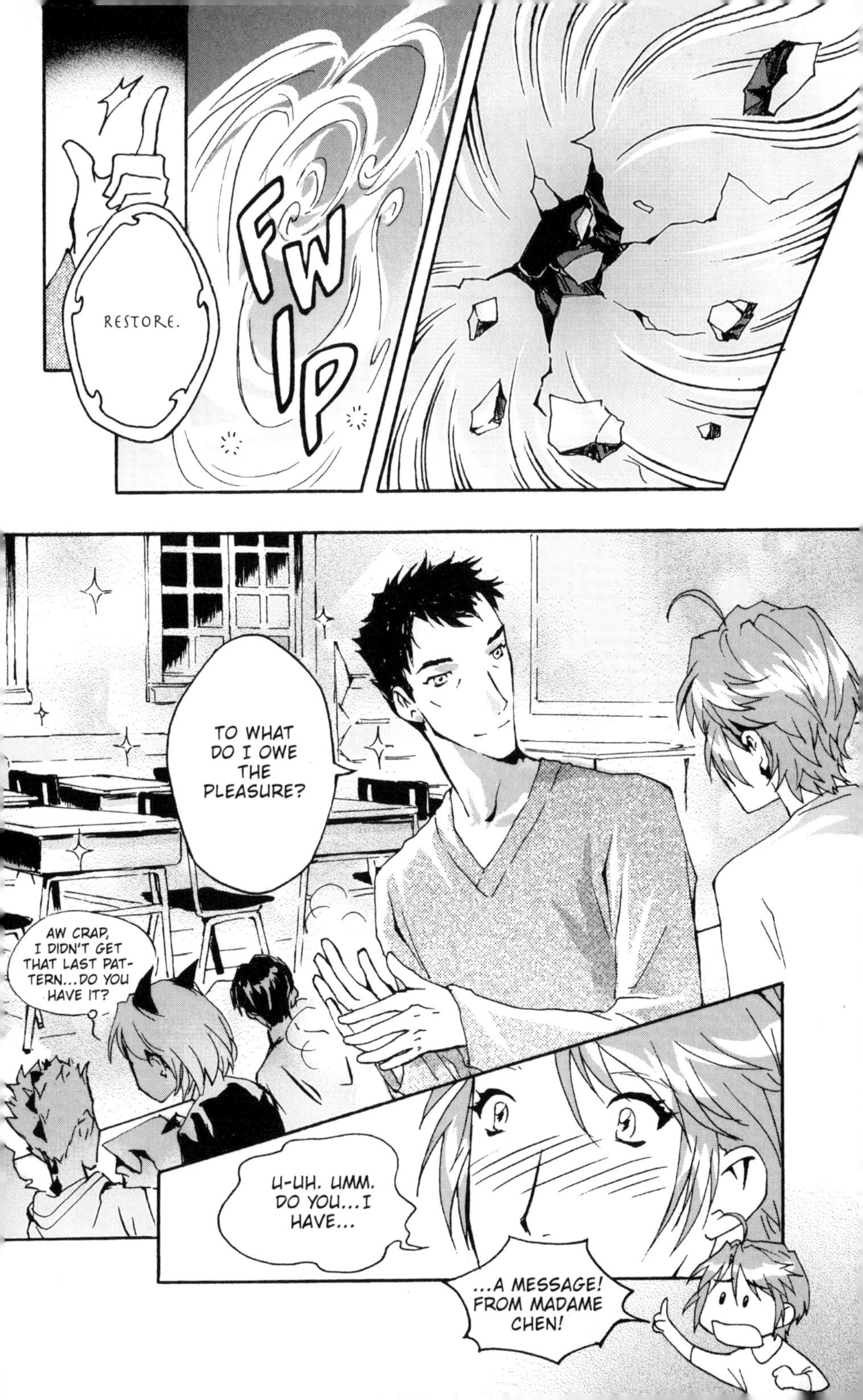
RESTORE.
FWIP
TO WHAT DO I OWE THE PLEASURE?
AW CRAP, I DIDN'T GET THAT LAST PATTERN...DO YOU HAVE IT?
U-UH. UMM. DO YOU...I HAVE...
...A MESSAGE! FROM MADAME CHEN!

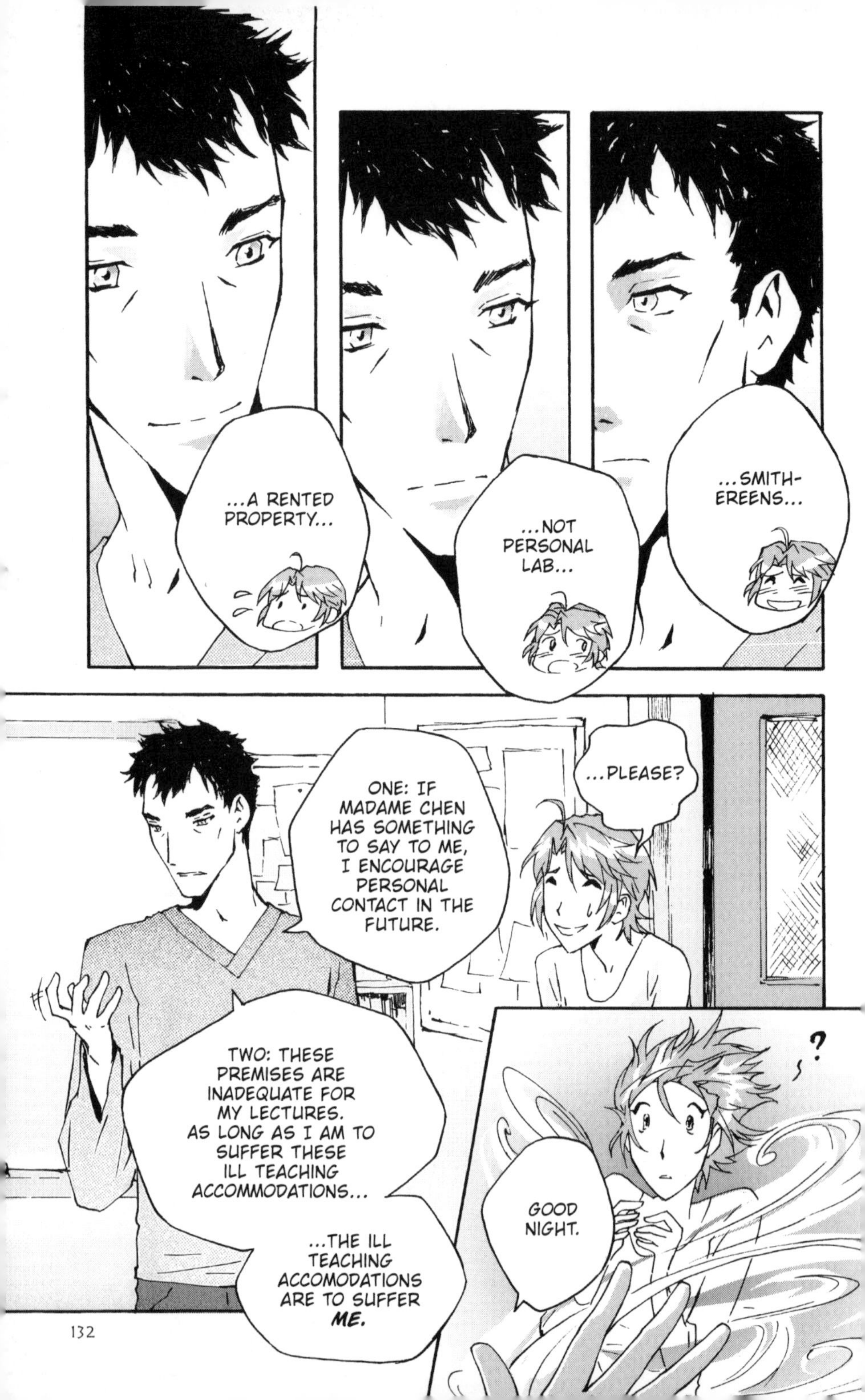

...A RENTED PROPERTY...
...NOT PERSONAL LAB...
...SMITH-EREENS...
ONE: IF MADAME CHEN HAS SOMETHING TO SAY TO ME, I ENCOURAGE PERSONAL CONTACT IN THE FUTURE.
...PLEASE?
TWO: THESE PREMISES ARE INADEQUATE FOR MY LECTURES. AS LONG AS I AM TO SUFFER THESE ILL TEACHING ACCOMMODATIONS...
...THE ILL TEACHING ACCOMODATIONS ARE TO SUFFER *ME.*
?
GOOD NIGHT.

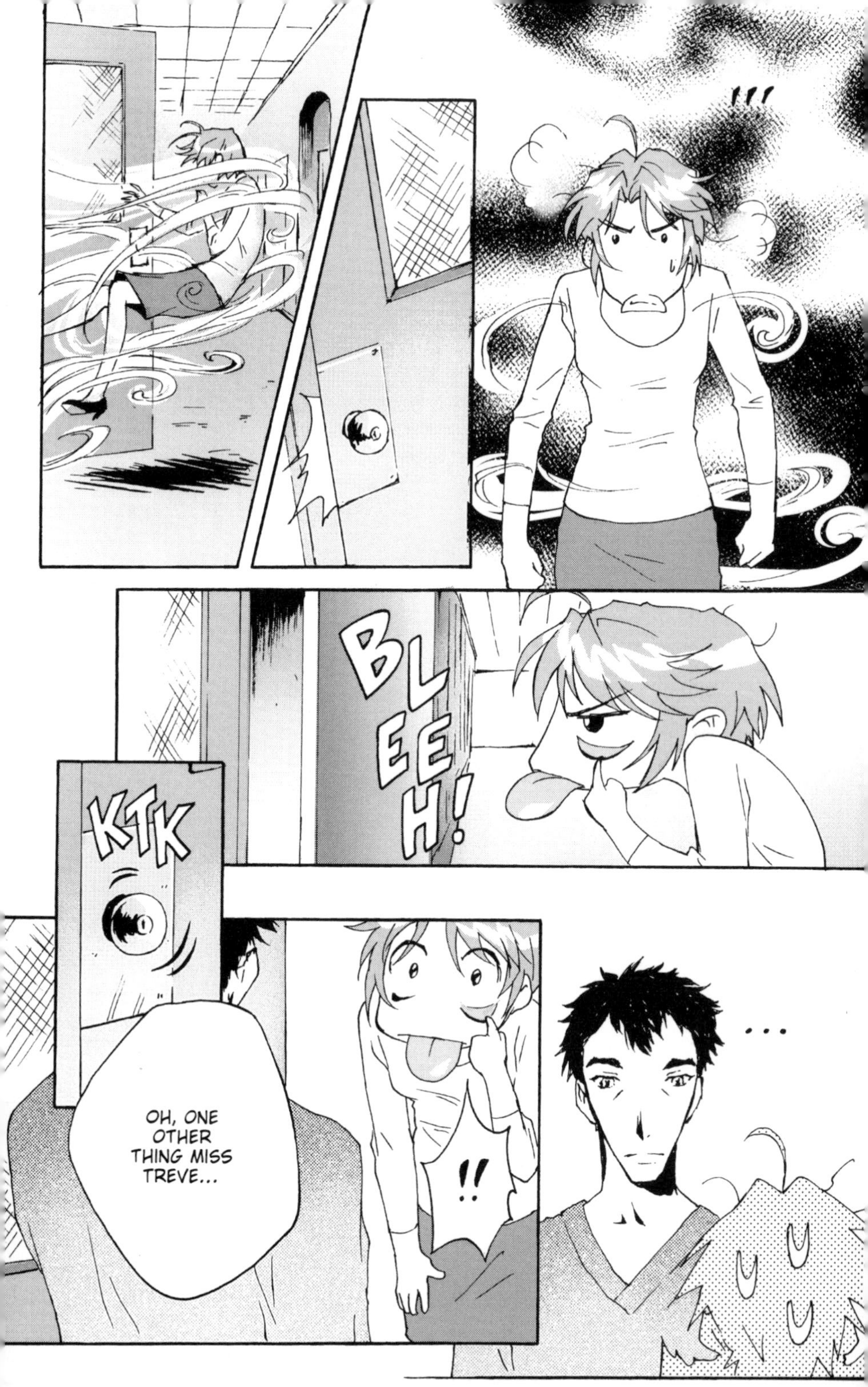
!!!
BLEEH!
KTK
OH, ONE OTHER THING MISS TREVE...
!!
...

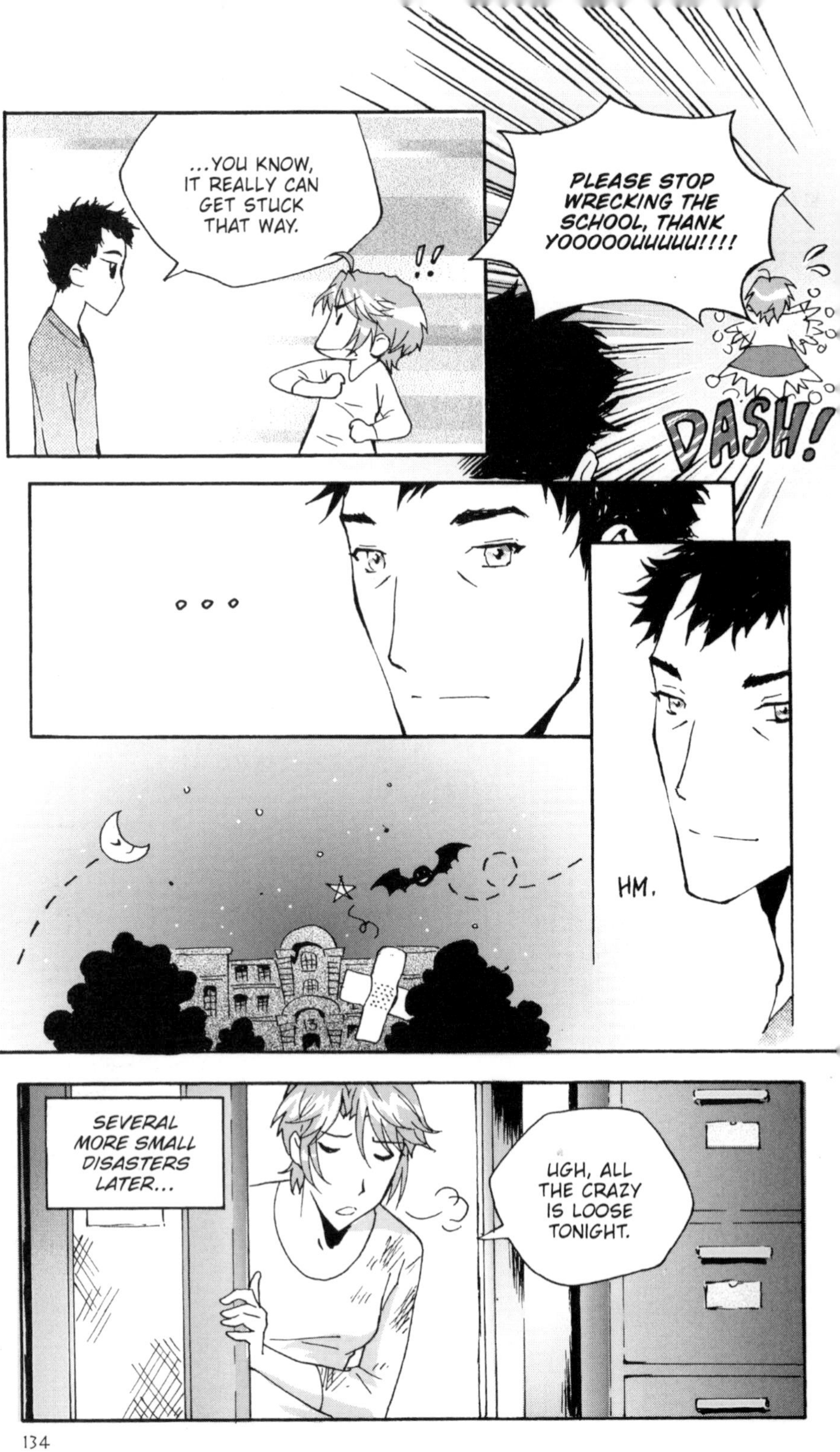
...YOU KNOW, IT REALLY CAN GET STUCK THAT WAY.
!!
PLEASE STOP WRECKING THE SCHOOL, THANK YOOOOOUUUUU!!!!
DASH!
...
HM.
SEVERAL MORE SMALL DISASTERS LATER...
UGH, ALL THE CRAZY IS LOOSE TONIGHT.

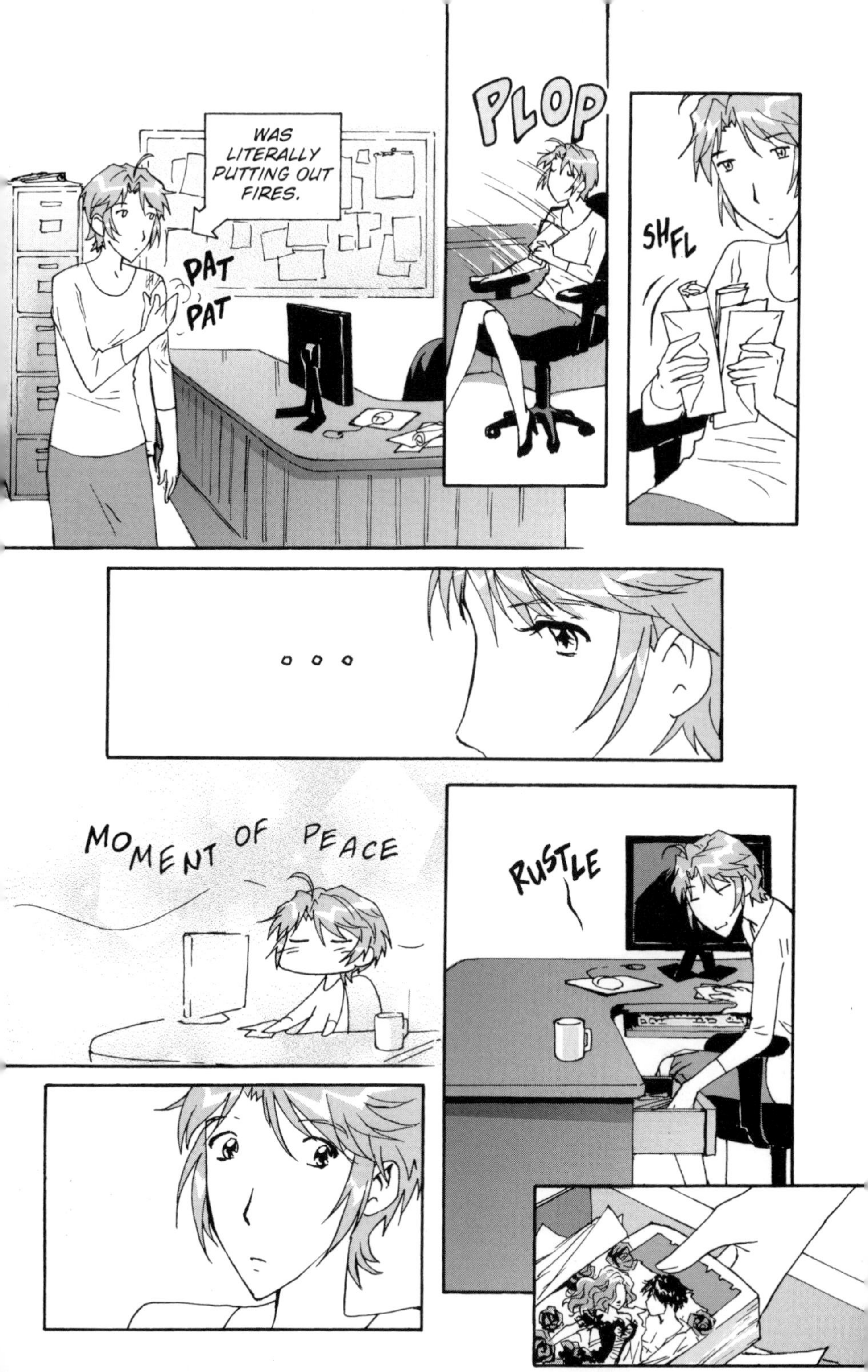
WAS LITERALLY PUTTING OUT FIRES.
PAT
PAT
PLOP
SHFL
...
MOMENT OF PEACE
RUSTLE

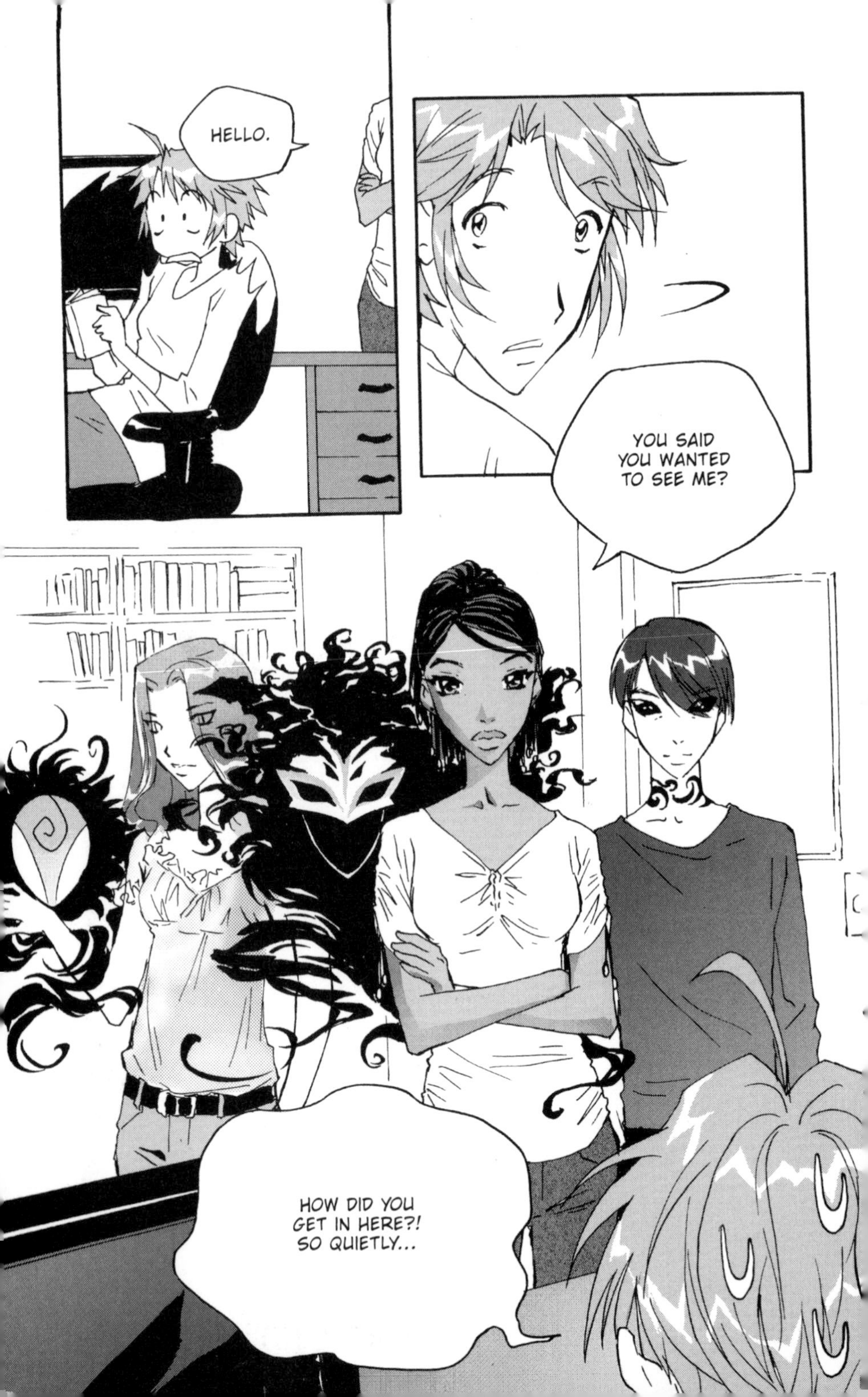
HELLO.
YOU SAID YOU WANTED TO SEE ME?
HOW DID YOU GET IN HERE?! SO QUIETLY...

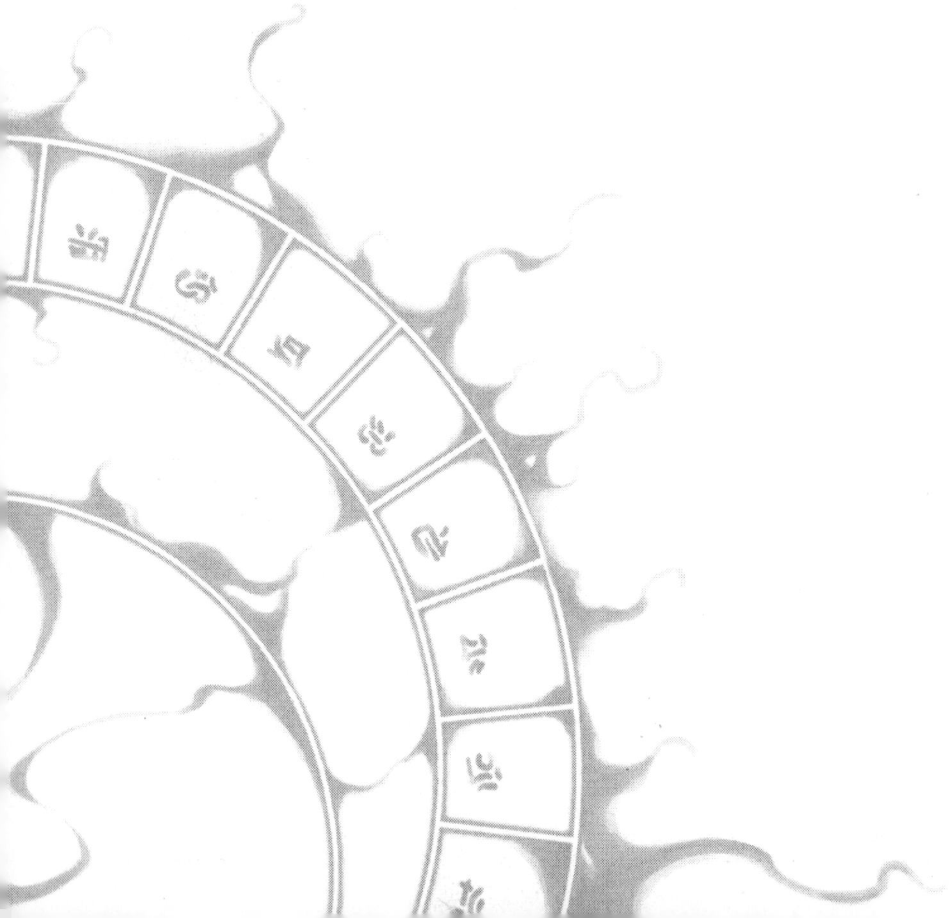

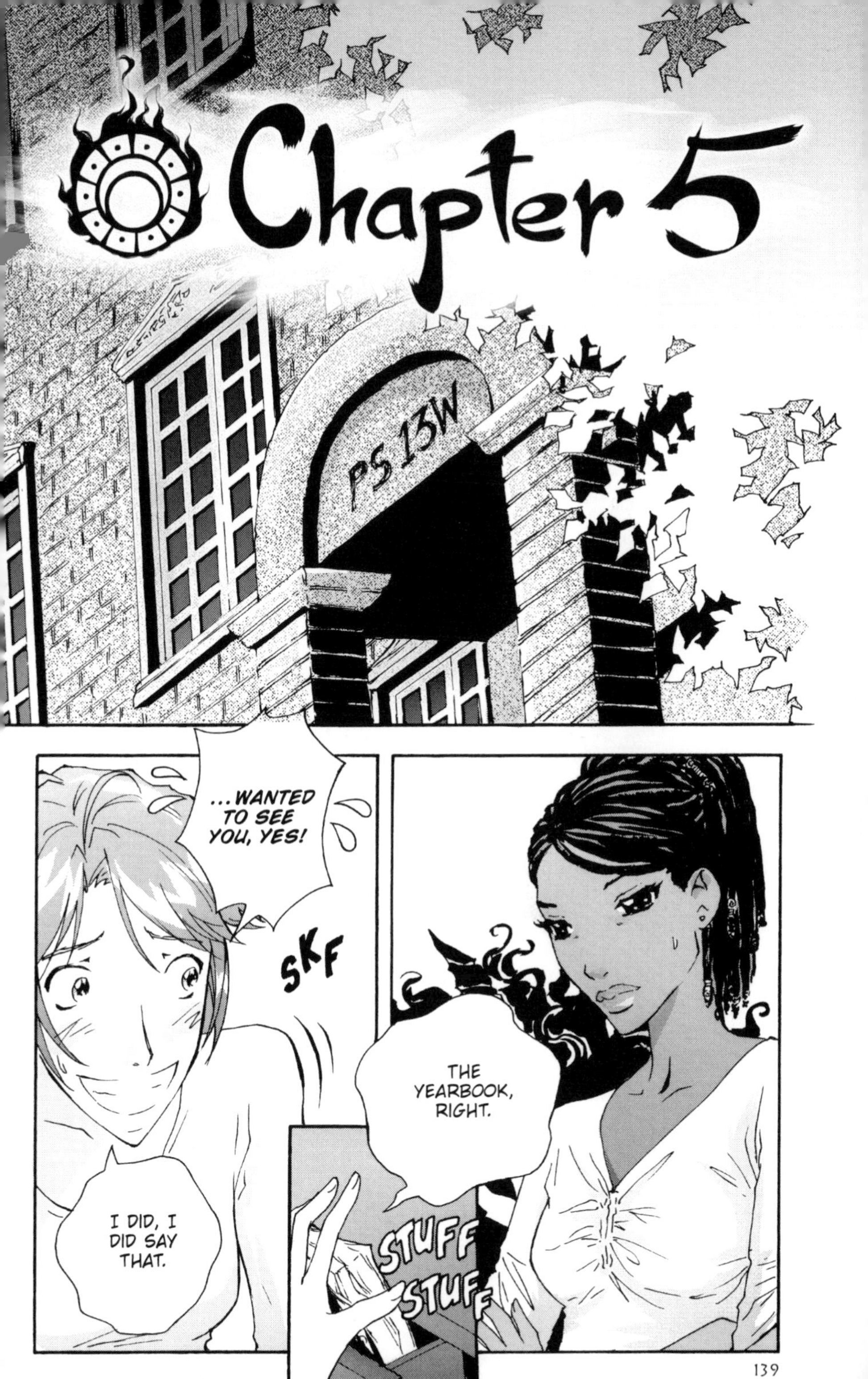

Chapter 5
PS 13W
...WANTED TO SEE YOU, YES!
SKF
I DID, I DID SAY THAT.
THE YEARBOOK, RIGHT.
STUFF STUFF

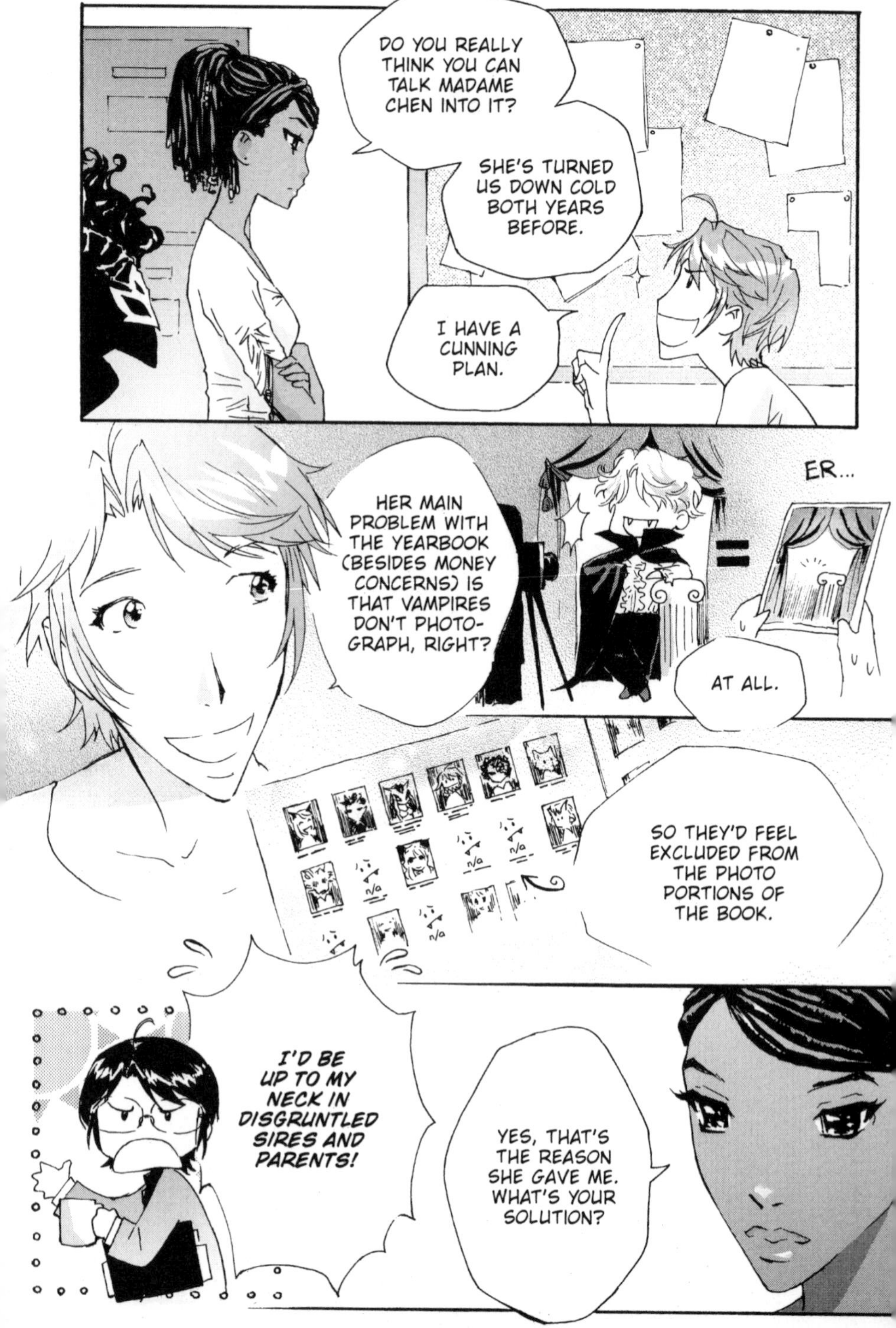

DO YOU REALLY THINK YOU CAN TALK MADAME CHEN INTO IT?
SHE'S TURNED US DOWN COLD BOTH YEARS BEFORE.
I HAVE A CUNNING PLAN.
HER MAIN PROBLEM WITH THE YEARBOOK (BESIDES MONEY CONCERNS) IS THAT VAMPIRES DON'T PHOTOGRAPH, RIGHT?
ER...
AT ALL.
SO THEY'D FEEL EXCLUDED FROM THE PHOTO PORTIONS OF THE BOOK.
n/a
I'D BE UP TO MY NECK IN DISGRUNTLED SIRES AND PARENTS!
YES, THAT'S THE REASON SHE GAVE ME. WHAT'S YOUR SOLUTION?

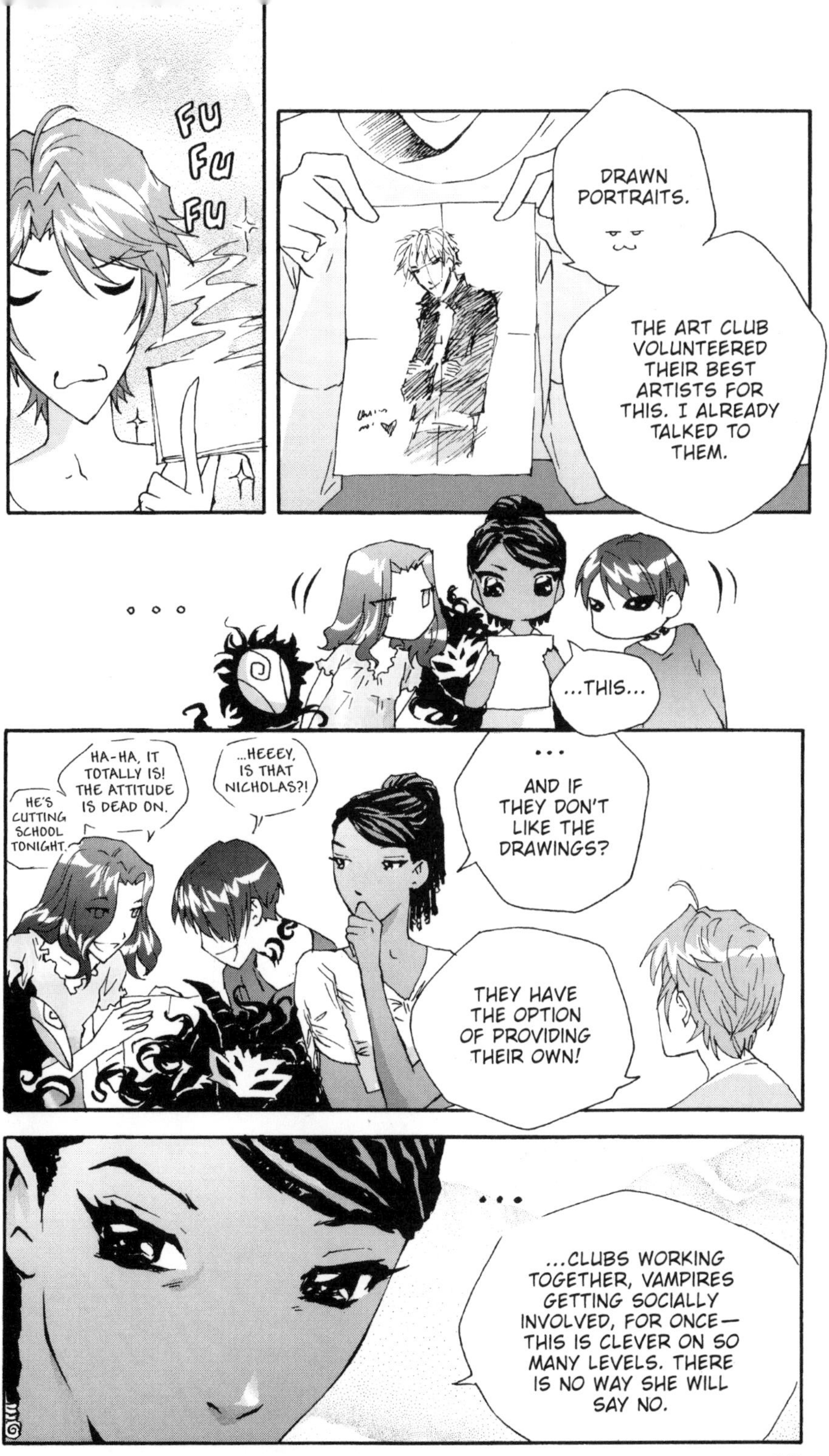
FU FU FU
DRAWN PORTRAITS.
THE ART CLUB VOLUNTEERED THEIR BEST ARTISTS FOR THIS. I ALREADY TALKED TO THEM.
...THIS...
...
AND IF THEY DON'T LIKE THE DRAWINGS?
...HEEEY, IS THAT NICHOLAS?!
HA-HA, IT TOTALLY IS! THE ATTITUDE IS DEAD ON.
HE'S CUTTING SCHOOL TONIGHT.
THEY HAVE THE OPTION OF PROVIDING THEIR OWN!
...
...CLUBS WORKING TOGETHER, VAMPIRES GETTING SOCIALLY INVOLVED, FOR ONCE— THIS IS CLEVER ON SO MANY LEVELS. THERE IS NO WAY SHE WILL SAY NO.

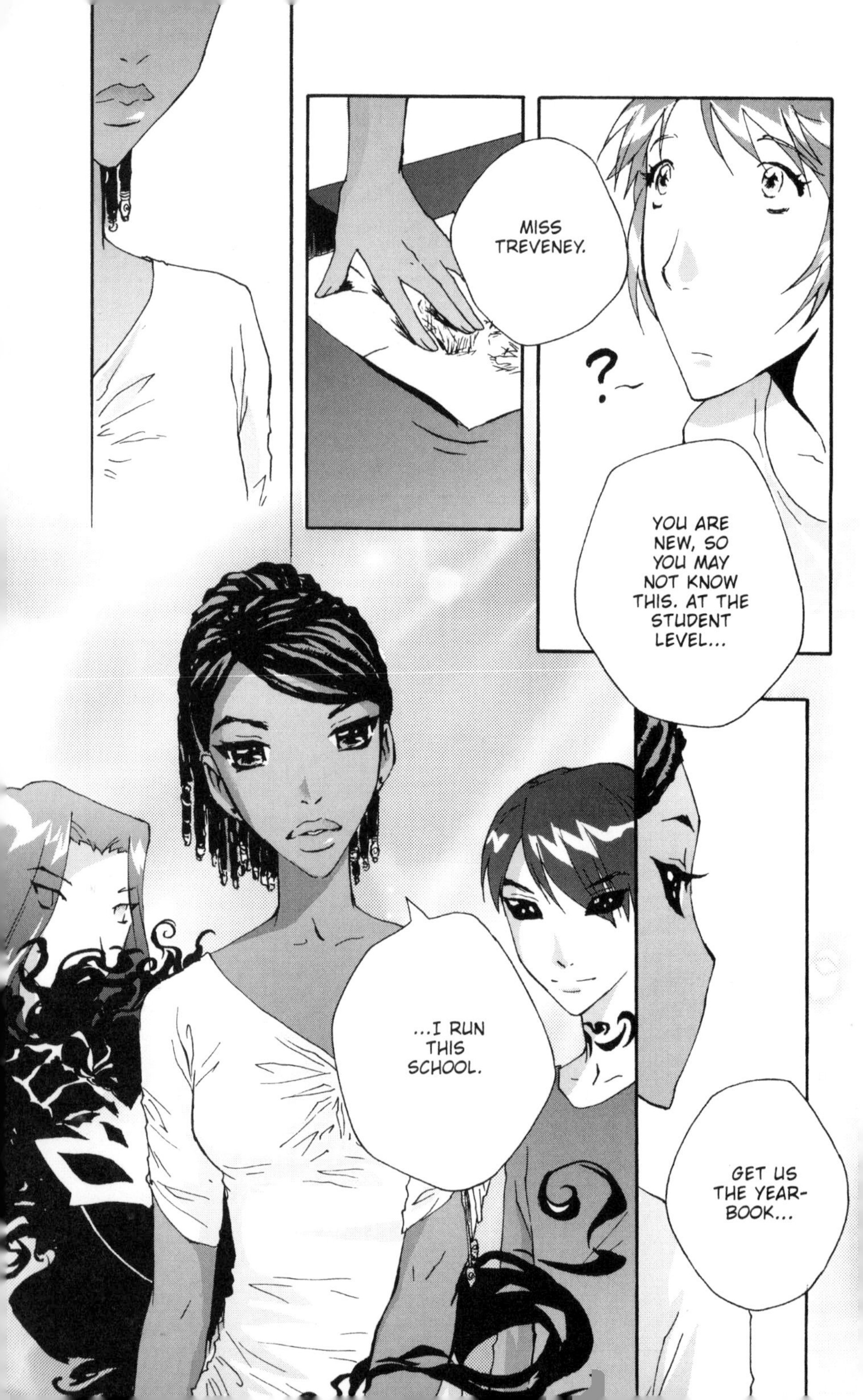
MISS TREVENEY.
?~
YOU ARE NEW, SO YOU MAY NOT KNOW THIS. AT THE STUDENT LEVEL...
...I RUN THIS SCHOOL.
GET US THE YEAR-BOOK...

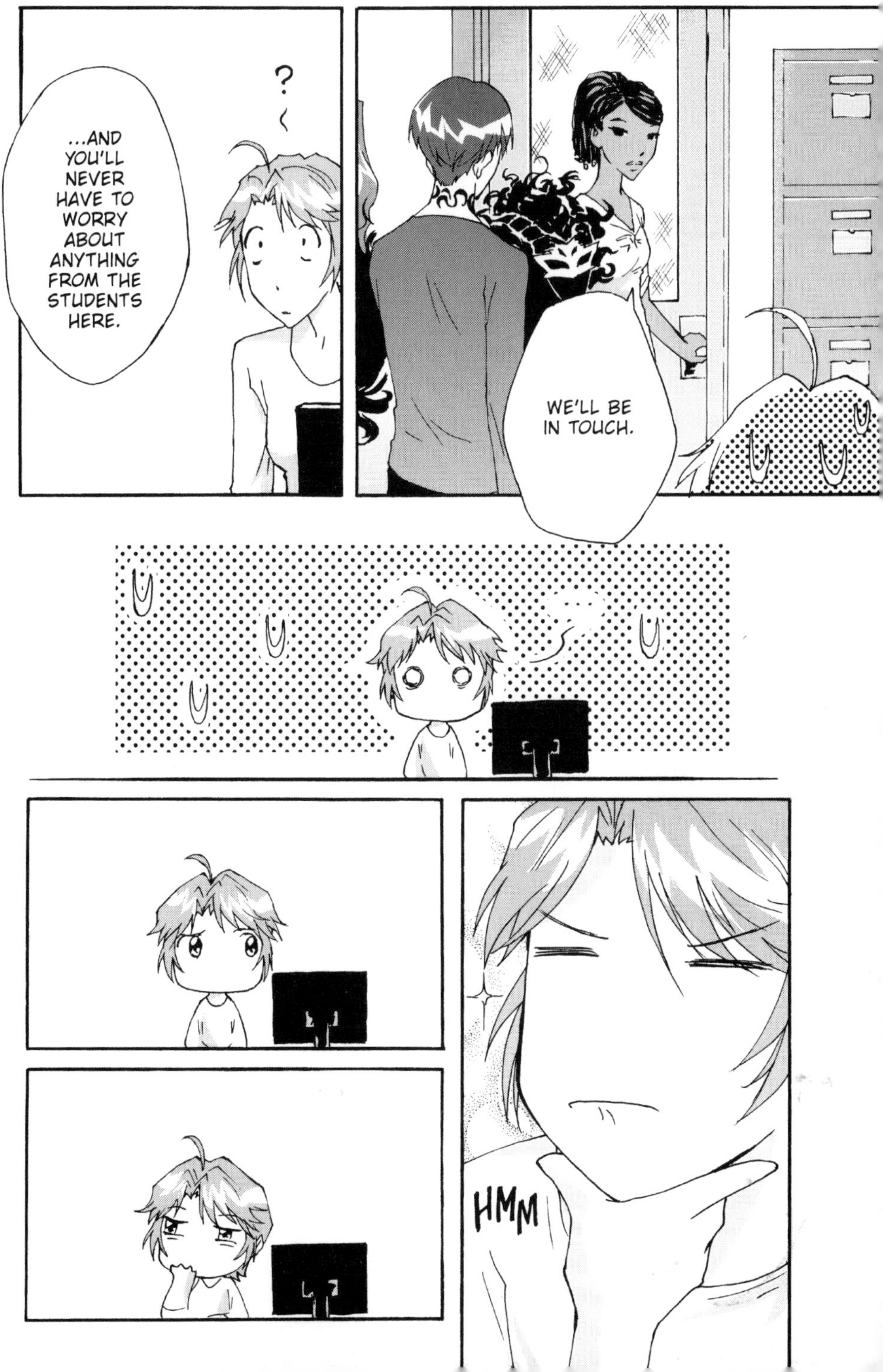
...AND YOU'LL NEVER HAVE TO WORRY ABOUT ANYTHING FROM THE STUDENTS HERE.
?
WE'LL BE IN TOUCH.
HMM

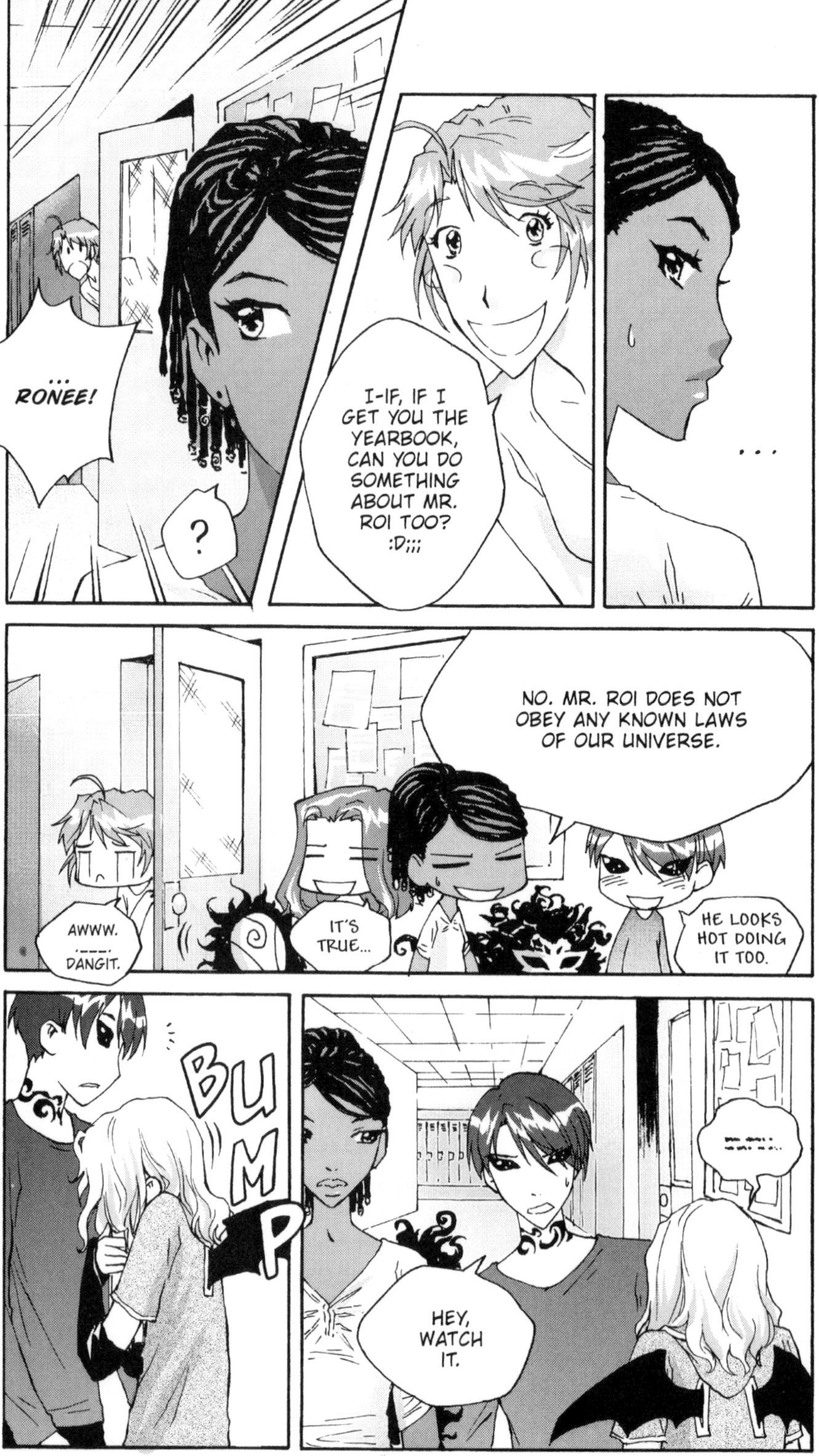

... RONEE!
?
I-IF, IF I GET YOU THE YEARBOOK, CAN YOU DO SOMETHING ABOUT MR. ROI TOO? :D;;;
...
NO. MR. ROI DOES NOT OBEY ANY KNOWN LAWS OF OUR UNIVERSE.
AWWW.
DANGIT.
IT'S TRUE...
HE LOOKS HOT DOING IT TOO.
BUMP
HEY, WATCH IT.

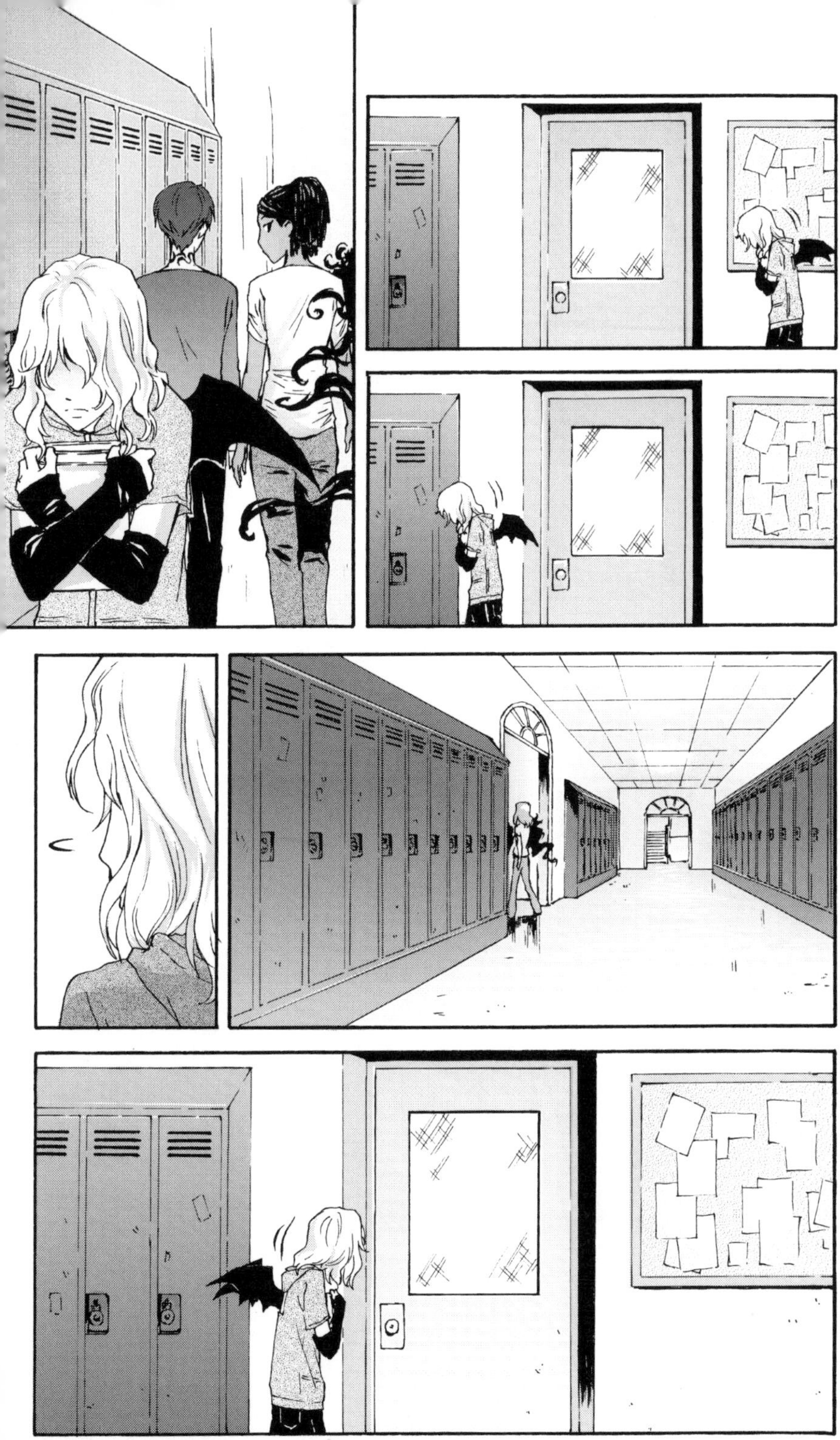

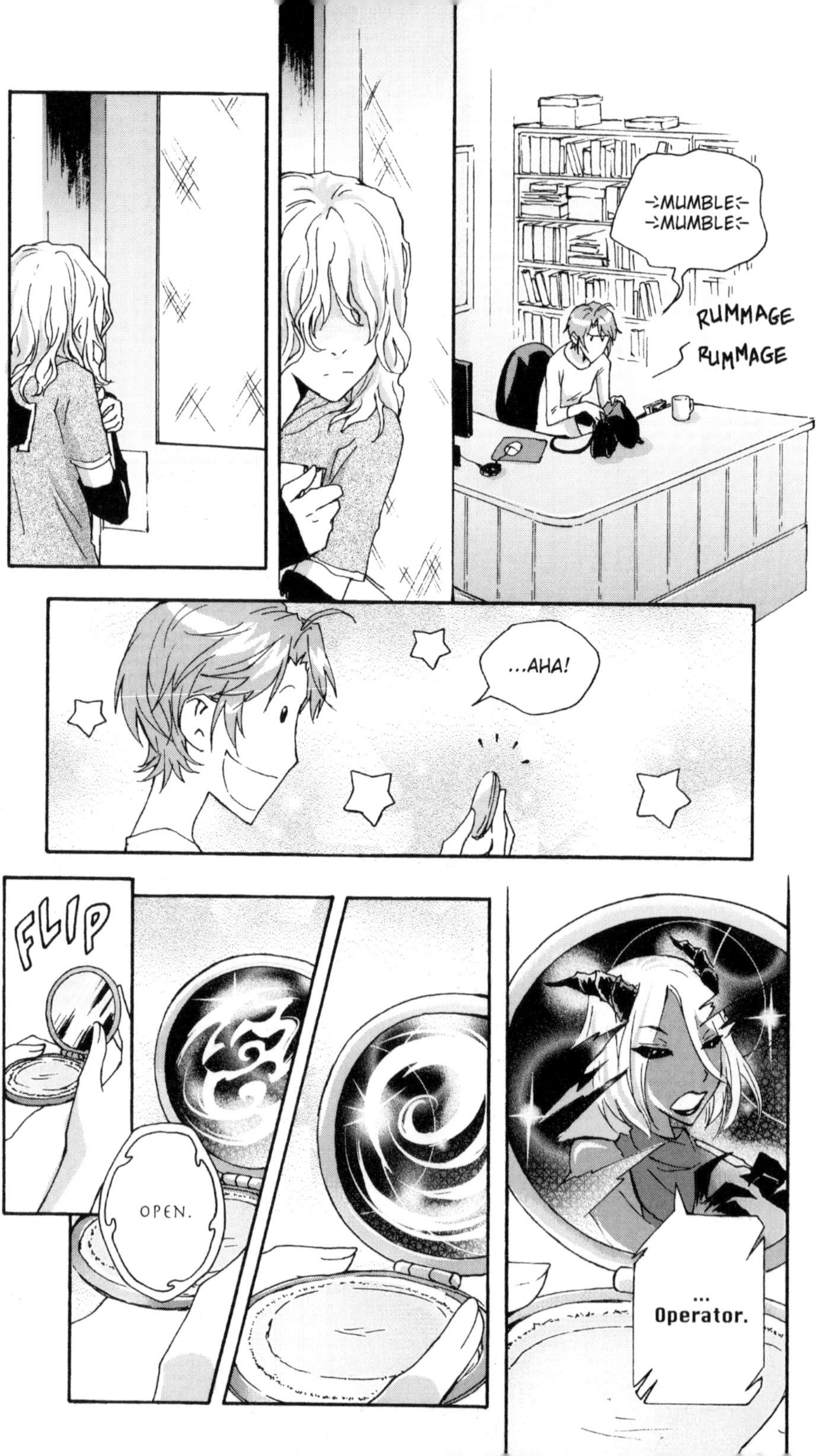

MUMBLE MUMBLE
RUMMAGE RUMMAGE
...AHA!
FLIP
OPEN.
... Operator.

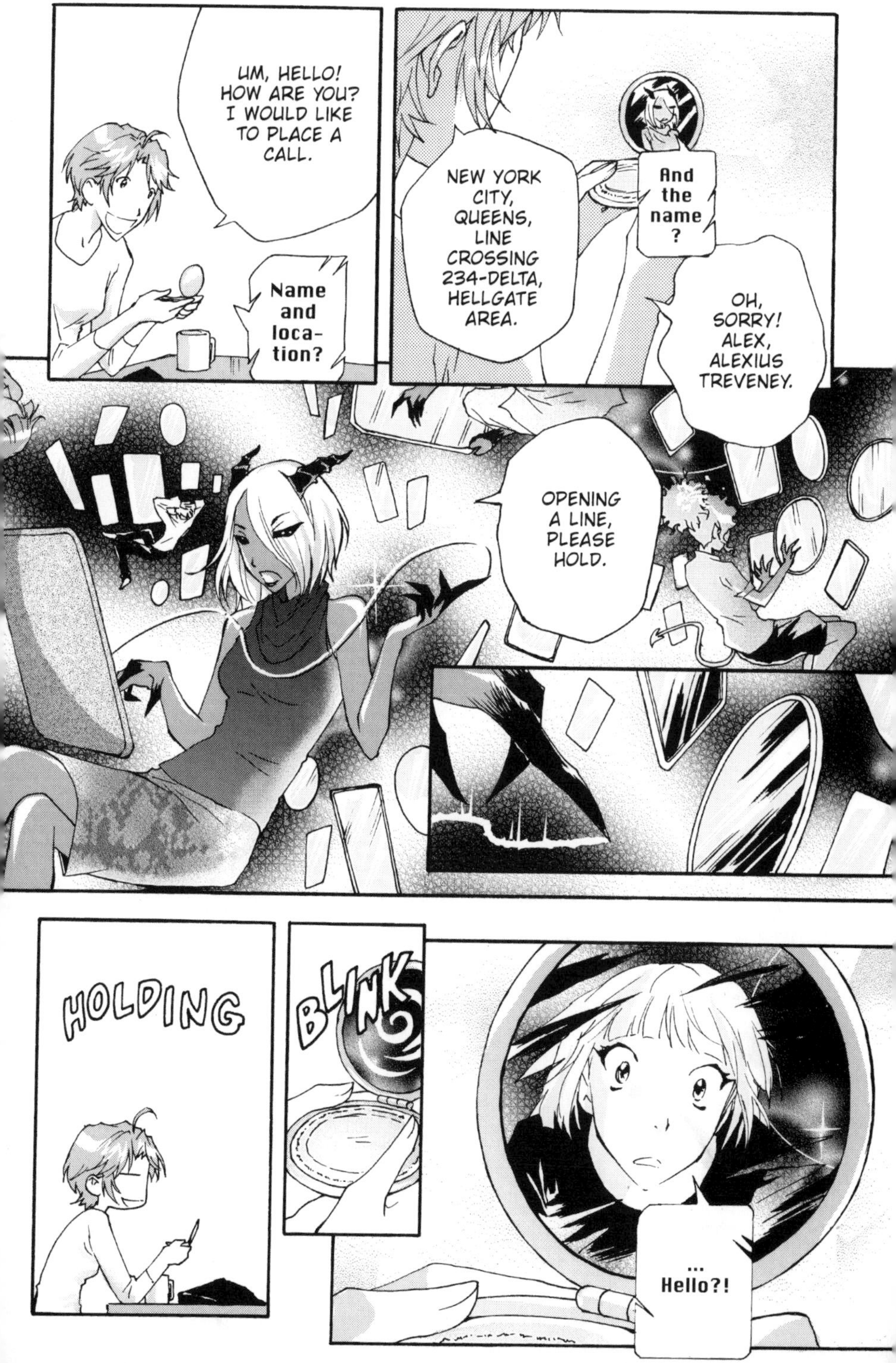
UM, HELLO! HOW ARE YOU? I WOULD LIKE TO PLACE A CALL.
Name and loca-tion?
NEW YORK CITY, QUEENS, LINE CROSSING 234-DELTA, HELLGATE AREA.
And the name?
OH, SORRY! ALEX, ALEXIUS TREVENEY.
OPENING A LINE, PLEASE HOLD.
HOLDING
BLINK
...Hello?!

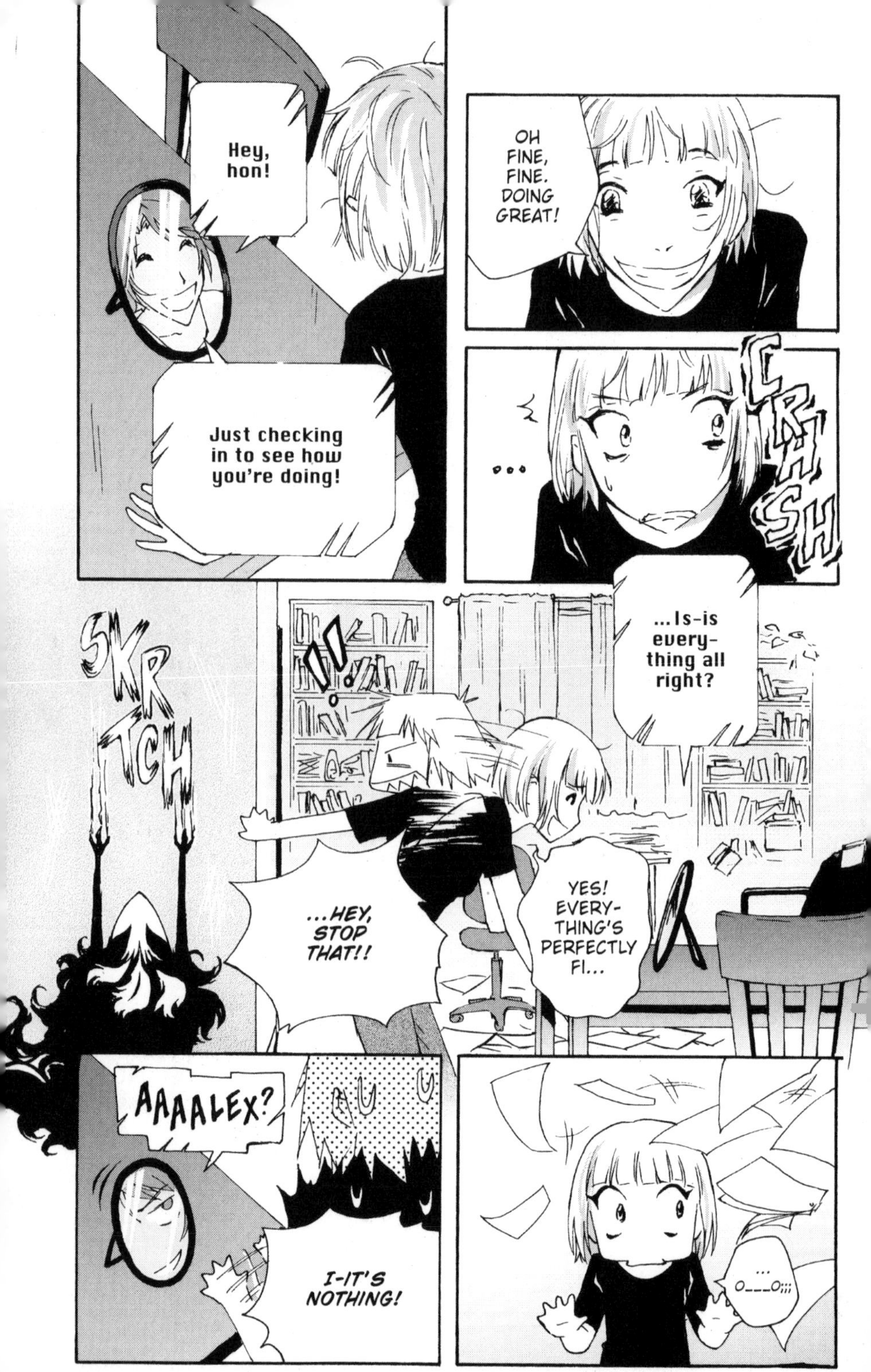
Hey, hon!
Just checking in to see how you're doing!
OH FINE, FINE. DOING GREAT!
...
CRASH
...Is-is every-thing all right?
SKRTCH
...HEY, STOP THAT!!
YES! EVERY-THING'S PERFECTLY FI...
AAAALEX?
I-IT'S NOTHING!
...
o___o;;;

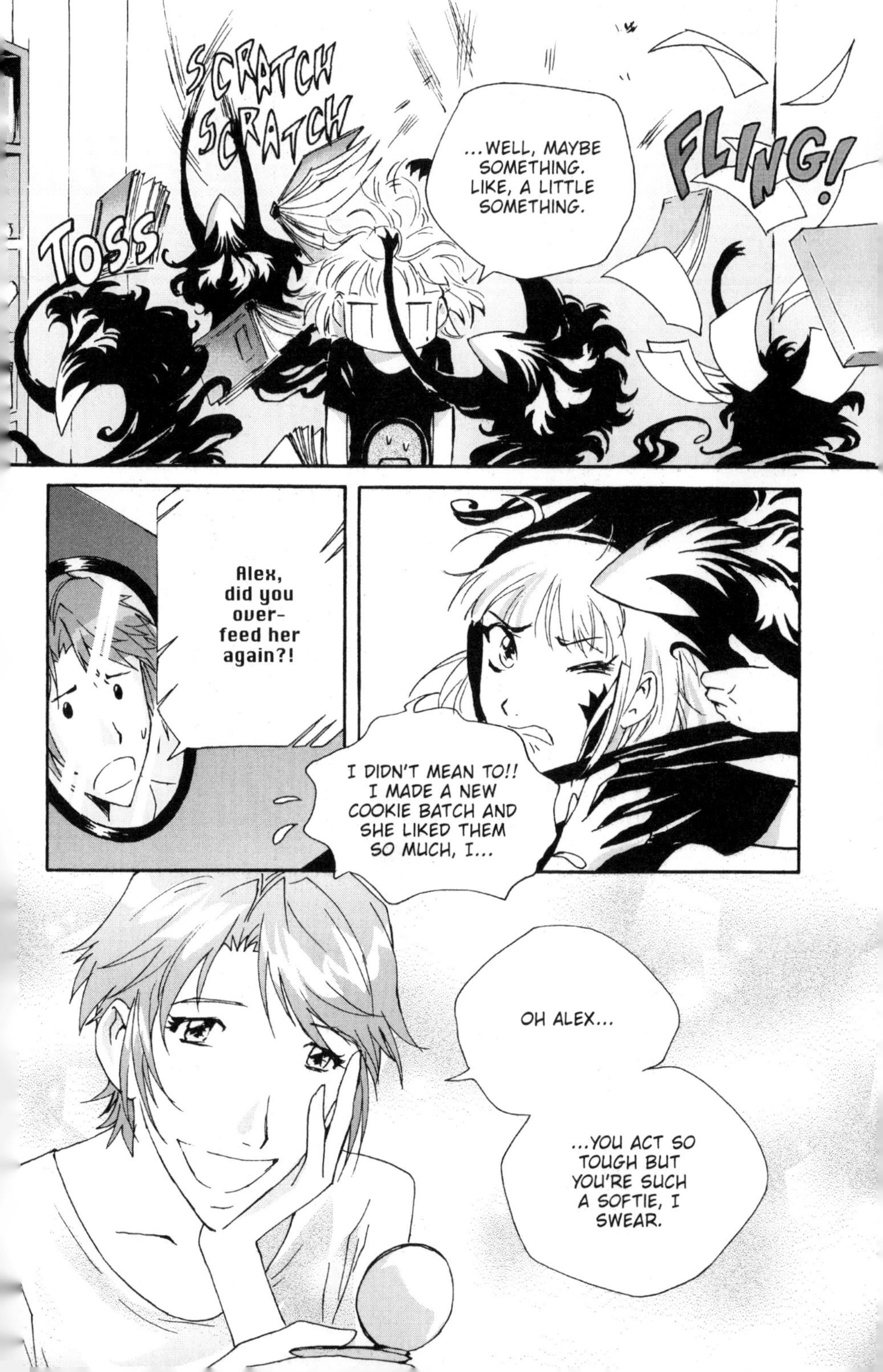
SCRATCH SCRATCH
TOSS
...WELL, MAYBE SOMETHING. LIKE, A LITTLE SOMETHING.
FLING!
Alex, did you over-feed her again?!
I DIDN'T MEAN TO!! I MADE A NEW COOKIE BATCH AND SHE LIKED THEM SO MUCH, I...
OH ALEX...
...YOU ACT SO TOUGH BUT YOU'RE SUCH A SOFTIE, I SWEAR.

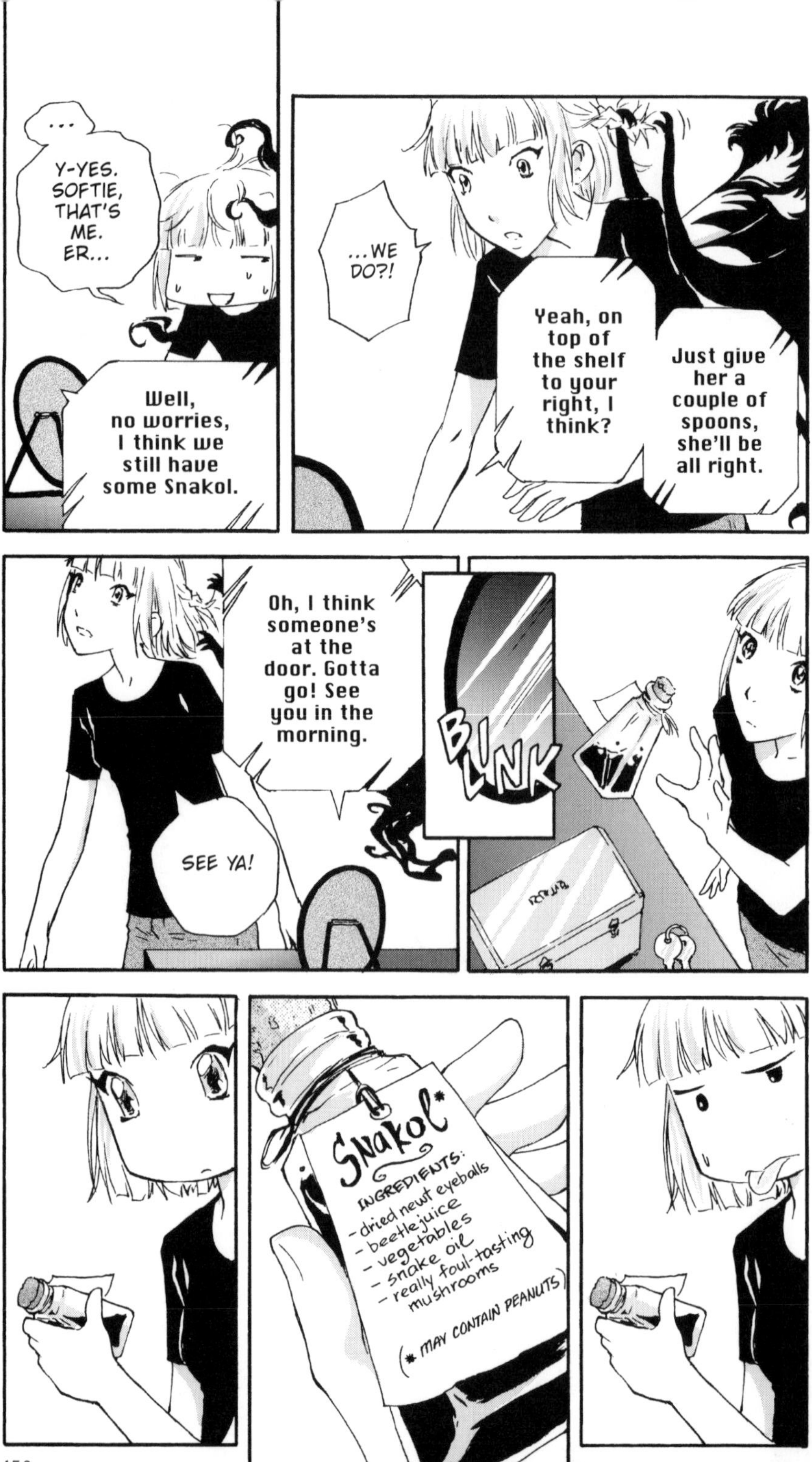
...
Y-YES. SOFTIE, THAT'S ME. ER...
Well, no worries, I think we still have some Snakol.
...WE DO?!
Yeah, on top of the shelf to your right, I think?
Just give her a couple of spoons, she'll be all right.
Oh, I think someone's at the door. Gotta go! See you in the morning.
SEE YA!
BLINK
Snakol*
INGREDIENTS:
- dried newt eyeballs
- beetlejuice
- vegetables
- snake oil
- really foul-tasting mushrooms
(* MAY CONTAIN PEANUTS)

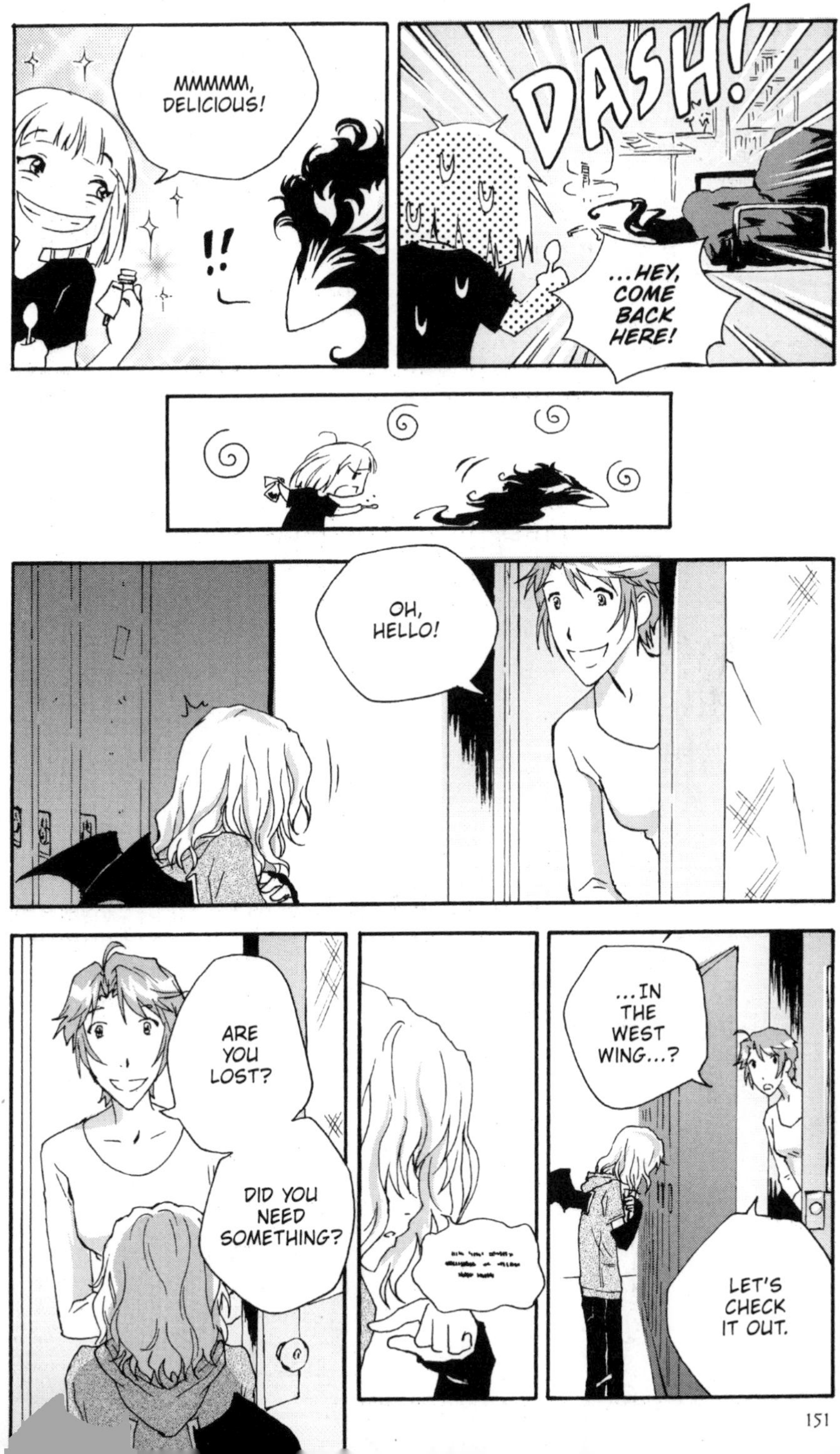
MMMMM, DELICIOUS!
!!
DASH!
...HEY, COME BACK HERE!
OH, HELLO!
ARE YOU LOST?
DID YOU NEED SOMETHING?
...IN THE WEST WING...?
LET'S CHECK IT OUT.

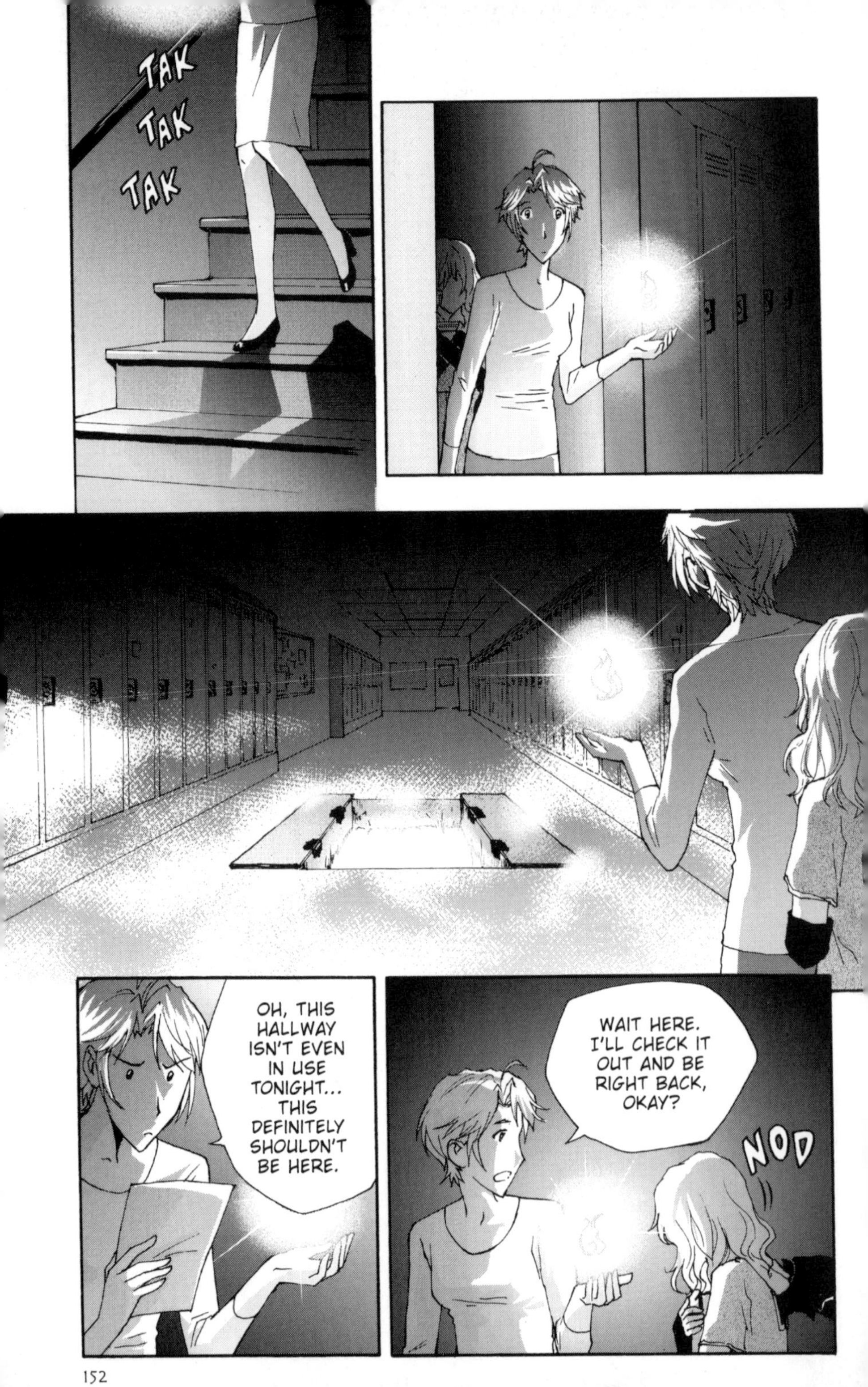
TAK
TAK
TAK
OH, THIS HALLWAY ISN'T EVEN IN USE TONIGHT... THIS DEFINITELY SHOULDN'T BE HERE.
WAIT HERE. I'LL CHECK IT OUT AND BE RIGHT BACK, OKAY?
NOD

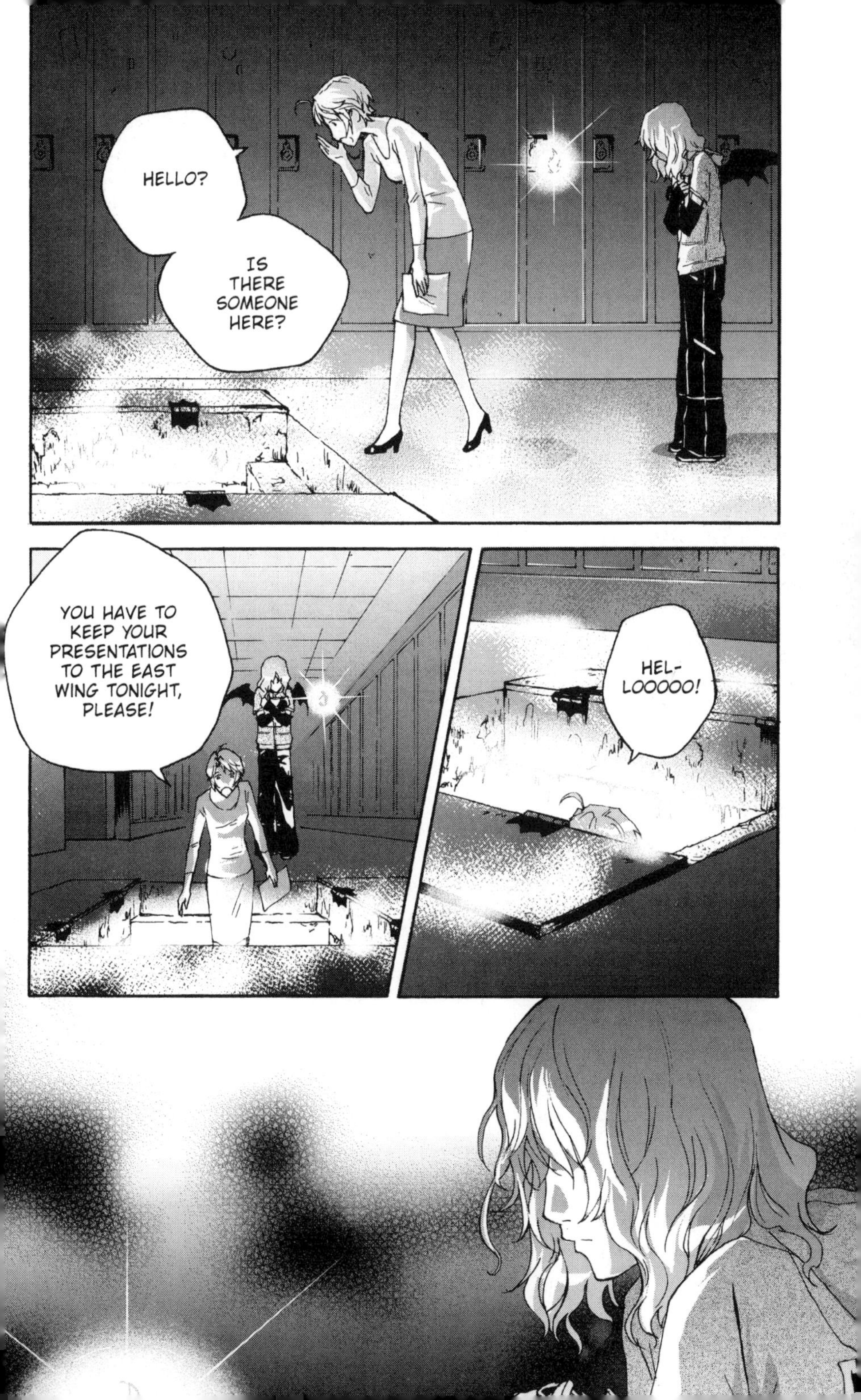
HELLO?
IS THERE SOMEONE HERE?
YOU HAVE TO KEEP YOUR PRESENTATIONS TO THE EAST WING TONIGHT, PLEASE!
HEL-LOOOOO!

CREAK
KTK

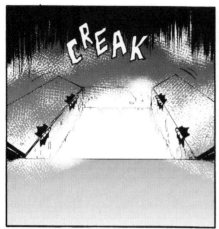

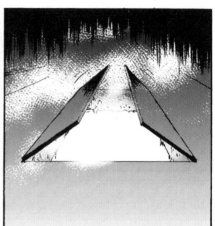

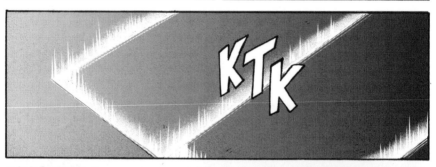

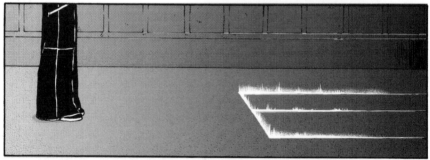

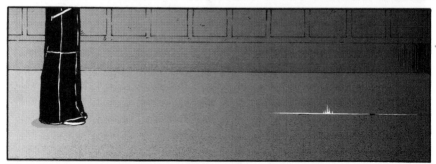

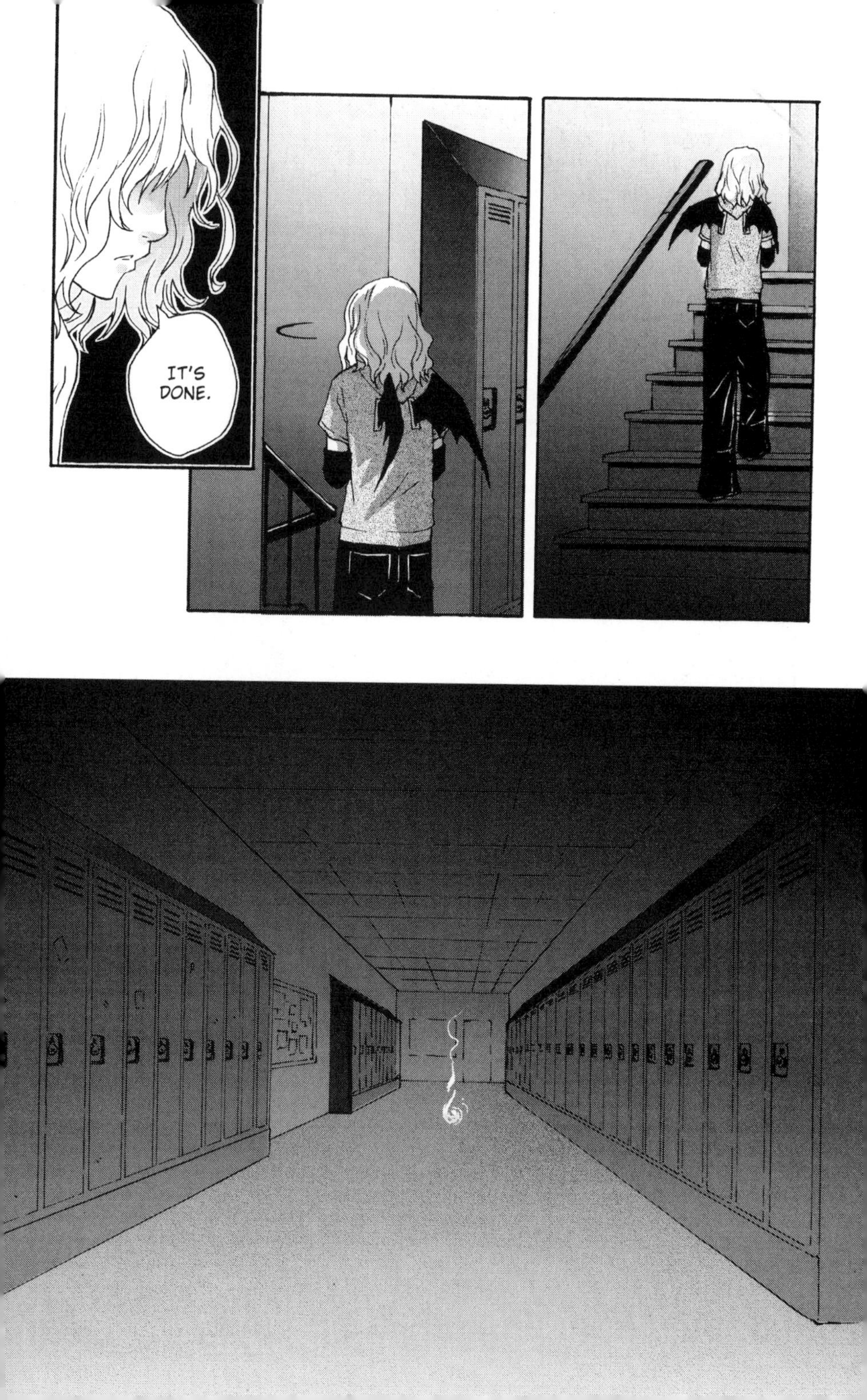
IT'S DONE.

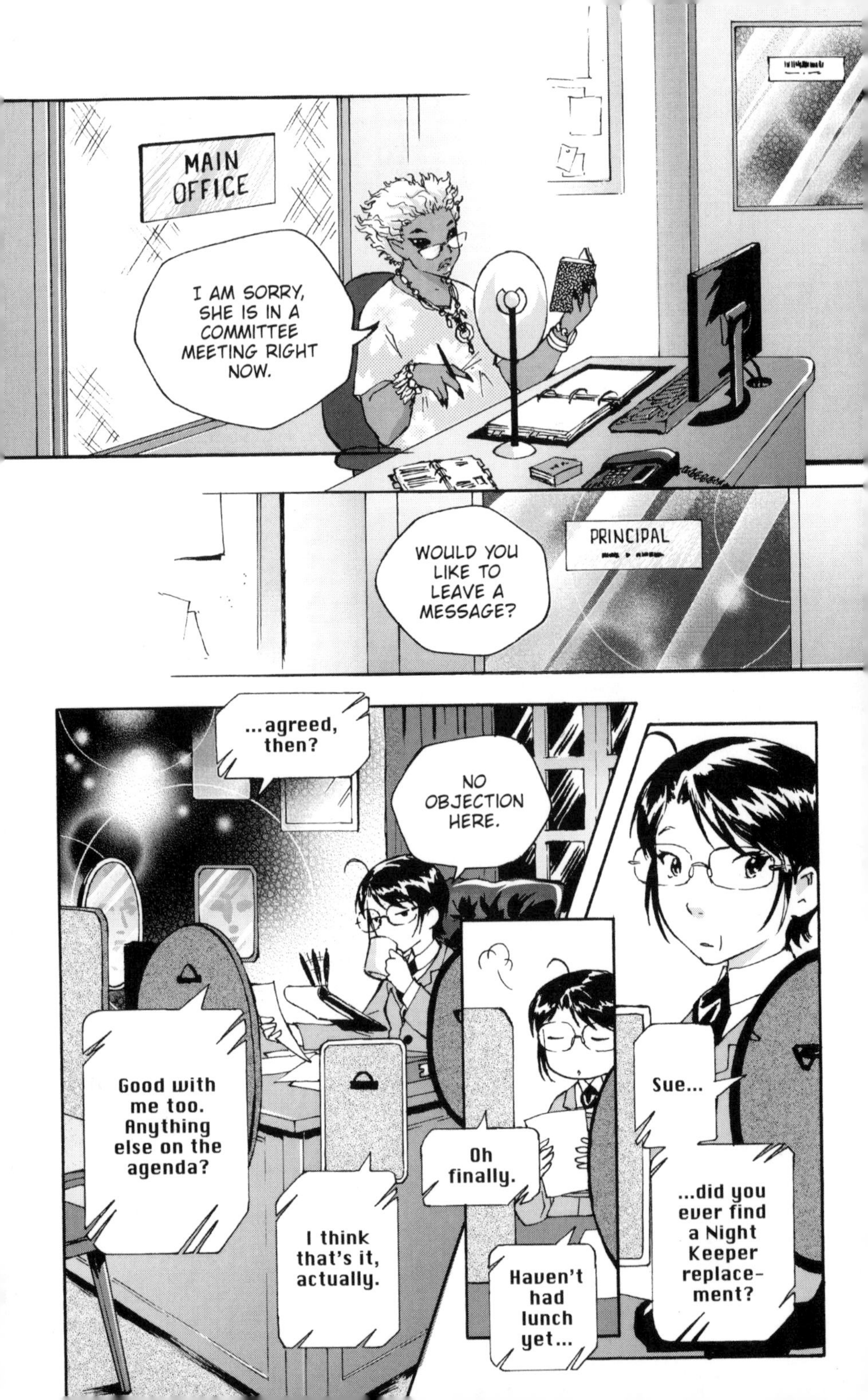
MAIN OFFICE
I AM SORRY, SHE IS IN A COMMITTEE MEETING RIGHT NOW.
PRINCIPAL
WOULD YOU LIKE TO LEAVE A MESSAGE?
...agreed, then?
NO OBJECTION HERE.
Good with me too. Anything else on the agenda?
I think that's it, actually.
Oh finally.
Haven't had lunch yet...
Sue...
...did you ever find a Night Keeper replace-ment?

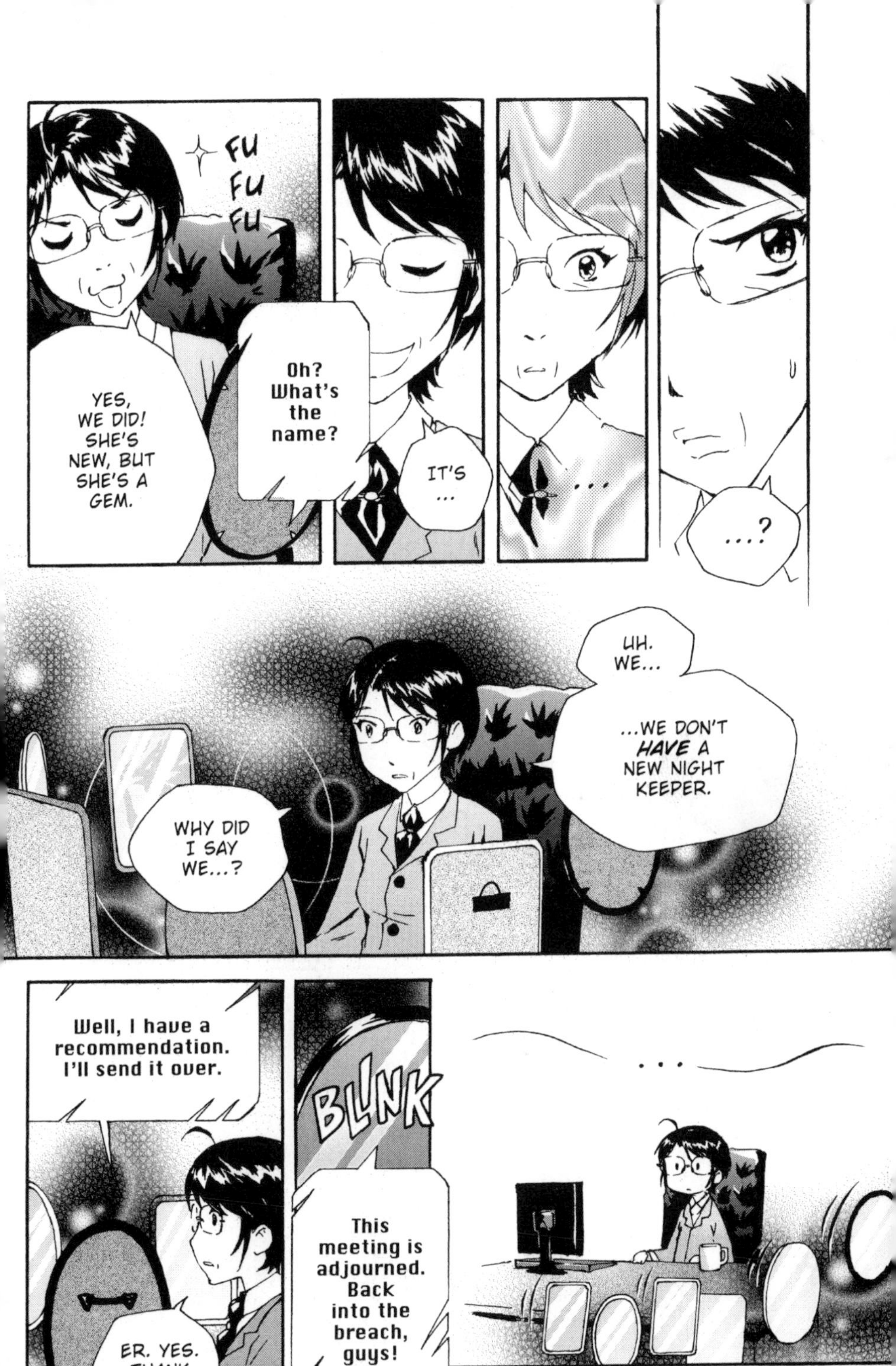
FU FU FU
YES, WE DID! SHE'S NEW, BUT SHE'S A GEM.
Oh? What's the name?
IT'S ...
...
...?
UH. WE...
...WE DON'T HAVE A NEW NIGHT KEEPER.
WHY DID I SAY WE...?
Well, I have a recommendation. I'll send it over.
ER. YES. THANK YOU.
BLINK
This meeting is adjourned. Back into the breach, guys!
...

SHELLY, DO WE HAVE A NIGHT KEEPER?

NOT SINCE YOU FIRED THE LAST ONE A MONTH AGO. REALLY NEED ONE, THOUGH.

HUH.

I WAS SO *SURE*. HM.

WELL, THERE IS DEFINITELY A CONTRACT... IT MUST HAVE A NAME.

FLIP FLIP

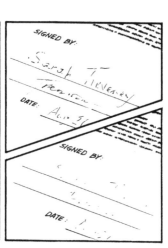

SIGNED BY:
Sarah Treveary
Treviw
DATE: Aug 3

SIGNED BY:

DATE:

IT'S BLANK? ...

...

... WHY WAS I LOOKING AT THIS AGAIN?

158

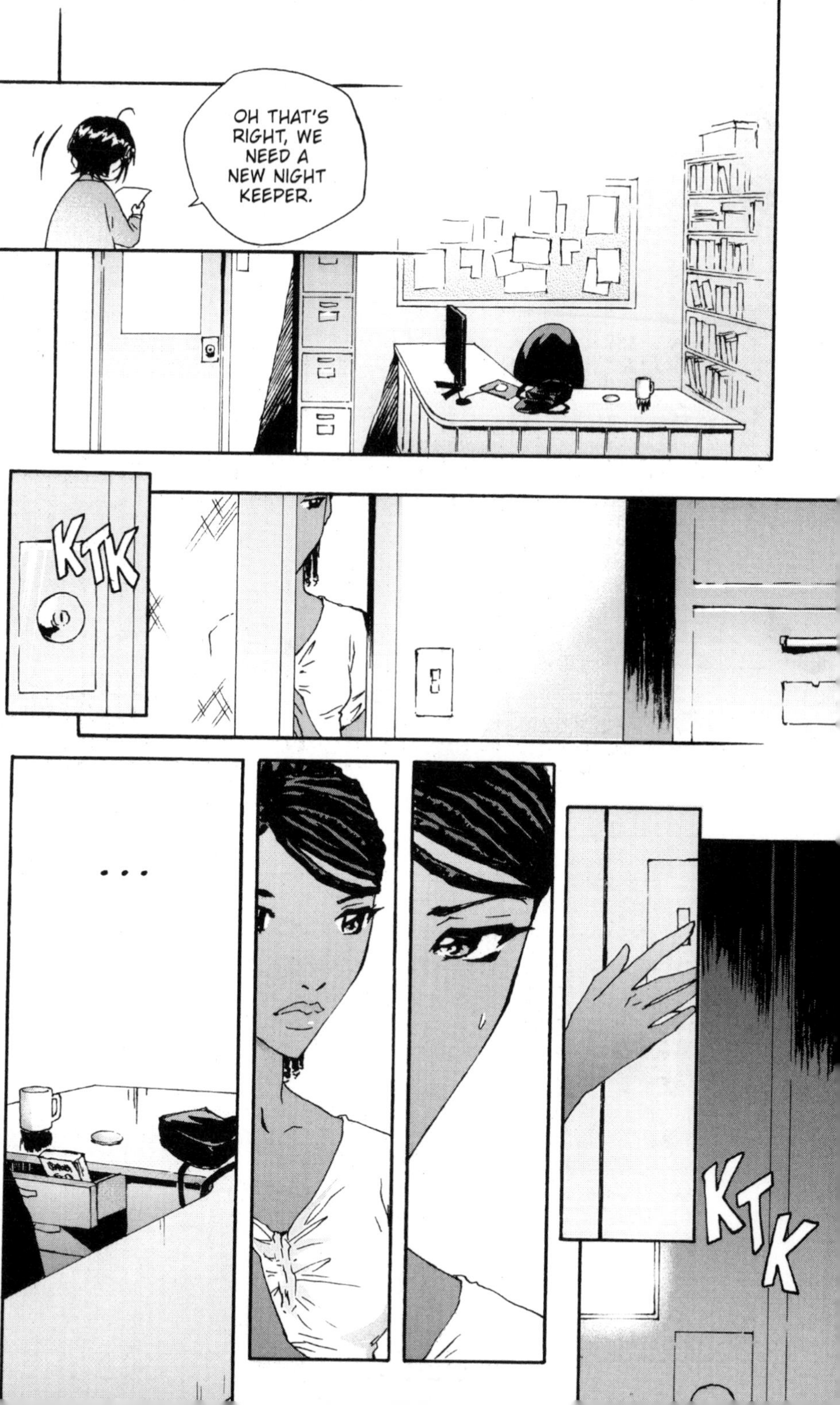
OH THAT'S RIGHT, WE NEED A NEW NIGHT KEEPER.
KTK
...
KTK

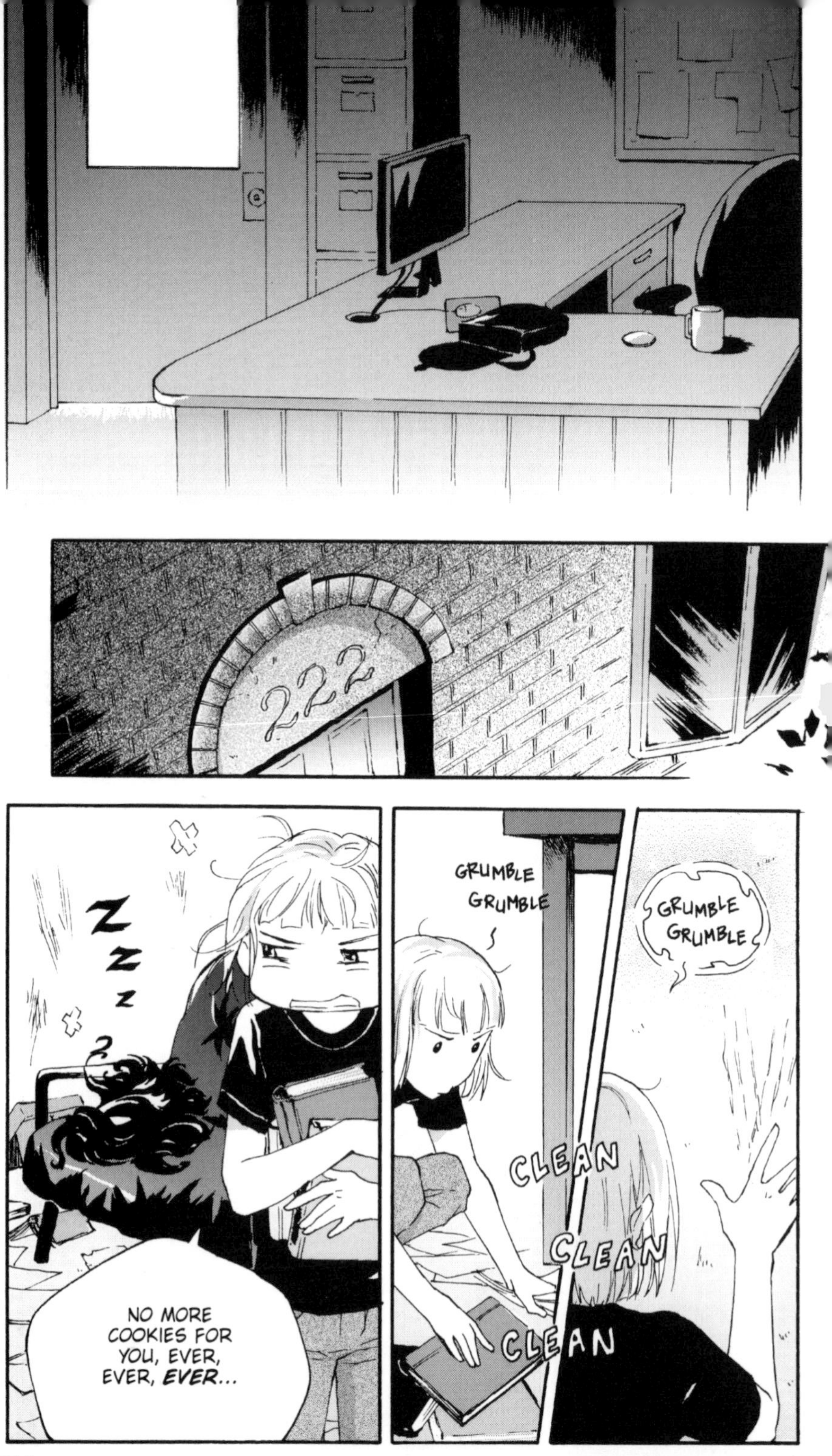
222
Z Z z z
NO MORE COOKIES FOR YOU, EVER, EVER, ***EVER***...
GRUMBLE GRUMBLE
CLEAN
CLEAN
CLEAN
GRUMBLE GRUMBLE

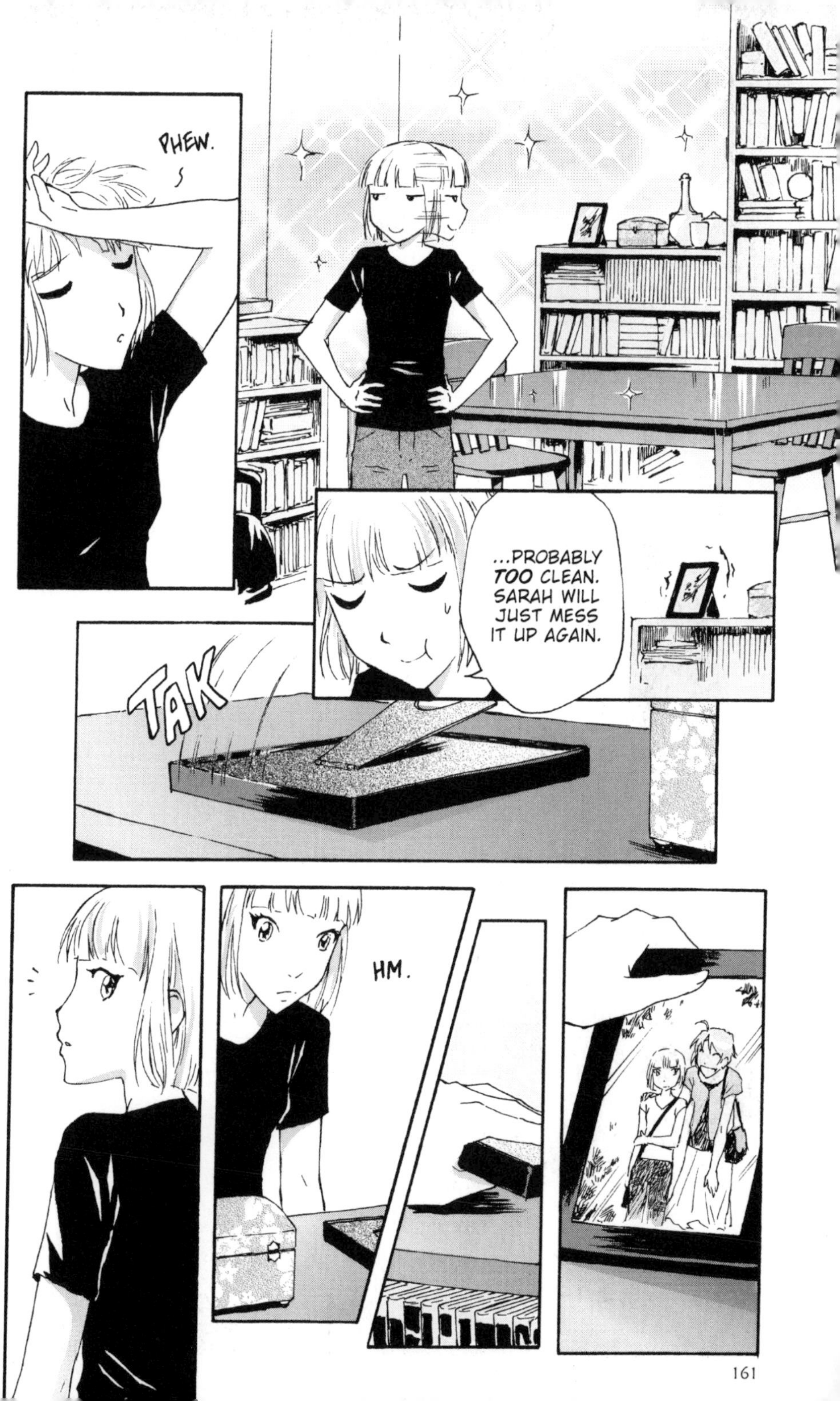
PHEW.
...PROBABLY *TOO* CLEAN. SARAH WILL JUST MESS IT UP AGAIN.
TAK
HM.

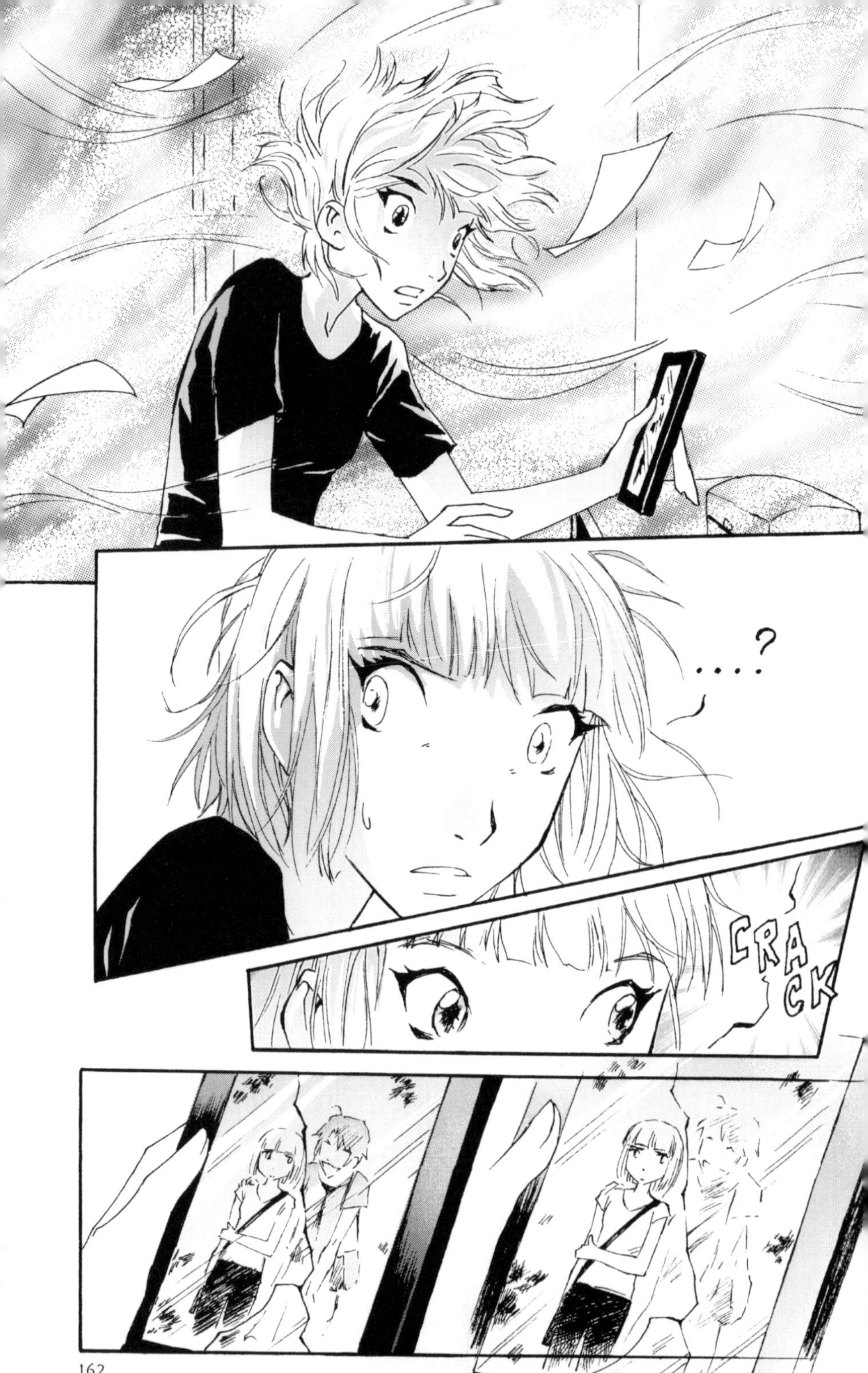
...?
CRACK

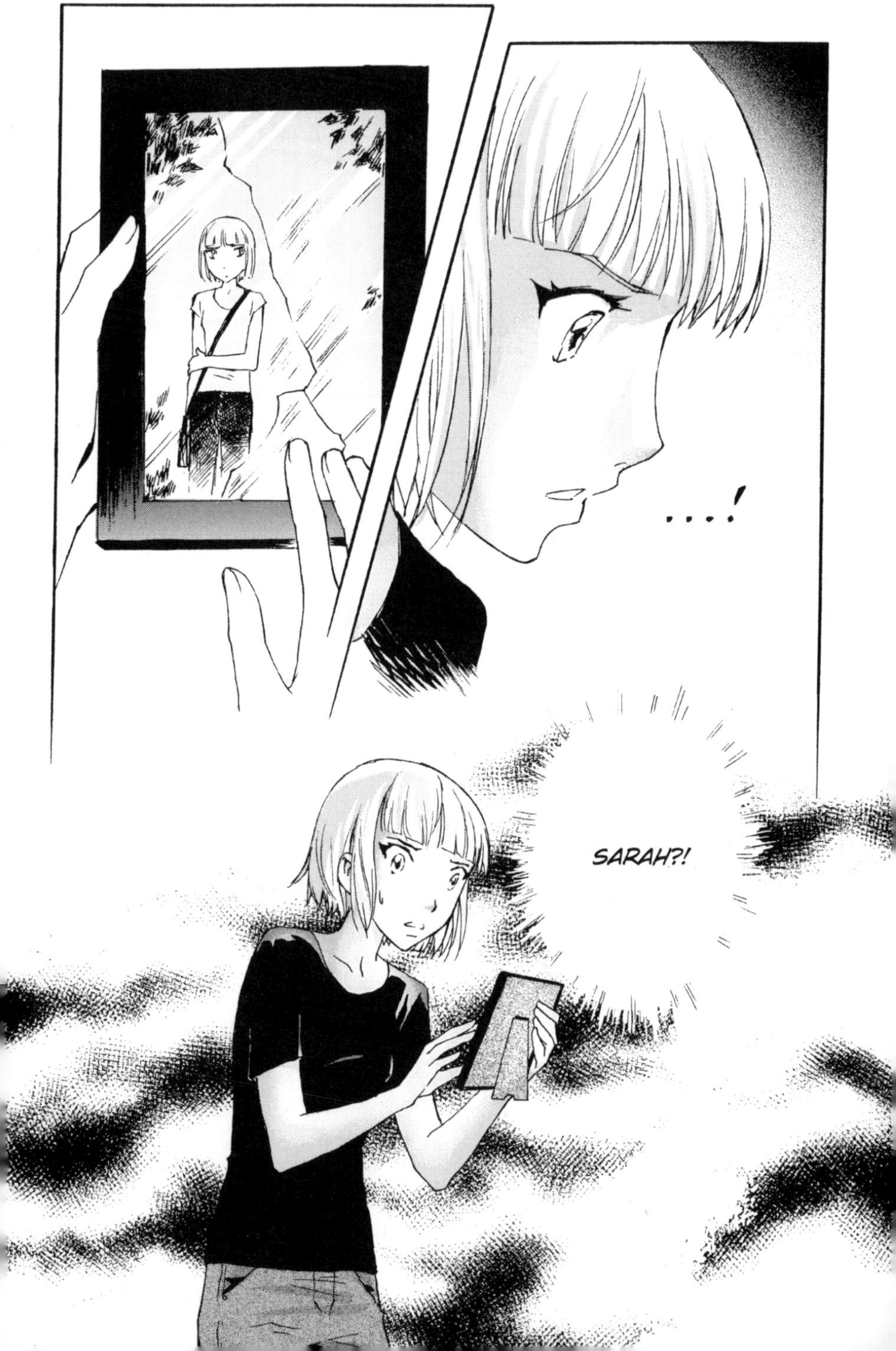
...!
SARAH?!

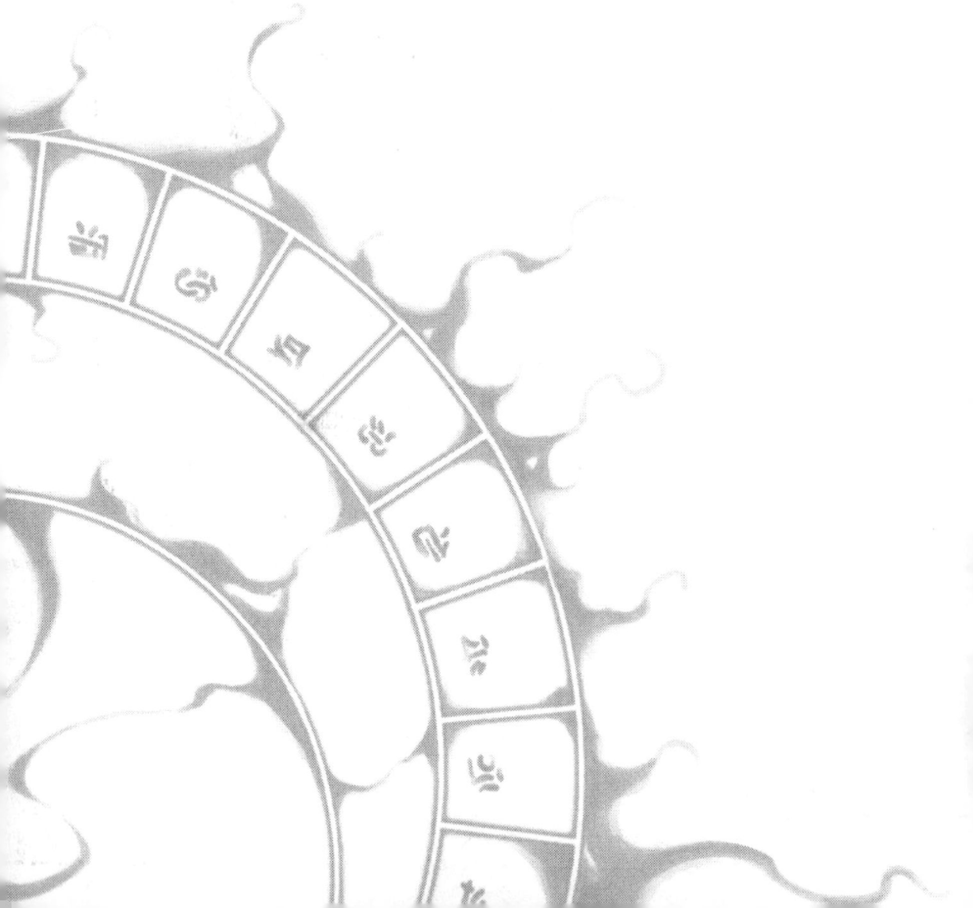

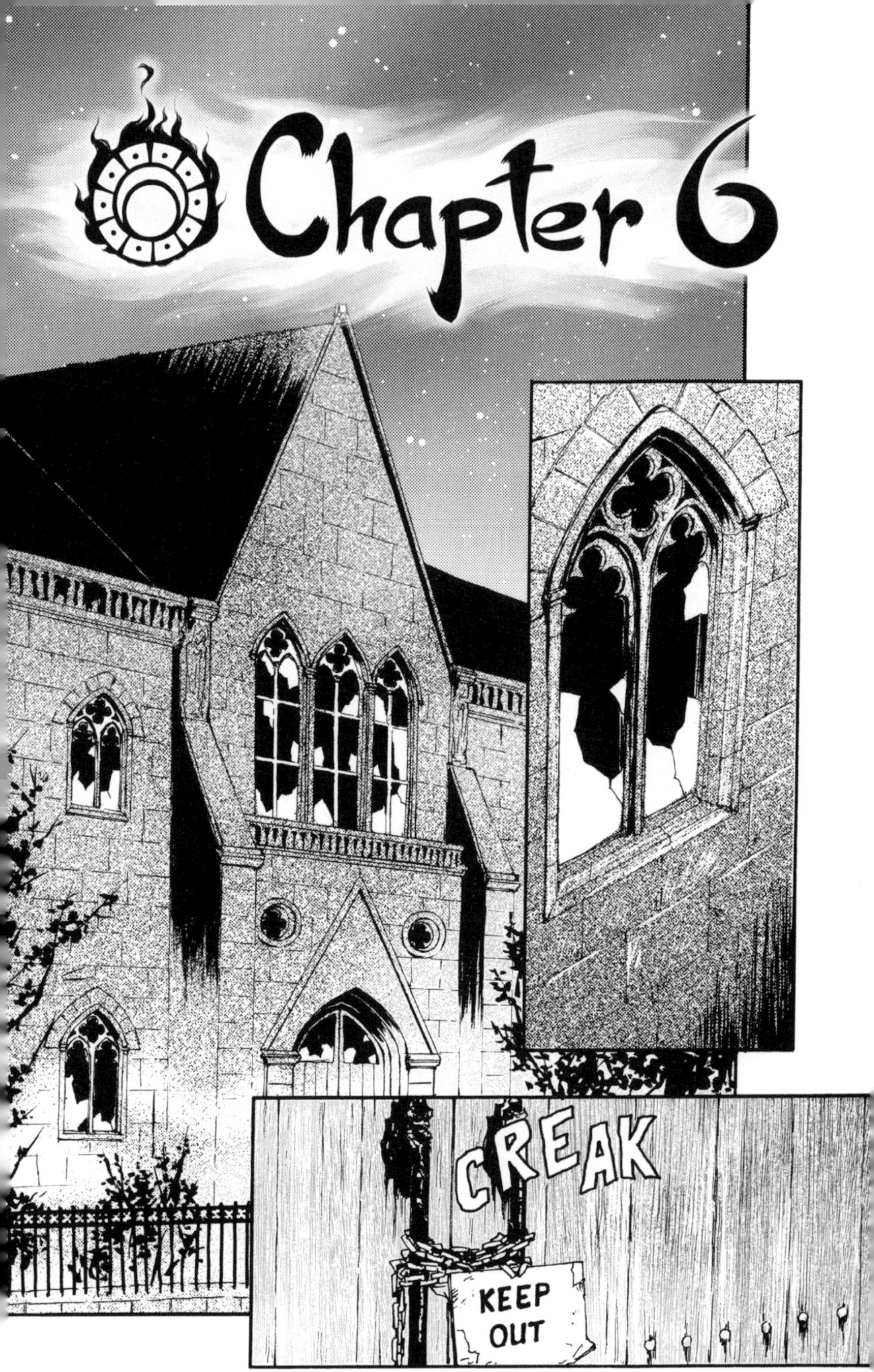
Chapter 6
CREAK
KEEP OUT

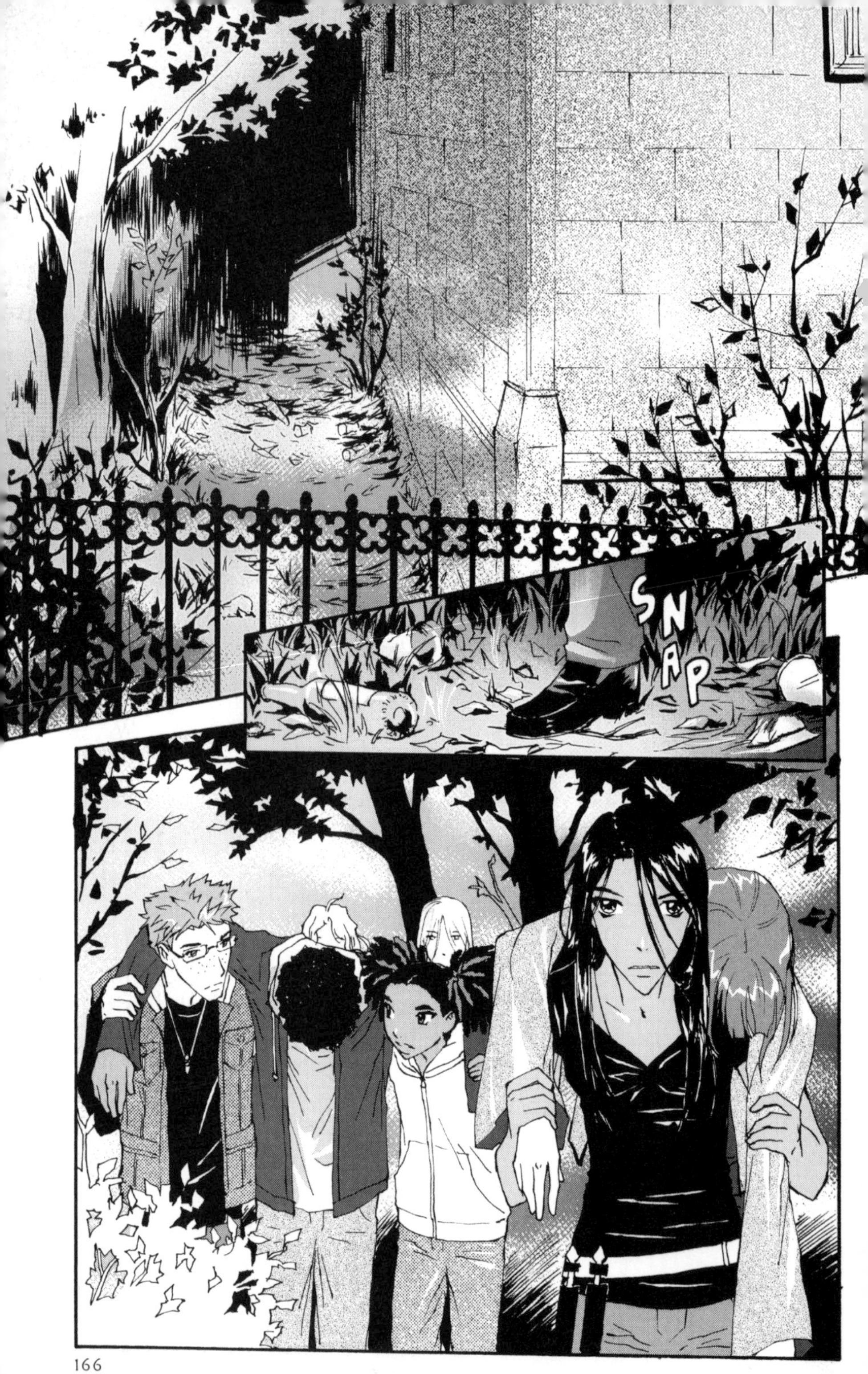
SNAP

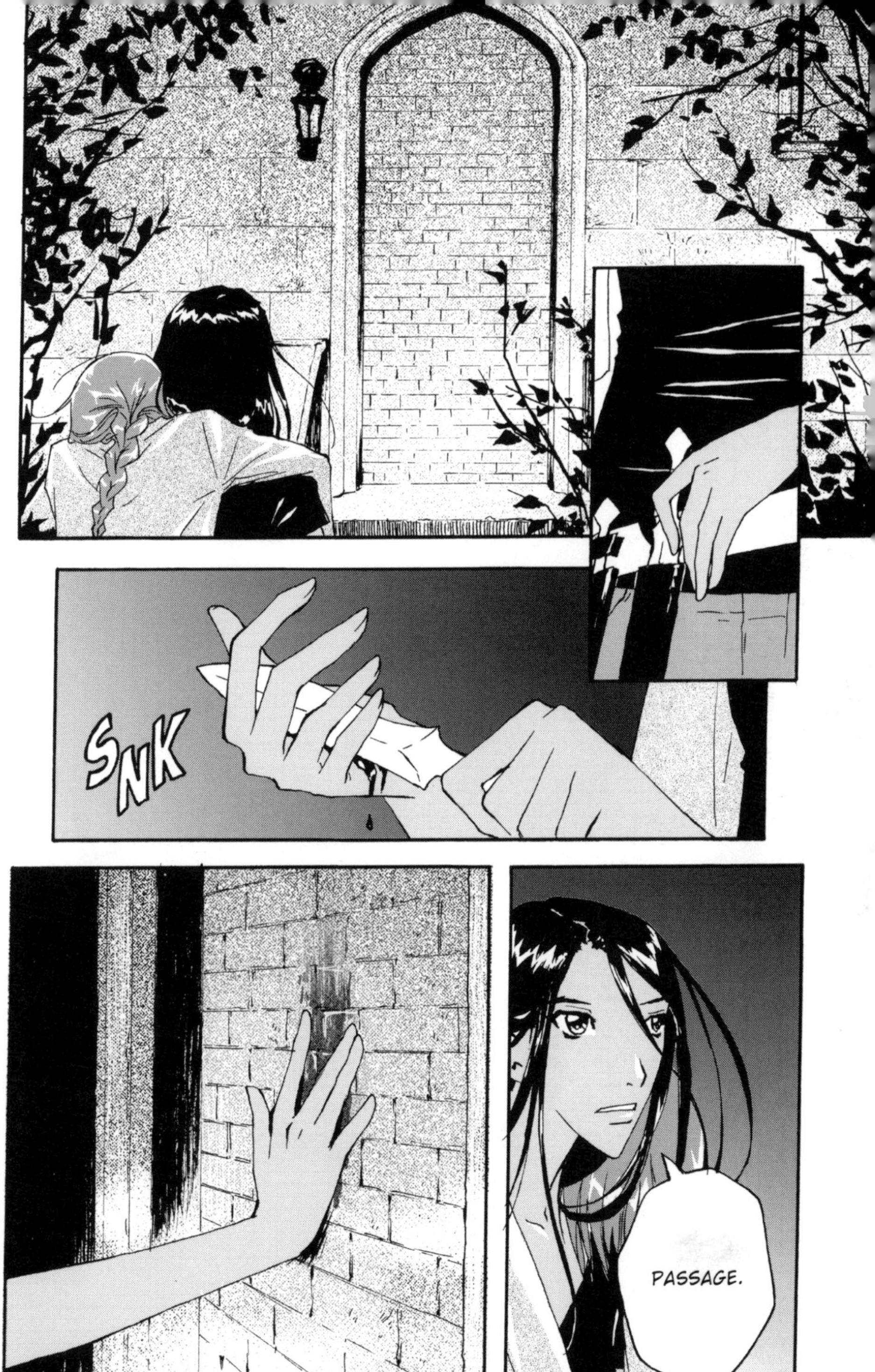

SNK
PASSAGE.

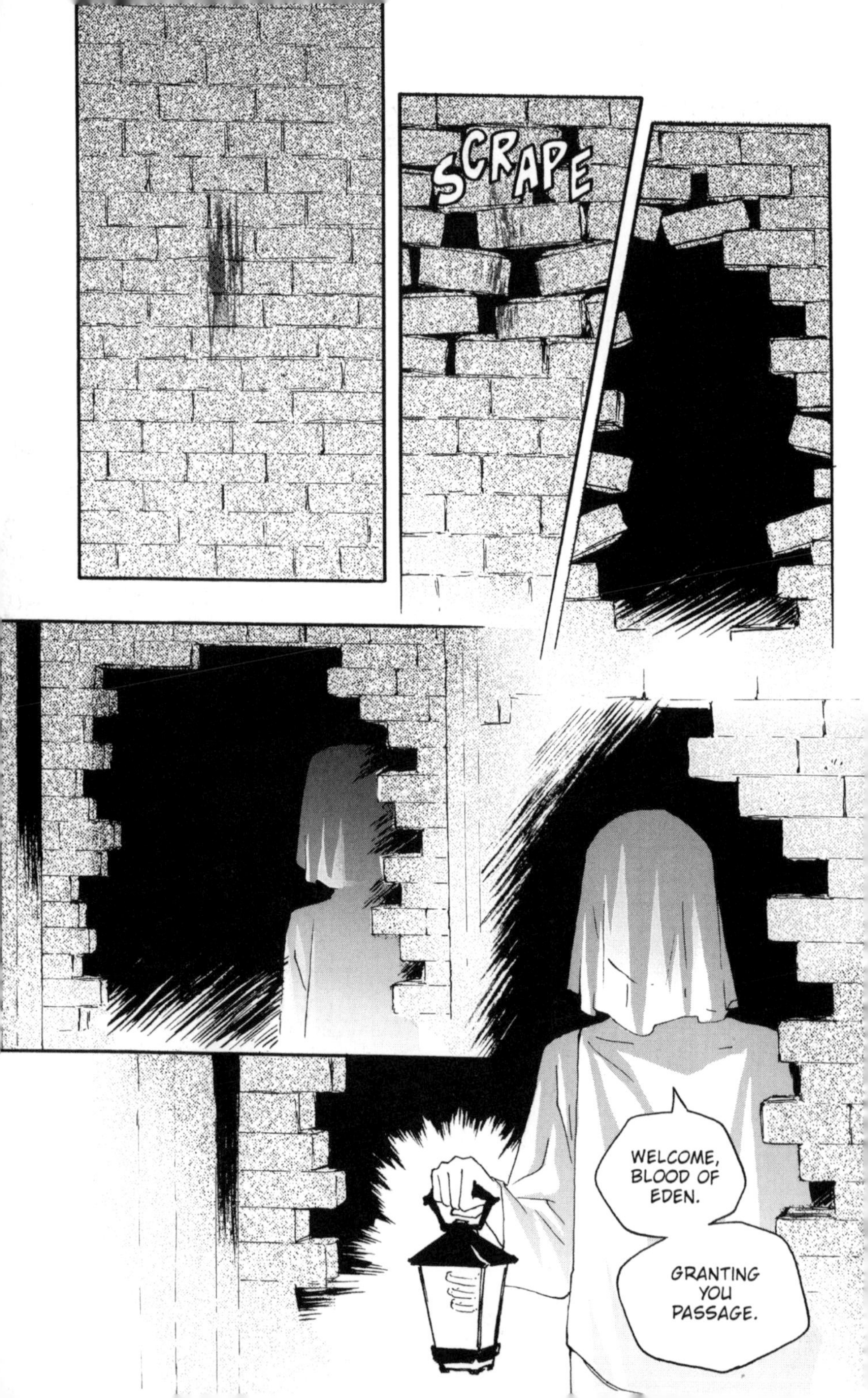
SCRAPE
WELCOME, BLOOD OF EDEN.
GRANTING YOU PASSAGE.

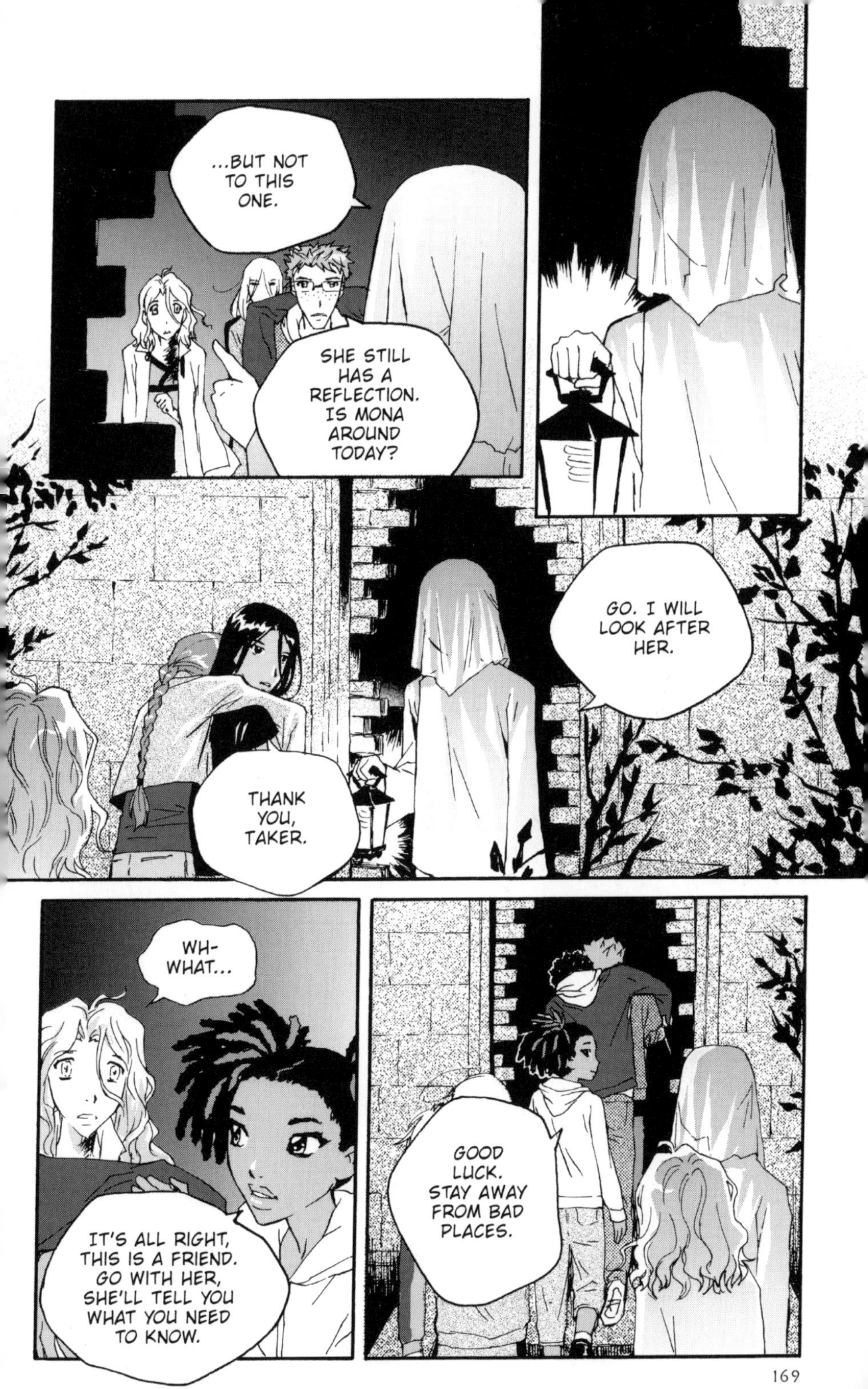
...BUT NOT TO THIS ONE.
SHE STILL HAS A REFLECTION. IS MONA AROUND TODAY?
GO. I WILL LOOK AFTER HER.
THANK YOU, TAKER.
WH-WHAT...
IT'S ALL RIGHT, THIS IS A FRIEND. GO WITH HER, SHE'LL TELL YOU WHAT YOU NEED TO KNOW.
GOOD LUCK. STAY AWAY FROM BAD PLACES.

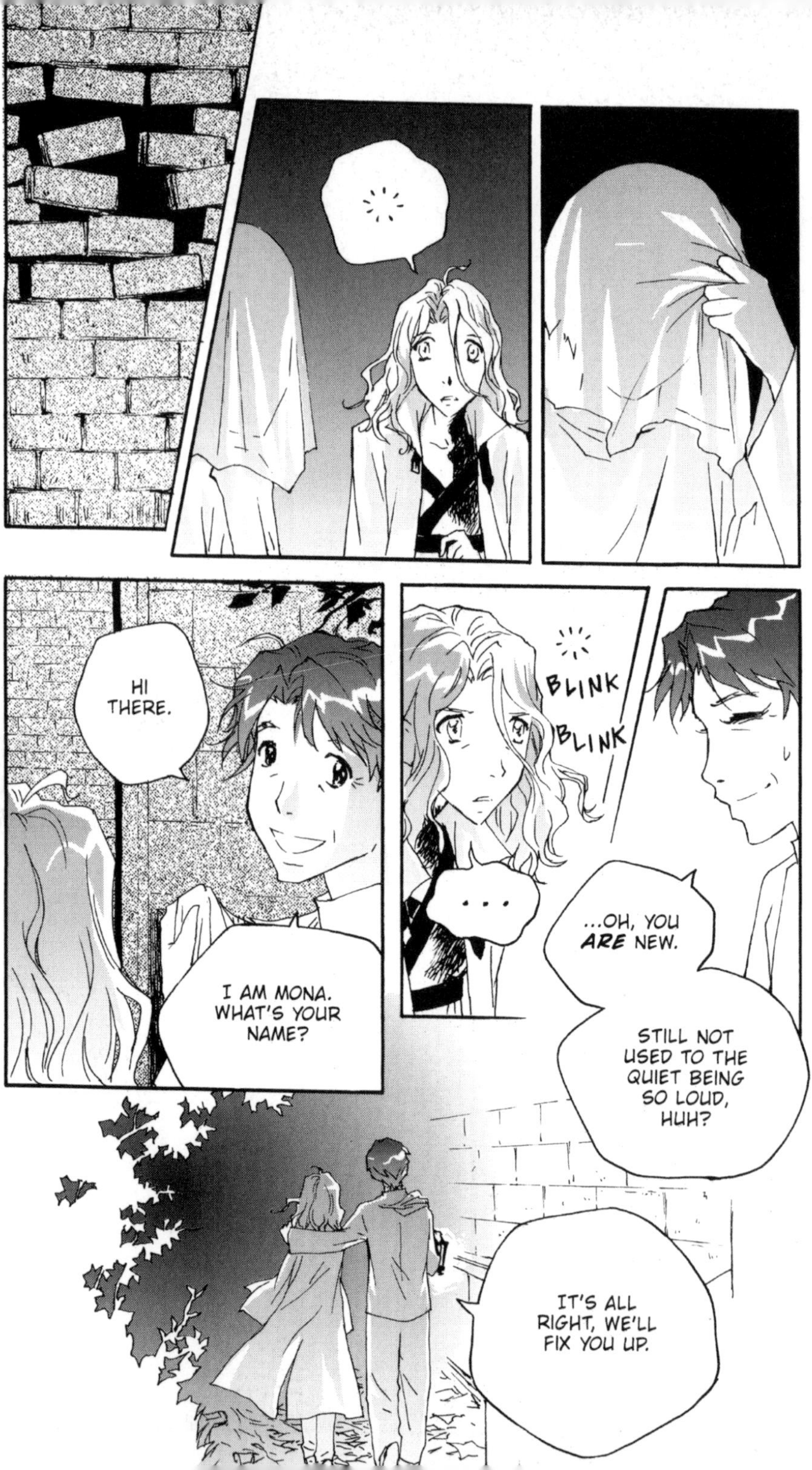
HI THERE.
I AM MONA. WHAT'S YOUR NAME?
BLINK
BLINK
...
...OH, YOU ARE NEW.
STILL NOT USED TO THE QUIET BEING SO LOUD, HUH?
IT'S ALL RIGHT, WE'LL FIX YOU UP.

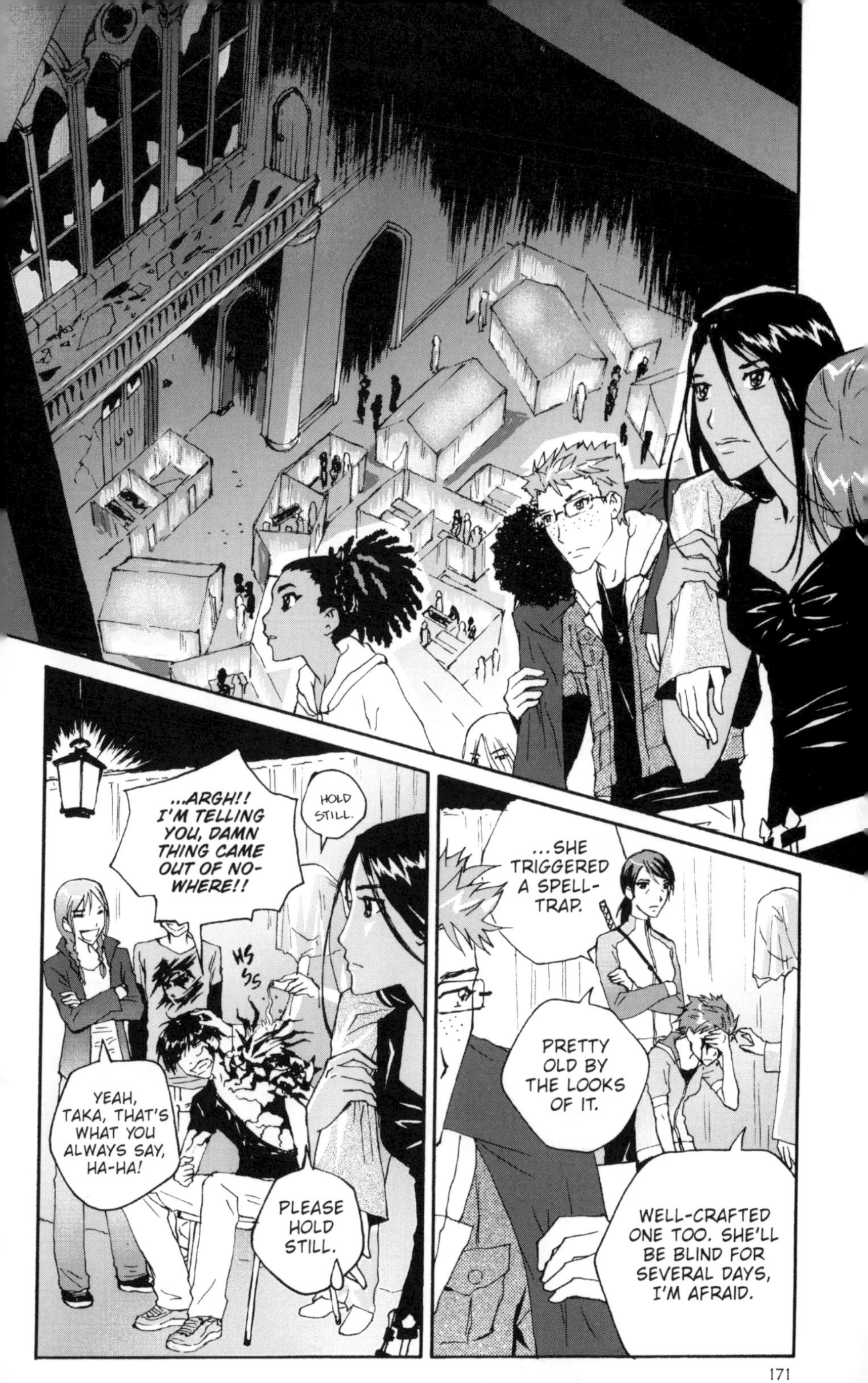
...ARGH!! I'M TELLING YOU, DAMN THING CAME OUT OF NO-WHERE!!
HOLD STILL.
HSSS
YEAH, TAKA, THAT'S WHAT YOU ALWAYS SAY, HA-HA!
PLEASE HOLD STILL.
...SHE TRIGGERED A SPELL-TRAP.
PRETTY OLD BY THE LOOKS OF IT.
WELL-CRAFTED ONE TOO. SHE'LL BE BLIND FOR SEVERAL DAYS, I'M AFRAID.

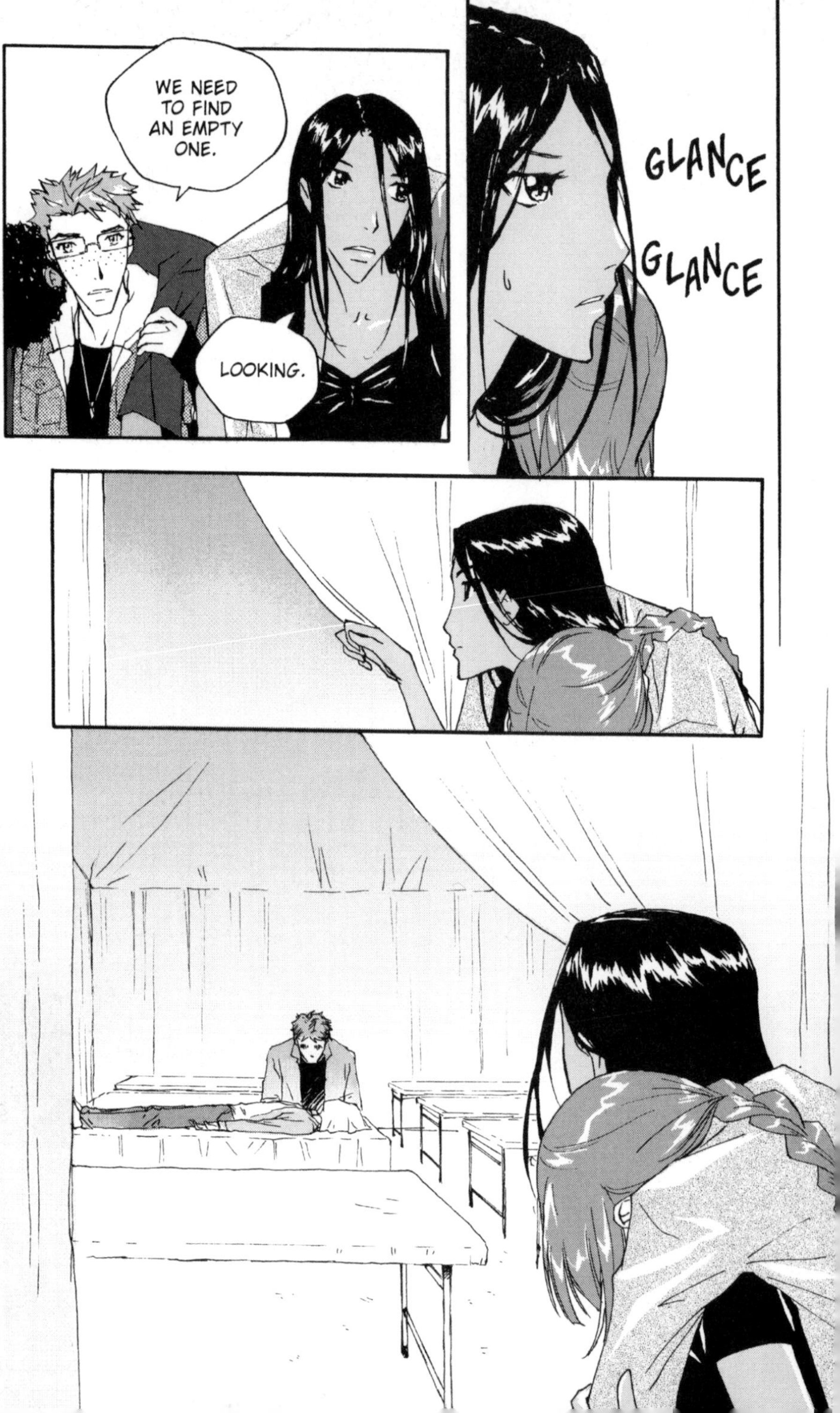

WE NEED TO FIND AN EMPTY ONE.
LOOKING.
GLANCE
GLANCE

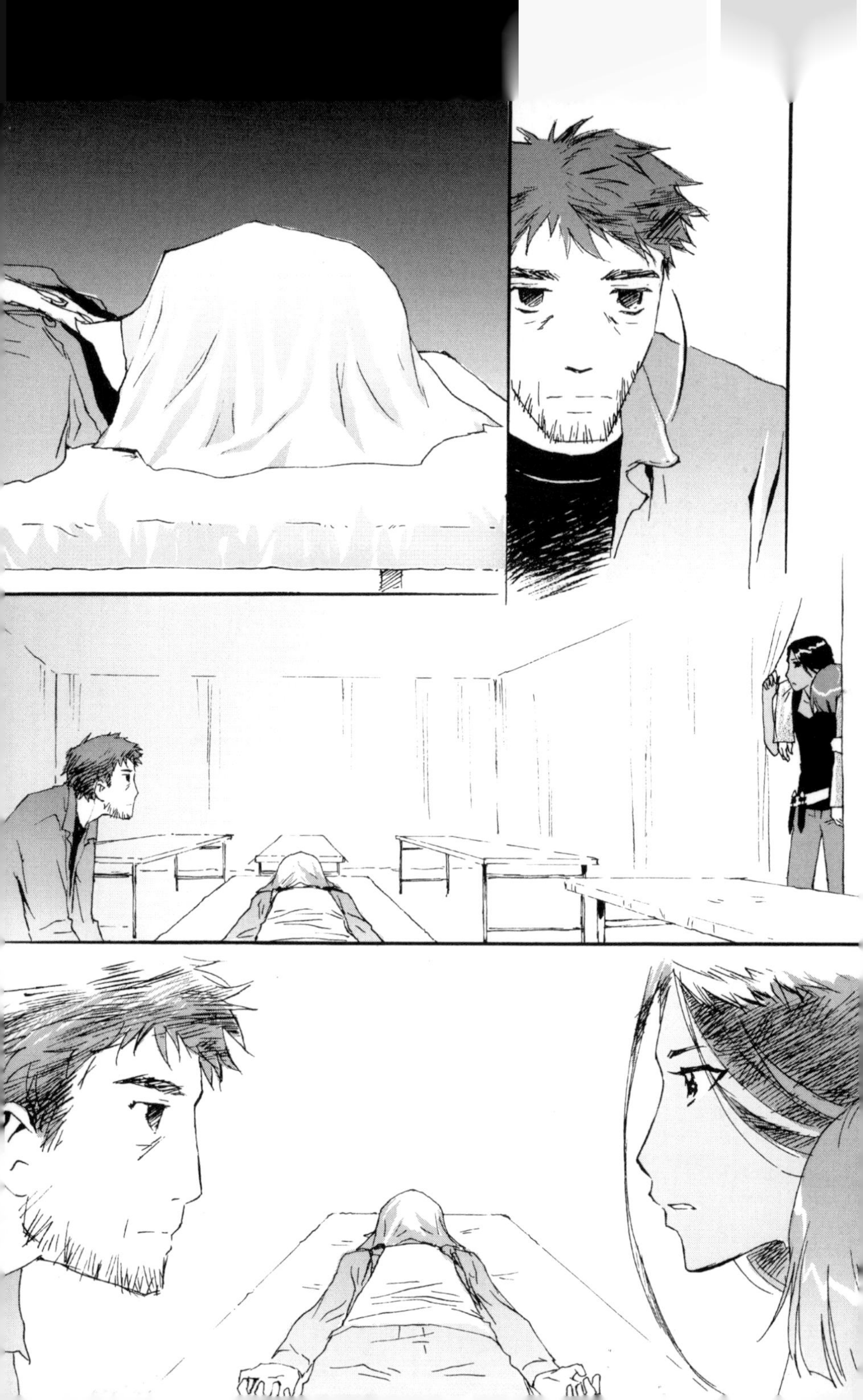

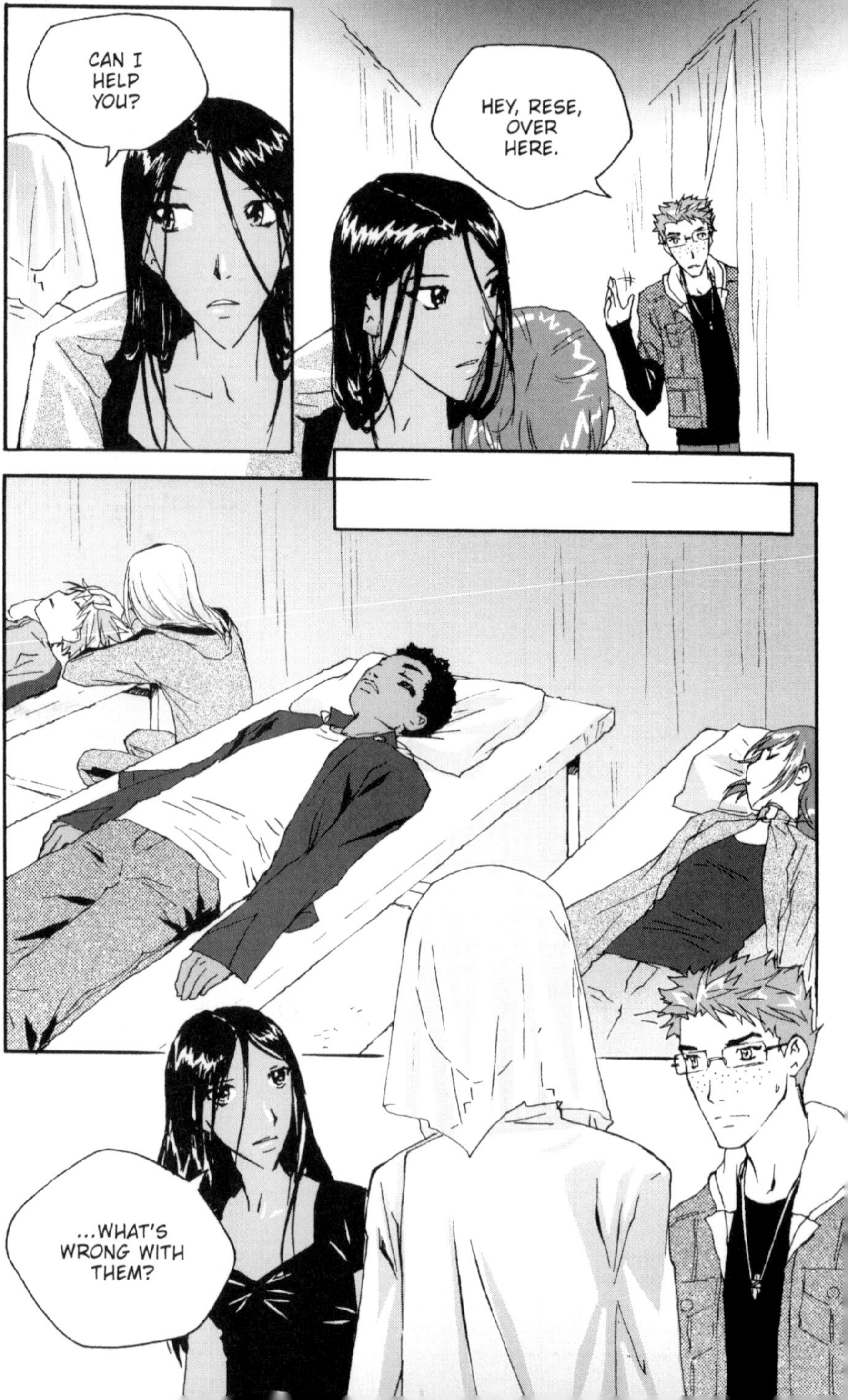
CAN I HELP YOU?
HEY, RESE, OVER HERE.
...WHAT'S WRONG WITH THEM?

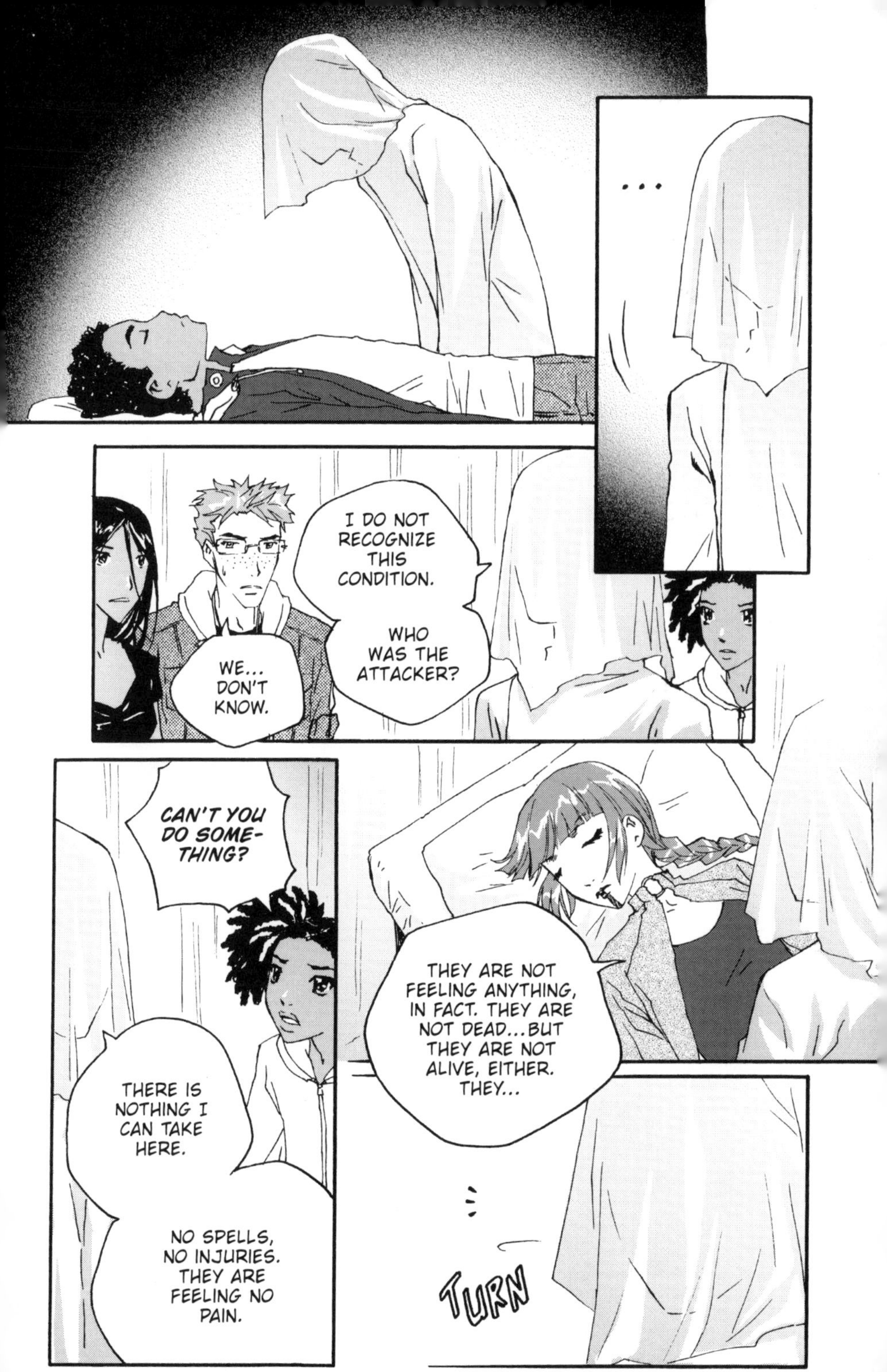
...
I DO NOT RECOGNIZE THIS CONDITION.
WHO WAS THE ATTACKER?
WE... DON'T KNOW.
CAN'T YOU DO SOME-THING?
THERE IS NOTHING I CAN TAKE HERE.
NO SPELLS, NO INJURIES. THEY ARE FEELING NO PAIN.
THEY ARE NOT FEELING ANYTHING, IN FACT. THEY ARE NOT DEAD...BUT THEY ARE NOT ALIVE, EITHER. THEY...
TURN

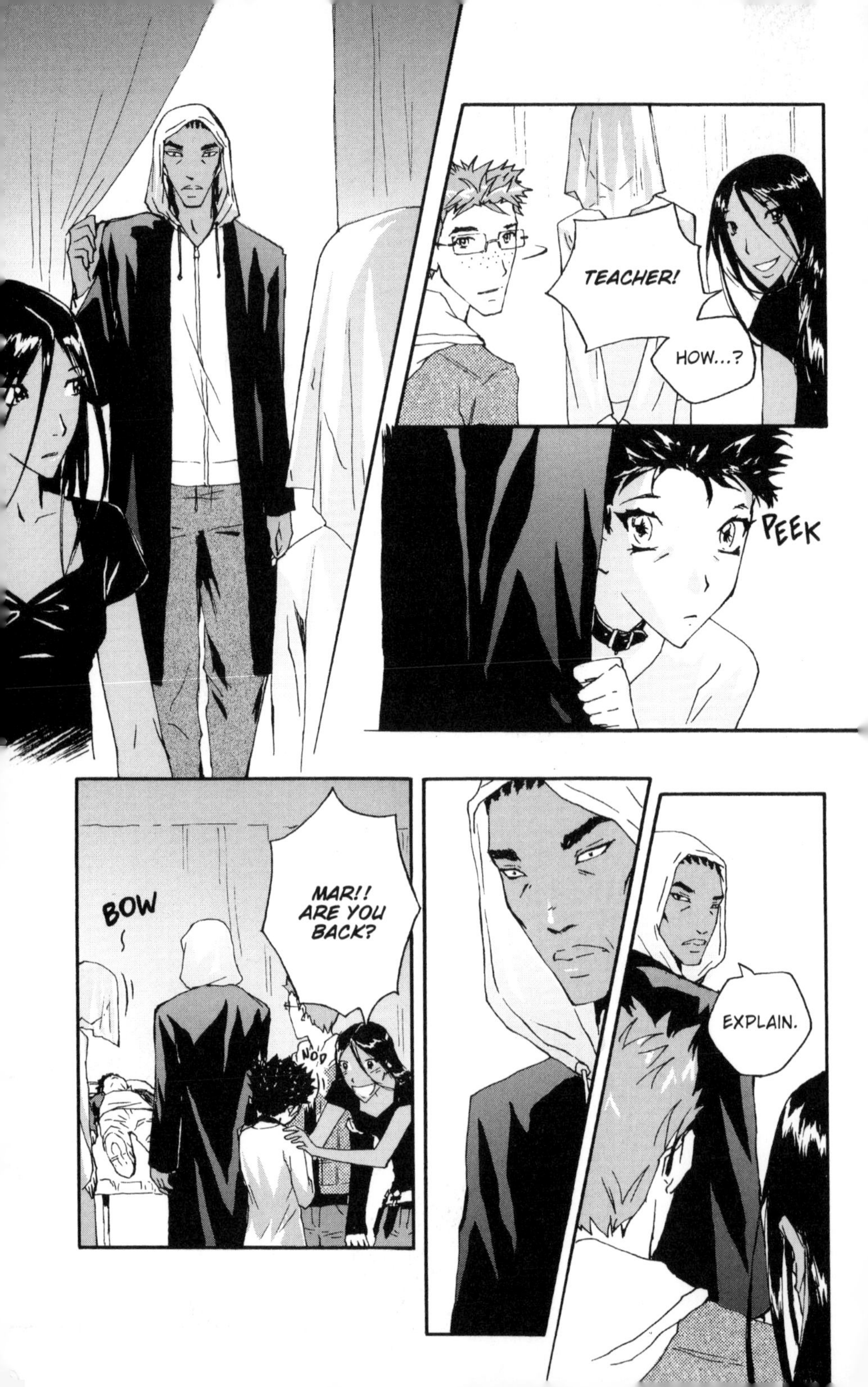
TEACHER!
HOW...?
PEEK
EXPLAIN.
MAR!! ARE YOU BACK?
BOW
NOD

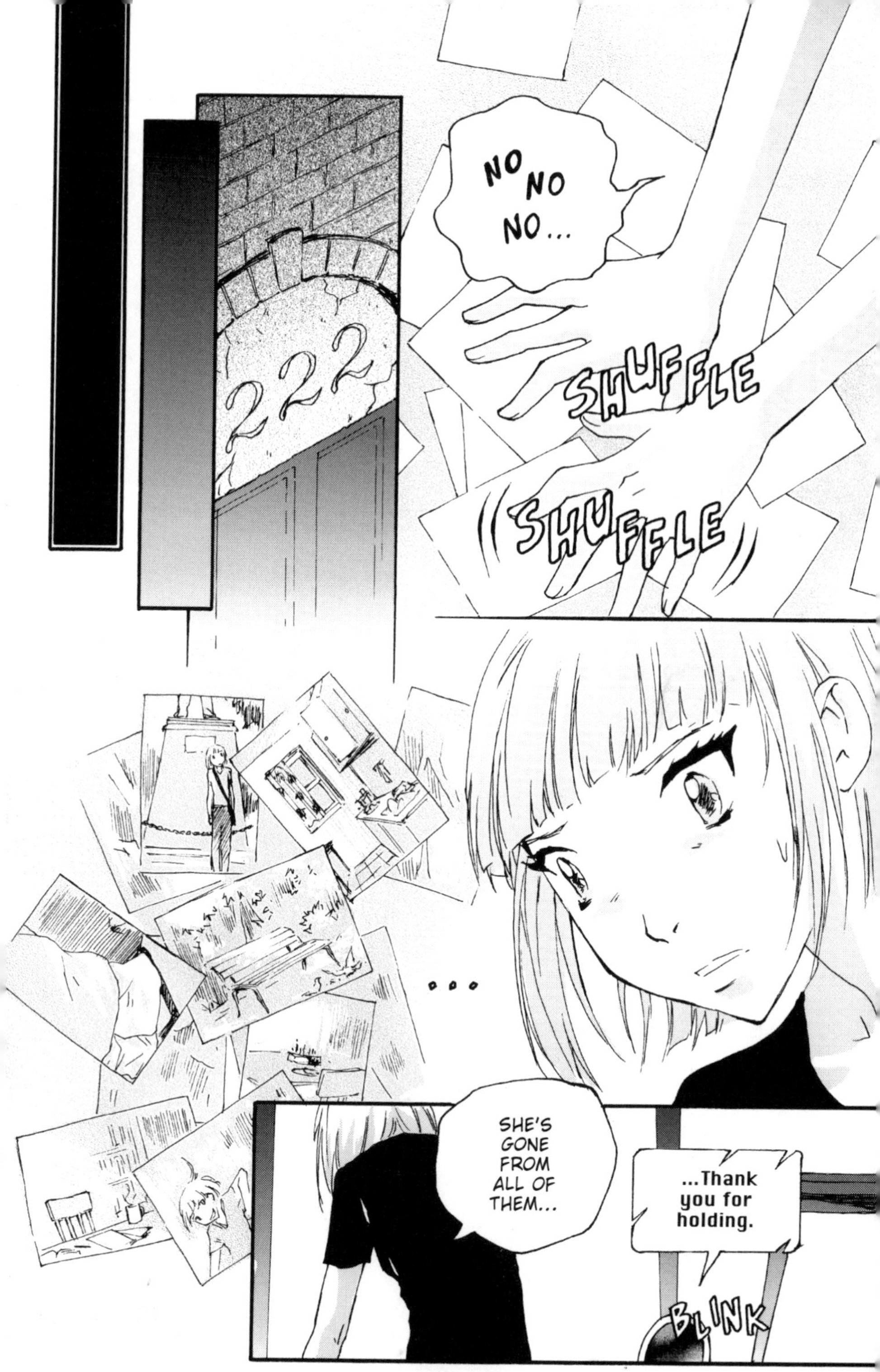
NO NO NO...
SHUFFLE
SHUFFLE
...
SHE'S GONE FROM ALL OF THEM...
...Thank you for holding.
BLINK

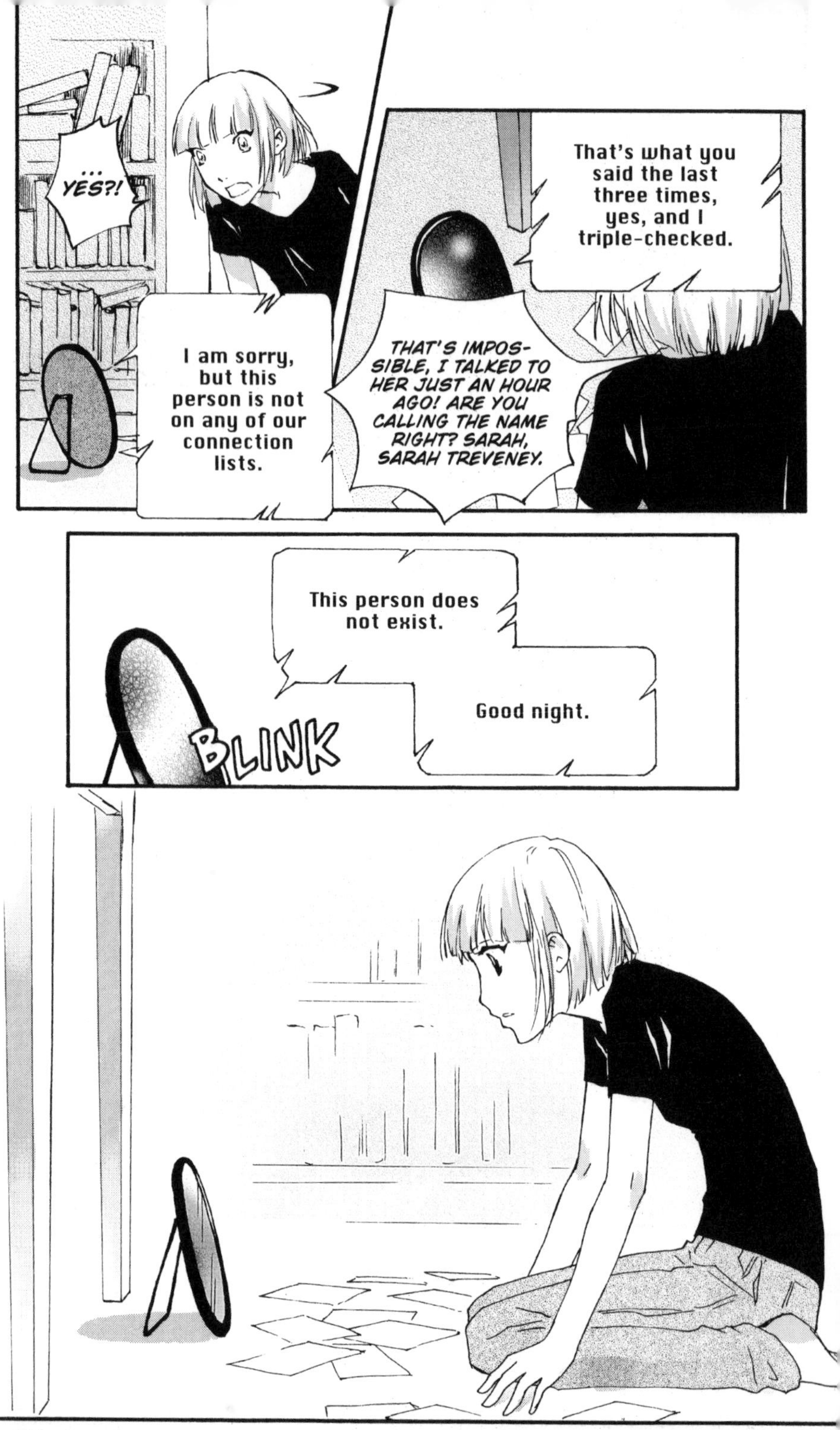

...YES?!
I am sorry, but this person is not on any of our connection lists.
THAT'S IMPOSSIBLE, I TALKED TO HER JUST AN HOUR AGO! ARE YOU CALLING THE NAME RIGHT? SARAH, SARAH TREVENEY.
That's what you said the last three times, yes, and I triple-checked.
This person does not exist.
Good night.
BLINK

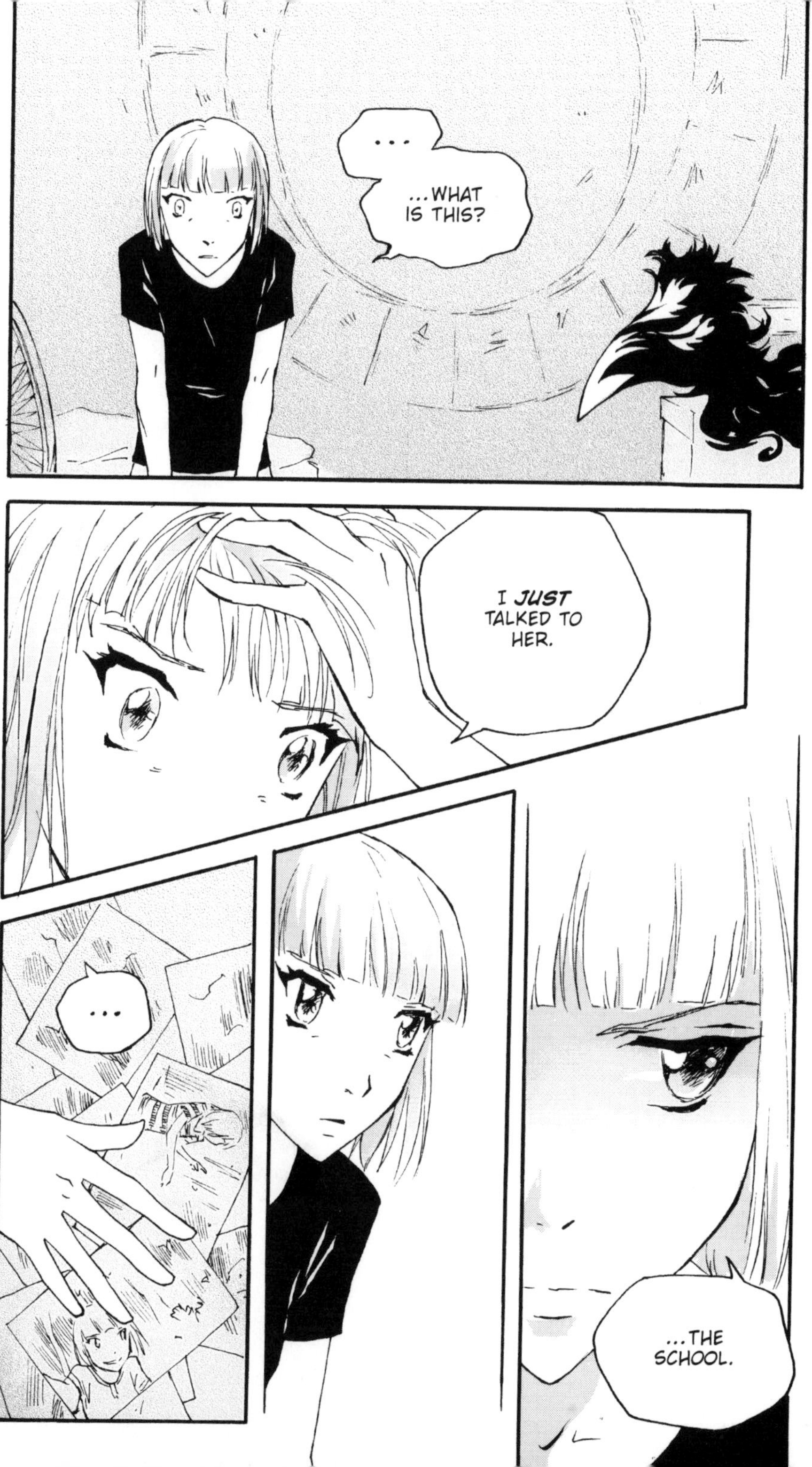
...
...WHAT IS THIS?
I *JUST* TALKED TO HER.
...
...THE SCHOOL.

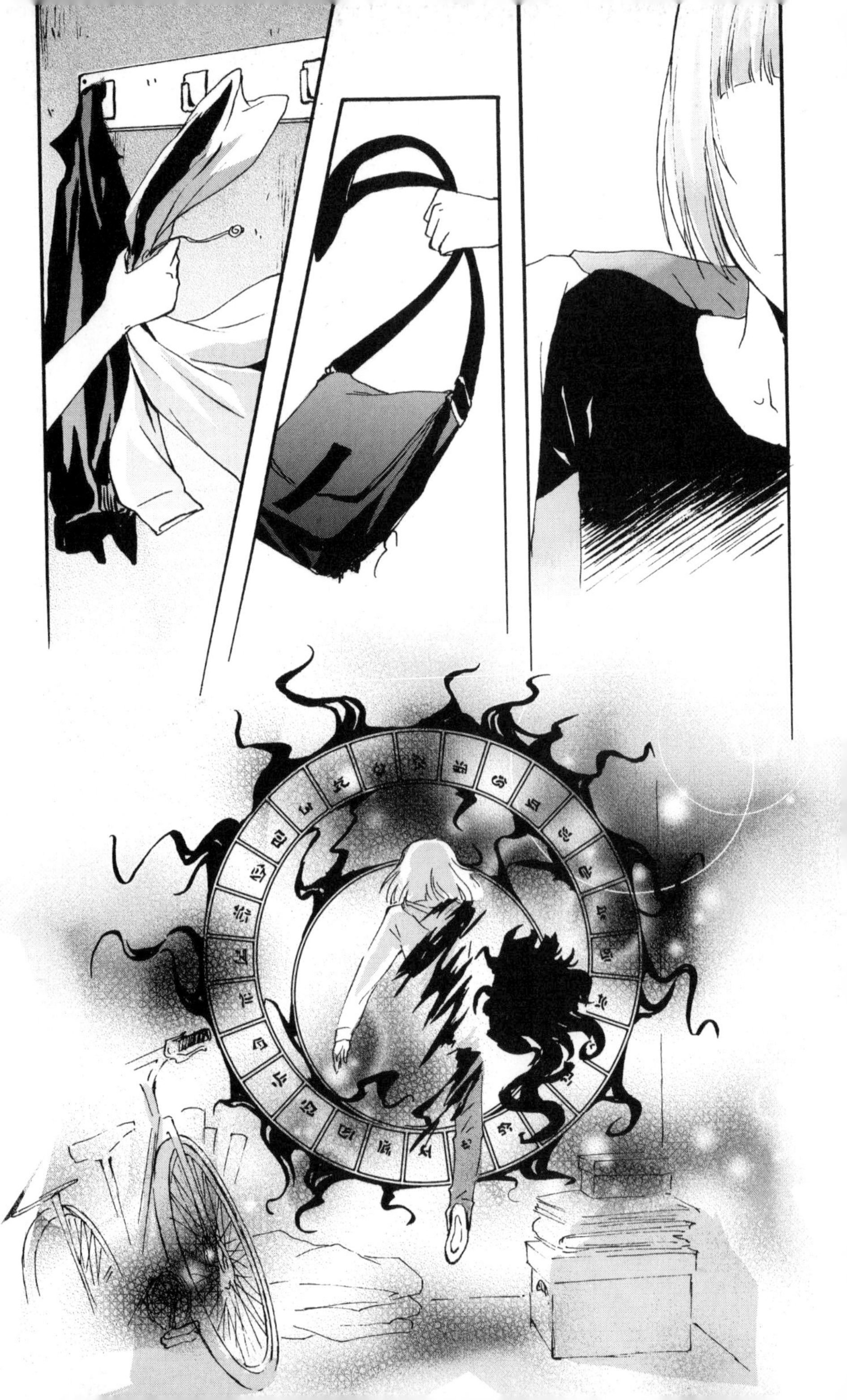

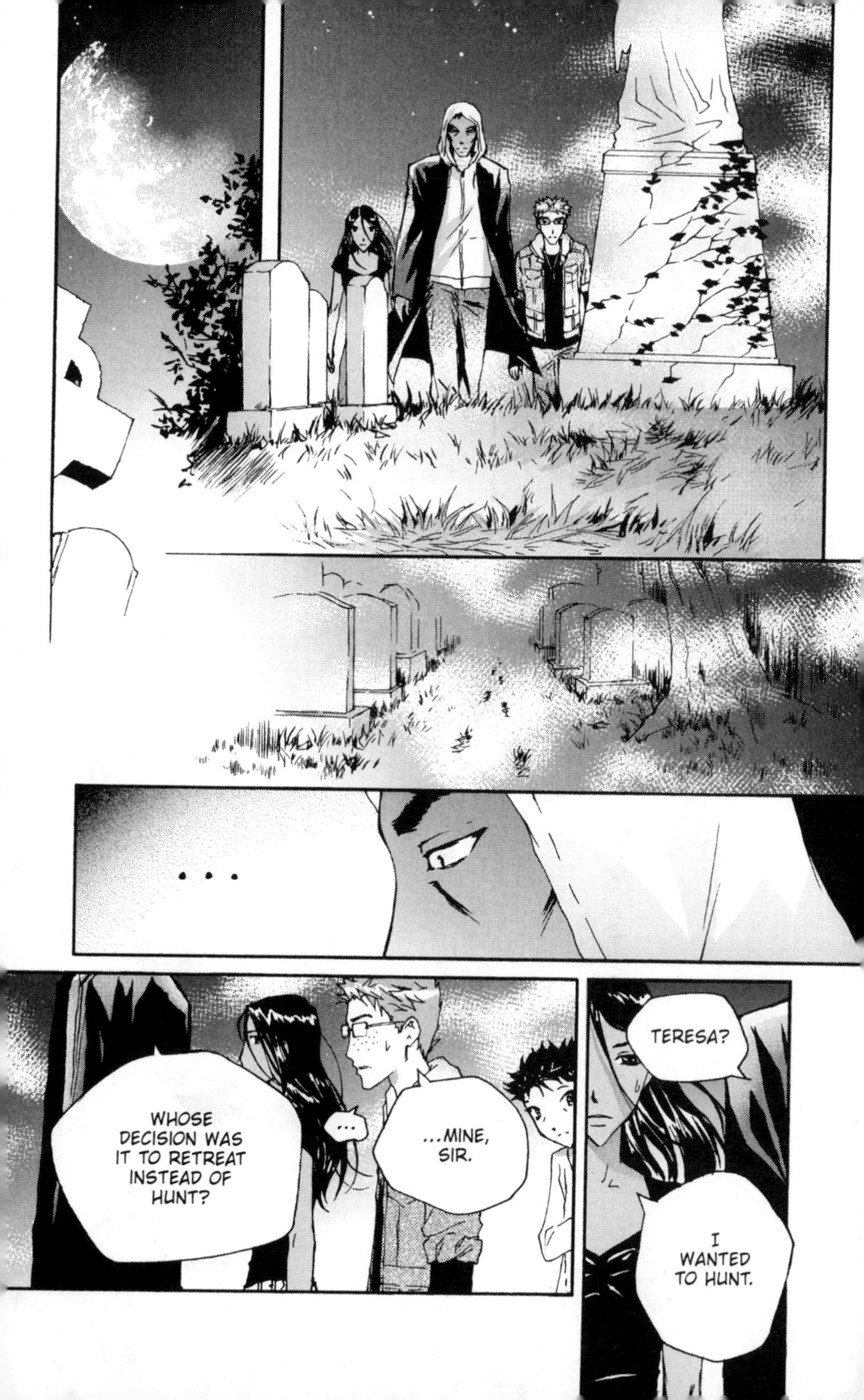
. . .
WHOSE DECISION WAS IT TO RETREAT INSTEAD OF HUNT?
...
...MINE, SIR.
TERESA?
I WANTED TO HUNT.

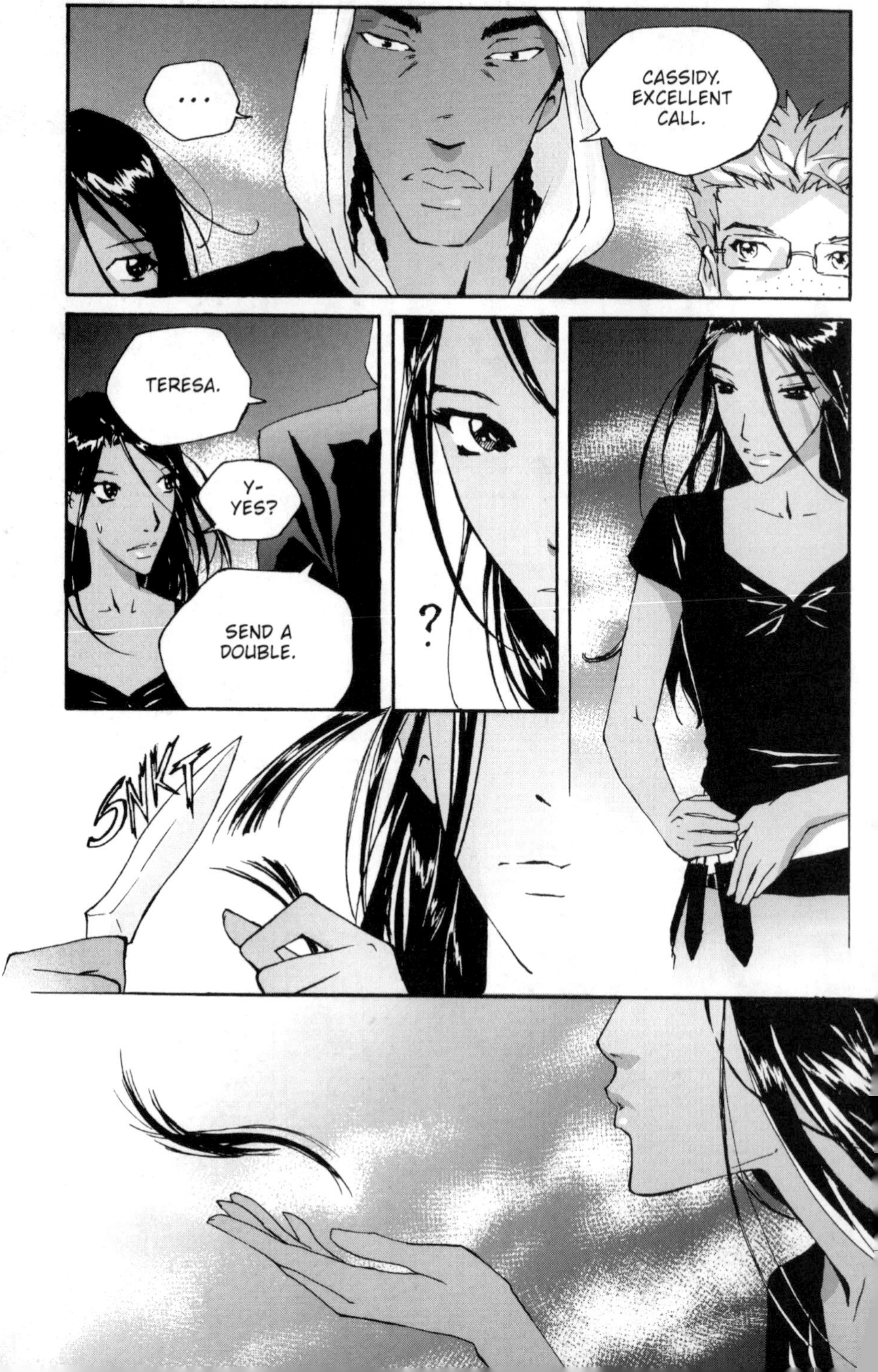
...
CASSIDY. EXCELLENT CALL.
TERESA.
Y-YES?
SEND A DOUBLE.
?
SNKT

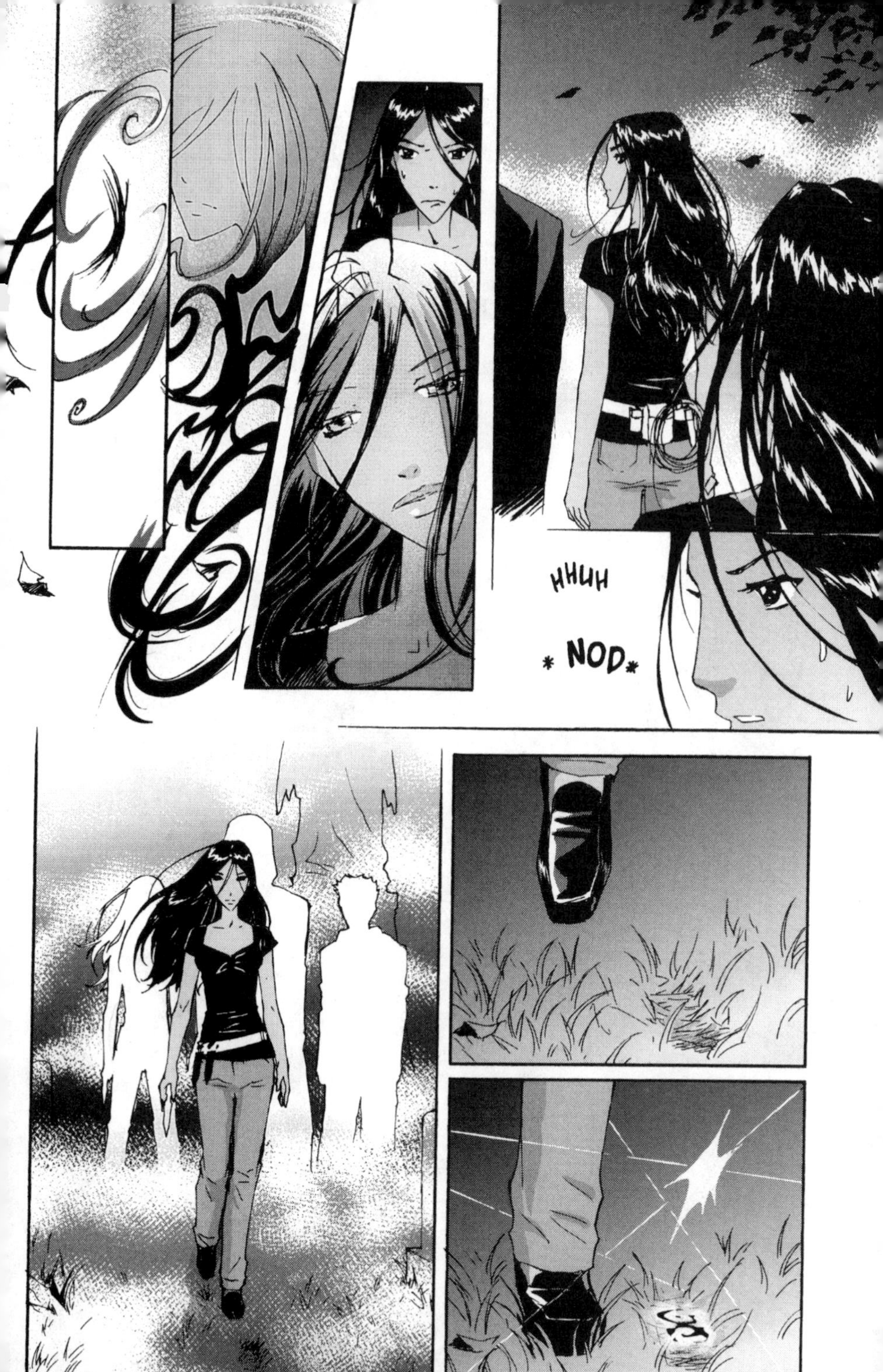

HHUH
NOD

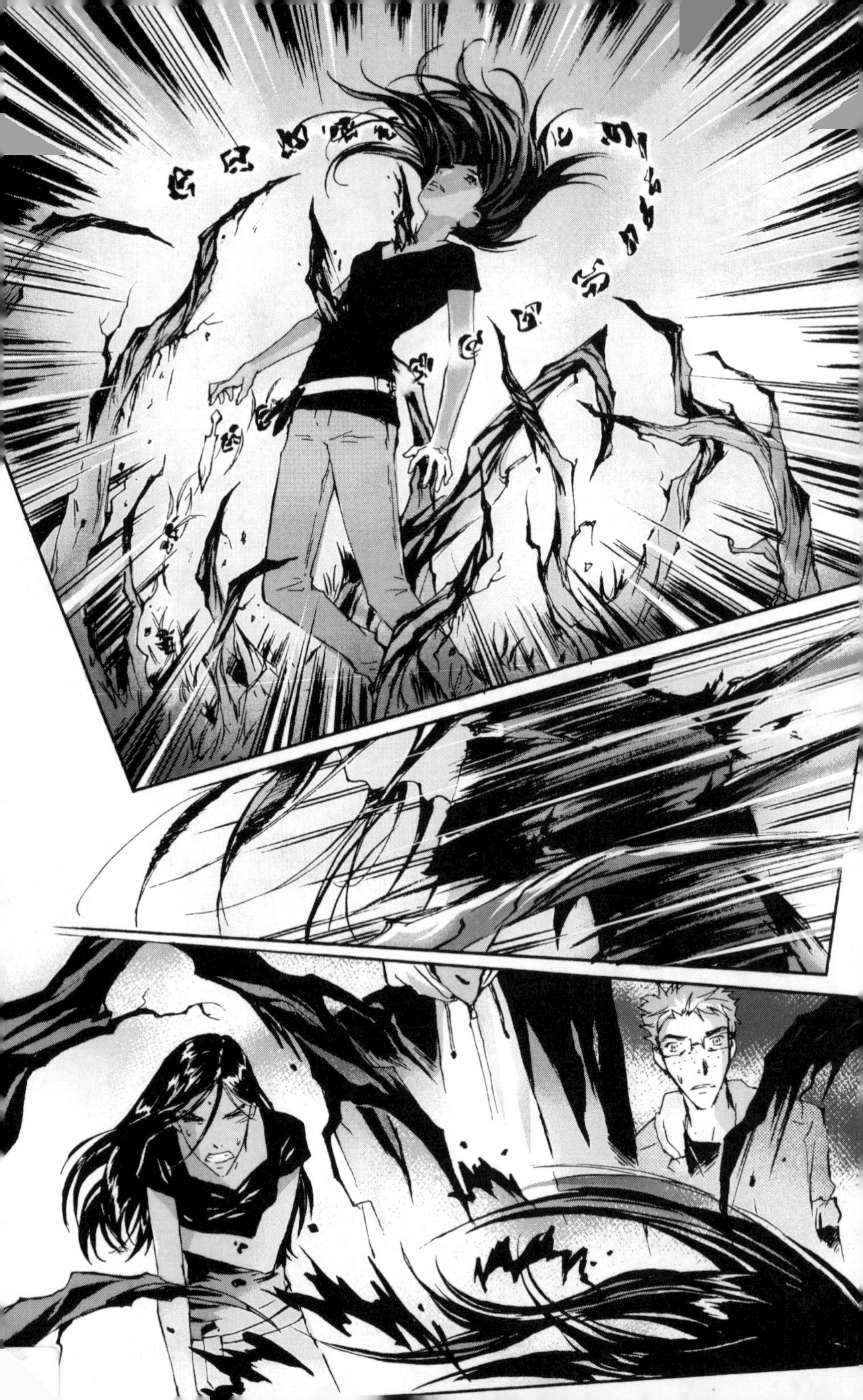

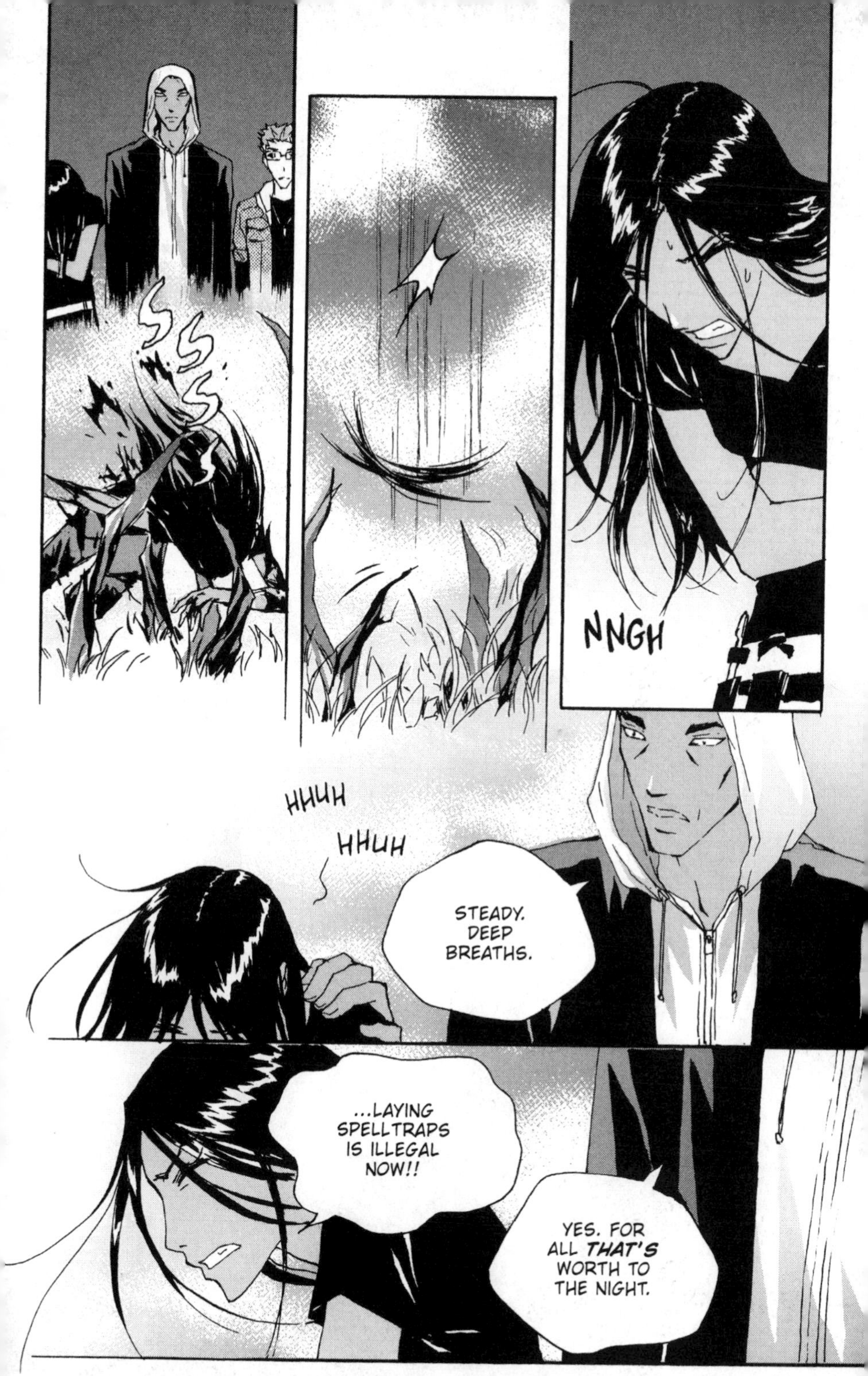
NNGH
HHUH
HHUH
STEADY. DEEP BREATHS.
...LAYING SPELLTRAPS IS ILLEGAL NOW!!
YES. FOR ALL *THAT'S* WORTH TO THE NIGHT.

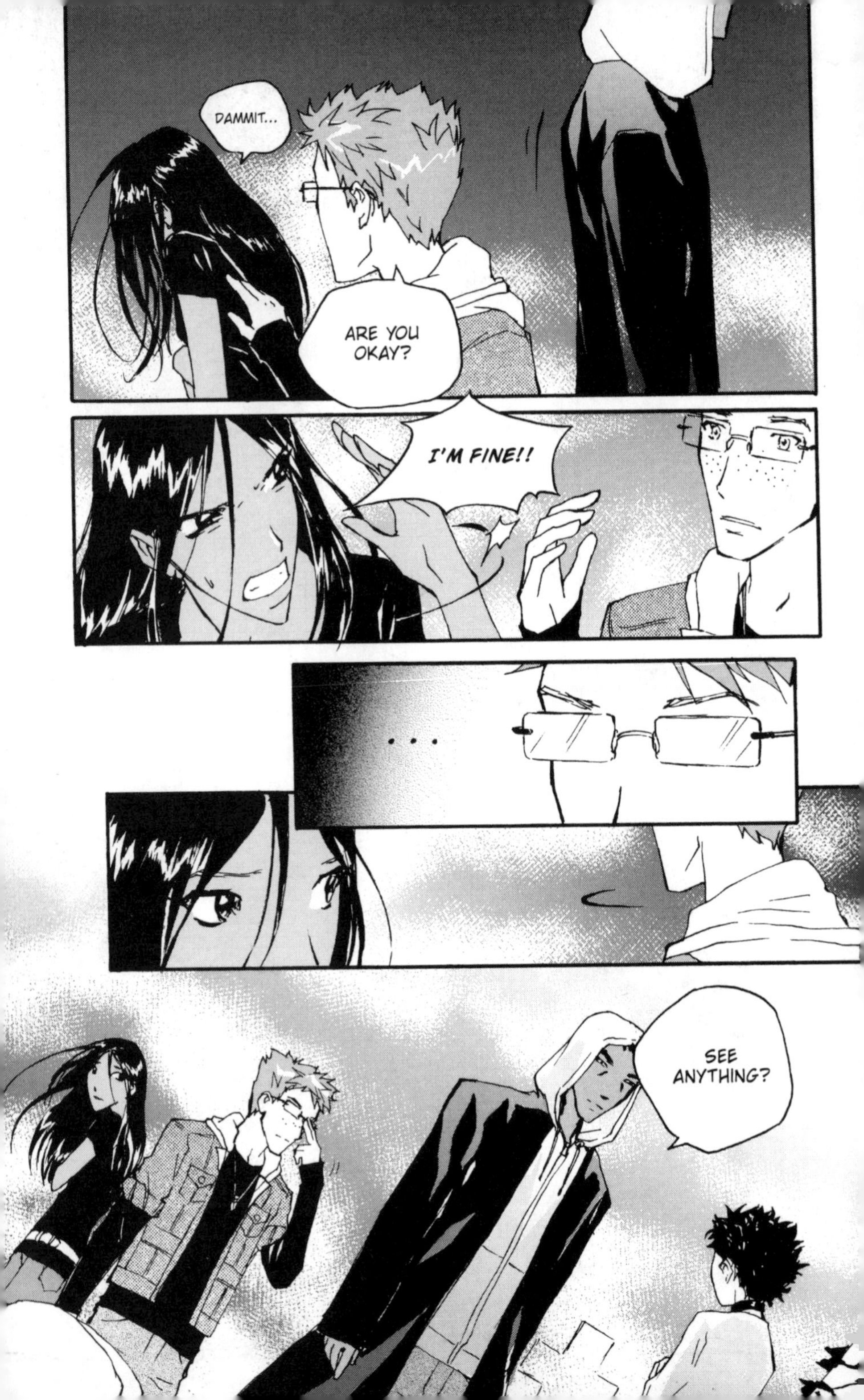
DAMMIT...
ARE YOU OKAY?
I'M FINE!!
...
SEE ANYTHING?

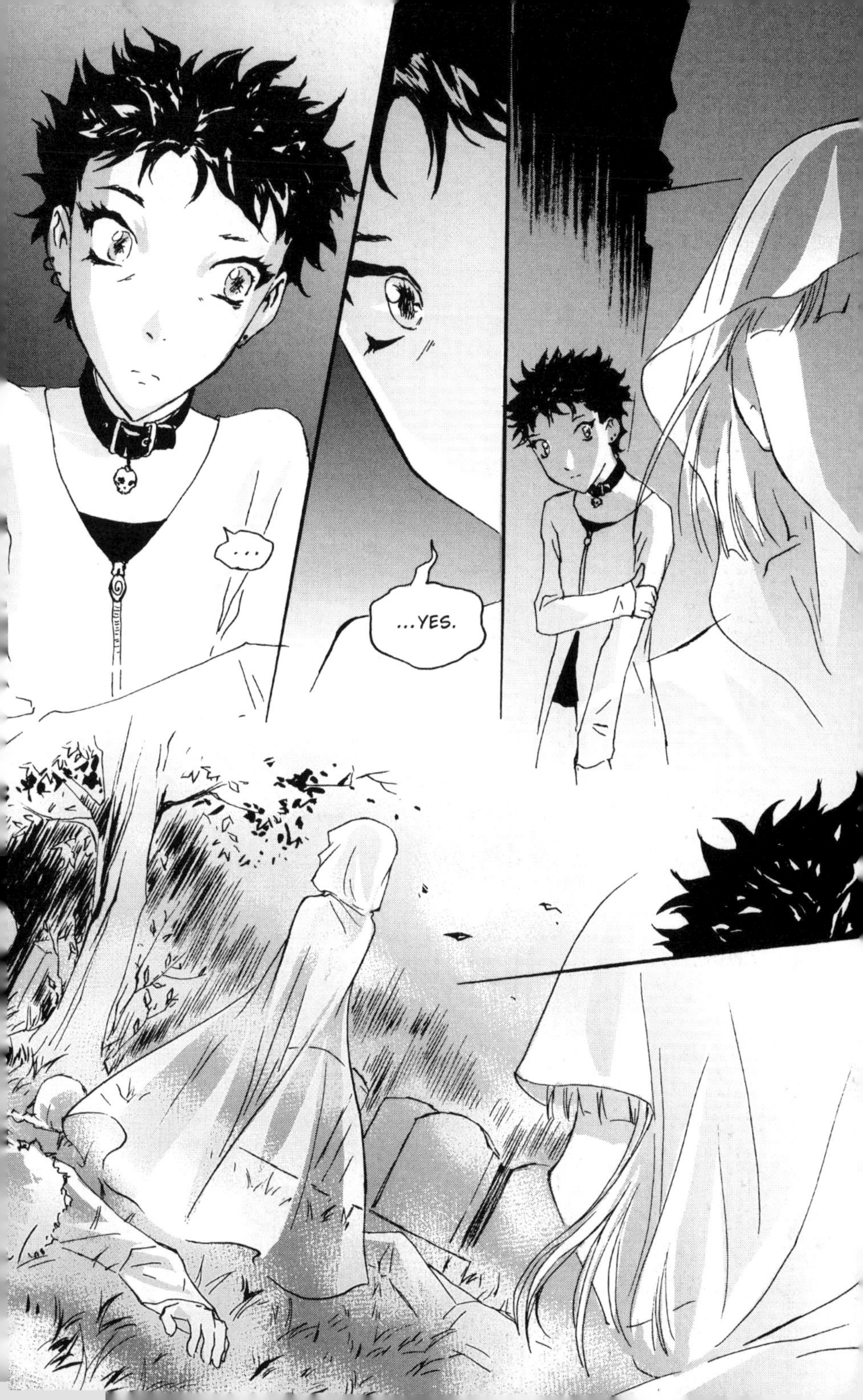
...
...YES.

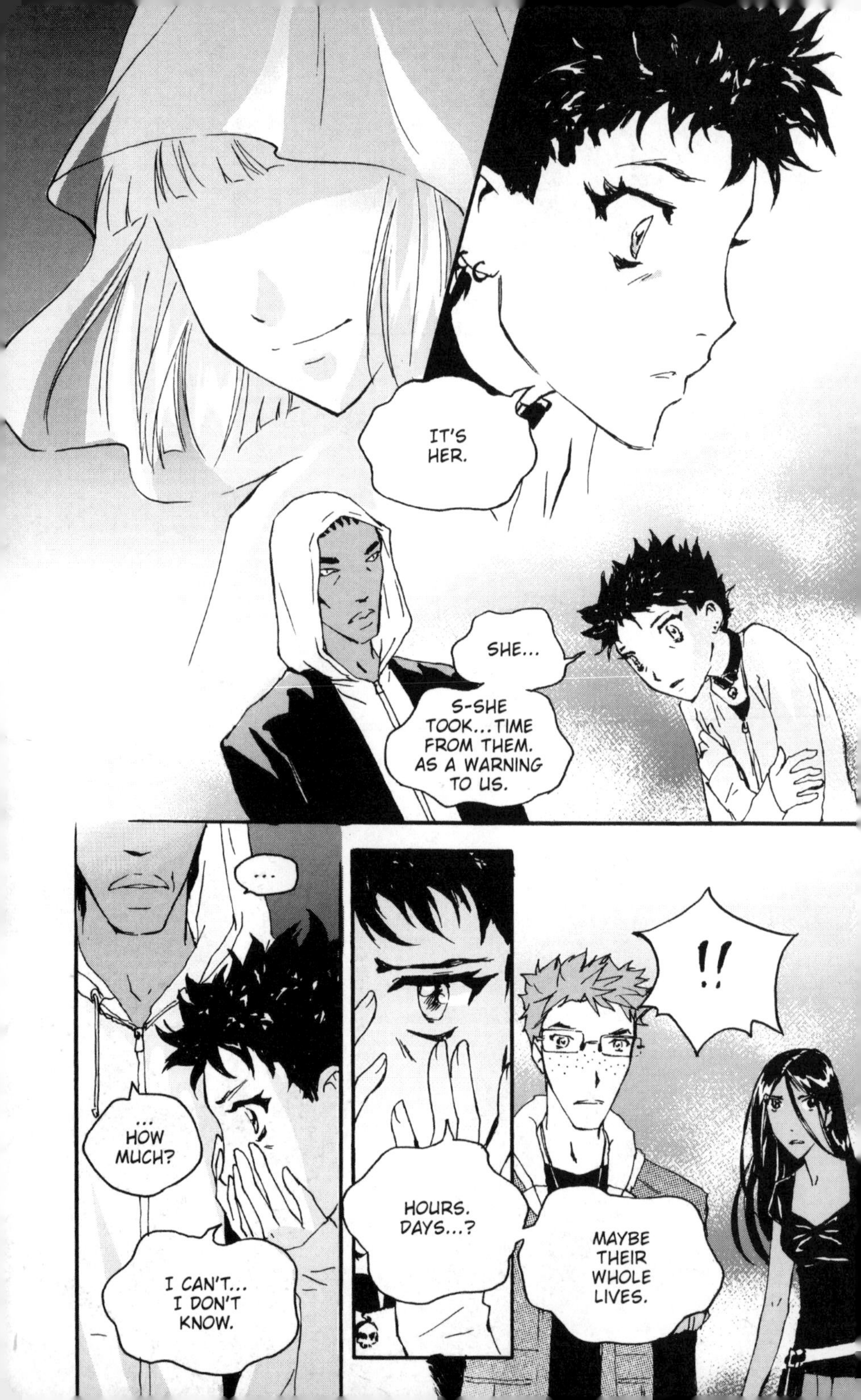
IT'S HER.
SHE...
S-SHE TOOK...TIME FROM THEM. AS A WARNING TO US.
...
... HOW MUCH?
I CAN'T... I DON'T KNOW.
HOURS. DAYS...?
!!
MAYBE THEIR WHOLE LIVES.

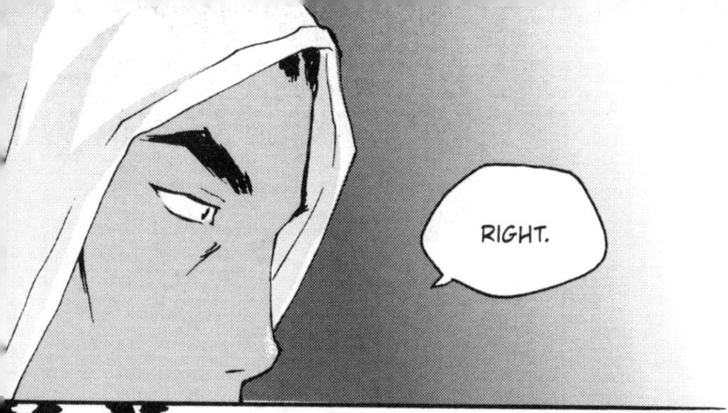
RIGHT.

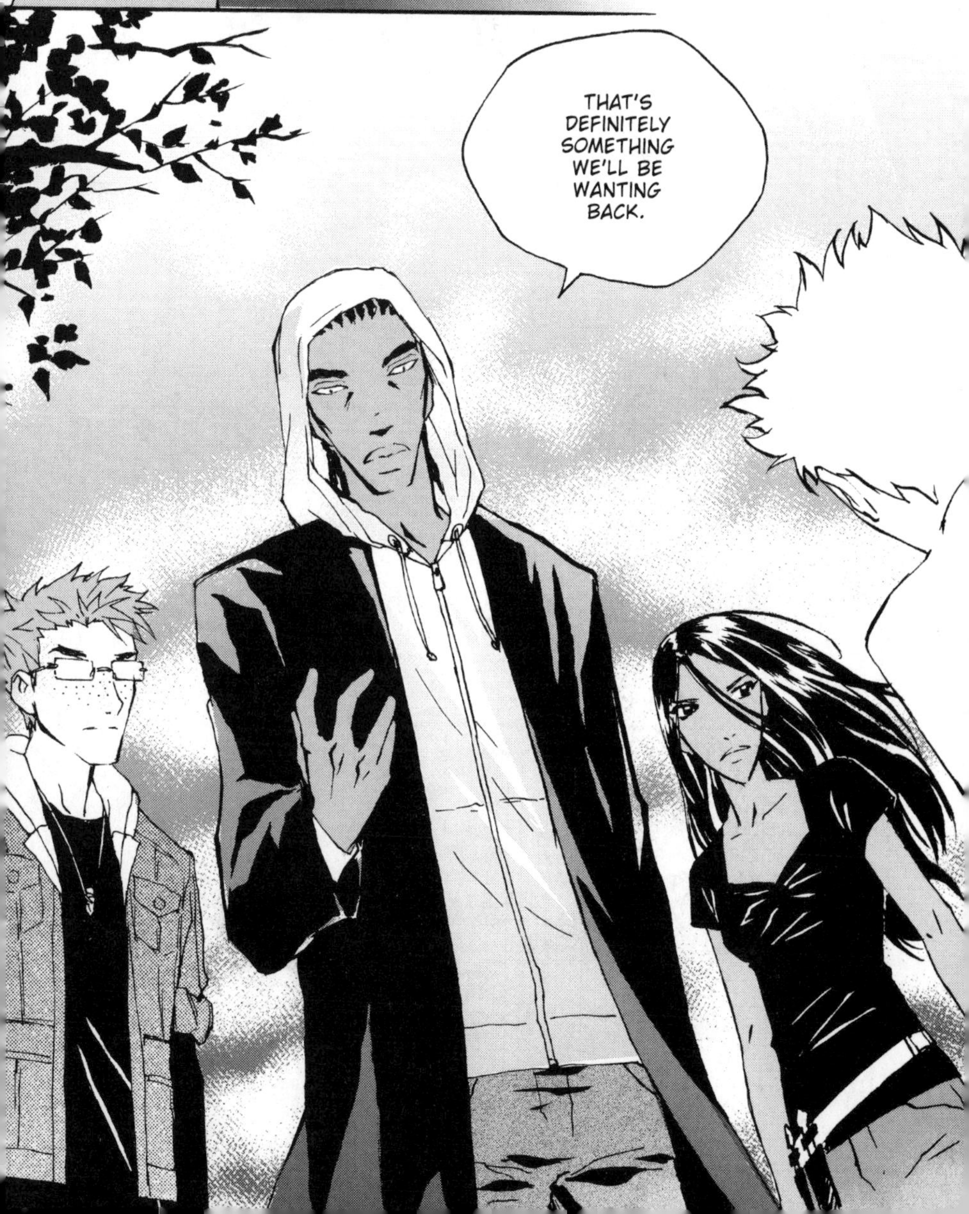
THAT'S DEFINITELY SOMETHING WE'LL BE WANTING BACK.

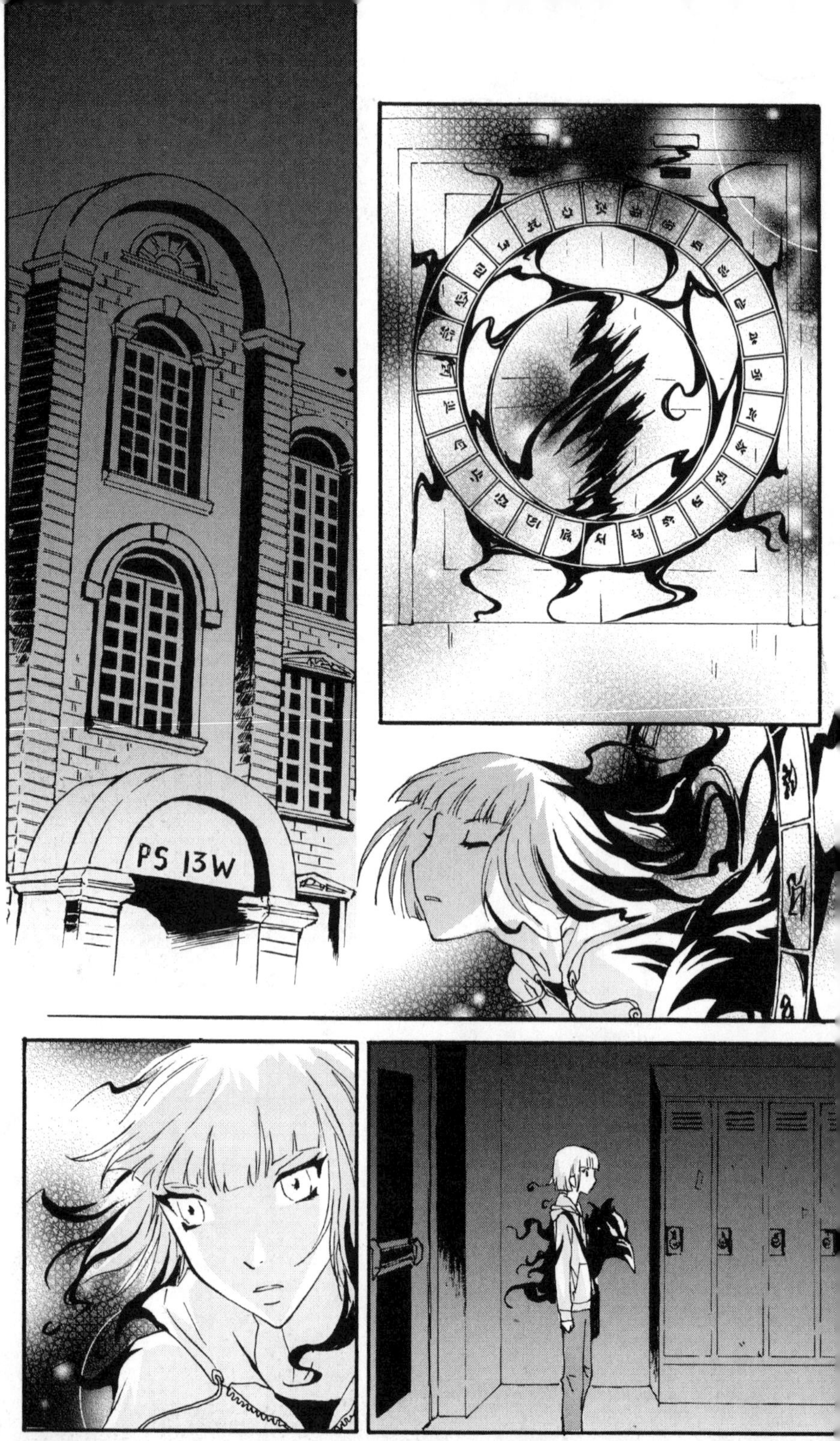
PS 13W

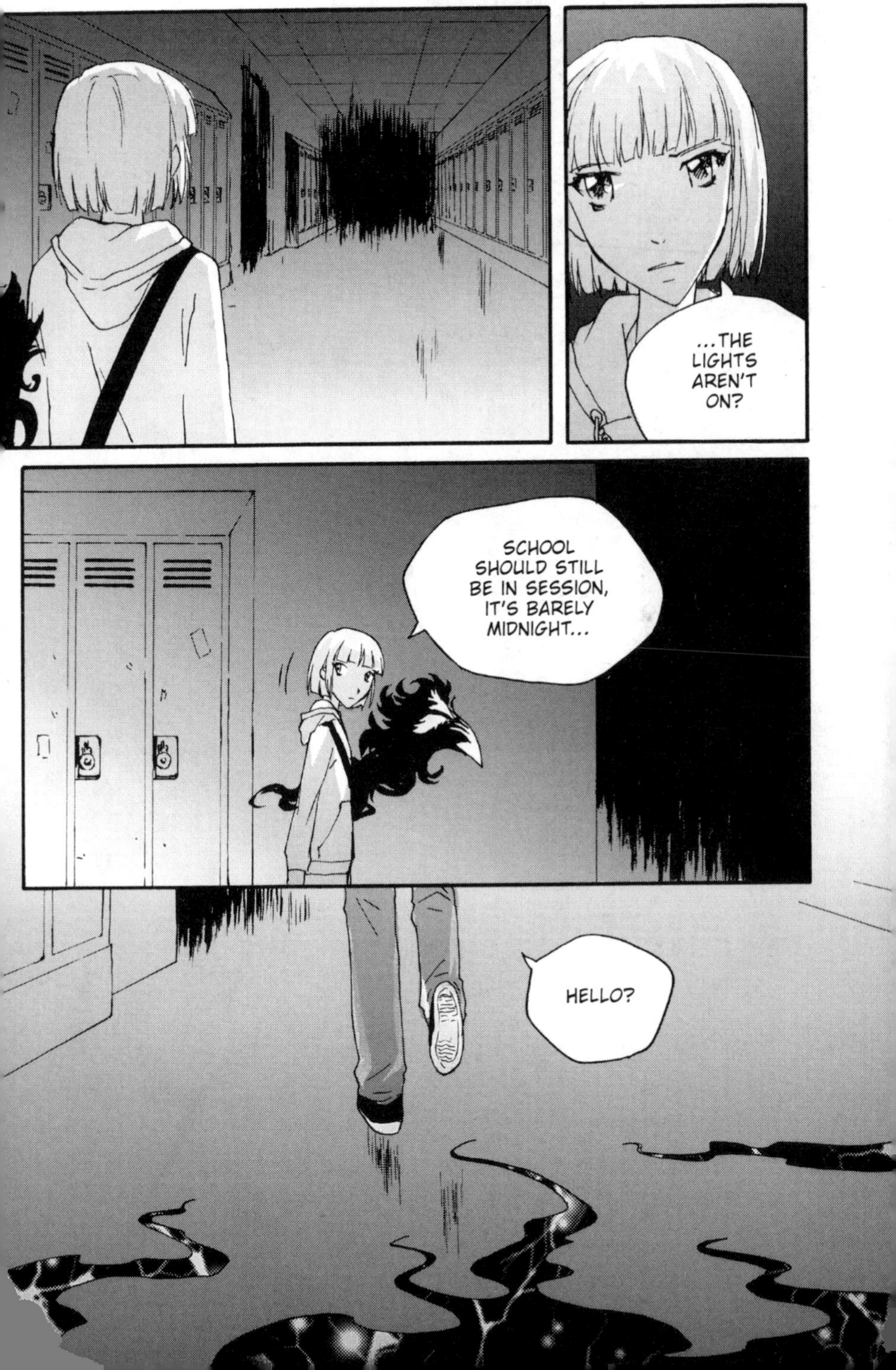
...THE LIGHTS AREN'T ON?
SCHOOL SHOULD STILL BE IN SESSION, IT'S BARELY MIDNIGHT...
HELLO?

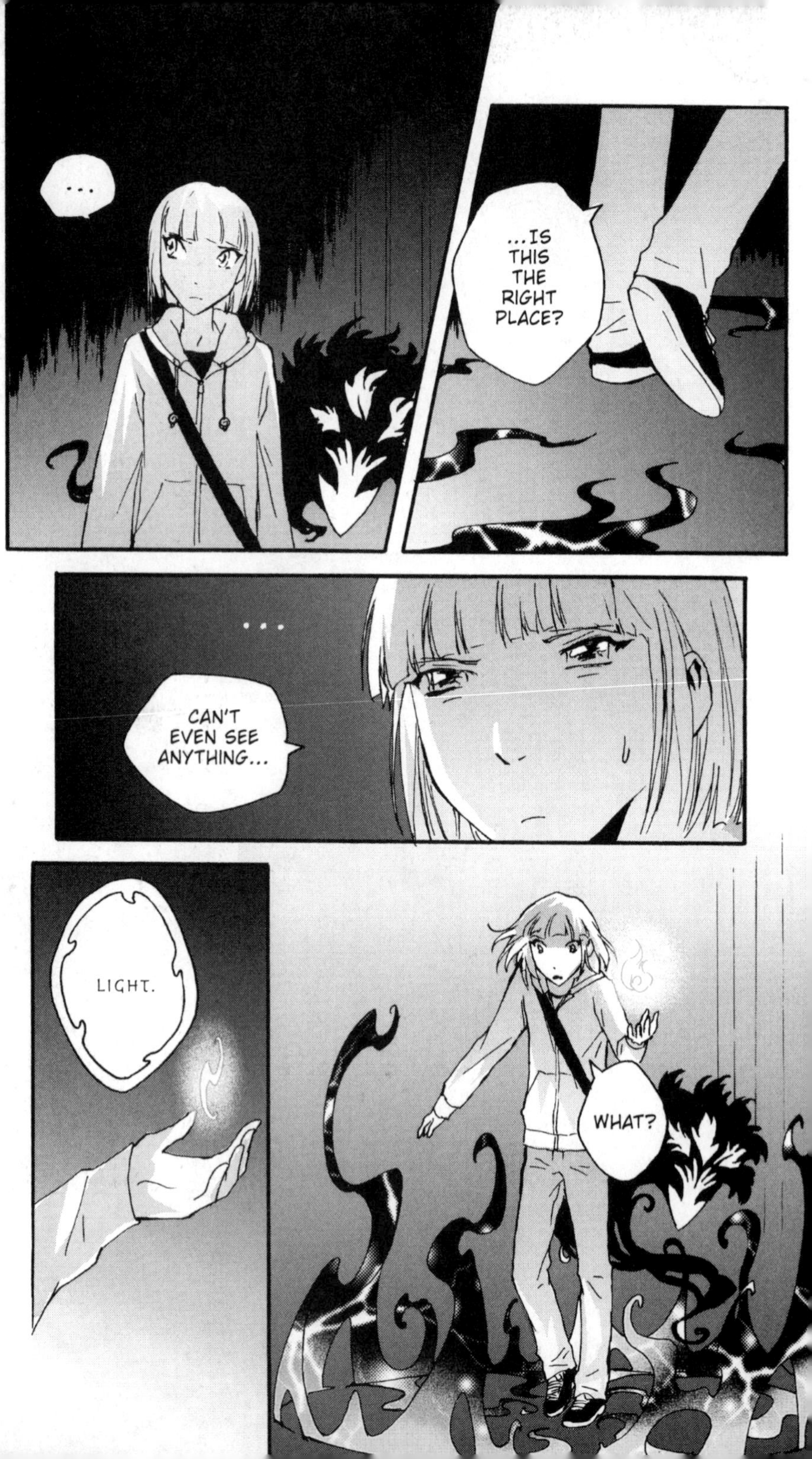
...IS THIS THE RIGHT PLACE?
...
...
CAN'T EVEN SEE ANYTHING...
WHAT?
LIGHT.

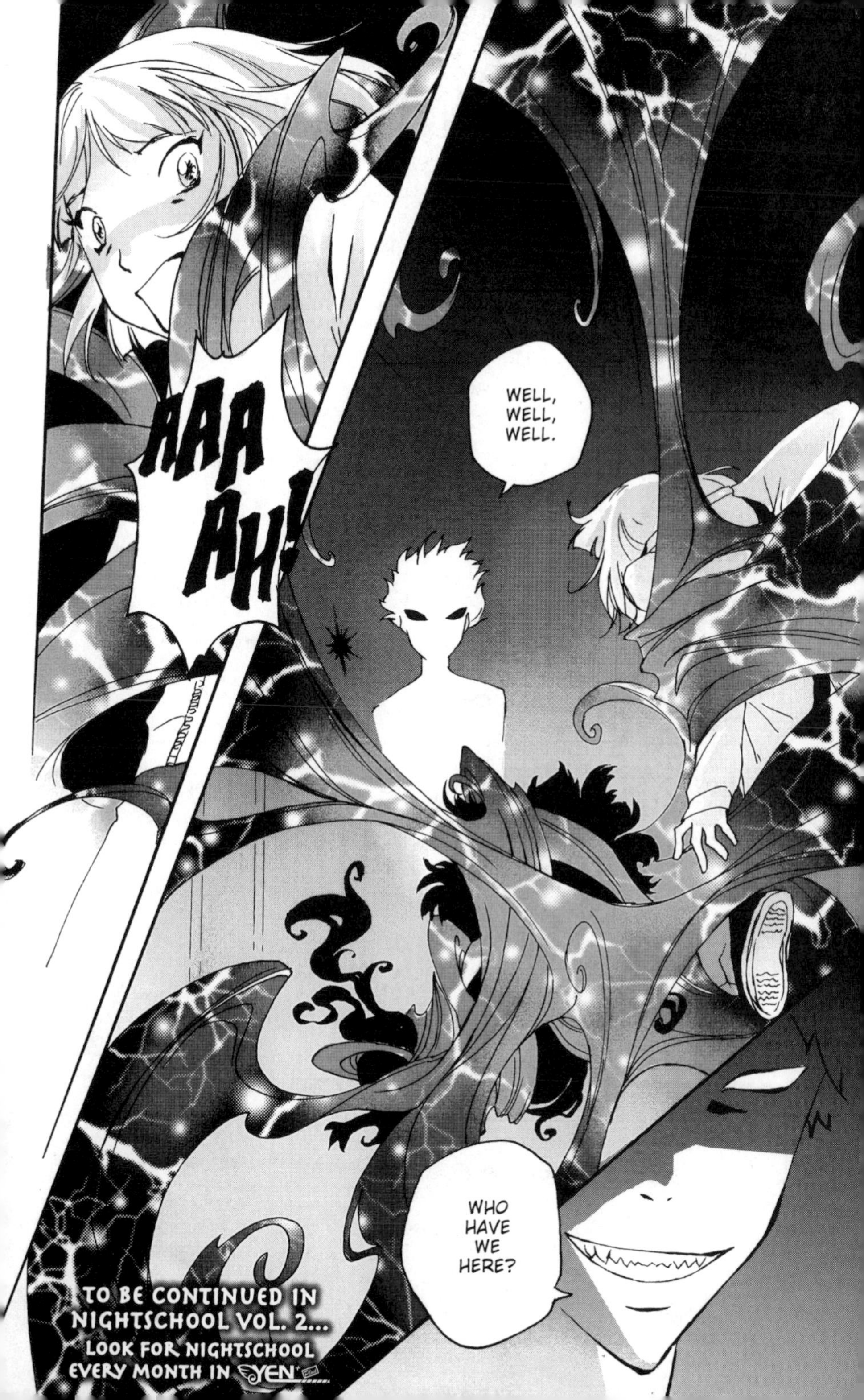
AAAAH!
WELL, WELL, WELL.
WHO HAVE WE HERE?
TO BE CONTINUED IN NIGHTSCHOOL VOL. 2...
LOOK FOR NIGHTSCHOOL EVERY MONTH IN YEN+

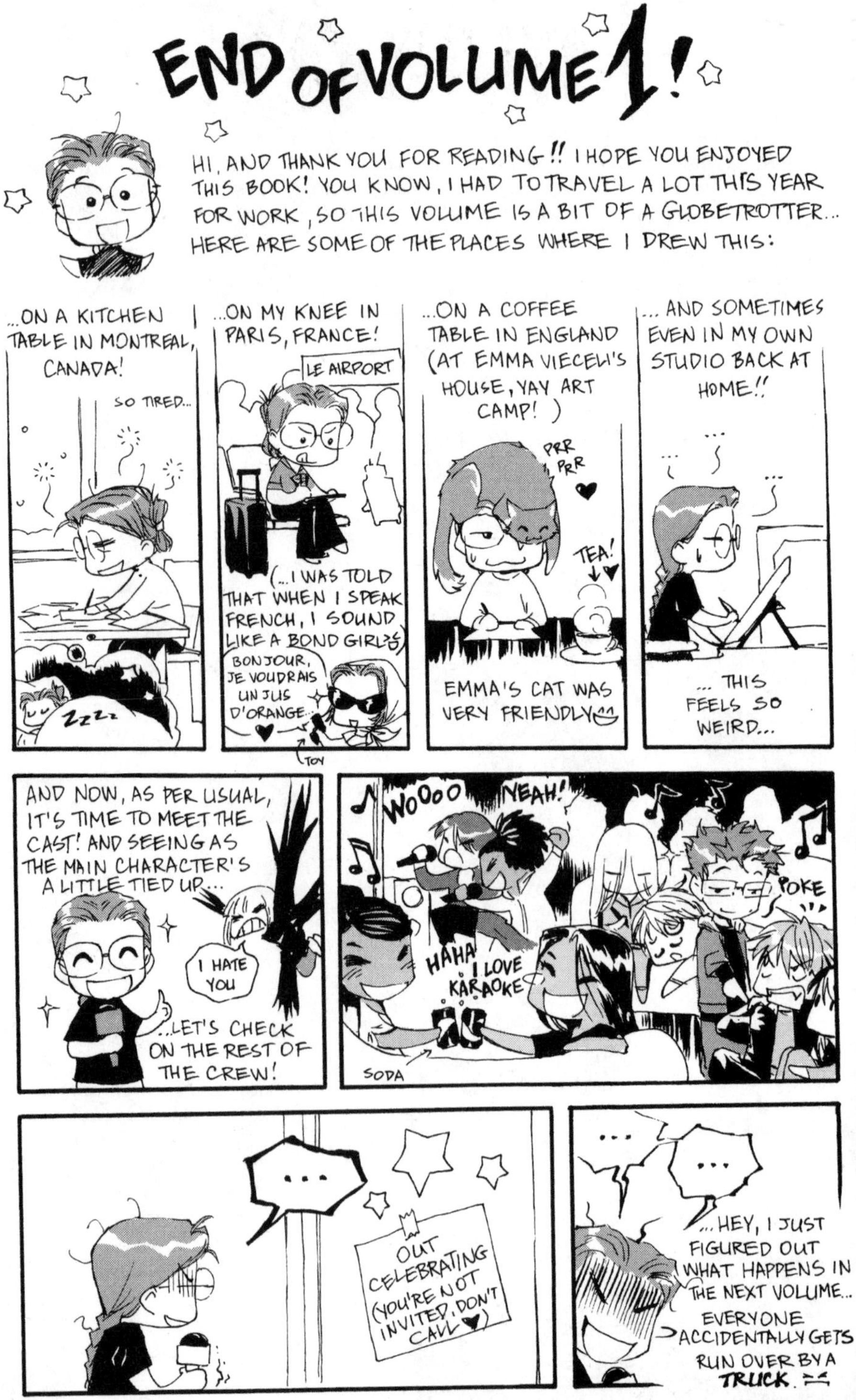
END OF VOLUME 1!
HI, AND THANK YOU FOR READING!! I HOPE YOU ENJOYED THIS BOOK! YOU KNOW, I HAD TO TRAVEL A LOT THIS YEAR FOR WORK, SO THIS VOLUME IS A BIT OF A GLOBETROTTER... HERE ARE SOME OF THE PLACES WHERE I DREW THIS:
...ON A KITCHEN TABLE IN MONTREAL, CANADA!
SO TIRED...
ZZZZ
...ON MY KNEE IN PARIS, FRANCE!
LE AIRPORT
(...I WAS TOLD THAT WHEN I SPEAK FRENCH, I SOUND LIKE A BOND GIRL)
BONJOUR, JE VOUDRAIS UN JUS D'ORANGE...
TOY
...ON A COFFEE TABLE IN ENGLAND (AT EMMA VIECELI'S HOUSE, YAY ART CAMP!)
PRR PRR
TEA!
EMMA'S CAT WAS VERY FRIENDLY
...AND SOMETIMES EVEN IN MY OWN STUDIO BACK AT HOME!!
...
...
...
... THIS FEELS SO WEIRD...
AND NOW, AS PER USUAL, IT'S TIME TO MEET THE CAST! AND SEEING AS THE MAIN CHARACTER'S A LITTLE TIED UP...
I HATE YOU
...LET'S CHECK ON THE REST OF THE CREW!
WOOOO
YEAH!
POKE
HAHA
I LOVE KARAOKE
SODA
...
OUT CELEBRATING (YOU'RE NOT INVITED, DON'T CALL)
...
...
...HEY, I JUST FIGURED OUT WHAT HAPPENS IN THE NEXT VOLUME...
EVERYONE ACCIDENTALLY GETS RUN OVER BY A TRUCK.

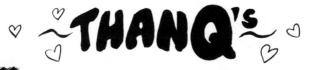

THANQ's

Barry McCarthy -- my high school art teacher. Thank you, Mr. McCarthy, for showing me that I could be an artist and for letting me draw cartoons. (And for making me draw stuff other than cartoons... You were right, it was important :D;;;)

My family and friends -- for being the rocking foundation of the whirlwind that is my life, I couldn't do this half as well without you.

(...Especially without Dee, my long-suffering tone artist with a hunted look in her eyes, and Sasha, my invaluable little sister and life-saver <3)

Yen Press crew ♥ -- this book would not be the same elsewhere. Thank you for helping me run amok on the pages of Yen Plus!!

(...Especially to my editor JuYoun, for guiding me through this very different writing process and for putting up with my loose grasp on the concept of "deadline"... Yes, Lillian, I see you smiling there!! Also, huge thanks to Kurt, for supporting my work all these years and for the encouragement at a time when I really needed it. Thank you, sir!)

Judy! -- my wonderful agent. Thank you for always looking out for me! *HUGS*

Dave and Raina -- those reference pictures helped So Much, I can't even say. Yay!!

Everyone who read this book! ^^ --you, dear readers, are a huge reason for why I am able to do this. Thank you so much for reading, for writing wonderful letters and for sending such amazing art.

I LOVE YOU!!

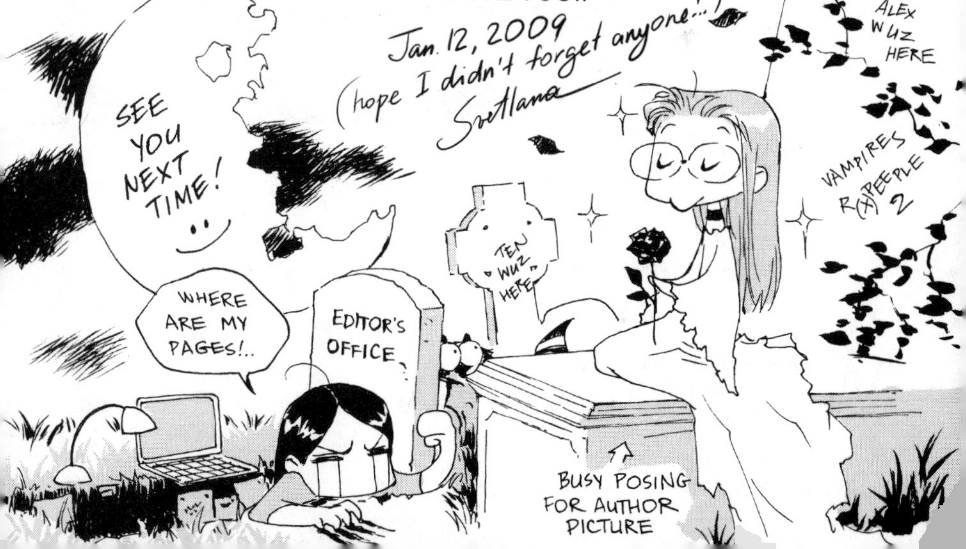

Jan. 12, 2009
(hope I didn't forget anyone!..)
Svetlana
ALEX WUZ HERE
SEE YOU NEXT TIME!
VAMPIRES R(X) PEEPLE 2
TEN WUZ HERE
WHERE ARE MY PAGES!..
EDITOR'S OFFICE
BUSY POSING FOR AUTHOR PICTURE

NIGHTSCHOOL
THE WEIRN BOOKS ①

SVETLANA CHMAKOVA

Toning Artist: Dee DuPuy

Lettering: JuYoun Lee

NIGHTSCHOOL: The Weirn Books, Vol. 1 © 2009 Svetlana Chmakova.

Yen Press
Hachette Book Group
237 Park Avenue, New York, NY 10017

Visit our Web sites at www.HachetteBookGroup.com
and www.YenPress.com.

Yen Press is an imprint of Hachette Book Group, Inc. The Yen Press name and logo are trademarks of Hachette Book Group, Inc.

First Yen Press Edition: April 2009

ISBN: 978-0-7595-2859-8

10 9 8 7 6 5 4 3 2 1

BVG

Printed in the United States of America